Practice a Rick

The *Witch's Circle* describes all aspects of a unique system of Wiccan ritual practice enriched by astrological symbolism. Whether you are just learning about Wicca, or have conducted many rituals of your own, this book will help you directly experience what lies at the heart of the Wiccan tradition: the connection between your life and the natural cycles of Earth and the heavens.

Everything you need to know to set up and run a Wiccan circle is provided in The *Witch's Circle*: fully scripted rituals for an entire year of Esbats and Sabbats; special rituals for handfastings, dedications, and other occasions; ritual aids such as music, chants, and meditations; and instructions for everything from setting up the altar and making ritual robes to spellcasting.

Use the insights and wisdom in this book to give an even deeper meaning to your ritual practice and your worship of the Goddess and God.

"A remarkable fusion of astrology and Wicca. This is an especially suitable combination because Wicca is so involved with the cycles of the earth, which is what many of the so-called cycles of the heavens really are."

—Robert Hand
Professional astrologer and author

"[Gives] a greater depth to understanding how the cycles of the sun, moon and earth are the basis for the sacred celebrations practiced by the Craft. A must for Pagans."

—Demetra George
author of *Mysteries of the Dark Moon*

About the Author

Maria Kay Simms, a professional astrologer for twenty-two years, is widely known throughout the astrological community as the author of several astrology books and as administrator of the prominent astrological computer service and publishing house, Astro Communications Services, Inc. of San Diego. In more recent years, she is also known as Lady Mari, High Priestess of Circle of the Cosmic Muse. The Circle is part of a growing network of Wiccan groups practicing a tradition that has been dubbed "West Coast Eclectic." Maria is an Elder Priestess (credentialed minister) of Covenant of the Goddess.

To Write to the Author

If you wish to contact the author or would like more information about this book, please write to the author in care of Llewellyn Worldwide, and we will forward your request. Both the author and the publisher appreciate hearing from you and learning of your enjoyment of this book and how it has helped you. Llewellyn Worldwide cannot guarantee that every letter written to the author can be answered, but all will be forwarded. Please write to:

Maria Kay Simms
c/o Llewellyn Worldwide
P.O. Box 64383, Dept. K657-2, St. Paul, MN 55164-0383, U.S.A.

Please enclose a self-addressed, stamped envelope or $1.00 to cover costs.
If outside the U.S.A., enclose international postal reply coupon.

Free Catalog from Llewellyn

For more than 90 years Llewellyn has brought its readers knowledge in the fields of metaphysics and human potential. Learn about the newest books in spiritual guidance, natural healing, astrology, occult philosophy and more. Enjoy book reviews, new age articles, a calendar of events, plus current advertised products and services. To get your free copy of *Llewellyn's New Worlds of Mind and Spirit*, send your name and address to:

Llewellyn's New Worlds of Mind and Spirit
P.O. Box 64383, Dept. K657-2, St. Paul, MN 55164-0383, U.S.A.

Witch's Circle

Rituals and Craft of the Cosmic Muse

(formerly titled *Circle of the Cosmic Muse*)

Maria Kay Simms

1996
Llewellyn Publications
St. Paul, Minnesota 55164-0383, U.S.A.

FIRST EDITION
First Printing, 1994
(formerly titled *Circle of the Cosmic Muse)*
SECOND EDITION
First Printing, 1996

Cover Art: Eris Klein
Cover Design: Anne Marie Garrison
Illustrations: Maria Kay Simms
Photography: Christiane Covington
Book Design and Layout: Jessica Thoreson

Library of Congress Cataloging-in-Publication Data
Simms, Maria Kay, 1940–
    Circle of the cosmic muse: a Wiccan book of shadows /
    Maria Kay Simms.
        p.   cm.
    Includes bibliographical references and index.
    ISBN 1-56718-657-2
    1. Witchcraft. 2. Simms, Maria Kay, 1940– . 3. Rites and
    ceremonies. 4. Astrology. 5. Magic. 6. Goddess religion.
    I. Title.
BF1571.S55   1994
299--dc20   93-46303
                                              CIP

Llewellyn Publications
A Division of Llewellyn Worldwide, Ltd.
P. O. Box 64383, Dept. 657-2, St. Paul, MN 55164-0383

Printed in the United States of America

Dedication

To the Goddess of many names,
Our Mother,
whom I first came to know as
Mary

and

To the God of many names
Her Son and Consort,
Our Father

May this offering contribute
to
♈ Initiative
♉ Patience
♊ Communication
♋ Nurturing
♌ Drama
♍ Skill
♎ Balance
♏ Empowerment
♐ Enthusiasm
♑ Growth
♒ Innovation
♓ Compassion

and

Unity

In Perfect Love and Perfect Trust

Other books by Maria Kay Simms

Twelve Wings of the Eagle, ACS Publications, 1988
Search for the Christmas Star (with Neil F. Michelsen),
ACS Publications, 1988
Dial Detective, ACS Publications, 1989
Your Magical Child, ACS Publications, 1994

Forthcoming books by Maria Kay Simms

Future Signs, ACS Publications, Oct. 1996

Table of Contents

A Family Tree

This book started out to be a "Book of Shadows" of my rituals based on astrological themes. Somehow, along the way, it became a story of my own spiritual evolution, then the development of my circle, and also the changes and evolution in my mother circle and its other daughter circles.

Throughout the text are numerous references to people within these circles. Usually I call them only by their circle names—and at some point during the course of my story, some of those names changed! A few are cited by their legal names. If this was a work of fiction that you could be expected to read from beginning to end, the use of all these names would, perhaps, make sense. It has been pointed out to me, however, that since this book is non-fiction, many readers will dip into it somewhere in the middle, according to an interest of the moment, and may find "who's who" to be confusing.

To help you sort them out, here is a "family tree" of the circles, in order of origin, followed by the members of each circle that are specifically named or cited within the text of this book. If a person is referred to by more than one name in the text, the alternate name appears in italics after their current circle name. Names cited in the

text do not appear here unless they are actually members of one of
the circles.

Circle of the Soaring Spirit, Mother circle of Circle Atheneum
Lady Olwen-Vivianne • Lord Hephaestus

Circle Atheneum
Lady Beckett • Lord Landerthorn
Habondia • Vespertia • Sidhe-the-Ri • Wolf Spirit

Circle of the Cosmic Muse, First daughter circle of Circle Atheneum
Lady Mari *Maria* • Lord Willow *Mark Adams*
Ibis • Rowena • Ariel *Anne Marie Shiosaki* • Maritha • Jered *Tear* •
Otter • Irisa • Lavender • Hare • Dara • Sar • Christiane (photog-
raphy) • Meadow *Molly* (my middle daughter of three, who Dedi-
cated at Circle Atheneum before my circle was formed)

The Circle of the Wildewood, Second daughter circle of Circle
Atheneum
Lady Aanja *Freya* • Lord Falkan *Daryl Fuller*

Circle of the Fates, Third daughter circle of Circle Atheneum
Lady Joy-of-Heart • Lord Brujo

Circle of the Cosmic Dance, First daughter circle of Circle of the
Cosmic Muse
Lady Terra *Terry Lamb*

Amber Grove, Fourth daughter circle of Circle Atheneum
Lady Shelayne *Greraven* • Lord Oberon *Eldar*

Acknowledgments

So many people have assisted me in creating this book! It has grown out of my experiences, influenced by all of those with whom I have shared those experiences. To my friends and family who are not specifically named on this page, my deep appreciation for your understanding and support. To the authors and artists whose work reaches many whom they never meet, whose work and ideas have contributed to my own, thank you for "being there" for me and my circle.

Special acknowledgment and thanks to:

Becky Turner (Lady Beckett), High Priestess of Circle Atheneum, with whom I trained as a Wiccan priestess. You will hear much about her throughout the text, and you will read her version of the Rede, The Wiccan Way. She has also specifically assisted the birth of this book by reading my manuscript, contributing her suggestions, and giving me constant, loving encouragement.

Mark Adams (Lord Willow), my High Priest and life partner, to whom I was handfasted in 1993. Mark has also read my text, offered suggestions, contributed to the creation of many of the rituals, wrote one of them, and is a steady source of balance, energy, love, and strength.

Maritha Pottenger, Editorial Director and my "second-in-command" at ACS, has not only understood my desire to do this book, and encouraged me during the preparation of it (even though it took time that I might have spent on an ACS project), but has also contributed her editorial suggestions to early drafts of the manuscript and her supportive presence and energy to the experiences of the rituals within our circle.

Daryl Fuller (Lord Falkan), ACS Managing Editor, has also contributed his encouragement, and valuable technical (computer) support, especially in helping me get the songs in this book into proper musical notation.

For Rob Hand's moral support and willing help in serving as High Priest at my first (and most emotionally difficult) large group ritual, the memorial farewell to my beloved husband, Neil F. Michelsen, and for his subsequent assistance with presentations at astrological conferences, I am deeply grateful.

For their substantial contributions to my training as Wiccan priestess, I offer my loving thanks to Habondia (Crone) and Lord Landerthorn (High Priest) of Circle Atheneum.

Terry Lamb (Lady Terra) and Anne Marie Shiosaki (Ariel), my first and current Maidens, have given much love and help with our circle activities, and have allowed me to include portions of their own writing in this book.

Encouragement, assistance, and ideas used in this book have been generously given by Darlene Fuller (Lady Shelayne), who devoted much of her time in the development of my circle by serving as my Crone, and by my other sister High Priestesses, Kathryn Fuller (Lady Aanja) and Lady Joy-of-Heart.

Without the people of the Circle of the Cosmic Muse—Ariel, Christiane, Cuth, Dara, Greraven, Hare, Ibis, Irisa, Jered, Jade, Lavender, Liz, Maritha, Orpheus, Otter, Rowena, Sar, Soler Sail, Terra, Theseus, and of course, Willow—who took part in the rituals presented in this book, I could offer you only prose and proposals—but with their good energy and participation, the rituals and magick have come to life.

Thanks to Llewellyn's Nancy Mostad, Marilyn Matheny, Andrea Godwin for her publicity work, and especially Jessica Thoreson, my editor, for their kindness, skill, and hard work in producing my book;to Joe Bethencourt for permission to quote from his collection of song lyrics; and to Christiane Covington for her fine photography.

Last, but most certainly not least, I wish to acknowledge with love the contribution of my mom, Anna Haurberg Simms, who has helped me with everything I have ever attempted by first teaching me to be creative and independent, and to believe that I could accomplish anything I sincerely set out to do—and who, no matter how strange some of those things might have seemed to her, has always maintained that "If Maria is doing it, it must be okay!"

Maria Kay Simms (Lady Mari)

Introduction: The Muse of the Cosmos

This book is intended primarily to be a practical one. It includes a full year of Full Moon and Sabbat rituals that were actually performed with my Circle of the Cosmic Muse, as well as a few special rituals that I have conducted or participated in. You'll also find chants, music, and instructions for just about everything involved with ritual, from setting up an altar and casting the circle to making simple ritual robes. It's my hope that this "practicum" will be useful to those of you who are just beginning, and also to those of you who have already conducted many rituals of your own.

Writing and doing sacred ritual is a creative act that is at once spiritually meaningful, self-empowering, self-healing—and fun! (Whoever may think that religion should not be fun has obviously not been involved with Wicca!) I hope, through this work, to support and encourage the creativity of others.

It must be said that no one creates in a vacuum, and very few thoughts (if any) are completely original. We all take ideas from each other, even if we honestly don't remember where we got them! Many of the ideas I've presented here are my own, meaning that if they were sparked by the work of someone else, I'm not consciously aware of it. Such ideas emerge from the sum total of my life experiences. When I am aware that my words or a concept have come from others, I have credited them—or if I did not know the source, I have attempted to discover it, and have credited it as best I can.

Before the actual rituals are a few chapters that offer a liberal dose of my opinions and philosophy, which may agree with yours in some cases and not in others. And that's okay. That is just one of the nice things about the new "old religion"—it's okay to disagree! I include this material because while I know that many of you will already be predisposed to my world view, I must expect that some will not. The opening chapters answer some of the questions I've received from people who are new to the Craft, and they provide some background on the astrological theme of my particular circle.

I am an astrologer—one who is serious enough about my field to have invested 20 years (as of this writing) in studying it, and to have earned professional certification from the two largest astrological organizations in this country. My previous books are astrology books and I am the administrator of a business that is familiar to every astrologer, Astro Communications Services, Inc. (usually called ACS or just "Astro"), the computing service and publishing company that was founded by my late husband, Neil F. Michelsen. I am also a Wiccan High Priestess. I say this while realizing that seeing it in print may discomfort even some of my astrologer friends who already know it, let alone some colleagues who don't.

Many astrologers, still having considerable trouble gaining public acceptance of the "A" word, would much prefer that astrology not be associated with the even less publicly acceptable "W" word! (More about "those words" later.) Also, while astrological symbolism can certainly be applied to religion (every major religion has some astrology in its roots), and some have called astrology the "Divine Science," certainly no one religion "owns" it. Astrology, in itself, is not a religion—most of its contemporary applications are strictly secular. As a study of time and of the correspondences between celestial and earthly cycles, and as a colorful language of symbolism, it has proved to be a useful tool for many purposes.

My Circle of the Cosmic Muse gets its name from the fact that we use the cycles and symbolism of astrology as a primary theme of inspiration for the development of our rituals. So if you know nothing about astrology before you read this book, you'll know quite a bit when you finish, without really trying—just as the members of my circle who had no prior background in astrology have learned through participating in the rituals. If you know a lot about astrology, this book may still give you some insights into the many ways that its symbolism is universal, capable of "striking a chord" with anyone at any time, regardless of the makeup of that person's individual horoscope.

Yet this is not an astrology book. It is a book about a new form of spiritual practice that is based on ancient religious rites planned around the holy days that were marked out by the natural cycles of Earth and Cosmos. All forms of religion use astrology for their holidays, whether they remember it and acknowledge it or not. Modern Pagan groups are quite conscious of astrological correspondences in their rituals, but for the most part, emphasize other things. Astrology is our primary theme because I, and some of the members of my circle, work with astrology on a daily basis. We use symbols that are meaningful to us. And so it should be. My intention, then, is not to make you into an astrologer, but rather to share with you the development of this particular theme in the hope that it will inspire you to create more rituals that have special meaning for you, in whatever theme you may choose.

Most of the rapidly growing numbers of people who are attracted to Wiccan circles, Medicine Wheels, and other non-traditional religious rites have come to these practices because conventional religions have ceased to be relevant to them. They yearn for spiritual practice and community and answers for the many unexplained "whys" of life, yet they can no longer feel at home with the intolerance, hypocrisies, and endless guilt infliction that are so much a part of the churches in which they were raised.

This is why it is of utmost importance that Wiccan ritual be relevant. To be sure, it is, in most cases. Yet some rituals can become so caught up in the ancient seasonal God and Goddess mythology or in archaic and flowery language that they almost lose the connection to the world in which we actually live, and the event becomes more of a pageant than a true spiritual experience for the participants. The language of symbolism that is astrology has worked for me in helping to establish relevance in the writing of ritual. Perhaps it will also work for you; perhaps something else will work better. In any case, I hope that in the rituals presented here, it will not be the symbols that will draw your primary attention, but rather, the aspects of yourself and others which are symbolized. That, of course, is what truly matters.

As above, so below
As within, so without
As the Universe, so the soul …

—Hermes Trismegistus

A Search for the Goddess

People often ask, "How did you get started in all this? ... " And I have always been interested, as well, in how others have found their way to active participation in Goddess religions. So to begin with, here is my story.

It was at the beginning of the 1980s, years before I began to formally study Wicca, that I was first drawn to the idea of the reemergence of the Goddess. I am not sure just how it began—perhaps partially through my own evolving consciousness and partially from something I'd read about the feminist spirituality movement. At that time I was living in southwestern Connecticut and was quite active as an astrologer—consulting, teaching, doing radio shows and public lectures, etc. I was also (in my own rather unorthodox way) a practicing Catholic, with my three daughters all in catechism classes in our local parish.

My religious background has been unsettled, one could say. An astrologer might call it a reflection of my Sun, ruler of my 9th house of religion/philosophy, in a close opposition aspect with Uranus, the planet of sudden changes, rebellion, and innovation. I was raised in a very small town in Illinois. It had a population of 750 then, and four churches, all Protestant. My mother had been raised Lutheran, but there was no nearby Lutheran church. My father, who was very close to nature, considered the forest his primary cathedral. His name, Frank, derived from Francis (the kindly saint often pictured among birds and animals), was appropriate. In his later years, even the robins in our yard would come up to eat from his hand. My parents felt it was "good" for my younger brother and I to go to Sunday School, so we were sent up the street to the Methodist church. I was always drawn to religious activity, and so I was very active in the Methodist Youth Federation as a young teen, attending camp and regional meetings, as well as local activities. During high school I began to get "turned off." In a small town everyone knows everyone else's business, and it began to strike me as hypocritical that some of the people who were teaching in the church were not practicing what they preached in their own lives. And it bothered me a great deal that so much time was spent in our youth classes, both locally and regionally, warning us of the great danger of dating Catholics, for fear that we might become entrapped in the horrible conflicts of a mixed marriage—or worse, be coerced into becoming a Catholic! This intolerance, fear, and running down of other religions rather than teaching one's own just did not jibe with the concept of the gentle, tolerant, and compassionate Jesus whose portrait hung in the church.

This, I suppose, was my particular teenage rebellion. Nearly every teenager rebels against something—beginning at the well-known adolescent crisis, which "coincidentally" happens at the first time in one's life that the planet Saturn opposes its birth chart position. By the time I graduated from high school and went off to Illinois Wesleyan University (chosen not because it was Methodist-founded, but because it was highly rated for the arts and because I had a full-tuition scholarship), I had become an agnostic.

After two years, I began to think that being an agnostic was unsatisfying and rather wishy-washy, yet I wasn't able to call myself an atheist with any conviction for I could acknowledge an unfocused inner yearning for that which was beyond the visible world. So I sought to discover if there was a religion in which I could feel "at home." Over the next year I visited just about every church and synagogue within a reasonable range of the university. I also took a class on the philosophy of religion, with a group made up mostly of young men who intended to go on to seminaries. It was one of the tougher courses I took during my entire four years, but it gave me a lot to think about. Finally, I found myself going most often to the Catholic church, where dialogue mass was sung in Latin, with a wonderful choir directed by a Wesleyan professor, who was director of Collegiate Choir, and including most of his Catholic music major students. As an art major, I had also studied much about the many masterpieces of painting, sculpture, and architecture that had been created for the church. It was all so beautiful, so mystical, so esthetically spiritual, with the music, the candles, the incense. Okay, not the best reasons for choosing a religion, you might say, but I really did enjoy going there.

When, in my senior year, I became engaged to a Catholic, it was fairly easy to decide to convert. I took instruction for more than a semester from a young and very patient priest. We spent, I remember, around two months or so discussing whether or not there was a God. Once I became reasonably satisfied with that issue, the rest of the basic theology went a bit more smoothly, but the year ran out before we got into much of the dogma. Nevertheless, I decided to become a Catholic, and was married in a high mass the summer after graduation.

As a young married woman who had no wish to have children immediately, I quickly ran up against items of the Catholic dogma that made little sense to me. It amazed me, however, that my husband (and others I knew who had been raised as Catholics) was able to dismiss the rules against artificial birth control without a second thought. "Nobody taught me that when I took catechism." "But you were confirmed when you were twelve. Of course they didn't teach you that. But you can read it practically any day of the week in the newspapers quoting the pope." "So? That's the newspapers. No priest ever told me. Don't worry about it."

Over the years there were many inner arguments over various points, and short periods where I left the church to try at one time Unitarian, and then later, because I missed the "high church" ritual, Episcopalian. But for the most part I stayed, feeling that my three daughters, all baptized Catholic, were better off learning a religion, even if they rebelled later, as I had, than to not learn any tradition at all.

I really never achieved much inner peace with religion until after I had become exposed to astrology and metaphysics in my early thirties. Astrologers can be found as active participants in all kinds of religions—Christian, Jewish, Hindu, Buddhist, Wiccan, you name it—or in no structured religion at all. I have yet to meet one, however, who described himself or herself as an atheist. One simply cannot study astrology, exploring the correspondences of Earth and Cosmos, and deny the existence of some Divine Order. Eventually I learned to flow with my role within that Order, listen to the "still, small voice within" and, when I attended mass, simply shut out the noise that didn't make sense to me, and enjoy what did.

In 1982 I was to have a daughter and a stepson in the confirmation class of the parish in which we lived in southwestern Connecticut, and the classes were to meet in various private homes, in the hope of a more refined and comfortable atmosphere than had been previously experienced in the school classrooms. Rather than chauffeur the kids across town every week and have two hours to wait, I had already volunteered to allow their class to meet in our home. When the parish came up with a shortage of confirmation catechists, the Director of Religious Education (DRE), who heard that I'd been a high school art teacher in the past, asked if I would consider teaching the group that was meeting in my home. (This parish confirmed at high school sophomore age, hoping for a little more depth of understanding than could be expected of twelve-year-olds.)

I said that since I was setting aside the evening anyway, I would be willing to teach, except that as a very visible astrologer in the community, and a divorced-remarried Catholic, I might cause some objections. She asked the pastor (who had a reputation for being very conservative) and he said, "Let her teach. If the parents complain, send them to me." He later explained to me that if he were to deny rites to all in his parish who had divorced and remarried he would lose many of his most active and willing participants in parish work. He felt it was best left up to a matter of personal conscience.

As for the astrology—well, that is only one demonstration of the fact that any Christian denomination varies greatly from one church community to another. (Believe me, I have been to enough churches in many different states to say that with conviction.) In this parish, the nuns pinned up a newspaper interview of me-as-astrologer on their bulletin board, the DRE found it "interesting," and the associate pastor went on a radio show with me at Christmas time to discuss the Magi and what the Christmas Star might have been. A year before I had participated in a three-month long "Letters to the Editor" debate over some positive coverage of astrology in a local newspaper. The fundamentalists who were prayerfully decrying the newspaper's presentation of this "work of the devil" and quoted verse upon verse to support their views, became so hysterical that they called me a fanatic when I calmly took each verse and placed in back into the context of the chapter from which it had been wrenched, and demonstrated that it really didn't condemn astrology at all. One day, some months later, I happened to glance at a notice from a Catholic parish of another town and saw that two of the most hysterical "fundies" who had written those letters had just been elected officers of the Holy Rosary Society!

As I said at the beginning of this tale, it was during these years of the early eighties that I became increasingly drawn to the Goddess, longing for an expression of deity with whom I could truly identify. I think now that the only reason that I stayed with the Catholic church as long as I did was because the Goddess at least was present there in the personification of Mary. (Yes, I know that isn't the "party line," but ask a number of nuns what they think!)

Also, I have to say that I stayed within the Catholic church longer than I might have because that particular parish accepted me. It was possible to think, in that place at that time, that the possibility for change in the "system" was more likely through working within it than through rejecting it. I was a confirmation catechist for three years and enjoyed it. The books that I was given to teach from were quite different from the strict "old church." They even suggested such activities as discussions on comparative religions and on the concept of God as Mother. The presentation of theological concepts were written in such a way that I had little trouble reconciling them with my metaphysical beliefs. My students preferred my guided mediations to rote prayers, and the DRE was so pleased that she had me teach the technique to the other instructors. We also had fun doing various community service projects, such as working in soup kitchens during Lent, and refurbishing toys for disadvantaged children at Christmas time.

During '82 and '83 I also wrote my first book, *Twelve Wings of the Eagle*,[1] which traces changing concepts of deity and religious symbolism throughout history against a framework of the ages of the zodiac. The book contains a great deal of biblical exegesis, for I found much symbolism that relates to the ages in Genesis, Exodus, and the Gospels. It also contains a strong Goddess-emerging sub-theme, proposing that before the end of the present Age of

Pisces, the "pendulum swing," or mass religious paradigm, is inevitably moving toward a primary emphasis on Goddess, just as society is inevitably returning toward a matrifocal emphasis. As an outgrowth of writing the book, I also gave a number of astrology lectures at conferences and meetings in several states on the theme "Pisces Rising—Return of the Goddess."

By the beginning of 1984, I had emerged from my intense involvement in writing the book and realized that writing it had, in part, been an act of withdrawal from some serious problems in my life and in my marriage. I remember that it was on the feast day of the Mother of God, January 1, that I went alone to the church and meditated before the altar of Mary, holding my manuscript in my hands. I dedicated myself to Her as Goddess, asking for Her guidance through the inner voice, promising to follow it and accept Her path, wherever it might lead. I also silently offered my trust that if She wanted my manuscript published, She would send me to the right publisher at the right time. I've never told anyone exactly that part of my story before—and in a way, I'm surprising myself a little that I am telling you all of this now. This is not quite characteristic for a Sun in Scorpio to reveal so much of herself.

Within the next week I had effortlessly taken some specific actions to change a major problem (which I shall decline to explain, for that detail involves others who may not wish to be so public) that I had been unable to effectively act upon before. Later that month my father died, and I gathered with all of my family at his funeral back in Illinois. I remember reflecting on why I, from such an uncomplicated, stable, and loving environment, had chosen so many complications within my own life. I had an overwhelming feeling that a very major chapter of my life was ending, that I was stepping into the unknown, but with no fear.

In the years since, I have been through a number of life passages that most people would call major crises, and a number of astrological indicators that a lot of astrologers would identify as pretty tough. I can only say that the Lady within has enabled me to maintain a serenity that I never achieved before I stopped trying to manipulate my life and instead allowed Her flow to prevail. And never in my wildest imaginings back on that January day, could I have dreamed that I would be where I am now.

Twelve Wings was not published until 1988. The book had to wait for my life to settle down after a year in Illinois in which I helped my mother through a serious illness and neurosurgery, and in which I obtained a divorce. In 1986 I moved to Florida for a new job, only to move once again in 1987 to become the Art Director of ACS Publications—and to marry the publisher. The Lady had led me to my publisher in a manner quite different from anything I had ever thought to anticipate!

After leaving Connecticut, I never again found another Catholic parish in which I felt comfortable. I tried at first, for the sake of my youngest daughter, when she was at the age for First Communion. I even sang in a choir for awhile, but did not like what my daughter related from her catechism classes—the original sin, guilt-inducing concepts that were becoming further and more irreconcilably separated from my own world view.

The Catholic refusal to consider women priests was, to me, completely indefensible on any ground, scriptural or otherwise. I had met nuns who wanted to be priests and would have been wonderful, understanding, effective, caring priests; I remembered the fine DRE from Connecticut who certainly should have been a priest. I became truly angry over the lame excuses that were given to support the all-male priesthood, such as "Jesus wasn't married. If he was, the Gospels would say so." This conveniently ignores the fact that nothing whatever is said in the Gospels about Jesus' life from age twelve to at least thirty. And "all of the apostles were men." This ignores the fact that the Bible doesn't even agree on who the "twelve" were. Different books of the Bible have different lists. The Gospels do allude to women also traveling with Jesus' band, including Mary Magdalene (who is never identified as a whore). One of the non-canonical Gospels discovered at Nag Hammadi shows the Magdalene as a primary apostle, whom Jesus "loved more than the disciples."[2]

In any case, the usual scriptural references against a female priesthood, in my mind, carry virtually no weight against the much more specific implication of John 4. This is the story of the Samaritan woman at the well, who is the very first person to whom Jesus clearly identifies himself as the Messiah, and sends on into the town where she spreads the "good news" (Gospel means "good news"). Jesus, by this action, could certainly be taken to have given this woman the mission to be the first Christian preacher! And if that is not enough, the first person to whom Jesus revealed himself after his resurrection was a woman, Mary Magdalene (Matthew 28, Mark 16, John 20).[3]

Finally, I simply gave up.

My views are no more unorthodox than some of the nuns with whom I am acquainted. They continue to work within the system, hoping for change as I once did. I respect that, and also understand that they not only have a vested interest in the possibility of change within that system, they also have some small chance of influencing it. As a Catholic laywoman, however, my voice was completely non-existent.

Soon after moving to San Diego I discovered the Pagan community by attending a few "public" rituals with an astrologer friend. (Public, in this case, means that word was quietly circulated around among circles that a ritual would be held and guests were permissible.) Within a few months I found a circle in which I felt comfortable and began to formally study Wicca. Here I found that the music, candles, incense, and mysticism that I had once loved within the church were being used to worship the Goddess—and to celebrate *my* world view! I felt as though I had "come home."

During my first few months at ACS, one of my projects was to prepare the camera-ready pages for *Twelve Wings* (which had been accepted for publication in late 1986). It was tempting to do some rewriting, since my ideas had obviously become even more unorthodox since I wrote it. But I decided to let it stand—and basically I still agree with it. In retrospect, I can read what I wrote and see that my world view was already Neo-Pagan, even though I didn't know it at the time and therefore did not identify it as such. And that is good, for as it is, it is a "bridge book," quite helpful (I've been told) for those whose hearts are in the emerging world view but whose heads are still stuck in the religious traditions of their childhood, or vice versa. For such people the book tends to reconcile the differences and make them more comfortable. The people for whom *Twelve Wings* would be a bridge are unlikely to be comfortable with this book, but for others perhaps this one could be their "bridge." Most people need to ease into new ideas slowly. That is why major religious paradigms take so long to change. People on the verge of change in thinking often need to know that other people think the same way. "I'm not nuts; it's okay, I'm not alone. I can cross that bridge without falling into the void."

One of my own bridges that helped lead me from *Twelve Wings* to this present book was meeting a former nun during a trip to

Houston to speak at an astrology conference. Lucia runs Lucia's Garden, an herbal garden and Goddess shop, in which she, who is now called a priestess, conducts Moon rituals and sponsors many related activities.[4]

Another bridge was crossed shortly after I moved to San Diego when I read Margot Adler's *Drawing Down the Moon* definitions of animism, pantheism, and polytheism in the Pagan world view. She said, essentially, that animism means that all things partake of the life force, pantheism means that the deity is immanent within nature, and polytheism means that reality (divine or otherwise) is multiple and diverse.[5] I distinctly remember putting the book down and pausing for a moment in revelation—"That concisely identifies just what I believe. I guess I must be a Pagan!"

With all the changes that have taken place since *Twelve Wings,* however, my belief has not changed that the way in which the masses perceive deity and themselves in relation to deity corresponds to the precessional ages of the zodiac. This perception influences the symbolism of the keynote religions and the social/political values of dominant civilizations that emerge within an age. I won't even pretend to speculate on why this is. No one really knows whether we humans are influenced by the Cosmos, or whether the concepts that we project upon the Cosmos are only a reflection of our collective inner selves. "As above, so below" is a familiar adage—but which is the mirror? And what is reality? Suffice it to say, for now, that there is a correspondence.

Endnotes

1. Simms, Maria Kay. *Twelve Wings of the Eagle.* San Diego: ACS Publications, 1988.

2. Robinson, James M., Ed. *The Nag Hammadi Library.* San Francisco: Harper & Row, 1977.

3. *The New American Bible,* Catholic Edition. New York: Thomas Nelson Publishers, 1971.

   The New English Bible. Cambridge University Press, 1970.

   Actually, just about any translation of the Bible would do, in referencing my comments here. I cite the two listed above primarily because they are my favorites—both written in clear language closely translated by teams of scholars from the oldest possible sources.

4. Lucia's Garden, 2942 Virginia, Houston, Texas, 77098.

5. Adler, Margot. *Drawing Down the Moon*. Boston: Beacon Press, 1979, page 25.

A New Age is Emerging–
But What Is It?

Like many others, I have occasionally referred to the rituals I do as "New Age" religion. Why? Probably because New Age doesn't raise red flags nearly as quickly as the words Pagan or Wicca or Witch-craft. Yet I thoroughly dislike the term "New Age." This chapter will explain why, and in so doing, introduce you to the astrological symbolism that forms the backdrop for the new religious paradigm that is emerging.

For several years New Age has been a catch-phrase for all types of out-of-the-mainstream studies that were for many years previously lumped under the terms metaphysical or occult. New Age became a mass media term with the help of Shirley MacLaine and the craze for crystals. For awhile it was a fad—enough to raise the ire and the fear of the Christian fundamentalists. Every chain bookstore expanded its New Age section and moved it up near the front. Then the crystals moved into the department store jewelry racks, the fad faded, and at ABA (American Booksellers Association Convention) in 1990, the question was "Is the New Age dead?" At

the 1991 ABA, the New Age Publishers Association reacted by discussing whether it should perhaps think up an alternative name for
"New Age."

No, the movement isn't dead—far from it. Those of us who
were involved in metaphysical studies for years before the media
hype know that interest continues to grow steadily and strong. If the
chain stores see a slackening of book sales, I'd bet it is mostly
because they do not carry enough depth. Once people become interested beyond the superficial fad level they quickly discover that most
of the best books are the small press books that are plentiful in any
metaphysical book shop, but are usually overlooked by the chains.

I do think, however, that a new name for the emerging world
view needs to be chosen. New Age was wrong from the start. It refers
partly to the fact that we are about to enter a new millennium, but
beginnings of new millenniums, contrary to public expectations, do
not herald cataclysm—nor have they magically brought about mass
changes of thinking. Such changes are gradual and very slow. The title
of "New Age" also came about because of a mistaken association of
the approach of the year 2000 with the Age of Aquarius.

The term "Age of Aquarius," after the hit song from the post-
flower-child musical *Hair,* stuck in the popular idiom and became,
for many "New Agers," a Utopian ideal that has an interesting sim-
ilarity to the fundamentalist Christian hope for the "Second Coming" and "the thousand years of peace" that will follow. Both ideas,
each in its own way, fantasize a golden age (within our own lifetimes, of course!) when we can escape from all of the ills of the past
and the present day and "peace will guide the planet and love will
rule the stars." Now, fantasy and escapism (as most any astrology
textbook will tell you) are traits that would most likely be attributed
to Pisces—which is the sign of the age we are in, and will be in, for
about 700 more years! To speak of the "dawning of the Age of
Aquarius" is just a bit premature.

Precessional ages are derived from the slow clockwise displace-
ment of the point of the vernal equinox (and the zodiac of signs)
against the zodiac of constellations. The sun at vernal equinox now
rises in the head of the west fish. It will not leave the constellation of
the Fishes and rise in the Waterbearer until about the year 2700.[1]

It is true that some less technically-oriented astrologers have
written of Aquarius as already here or coming soon, supporting their
views with cultural examples that they interpret as Aquarian, such as

communism, large corporations, space travel, electricity, hippies, etc. I submit that one can take any sign and find many things in our culture that could be associated with it. (In fact, in the rituals to come you will see how each sign can be universally meaningful.) However, those who are actually looking at the astronomical positions upon which the concept of precession is based will not differ greatly from my time estimate. No system of astrology that I know of places its "zero point" as entering Aquarius for a long time yet to come.

During the time I was writing my book *Twelve Wings of the Eagle* (which traces the precessional ages through history, myth, and scripture) I was at first amused to hear or read numerous New Age teachers speak of the Age of Aquarius as being already here—or certainly arriving with the new millennium—and to describe its virtues with words like wholistic, mystical, compassionate, Universal Love—all words that an astrology text would more likely use to describe the highest expression of Pisces. More recently, though, I've been particularly dismayed to read two authors, whose books I am citing in a later chapter as excellent resources, analyze the "outgoing age" and the "New Age" in terms that cast Pisces as the total villain of patriarchy, power, exploitation of the earth, and just about everything else they dislike, and credit meditation, ecology, the women's movement, and just about everything else they support to the "soon-to-arrive Age of Aquarius."

Because of the problems and possible backlash that I see with perpetuating this misconception, I will try once more, at least in this chapter, to make my case for learning to understand the age we are in and to consequently improve it, rather than escaping into a fantasy world (a Piscean trait) by projecting all hopes for change onto an age that even our children's children won't live to see.

To me, the concept of balance is very important. How can we propose to impose Age of Aquarius as a present-day identity and completely throw out the very basis by which precessional ages are measured? In the New Age rush to emphasize right-brain intuition as a counter-balance to the problems that have ensued over an over-emphasis on left-brain logic, shall we now completely throw out the left brain? If we do, the paradoxical joke is that we would then be ignoring the fact that most any astrology text will identify Pisces as an intuitive (right-brain) water sign and Aquarius as a logical (left-brain) air sign! By any known system of measurement, part of the constellation Pisces still rises before the Sun at vernal equinox. If we accept that as having any scientific validity, then why not also attempt to understand the emerging world view as a further reflection of the Piscean paradigm that is not yet fulfilled?

You see, this plea for a reconsideration of the Age of Pisces goes way beyond the issue of when the Age of Aquarius actually does begin. For one thing, even if the authors point out that they are speaking of an age and not of a person who has the Sun in Pisces, still, an implication of Pisces equals bad and Aquarius equals good comes through. This is terrific for the Aquarians. They love associating themselves with light and love and peace. Who wouldn't? It's rare, these days, to hear anything about a possible dark side to Aquarius.

Yet every sign has its "light" and "dark" sides. Most people, at one time or another in their lives, manifest the best and the worst of their dominant signs, as they learn and grow. As the collective consciousness evolves, it, too, expresses the best and worst of the symbols of its zodiacal age. It is simply not true that Pisces is at fault and an Aquarian dispensation would be the correction of all those faults. Even more significantly, the rejection of Pisces and the premature embrace of Aquarius is, albeit unconscious and unintended, yet another devaluation of the feminine and a negation of some of the very ideals the New Age movement purports to embody: living in the Now, being in touch with feelings, and most importantly, healing our planet with the flow of Universal Love.

Why do I say these things? Let's look at some basic keywords for the two signs, as astrological tradition defines them. Pisces is a feminine, water sign. The so-called feminine polarity is associated with receptivity, subjectivity, and yin. Water symbolizes "right-brain" functions like intuition and feelings. Aquarius is a masculine, air sign. The masculine polarity is associated with initiative, objectivity, and yang. Air symbolizes "left-brain" functions like rational, abstract thought.

Universal Love would best define the highest manifestation of Pisces, just as it was presented at the very beginning of the age: "Love thy neighbor as thyself." Now, the fact that many people—and church leaders—fell short of, and even distorted, that ideal does not change the fact that it *is* the ideal, the vision of the Piscean Age.

The vision of Aquarius would be more properly termed Universal Truth, in keeping with a rational, air/intellectual paradigm. One of the most often stated characteristics of Aquarius is emotional detachment. How might the truth of the Aquarian Age be stated? Could it be distorted, too? Of course it could! What the truth of Aquarius will be may very well depend upon our collective evolution within the Age of Pisces. Rather than reject Pisces, I think it is important that we reexamine what it has been, what it perhaps was intended to be, and what it should be in the future. My purpose here is to encourage the revision of the history of this age and of the New Age movement with its true symbols: Pisces, its "vision," and the complementary opposite and co-star, Virgo (another badly maligned sign), which reflects "reality"—meaning Pisces as the collective concept of deity, and Virgo as an expression of the culture that births the concept.

After all, Jesus, the avatar of the Age of Pisces, was born of the Goddess of the Sea, Mar-y (*Mar,* a root word for sea), who was also the Virgin, Virgo, Goddess of the constellations, and Mother Earth. This calls some major questions: how did our Lady of the Sea get demoted to a subservient mortal woman? And how did our fruitful Virgo of the Harvest become (in negative astrological interpretation) a nit-picking, critical, barren prude? And if this "New Age" isn't Aquarius, what is it?

Religion and the Ages

Whatever else an age of the zodiac might mean, the best evidence seems to link it to a paradigm so basic and long-lasting that it tends to be taken for granted. The collective concept of deity—or in other words, the way people think of their gods and of themselves in relation to their gods—reflects the cycle of the precessional ages. This happens even if the people have no idea what a Great Age is, and even if they have no knowledge of astrology. Few think about how deeply the concept of deity is buried at the roots of an entire culture, and how profoundly it influences sociological and political trends.

Many writers have pointed out tangible symbols that link religion with the ages of the zodiac. The sacred cattle of India, Hathor and Apis of Egypt, the Minotaur of Crete, all date to the Age of Taurus the Bull. The Aryan invaders of the Age of Aries the Ram brought their fire gods throughout the Middle East and even into India. Apis of Egypt was supplanted by Amon the Ram God, and Greece's Athena, born of her father, wore a helmet with ram's horns. In the exodus from Egypt, the Hebrews, led by God in a pillar of fire, sacrificed the bull as an offering, and consecrated their altar and priestly vestments with the blood of a ram.

As the Age of Aries drew to a close, the Lamb of God was sacrificed to atone for sin and rose to introduce the Age of Pisces and a new religion. The followers of the Fisher of Men identified themselves by the sign of the fish. Their clergy adopted fish-head hats, and their supreme pontiff is said to wear the "shoes of the Fisherman."

More interesting than bulls and rams and fishes, however, are the ways in which the characteristics that are associated with zodiacal symbolism seem to mirror the god concepts, and consequently the culture, of the ages. For example, the symbols of the zodiac are traditionally grouped into polarities. Six of the twelve signs are said to be masculine, positive, and yang, while the other six are said to be feminine, negative, and yin. The charge alternates around the circle. Astrological tradition places no relative value on one form of energy over the other. Both are necessary for balance. Taurus is feminine, earthy, sensual, and peace-loving. In the Age of Taurus the primary deities were goddesses, and societies were matrifocal, agricultural, and mostly peaceful. Aries, a masculine, fire symbol, is assertive, competitive, and wants to take the initiative and be "number one." In the Age of Aries male gods became dominant, and society became primarily patriarchal and warlike.

Pisces is feminine, watery, intuitive, mystical, compassionate, and visionary. The vision of deity that emerged through the teachings of Jesus at the dawn of the Age of Pisces softened the fiery Aries god-concept into a loving and forgiving parent-figure. All of the Ten Commandments of the previous order were merged into the one simple charge in the primary teaching of Jesus: "Love thy neighbor as thyself." Jesus made it plain that he considered everyone his neighbor, even the gentiles and outcasts.

The vision of Pisces is love—Universal Love, love that is not merely tolerant of those who are different than oneself, but love that feels a deep, mystical interconnectedness of self with all other beings through the presence of the life force within.

So, if that truly is Pisces, and Pisces is a feminine sign, I hear you asking, how did we get the patriarchal church that has so influenced the cultural suppression of women and of all things feminine? And why did wars of conquest continue?

Again, I remind you, this age is far from over. Ages and shifting world views change very slowly. Fire and ram symbolism appeared at the beginning of the Age of Aries, but it took nearly the entire age before the struggle for patriarchal dominance was won and the suppression of women into secondary roles became firmly established.

Now, I reiterate, no astrological archetype is "good" or "bad." The surging, bright energy of Aries is admirable and necessary for initiative when positively expressed, and its collective energy is reflected in the pioneering spirit that has spearheaded exploration. The end of the Arian Age, however, found much of humanity entrenched in a religious paradigm that expressed Aries at its fiery, masculine worst. God had become unequivocally male, and only man was created in His image. The Goddess had become secondary even in the Roman empire, and in the culture through which the new Piscean Age paradigm would most significantly emerge, She had vanished in the Fire that proclaimed to Moses (presumably in basso-profundo tones) "I Am that I Am!"[2]

Jesus tried to soften his peoples' concept of God into an always forgiving father-figure, but the new religion was rooted in the fiery, punishing God-concept of the old age. The men who established the Christian hierarchy may have accepted the teachings of Christ in theory, but they acted according to unconscious habits of thinking carried over from the Aries dispensation. A changing paradigm, a new vision—or "Word"—was to be disseminated, but how did they act to do this? Witness the un-Christlike wars, slaughter, and heretic burnings of the early churchmen's actions that they claimed were done in the name of spreading the teachings of Christ.

Marion Weinstein says, in the beginning of the section of *Positive Magic* in which she tells us all of the things that are wrong with the Piscean Age but improved with Aquarius, that Jesus never intended this, but Christianity evolved according to choices made in the age that followed him.[3] I submit that Christianity evolved according to choices made according to the habits of thinking, the "programming," that carried over from the Arian paradigm.

Think about it... how old are people before they make choices that are not based on their past programming? At the very least they are around thirty, the age at which for the first time Saturn has traveled all the way around the zodiac and returned to the same degree as it was in their birth chart. Usually it is even later, at around the time of the so-called "mid-life crisis" when all of the outer planets make one hard aspect after another to their birth chart positions. Even the truly free choices made at thirty tend to go through various periods of testing before mature self-awareness emerges. How long do most people normally live? Say about 75 years? The mid-life crisis is at around 42. The Age of Pisces is about 2700 years long. Let's make an analogy of the age of a person and the age of an Age. 2700 divided by 75 gives us 36, which we can equate to one year for a person. For the Age to be the equivalent of 30 years old, we would have to look at the Renaissance. This is exactly the time when the nearly absolute power of the Church began to crumble, after the invention of the printing press had brought scripture to the masses for their own interpretation.

To continue the analogy: some have suggested that a woman should be especially honored at around age 50 (or the onset of menopause) as she enters the phase of the Crone (Wise Woman). Age 50 would equate to AD 1800. Did our feminine Age of Pisces begin to show her wisdom then? In *Beyond Power,* Marilyn French tells us that the feminist movement in America is deeply rooted in the struggle for abolition. The Grimkes, Angelina and Sarah, were among the first to speak out against slavery in 1836. In 1854, she goes on to say, Susan Anthony began the women's suffrage movement.[4] Now, 36 times 65 is 2340. Goddess! We are still in our prime! "Years" to go before "retirement" age! Plenty of time yet to work toward the fulfillment of the Piscean spiritual vision.

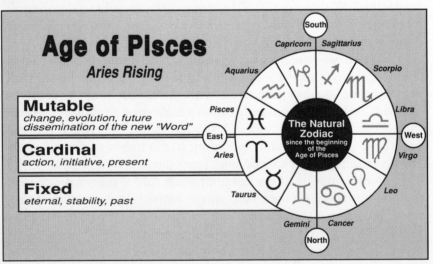

Note that "East" is on your left. A horoscope is not drawn like a road map. It is set up as if you are standing on Earth, looking up at the constellations of the ecliptic arcing across the southern sky. Therefore south is at the top and planets rise in the east to your left.

The so-called "natural zodiac" can be used to illustrate the relationship between vision and action. Aries rises, the first sign of the zodiac and the Cardinal Ascendant. The cardinal signs Aries, Cancer, Libra, and Capricorn are associated with the cardinal points of the compass: east, north, west, and south, respectively. This was not always the case. In the Age of Aries the cardinal points and guardians of the east, north, west, and south were Taurus, Leo, Scorpio, and Aquarius. The highly influential Babylonian astrologers used the star Aldebaron (the Bull's Eye of Taurus) and its direct opposite star, Antares in Scorpio, as the reference point for their zodiac.

The constellation for which an age is named is the one that rises before the sun at vernal equinox. The constellation that rises with the sun is cardinal east. Because the Sun is so bright, you can't see the more distant light of the stars, once the Sun has risen. Lost in the blinding sun rays, the cardinal constellation can no longer be seen, and was said, by the ancients, to be "sacrificed." Thus, at the end of the Age of Aries, the Ram—the Lamb of God—was sacrificed to bring in the new order. [5]

According to astrological tradition, the zodiac signs are said to have one of three qualities: cardinal, fixed, or mutable. Keywords for the "family" of cardinal signs (in this age: Aries, Cancer, Libra, and Capricorn) are action and initiative. The fixed signs (in this age: Taurus, Leo, Scorpio, and Aquarius) represent stability, and the mutable signs (in this age: Gemini, Virgo, Sagittarius, and Pisces) symbolize change and the dissemination of ideas. The zodiac symbol for which our Age of Pisces is named is mutable. Rising just before sunrise at vernal equinox, Pisces then symbolizes the new Word, the new ideals that are to be disseminated, the change in consciousness that is to be the new paradigm of spiritual evolution. This, then, symbolized the new Word at the advent of the Christ—the new Word that has been so misunderstood and distorted by so many. The nose of the western fish in the Pisces constellation still rises before the Sun—about 4-5 degrees of the Pisces constellation. Nearly 800 more years will pass before the precession of the equinoxes will cause the entire Pisces constellation to be "sacrificed" to the rising Sun. Only then will we truly be in the Age of Aquarius. At that time, will the predominant world view of the masses have finally grasped the full meaning of the Pisces dispensation—or not?

In the Age of Aquarius, Pisces will be rising at vernal equinox— the new "natural Cardinal Ascendant" and principle of action. We have seen the abuses of a negative Aries model for the cardinal action principle. Let's fantasize what a similarly negative Pisces model might be. Huxley's *Brave New World* comes to mind as a perfect prototype of an Aquarian idea (individual interests subordinated to the welfare of the group) with a Pisces Rising mode of action. Everyone escaped by spacing out on a drug called Soma.[6] Escapism and substance abuse, in any astrological text, is attributed to misuse of Piscean energy.

In our present day, as only a small portion of the Fishes rise before the Sun, and most of the constellation rises with it, a new collective concept of what constitutes "right" action seems to be emerging. That doesn't mean that Aries will no longer be a pioneer, or that Pisceans are becoming fiery and aggressive. It means that the collective consciousness is slowly but surely moving toward a time when the perception of the best way to act in order to achieve goals would be more Piscean in character than Arian. It means, for one example, that the majority of people no longer support impulsively charging forth to either conquer or defend. The Cold War has effectively ended, and there are signs that the superpowers are at last talking seriously about disarmament. (It remains to be seen whether a new system of astrology will someday emerge that will actually acknowledge Pisces as the Cardinal Ascendant.)

The Pisces-Virgo Polarity[7]

Another way to look at our age is through the symbolism of the Pisces-Virgo opposition. The Christian religion grew out of linear and dualistic concepts that emerged in the previous age, with Zoroastrianism around 500 BC. (It is interesting that it was about the time of the classical Greeks that the Pisces constellation was revisioned as two fish, where it had earlier been imaged as only one, yet the early Christians chose one fish as their symbol, still used today.) It was only natural that if a Piscean vision was to be "God," then its opposite, Virgo, would represent "not-God," or mortal humanity. We, collectively, are Virgo. Our advanced technology and highly developed specialties express her astrologically traditional attributes at their highest level of efficiency. But in the process, our very humanity is reduced to a computer number. Virgo out of balance with Pisces is descriptive of society's ills as well. Virgo is notorious for "missing the forest for the trees." Are we so caught up in mountains of trivia, in narrow fields of specialty, in details of living in our own small place on the planet, that we have lost sight of the whole? An astrology text might describe the faults of Pisces as lack of firm principles, vacillation, self-delusion, escapism, and a superficial sentimentality in place of true empathy. Do these not sound like familiar ills of the masses in these times?

Note that in Pisces and Virgo we have a challenge of balance between two feminine symbols. Opposition signs in the zodiac are complementary opposites. They have major issues in common, but ways of dealing with them that are different. The Virgo-Pisces polarity is involved with service. Ideally, Virgo the realist is unselfishly dedicated to fulfilling earthly human needs. Pisces the visionary is selflessly devoted to the needs of the spirit. The collective task of this age is to evolve to the highest expression of Virgo, and to then reach out toward the fulfillment of our Piscean vision. In the process, society expresses the best and worst of both ideals.

For example, a vast proportion of our technology is still used to build weaponry that is capable of reducing humanity to ashes. Small wonder that Piscean escapism (at its worst, augmented by drugs and alcohol) has run rampant. It is important to pause and reflect upon why we are building these things—or permitting them to be built by our silent acquiescence to those who hold positions of power. Our technology should serve the spirit and vision of humanity, not threaten to destroy it.

In the reality of our physical world, we humans come in many varied kinds—and how our Virgoan minds love to categorize and discriminate and criticize each others' differences! We differ in color, in nationality, in religion, in education, in language, in size, in taste—the list could go on and on. But suppose we were visited by a race of extra-terrestrials? Would we seem so different from each other to them—or would they simply regard us as all members of one species? Should we not concentrate our energy into discovering the ways in which we are similar? Perhaps, then, the empathy and compassion of our Pisces vision would come more easily, and the nebulous fears of negative Pisces would diminish.

The Demotion of Virgo and the Goddess

The Christian church, a major contributor to the distortion of the Virgin in this age, insists that she is mortal. Even though raised to Queen of Heaven, she is still not considered to be in the same class as Jesus, who is proclaimed to be one and the same as God before all creation. Astrological tradition calls Virgo a "barren sign," given to pickiness and pristine orderliness. Let's look at what she was before.

Pre-Christian religions considered Virgin to be an aspect of the Triple Goddess, and the term "virgin" did not necessarily mean chaste, but rather free and independent, property of no one. The Virgin of the constellation is mythologically the Earth Mother from whom all life emerges. She is the womb of time through which humanity must evolve. She represents the seed that is planted, and the labor and struggle of growth. And she is the bounty of the harvest, pictured as she is with a sheaf of wheat or an ear of corn. A "barren sign?" No! The virgin earth bursts with all of the potential of life and creation.

Probably the main zodiacal explanation that reflects the suppression and distortion of the feminine potential is that it is the Virgin herself who is now the symbol of opposition to our Pisces vision of deity. Once upon a time the Goddess, she became only a mortal and fit to be saved only by the benevolence of a Father God. However virtuous the maiden might be, she was still considered to be the descendant of Eve, who according the Biblical authors of Aries-time, led man to his downfall. According to that reasoning, if Pisces (Christ, God) is all good, than his opposite, Virgo the Maiden, must be bad—or even if she is virtuous, she must certainly be kept in her place!

As Simeon prophesied to Mary at the circumcision of Jesus:

> *This child is destined to be the downfall and the rise of many in Israel, a sign that shall be opposed, and you yourself shall be pierced with a sword, so that the thoughts of many hearts may be laid bare.*

> —Luke 2:34-35[8]

The sword must pierce the very heart and image of the Divine Mother, who would now take her turn as the opposition symbol to the deity of the age. The Virgo-mortal can "fall" or "rise" as the message of Pisces is revealed in the heart. Whatever have we done to our Virgo-selves?

Astrologically, the characteristics of the Virgin became distorted at the dawn of this age when Ptolemy assigned arbitrary planetary rulers for the signs. Leo and Cancer, at the zenith at the warmest part of the year, were assigned the Sun and Moon. The adjacent signs on either side, Gemini and Virgo, were to be ruled by Mercury, the closest planet to the Sun.[9] So it was that in our time Virgo became associated with the sexless, intellectual, analytical Mercury instead of her more natural crescent Moon. Mary-of-the-Gospels was also assigned her destiny by the winged "messenger of God."

For centuries collective society acted out its distorted and suppressed and misunderstood Virgo. When one so severely suppressed finally escapes, she is likely to emerge as a very angry lady, and the vehemence of the early feminist movement is just one example of her many extreme reactions. Now past the initial angry eruption in which many feminists, in their zeal to gain equality with men, emphasized almost "macho" behavior, the feminist spirituality movement has led us toward a higher identity with the full and rich womanhood that was the Mother Goddess before her fall. Progress in the spiritualization of Virgo that is necessary to reach the ideals of Pisces can be seen in the slow but inevitable trend to focus not on the masculinization of women, but rather to change our culture so that the concerns of the Goddess (such as ecology, disarmament, the nurturing and education of the young) receive the status and priority they deserve.

As a significant part of the process it is important to reclaim Mary from the patriarchal church. She, who is Virgo and also Pisces, and who appears in the Gospels in the roles of Virgin, Mother, and Crone, must be restored to Her rightful role as Goddess.

The New Renaissance

Pisces has been an age of extreme shifts in world view, and is now seeing yet another major shift, all within the larger paradigm that was introduced at the beginning of the age. Illustrated on the next page is a symbolic pendulum of this age that includes its vision, Pisces, at the top of the center balance pole, and its reality, Virgo, at the bottom.[10] At the extreme outward swings of the pendulum are

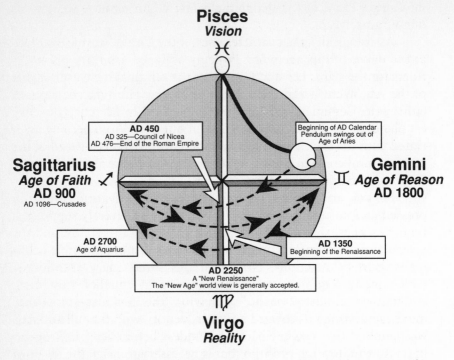

the two squares of the mutable cross, Sagittarius and Gemini, the characteristics of which quite accurately reflect the two most extreme paradigm shifts within this age.[11] Imagine that our pendulum swings out of the Age of Aries, and in one full swing to the opposite extreme, a full swing back, and then one more, it completes the Age of Pisces and enters Aquarius. At the first passage of the center pole, the transition period from the Age of Aries to the Age of Pisces is completed with the fall of the Roman Empire and the Council of Nicea. At that council a central figure was a priest named Arius (how coincidental!), who insisted upon the absolute monotheistic concept that had emerged in the outgoing age. Arius was overruled by those who supported the Holy Trinity, with God, Jesus, and the Holy Spirit as "one and the same substance." He was condemned as a heretic and exiled.

The first extreme paradigm shift was in full flower as the pendulum swung to Sagittarius. (A key issue of the Sagittarius-Gemini polarity is wisdom. Gemini sees truth through reason and logic, while Sagittarius sees truth through revelation and faith.) Here we have the era that history books call the Age of Faith. The sciences were suppressed and the church reigned dogmatically supreme, its edicts to be accepted on faith, without question or doubt.

As the pendulum passed its center pole, again a period of balance between the extremes of the two squares was reflected in the Renaissance. (This, as said before, could be considered a "mid-life crisis" of the age!) The individual discernment and the concepts of reality (Virgo) that did not fit into official dogma had been too long suppressed. Like the "shadow" of Carl Jung's psychology, it was about to erupt. The printing press spread the Bible to the masses, no longer could one church control what the people believed, and the old dogmatic days were nearly over. Quite independently from the churches, great advances were being made in scientific observations. The pendulum would later swing to the opposite extreme with a vengeance.

The imaginary pendulum swung out to Gemini in the eighteenth century, called by historians the Age of Reason. The dominant paradigm became materialist science, which dismissed with scorn any intangibles that could not be analyzed under a microscope, seen through a telescope, measured in a test tube ... proved! The intellectual establishment discredited any assumptions about the nature of the universe that could not be supported by rigorous scientific investigation. Scientists had no time to consider unproven assumptions based on human experience or revelation. Interest in the intangible spirit waned to zero. Rationalism and materialism became reigning philosophies.

In this era, the pendulum is swinging back toward center. The absolutes of the mechanistic science world view are being questioned from within and without. New religious concepts of immanence and power-from-within are emerging that are more holistic, more in keeping with the keyword Piscean vision of synthesis. I think that shortly after the dawn of the new millennium a "New Renaissance" will find our culture in a new paradigm that reconciles the opposite extremes of faith and reason, and that truly restores the balance between the masculine and feminine polarity. This is the New Age that is dawning! Perhaps it will truly be a Renaissance ("rebirth") of the vision of Pisces in full flower as the mass collective consciousness finally feels what its feminine, watery, mystical flow of love was intended to be in the first place. Only then will humanity be prepared to act (Pisces rising as Cardinal Ascendant!)[12] in a manner that will allow the new "truths" of Aquarius to emerge in balance.

Endnotes

1. For those interested in more extensive information on precession and its correlation with history and mythology, see:

   Twelve Wings of the Eagle (which cites the end of the Age of Pisces as about AD 2700), San Diego: ACS Publications, 1988.

   Hamlet's Mill (a scholarly treatment of mythology and astrology/astronomy which speaks of the Age of Pisces as having "several centuries yet to go") by Giorgio de Santillana and Hertha von Dechend, Boston: Godine, 1981.

   Essays on Astrology (which by computer calculations based on the star maps of Ptolemy, cites 2800 as the end of the Age of Pisces), by Robert Hand, Rockport, MA: ParaResearch, 1982.

2. "I Am that I Am" is what the Bible, in Exodus, tells us God, speaking from a burning bush, said to Moses. "I Am" is the motto for Aries, which you will find in dozens of books, on astrological calendars, etc.

3. Weinstein, Marion. *Positive Magic: Occult Self-Help.* Custer, WA: Phoenix Publishing, Inc., 1981.

4. French, Marilyn. *Beyond Power.* New York: Summit Books, 1985.

5. This is the way the authors of *Hamlet's Mill* explained that observation was made that a new age had begun.

6. Huxley, Aldous. *Brave New World.* New York: Harper & Bros., 1932.

7. This section is largely reworked or repeated text from *Twelve Wings of the Eagle.*

8. *The New American Bible,* Catholic Edition. New York: Thomas Nelson Publishers, 1971.

9. Waverly translation, *Ptolemy's Tetrabiblos.* North Hollywood, CA: Symbols & Signs, 1976.

10. Illustration reprinted from *Twelve Wings of the Eagle.*

11. There are four signs in each of the three families: cardinal, fixed, and mutable. The four form a cross that divides the circle in quarters. The complete circle is 360°. One quarter of it is 90°, or a "square." In astrological terminology, a 90° aspect between two points is called a square. In the symbolic model illustrated, Pisces as the God-concept of the age is at the top. Virgo, 180° opposite, at the bottom of the circle, symbolizes "not-God" or mortality. The signs Sagittarius and Gemini, forming a horizontal bar, each 90° from the central axis formed by Pisces/Virgo, are used here to symbolized the extreme world views within the Age of Pisces. It is interesting —coincidental?!—that the historical times of the height of these extreme world views came at even intervals of the total period of the age.

12. When nothing more remains to be seen of the constellation Pisces just before sunrise at vernal equinox, Pisces will fully be (whether astrologers designate it so or not) the Cardinal East sign, the Cardinal Ascendant, and the constellation Aquarius will be the heliacal rising constellation, and reflect the mutable (changing) paradigm to which the masses must adapt. By then, if trends continue—which I propose they will—the Piscean habits of thinking will have mass acceptance as the right way to act. Hopefully, this will primarily involve the Piscean ideals of universal love—love thy neighbor as thyself; as ye harm none, do as ye will; do unto others as you would have them do onto you—and synthesis, compassion for all life, and mysticism. Or will society continue to overemphasize escapism, delusion, and martyred or "poor-me-the-victim" attitudes? Either choice reflects characteristics of Pisces.

The New World View

The Current Shift: Dualism versus Immanence

So a new world view is emerging—and with it, a new concept of the divine that currently ranges from considerations within some traditional churches of God as father and mother, through an emphasis on Goddess in the rapidly growing Neo-Pagan religions, to the outright exclusion of the masculine aspect of God within some Goddess-worshipping feminist spirituality groups.

Yet the shift from God to Goddess is only an overt manifestation of the new concept. The more basic change of thinking is not about *who* God is, but about *where* he/she/it is. It is about cycles and circles, rather than straight lines from beginning to end. And it is about synchronicity and relativity as basic assumptions about "how things work," rather than strict cause and effect.

Where is God?

In the fading God-concept of orthodox or fundamentalist religions, God (even when occasionally acknowledged as father-mother God) is always "out there"—separate and apart from the material world and from us mere mortals. God resides in "Heaven." People who are "saved" will go there after they die, where they (as often characterized in art from cartoons to museum masterworks) remain still separate from God, who reigns from his throne, forever out of reach. People who are not saved will go to the opposite place, a fiery Hell of eternal punishment.

The "out there" idea is extremely dualistic. If God remains outside the universe, and if God is all "good," where does that leave everything else? Why, the opposite, of course—"bad!" And thus we have a concept of the material world as being inherently evil, and of people being born in "original sin."

The dualism is carried to a further extreme with the concept of the total opposite of God: Satan. Satan is perhaps a natural projection of a people who have already projected the power and the responsibility for their goodness and their salvation onto a transcendent God. If God is the ultimate good, then Satan is the ultimate evil, and the ultimate solution to any lack of personal power or responsibility is simple. Pray to God for intervention and salvation, and either excuse any occasion for unhappiness as "God's will" or blame it on the interference of Satan. In any case, the responsibility and the power to effect desired change lies outside the self, outside the material world.

In the emerging world view, God/Goddess/the Life Force (whatever one prefers to call it) is immanent within the universe, alive within everything and everyone. Satan simply does not exist. One outgrowth of this concept is a perception of the universe and each newborn inhabitant as inherently "good," or in harmony with the flow of life. Through various life experiences one may learn to live primarily in disharmony, and therefore effect self and environment in a manner that creates unhappiness. This leads us to a second outgrowth of the concept, that the power and the responsibility to effect change (and therefore become happier) resides within each individual.

Dualism, within the new world view, does not exist in the same sense that it does in the Judeo-Christian tradition. In the new paradigm, the Life Force—the Whole—encompasses the full cycle of experience—birth, growth, harvest, death, birth again, and so on, around and around in an endless, eternal cycle. No part of the life experience is seen as an absolute "good" or "evil."

Yes, there is still dualism. Obviously, there are opposites in the world—male and female, light and dark, noise and silence, etc. But none of these things are labeled "good" or "bad." Dualism is perceived more in the manner of a battery charge, where both positive and negative poles are necessary to make the thing work. One's perception of what is "good" or "bad" in any situation or circumstance is relative to the harmony or disharmony of the whole.

Now, granted, within the outgoing world view, God (or more often, the Holy Spirit) is also referred to as immanent within the Universe, permeating everything. And within the emerging world view one also sometimes hears talk of transcending physical reality. The difference, though, is that in actual practice, the former view is primarily one of a transcendent deity, while the latter view is primarily one of an immanent deity.

The concept of transcendence, in the new view, does not set God apart from either self or the Universe. Rather, it proposes an essence of self, or spirit, that lives before and beyond physical incarnation in any one specific human body—a self who may choose to incarnate in more than one—or many—physical lives. (Belief in reincarnation—the ultimate human recycling!—is prominent in new paradigm thought.)

Another way in which transcendence could be defined within the new world view is in the capacity of mind to constantly expand beyond previously perceived limitations, and to further expand by drawing upon the energies of the group mind and upon the energies of the immanent Life Force.

Cycles and Circles versus Lines

The outgoing world view thinks in lines. God created the universe—a specific beginning. Someday it will come to an end. Lines have opposite ends, and thus the extremes of dualism. People are born once, the soul is born with the body (if soul and body are thought separate at all). When one dies, the soul may go to Heaven or Hell, but there is still only one body, and in the more fundamentalist view, that body will be resurrected at the Last Judgment. Other examples of linear thinking include mechanistic science, with its ultimately unprovable assumption that all effects have a cause, and highly hierarchical socio/political systems—the patriarchy.

The new world view thinks in circles. The wheel always turns, the cycles repeat again and again. There is no beginning and no end, only continuum. It is not necessarily true that any one thing must cause another; the two may be merely synchronous, or correspond to each other. Reality is subjective. Now, these concepts are no more ultimately provable than the former. The point is that many aspects of any culture—religious, sociological, scientific, political—rest on basic assumptions that are a matter of faith, and not absolutely proven truths. Once the assumption becomes the prevailing view, it is taken for granted, and it spins off onto a myriad of things that are then "proven" according to the basic assumption that is unprovable!

Current manifestations of the growing tendency toward cyclical thinking include the ecology movement, modern physics, modern economics and the growing interdependence of one nation on another, belief in reincarnation, and Neo-Pagan religious movements.

Neo-Pagan Religion—What Is It?

Here we must begin to deal with various words that have acquired quite different meanings over the centuries. "Pagan" comes from the Latin root *paganus,* which means a person who lives in the country. When Christianity became dominant in the time of the Roman Empire, it was first fashionable in urban areas. People who lived in rural areas were the last to be converted, preferring to keep to the old ways. To call someone a pagan in those times meant about the same thing as if a "city slicker" today called a farmer a "hick" or a "country bumpkin." A little later, according to my daughter's Latin textbook, *paganus* was used to signify civilian, as opposed to *miles,* a soldier, because the Christians called themselves the "soldiers of Christ." Eventually, with the increasing dominance of Christianity, came the present day Webster's definition of "Pagan" as "one who has no religion." Webster's first definition of "religion" is "belief in or worship of God or gods." These definitions, it would seem, surely reflect the intolerant attitude of established religion—if you don't believe in God in the manner as defined by the ruling majority, you have no religion or, as in the implication of the definition of religion, you believe in "gods" (note lower case).[1]

In any case, the modern day definition of Pagan is quite unfair. The ancient Pagans most certainly did have a religion—one that honored and respected Mother Earth and saw Her in every plant and every creature. In recreating elements of the "old religion," Neo-("new") Pagans see the deity manifest and active in all aspects of nature, and of course they also see that divine spark within all people. This is immanence. One could also call it pantheism (Webster: "all forces and manifestations of the universe are God")[2]—the concepts are quite similar, if you bring God/Goddess within instead of projecting deity "out there." No doubt Christian dualists would differ with me on this point. They could accept the idea that God as Holy Spirit is operative within the Universe, and call that "immanence," but would reject the idea that God is in everyone and everything (pantheism), for that would give no satisfactory place for their belief in the existence of Satan.

This brings us to a second major characteristic of Pagan/Neo-Pagan religion (which I will henceforth refer to as just "Pagan"): polytheism, which Webster defines as "belief in more than one god."[3] Perhaps this was true of the ancient Pagans, but in regard to today's Pagan movement, we need to probe the meaning of that word a bit. Yes, we speak of Goddess and God, and we speak of them in many different names. Yet all of them are seen and understood to be only different aspects of the Whole—One divine force that is immanent within the Universe. This One is so big, so powerful, so awesome that we cannot possibly comprehend its totality. We are like the parable of the blind men examining different parts of the same elephant, all reaching a different opinion of what the elephant is. So in order to bring the One into a relationship with our lives that will be comprehensible, we personify the particular aspect that is helpful to us at that time. By weaving into our rituals a particular Goddess or God mythology, we learn about aspects of ourselves that will help us live more in harmony with our Universe.

Yes, we worship both Goddess and God, the feminine and masculine, the yin and yang aspects, of the One. Yet we do not project them "out there" as distinctly and forever separate from ourselves and each other. The Goddess and the God dwell within each of us, whether male or female. The Universe can no more work without both of these energies than a battery can work without a positive and negative charge.

So in this sense of understanding of the Universe, what on the surface may be called polytheism is really monotheism!

Now, let's take a look at a religion that considers itself to be monotheistic, believing in only one God. We've already covered the widespread belief among Christians in Satan, as a force separate and apart from God. (That's two.) Now, consider the Trinity. Of course, Father, Son, and Holy Spirit are said to be of one and the same substance—but how many Christians really, truly, understand that concept? (That's three—four, counting Satan!) And then we have the Catholic saints—many of whom are renamings of Pagan Goddesses and Gods. (I've lost count!) In addition to all of this we have the fact that Christianity is subdivided into hundreds of different denominations, largely because Christians have never really been able to agree on just how to define the nature of their "one" God. The only aspect that gets short shrift is Mary, proclaimed "Mother of God" by the Catholics but still clearly defined as a mortal, and nearly totally ignored by other denominations.

Pagans do not necessarily disbelieve in Jesus and Mary as important aspects of the One—I have both attended and conducted rituals where they were specifically honored (See Yule, page 163). What is rejected is the concept that there is only one way to conceive of God. Pagans are very tolerant. To them, "polytheism" means merely that there are many realities. I have my own set of beliefs—at this moment. I expect that some of them will change; the only constant in life is change! You have yours, too. That's okay.

Is Today's Pagan Religion "Old," or Is It Mostly New?

Much has been said about the antiquity of "the old religion." Many books are in print that have researched "herstory," piecing together remnants of a pre-Christian time when the primary deity was the Goddess of many names, and when society was matrifocal, agrarian, and peaceful. This is absolutely necessary to begin to restore some semblance of balance after centuries of male dominance and suppression of the feminine. I submit, however, that when we go on at length about following the "old path" in our spiritual practices and religious symbolism, we are just plain kidding ourselves.

Pagan religious rites of today probably bear about as much resemblance to medieval Witchcraft or ancient Druidic ritual as the practices of the present-day Catholic church resemble those in the periods of the Inquisition or the Crusades. Elements of the old are used, but what we are creating with them is brand new—a reflection of our time and our searching for a religion that is spiritually meaningful to us now. This is true of all aspects of Pagan religion—Wicca, the feminist spirituality movement, and even the currently popular Native American Medicine Wheels.

Summary of Current Forms

Wicca has become a general term for "the Craft," or contemporary Witchcraft. Actually a bit of the residue of male dominance has slipped in here, too, for the Old English *wicca* referred to the male practitioner; the female was *wicce*. Yet "Wicca" is in general usage to refer to the religion itself, encompassing both sexes.

Although many Wiccans define "Wicca" as being derived from a word for wisdom (Craft of the Wise), it is probably more correct that its root word is the Indo-European *wic,* meaning to bend. "To bend" implies "to change," and much of Wiccan practice is directed toward empowering the individual with the ability to create desired changes.

While "Craft of the Wise" may not be technically correct, according to the actual derivation of words, it still contains truth, both for the old times and the new. Witches of old were looked upon within their communities as being wise, and skilled in healing and practical magic. Today's Witches tend to be quite interested and involved in ecology, natural healing practices, psychic development, meditation, and general self-help and group support therapies. They place strong emphasis on personal responsibility.

Both Goddess and God are worshipped in Wicca, although Goddess is usually more prominent, and the primary leader of most groups is the High Priestess. (This may or may not have been true in the past; it is currently true largely because of the reaction to the imbalances of the patriarchal church that runs through all aspects of the Pagan revival movement.) Both male and female Wiccans are called Witches.

(In case some readers may be wondering, the term "warlock" is not used by Wiccans. It is derived from an old Anglo-Saxon word that means a traitor or liar, and was used to refer to a sorcerer who had made a pact with the devil. Since Wiccans do not believe in the devil, it is thought that the word "warlock" was long ago applied to Pagans by Christians who did believe in the devil and wished to suppress any but their own faith. In any case, if you hear anyone refer to a male Witch as a warlock, you are probably hearing someone who is not Wiccan, expressing his or her ignorance of Wiccan terminology.)

In a typical mixed Wiccan group, the concept of balance between feminine and masculine is important. The ritual is conducted by a High Priestess and High Priest together. Other members of the circle participate, perhaps "calling the quarters." Magickal practice is an accepted part of the Craft, although it is not the main aspect. More about that in Chapter 5.

Wiccan groups are quite small, for most meet in someone's home. A group of much more than a dozen is unusual; less than that is probably more common. Some groups follow a specific tradition, often handed down through families, generation to generation. Most groups are fairly eclectic. No collection plate is passed. Although a High Priestess may accept a fee for teaching a public class, perhaps at a metaphysical book shop, it is very rare for one to charge a fee for training the people whom she accepts as members of her circle.

Wiccan circles are quite autonomous. There are a few areas of common agreement on ethics, which will be discussed in a later chapter. There are some common elements that one can expect to find almost anywhere, such as moving sunwise within the ritual area and calling the elements (fire, air, earth, and water) to the four directions, but there is absolutely no central governing authority. Most Wiccan groups have a formal training program in the Craft, set by the High Priestess and/or High Priest, which takes the form of "degrees." This varies, but to my knowledge, Dedication followed by three progressive degrees is fairly common.

Although, as I've said, modern groups tend to be very eclectic, most of the common practices mentioned above can be traced to the Gardnerian tradition which was begun by English Witch Gerald Gardner in the 1950s.

Gardner is chiefly credited with the revival of Wicca in western culture. He wove his tradition from a mixture of various threads that included Golden Dawn ritual magick, Masonry, Rosicrucianism, folklore, and other older traditions and mythologies. He collaborated with High Priestess Doreen Valiente, a poet, who is generally credited with a greatly increased emphasis on the Goddess, and with the original writing of the widely known and much loved "Charge of the Goddess."

The primary ethic, and the one absolute law, that is common to all groups is "As you harm none, do as you will." More about that, too, in Chapter 4.

Feminist Wicca

Although I, personally, heard little of it until 1980, I now understand that beginning in the late 1960s, and gaining momentum in the 1970s, some leaders of the feminist movement sought to reclaim female power and raise consciousness by seeking a feminine form of divinity. They adopted elements of the "old religion" that worshipped the Goddess. The forms of Wicca that have emerged from the feminist spirituality movement are in many ways similar to Wicca, as described above, so I will not repeat myself on the similarities.

A primary difference is that feminist groups tend to be all female. Sometimes their practices are referred to as Dianic Wicca (after the Goddess Diana). Some groups work with the balance of masculine and feminine within. One of the women will take the role of High Priest. Yet some groups virtually reject the God, perhaps feeling that religion has been so badly skewed in his favor for so many centuries, that it is only right to now give exclusivity to the Goddess. Rejecting the God is probably more likely to be the practice of a lesbian or primarily lesbian group, although this is also likely to be an understandable choice for heterosexual women who have been abused by men. Some feminist Wiccans harbor a lot of anger against men; others do not, but just prefer to meet with all women.

Another difference is that many feminist Wiccan groups are formed by women who have had no formal training in Craft. They are often totally non-hierarchical, feeling that any structure that resembles hierarchy smacks of patriarchy. The role of High Priestess may rotate among all of the women in the group, and decisions are made by consensus. Such groups use elements of "traditional" Wicca—the traditions are easy to find; there are hundreds of books in print. Essentially, though, they make up their own rites, and often do so very beautifully and creatively, as is evidenced by the many books that have emerged from the movement.

In my opinion, the many published contributions of the feminist Witches have had a massive influence on the practice of contemporary Wicca, and indeed the entire Pagan revival. A number of the feminists, rather than remaining discreetly "in the broom closet" as mixed Wiccan groups tend to do, came out quite publicly and vocally about what they were doing and wrote books about it—lots of books. They wore the name "Witch" like a badge of honor, and defied any one to defy them. (More about this a little further ahead in this chapter under the heading "The 'W' Word.")

With this greater openness, some Wiccans from older traditions became more open, too. Interest in any book topic tends to breed more books. The number of Wiccan and Goddess-emerging books available today is overwhelming compared to when I had my book shop in the mid-70s. At that time, even I, an owner of a metaphysical book shop which sponsored lectures and classes on a wide variety of topics, carried practically nothing on Witchcraft. Nothing much was available on my distributor lists except that which sounded somehow "power-over" oriented, or otherwise suspicious of being "black."

The creativity of the feminist authors in making ritual relevant has influenced the practice of many Wiccan groups with both male and female members, including, of course, my own. And when I compare even some recently published books by male Witches with those published years ago, I see changes in approach that are very likely related to the influence of feminist Wicca.

There is a greater tendency within feminist Wiccan groups than within mixed groups to be actively involved with various political movements that are part of the feminist agenda, although mixed-group Wiccans are likely to be individually interested or involved in many of the same issues.

The feminist Witches are also largely responsible for raising public awareness about the "burning times." This is the dark period of the Catholic Inquisition when people, mostly women—sometimes whole town's populations of women—were arrested and burned after being tortured into confessions of Witchcraft. I think some of the published numbers into the millions are a bit far-fetched in regard to actual populations at that time, but numbers in the hundreds of thousands have been substantiated.

Medicine Wheels

There are more similarities than differences in the interests and practices of those who are drawn to Native American Medicine Wheel
rituals and those who are drawn to Wicca. I daresay that part of the
popularity of the Medicine Wheel (at least among those who are not
of Native American ancestry) is that "Native American" is fashionable and respectable in the general public eye, while Wicca still bears
the stigma of the evil fairy tale Witch.

Of course, some of the Medicine Wheels today are being led by
Native Americans who are teaching the true ancient traditions of
their tribes. But probably the majority of those studying and working with the Native American and Shamanic motifs have little or no
actual Native American blood in their veins. Of most of the Medicine Wheels I've attended at various conferences, I think it would be
fair to speak similarly to what I've already said about Wicca—the
present-day practices probably bear about the same amount of
resemblance to what actually went on in the ancient Native American tribes as contemporary Wiccan practice resembles an ancient
Celtic Druidic rite.

Medicine Wheel rituals, like Wicca, relate to the cycles of Earth
and sky, to respect for Mother Earth, to responsibility for oneself
and what one is creating in life, to the immanence of deity, and to the
search for a religion that is meaningful to replace that of the established churches that no longer suffice.

Other Groups

There are certainly other groups that generally share the world view
expressed here, but who would probably not identify themselves as
Pagans. It's even quite possible that some who identify with groups
like those I have just summarized may not think of themselves as
Pagans, either. Perhaps by the time the Age of Aquarius finally does
arrive, a new name might be invented for this new world view that
will satisfy everyone. Meanwhile, you will find a similar emphasis on
concepts of God or Goddess within, along with the consequent
emphasis on responsibility for self, in a wide variety of groups that
are exploring meditation techniques, Eastern religions, mind control,
self-help support, etc. Even a few churches now place such strong
emphasis on the concept of Christ-within or Christ-consciousness

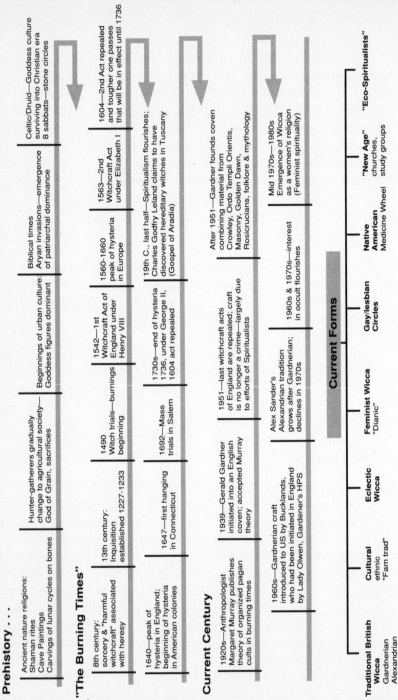

Evolution of Neo-Pagan Religion

Prehistory . . .

Ancient nature religions:
Shaman rites
Cave Paintings
Carvings of lunar cycles on bones

Hunter-gatherers gradually
change to agricultural society—
God of Grain, sacrifices

Beginnings of urban culture:
Goddess figures dominant

Biblical times
Aryan invasions—emergence
of patriarchal dominance

Celtic/Druid—Goddess culture
surviving into Christian era
8 sabbats—stone circles

"The Burning Times"

8th century;
sorcery & "harmful
witchcraft" associated
with heresy

13th century:
Inquisition
established 1227-1233

1490
Witch trials—burnings
beginning

1542—1st
Witchcraft Act of
England under
Henry VIII

1560-1660
peak of hysteria
in Europe

1563—2nd
Witchcraft Act
under Elizabeth I

1604—2nd Act repealed
and tougher one passes
that will be in effect until 1736

1640—peak of
hysteria in England;
beginning of hysteria
in American colonies

1647—first hanging
in Connecticut

1692—Mass
trials in Salem

1730s—end of hysteria
1736, under George II,
1604 act repealed

19th C. last half—Spiritualism flourishes;
Charles Godfry Leland claims to have
discovered hereditary witches in Tuscany
(Gospel of Aradia)

Current Century

1920s—Anthropologist
Margaret Murray publishes
theory of organized pagan
cults in burning times

1939—Gerald Gardner
initiated into an English
coven; accepted Murray
theory

1951—last witchcraft acts
of England are repealed; craft
is no longer a crime—largely due
to efforts of Spiritualists

After 1951—Gardner founds coven
combining material from
Crowley, Ordo Templi Orientis,
Masonry, Golden Dawn,
Rosicrucians, folklore & mythology

1960s—Gardnerian craft
introduced to US by Bucklands,
who had been initiated in England
by Lady Olwen, Gardener's HPS

Alex Sander's
Alexandrian tradition
grows after Gardnerian;
declines in 1970s

1960s & 1970s—interest
in occult flourishes

Mid 1970s—1980s
Emergence of Wicca
as a women's religion
(Feminist spirituality)

Current Forms

| Traditional British Wicca Gardnerian Alexandrian | Cultural ethnic "Fam trad" | Eclectic Wicca | Feminist Wicca "Dianic" | Gay/lesbian Circles | Native American Medicine Wheel | "New Age" churches, study groups | "Eco-Spiritualists" |

that they belong almost more to the so-called New Age than to mainstream Christianity.

The timeline illustrated on page 40 shows some of the archeological findings and historical dates that are in the background of present-day revivals of Pagan religion.[4] Again, however, I think it would be more honest to acknowledge that present day forms of Wicca have relatively small connection with the "burning times" or with the earlier religions noted on the timeline, other than the revival of three main ideas:

1. religion based on attunement with and celebration of natural cycles of Earth and Cosmos,
2. the divinity of Nature, and
3. personification of deity as the Goddess.

Other than these, most of our current practices are no more historically "ancient" than Gardner, if indeed that old. What is happening now is a new creation—a new religion—in response to the spiritual needs of our own time.

This summary is deliberately short, for it is not my main purpose in this book to detail the history and origins of Wicca. Margot Adler has done that very thoroughly in *Drawing Down the Moon,* and I recommend that you read it.[5] Other sources for historical background are also listed in the Annotated Bibliography.

Another book that gives good descriptions of the various Wiccan traditions is *To Know* by Jade.[6] I found Jade's book very informative, easy to read, and enjoyable (with the exception that she is one of the two authors mentioned previously who give the Age of Pisces such a hard time and attributes all of its virtues to Aquarius). She compares and contrasts various Wiccan traditions with each other and with feminist groups—even to the point of an amusing list of generalizations about how Wiccans compare with mainstream culture. Her list even included such detail as suggesting that Wiccans are more likely to have a Volkswagen, and to be non-technically oriented. I admit to having once owned a Volkswagen, but I don't share her experience that Wiccans tend to be "no-tech or low-tech." At least in the San Diego Pagan community, the typical Book of Shadows is likely to be a "Disk of Shadows," and there are also Pagan computer bulletin boards. Maybe it's only that my business is so involved with computers that I am more likely to encounter people who are similarly involved, but it seems to me that of the Pagans

I've met in San Diego, the majority are in computer-related career fields. A fairly close second in numbers would be the nurses or other health-care professionals, and theirs could hardly be called a low-tech field, either.

The "W" Word

Where did that old children's chant come from: "Sticks and stones may break my bones, but words will never hurt me"?

Frankly, I'd just as soon drop it—the "W" word—Witch. It carries more heavy baggage than it is perhaps realistic to ever expect it to shed. Some feminists have made a big, public point of "owning" the word, determined to reclaim it from its many negative connotations and forcing a change in how it is perceived, just as they seek to force changes in the status of women. They tie it to the idea of women claiming their power, saying that a Witch is a woman of power and that is why the word is so threatening to people who wish to deny the emerging feminine. While I empathize with that position, it must be admitted that power can be used in many different ways, even by those who call themselves "Witches," and some uses of that power are very different in their values from those of Wicca.

Whether we like it or not, on top of all the unpleasant images of Witches derived from children's fairy tales, Halloween cartoons, Hollywood horror movies, and the like, we also have to contend with the decidedly non-Wiccan cultists or Satanic groups who are also prone to call at least their female members "Witches." Or if they don't call themselves such, and they get in trouble with the law, certainly the arresting officers and media reporters do. And then there are the law-abiding but publicity-seeking types who have probably never had anything to do with a Wiccan group, but still call themselves "Witches" and make their living selling instructions for spells and potions and various other manipulations that make us cringe with disgust.

We can say a thousand-and-one times that Wicca is not like that, and that these people have nothing to do with us and never did, and we still won't make a dent in the general public impressions. The "W" word is definitely in the way of the kind of tolerance that would allow the legions of Wiccans who practice very privately to "come out of the broom closet."

For every Wiccan I know who is open about his or her religion, I know of dozens of others who dare not be open. They would lose jobs, lose leases and be forced to move, or literally be in physical danger from self-righteous people in their environments who claim to be good Christians "doing the Lord's work." This was the motive of one man I know of, who observed that a neighbor had several guests who met inside his home at each Full Moon, and that shortly after everyone went inside, the lights were dimmed. After a cat or two was found dead in the neighborhood, this "good Christian" jumped to the conclusion that the group that met at the Full Moon must be Satanists who were sacrificing cats. Did he ask his neighbor questions or do anything at all to verify his suspicions? No, he waited until the lights inside dimmed at the next Full Moon meeting and then he slashed the tires of all ten cars of his neighbors' guests. He then started vicious rumors that had every other neighbor frightened, until a friendly and open meeting arranged among the neighbors and members of the group who had been meeting there (but do so no longer) restored a semblance of peace. The tire slasher was not prosecuted; nothing could be proved, although everyone knew who he was.

In another recent San Diego incident, a Wiccan group holding a peaceful Sabbat ritual in a public park was stoned by a group of people who gathered on a hill above where the circle was formed. One stone just barely missed seriously injuring a toddler who was with his Wiccan mother in the circle.

I once attended a lecture by Margot Adler, in which she discussed the "W" word, admitting that it was easier for her to be open about being a Witch since as a New Yorker, she could "walk down the street stark naked if I chose and no one would give me a second glance." There are very few other places of which that could be said—even in so-called liberal southern California!

Even I, who am the employer and therefore immune from being fired, and a homeowner and therefore immune from a landlord finding an excuse to push me out, thought long and seriously before deciding to write this book, because of the possibility that it could bring about unpleasant repercussions on others close to me.

I well remember when one of my daughters (all of whom have attended some of my rituals and one of whom is now a Dedicate) said, "Mom, I know perfectly well that what you are doing is good and healthy and all that, but when you are talking to my friends at college or their parents, please don't identify yourself as a Pagan. You move in New Age groups where everyone understands you, but you have to remember that at least 85 percent of the rest of the people in this country would immediately associate 'Pagan' with 'Devil worshipper,' or at best, would consider you a fringe lunatic."

And then my mom and other family members still live in small towns in central Illinois where for many people my choice to become an artist was radical enough, to become an astrologer was really a head-shaker, and to become a Wiccan would be incomprehensible. Realizing that this book will find its way primarily into the hands of those for whom it is intended, those who are already seekers of the new world view, I can only hope that others with misconceptions who might cause problems for anyone close to me either will simply not see it, or if they do, will at least read it before they jump to conclusions. It is an unfortunate fact, though, that people who make the most noise over such things as books tend to react emotionally without really reading them, or considering the opposing view or the right of the viewer to hold it.

Forgive me for one more shot at those who would like to jump-start us into the Age of Aquarius, but I do think it important that "New Agers" at least occasionally emerge from the rarefied atmosphere of the "enlightened" to look around at the rest of the world. When practically the only people we ever talk to or choose to associate with, other than in necessary impersonal encounters of daily life, are people who share our world view, it is easy to forget that we are still a very small minority. My daughter's estimate regarding "85 percent of the rest of the world" is probably conservative. We still have a long way to go.

The Neo-Pagan or New Age world view of immanence and personal responsibility may well be the fastest growing religious movement today—I've heard that said, and I see plenty of evidence of it. It is growing because it answers the needs of people who are looking for a spiritual focus and can no longer find it within the dying world view of separatism, fear, guilt, intolerance, and blame that permeates so many churches. Yet you don't have to do much more than pick up a newspaper, visit a city school, walk down a street, or flip on the television to observe that the majority of our society is materialistic and secular. It has lost its soul, and a great many people do not seem to realize anything is missing—or if they do, they seem not to care.

They do what they must to survive financially, and other than that, they take the typical Piscean routes of escapism—many of them to the negative extremes of alcohol or drugs, and many more to the less damaging but still unproductive tactic of just tuning out reality and escaping into the fantasy world of the "tube" whenever they have a free moment.

Some well-meaning people who do care have taken a fundamentalist approach to the established religions, believing that the answer to today's problems is to reaffirm (and force through legislation, if necessary) the mores, rules, traditional families, obedience to religious authority, etc., that worked in the past. Ultimately, clinging to the past will not work, for it is out of sync with the much larger paradigm shift of the totality of this age, which is moving inevitably (although slowly, for our short lifetimes) in the Way of the Goddess.

So, while we can feel good about being on the cutting edge of change, we need also to retain some perspective in regard to how far that edge may be from the center point at which the shift in consciousness may reach the masses. That, my friends, is when we'll have a New Age. And by then, some new religious symbols that will keynote that new age, as the Fish did at the dawn of this one, will be widely recognized. If it turns out to be the Aquarian Waterbearer, I think he may have magically changed into a She (Pisces Rising), and She'll pour out waves of light!

Back to the "W" word: within the "family," the members of my circle use it—and that other "loaded" word, "coven"—quite freely, but we generally refer to ourselves in public as "Wiccans," and to our group, as a "circle." I really think this is best, as a general practice, though I know there are Wiccan Witches who vehemently disagree, but like it or not, all Witches are not Wiccans. If we could begin to establish that difference in the public mind, perhaps one day we could all freely hold rituals in public places without concern about being stoned. And perhaps we could celebrate our new religion that is loosely based on ancient European traditions with the same openness that others celebrate essentially the same new religion in the more socially acceptable forms that are loosely based on ancient Native American traditions, with leaders who call themselves Shamans rather than Witches. So why don't I just call myself a Shaman and start a Medicine Wheel group, you may ask? Maybe it's the half of my ancestry that goes back to Ireland, perhaps even to ancient Celtic traditions. Maybe it's a past life—who knows? I just feel more "at home" with Wicca.

I advise my coveners that family, neighbors and acquaintances are more likely to accept or feel comfortable with "Wicca" and "circle," especially if they are also seeing you as a person they like— cordial, considerate, a "good" neighbor. Putting out the word "Witch" before they get to know you can throw up a barrier that is difficult to break down. At the same time, I also tell those who seek to enter my circle that they must be prepared to accept and own the word "Witch." Unless you are independent, a bit unconventional, and comfortably self-assured enough to handle the possible consequences of being publicly identified as a Witch, you should probably not seek to become involved. I am quite open about identifying myself as a Witch in some public settings. In others I call myself Wiccan, and in still others I may only speak of my work in "sacred circle ritual"—at least until the dialogue progresses to a sufficient rapport to elaborate. One who forges brazenly into an unready world sporting black with a large pentagram cannot fairly blame that world for lack of understanding or non-acceptance. My advice: use common sense.

White Witches versus Black Witches

The "White Witch" mentality that exists within some Wiccans is yet another issue that relates back to my previous statement about how old our traditions really are. To hear some Wiccans tell it, all Witches are innocent, harmless, positive, and good, and all those fairy tales and Halloween and Hollywood images are a result of the atrocities of the medieval Inquisitors and the patriarchal Witch hunts of the burning times, and perpetuated by patriarchal Christianity. Please, let us not kid ourselves. Certainly there were great injustices in those times, but this is now, and Wicca today is primarily a reflection of where we are now. I do not think that the path to public acceptance is through a denial of basic common sense.

The fact is, all people, and consequently, all of our collective groups, have a dark side; in psychological terms, the Shadow. Wiccans are no exception. When the dark side is repressed and projected "out there" to blame things on something else, it is likely to backfire with a vengeance. It could be said that the very repression of what patriarchal society considered to be dark, the feminine, is why the feminist movement exploded into being with such anger. That which was denied became like the Shadow of the collective consciousness. Let us not set our collective selves up for an unexpected boomerang in the other direction.

People who set out to increase their level of awareness and abilities for mental focus and creative visualization—in other words, their power—as Wiccans do, also incur a heavy responsibility. Sometimes power builds; sometimes it destroys. Sometimes destructive power brings about a desirable result. But who decides? You do. And remember, "As you harm none, do as you will."[7]

Sometimes a choice must be made in which a perception of "harm" to someone involved with one of your options is impossible to avoid, yet you must choose. Then what? Your conscience must be constantly and closely examined, and you must be prepared to take responsibility for the consequences of what you choose.

I once heard a television interview of well-known Wiccan author Ray Buckland, in which one of the phone-ins stated his impression that the trouble with Wicca is that it had no ethic at all. Buckland responded with a statement of the great significance of the key concept of the ethic that is generally known as the Wiccan Rede: "As you harm none, do as you will." The caller returned with doubt to the effect that this was just too loose; it gave one no guidelines. Unfortunately, the discussion was cut off to bring on another caller. Television works in sound bites, rarely allowing anything to be covered in depth. It is undoubtedly easier for many to follow a religion that makes lots of rules. One can then avoid responsibility for many difficult choices. If you do as you are told is "right," and harm or unhappiness for someone—or even yourself—results, it can be accepted as "God's will."

Let's face it, like just about everyone, a Witch is capable of being a bitch, even though normally well-intentioned. (May all dog-lovers forgive me this use of another misused—but nicely rhyming—word of popular idiom.) The difference for you as a Wiccan is that you have no devil that you can say "made you do it!" To deny that somewhere deep within you have a potential for such emotions as anger, fear, envy, or that you may sometimes speak or act without thoroughly thinking through all of the ramifications, would be to deny your very humanity.

To pretend we are all good, and victims of the oppressive patriarchy or of intolerant fundamentalists, is the very antithesis of claiming our inner power. To be a Witch who learns to handle energy wisely and well requires serious thinking and self-examination, humility, and a great deal of *agape*—the Universal Love for all humanity, as differentiated from *eros*, which is the emotional love of attraction that often blows hot or cold.

Claiming Our Power

The time has come for us to claim our power—our right to practice our beliefs in peace within this country whose Constitution is supposed to guarantee freedom of religion.

We must begin by being honest with ourselves, and then, in the spirit of the tolerance and acceptance of other's differences that we would like to receive from others, we must reach out much more widely to network with each other.

We all place a high value on our autonomy, and there are justifiable fears that organization will lead to central control—justifiable because this is what has happened to so many institutions in the past. Yet so long as our circles stay isolated, secretive, and in little contact with each other, we will continue to have an environment where many must publicly hide or deny their very spiritual identity in order to protect their jobs, homes, and loved ones from intolerance.

We are all much more alike than we are different. Let us not fall into the trap of nit-picking at each other over differences in traditional forms, or even whether we are female, male, heterosexual, homosexual, old, young, or what have you. I believe it is possible for us to network and support each other and still retain autonomy of form and practice within our individual circles.

The advantage of networking and of a perception emphasizing our unity rather than our differences is the very simple fact that there is strength in numbers. Realistically, it will probably be some time yet before many of those who practice Wicca will feel free to do so publicly. Yet there is no doubt in my mind that if we had a means to draw upon our numbers in just about any area of the country, we would have to be recognized as a legitimate and therefore legally protected minority religion—with actually a lot larger numbers than quite a few others that are recognized minority religions! Think about it.

Endnotes

1. My daughter's textbook is *Our Latin Heritage,* by Hines, Welch and Bacon, New York: Harcourt, Brace, Jovanovich, 1966.

   This paperback dictionary that I had at hand when I was writing the "world view" chapter: Guralnik, David B., Ed., *Webster's New World Dictionary of the American Language*, New York: Fawcett, 1979.

   I recently compared the old paperback dictionary with my newer (1991) Merriam Webster *Webster's Ninth New Collegiate Dictionary,* Frederick C. Mish, Editor-in-Chief, which has slightly (in my opinion) improved wording for the words I'd looked up earlier. Most notable: "religion" is defined as "the service and worship of God or the supernatural." However, Pagan is still appearing only as "pagan" (note lower case), defined as "country dweller ... one who has little or no religion and who delights in sensual pleasures and material goods." (Can't deny the sensual pleasures part.)

   "Wicca" doesn't appear at all, except in italics, lower case, after "witch," which is defined as "1. one that is credited with usu. malignant supernatural powers; esp: a woman practicing usu. black witchcraft often with the aid of a devil or familiar, sorceress—compare warlock, 2: an ugly old woman; hag, 3: a charming or alluring girl or woman." (Well, now— maybe half right on that last one, missing only our sensitive and sexy menfolk!)

   Obviously, *Webster* needs our help! This also serves as yet another indicator of how far Wiccans are from mainstream acceptance of our religion—and how important it is for more of us to network with each other and communicate with the public.

2. Ibid.

3. Ibid.

4. This diagram was prepared for a circle class handout. I no longer remember exactly where I got these dates, but my Annotated Bibliography should cover all the books from which I may have learned this information.

5. Adler, *Drawing Down the Moon.*

6. Jade. *To Know: A Guide to Women's Magic and Spirituality.*
    Oak Park, IL: Delphi Press, Inc., 1991.

7. This phrase capsulizes an important ethic of Wicca. It will be
    discussed in greater depth in the next chapter.

The Ethics and Practice of Contemporary Wicca

This chapter will elaborate on material which was touched upon in the summary of Wicca in the previous chapter. Here, though, you will read details based upon the particular tradition in which I was trained, and have, in large part, passed on to my Circle of the Cosmic Muse, with some modifications. Lady Beckett has dubbed this tradition "West Coast Eclectic," and we've since heard that label adopted by other groups in southern California.

Beckett is High Priestess of Circle Atheneum, in which I have trained through Third Degree and have never completely left, in spite of my official "spinning off" and acknowledgment by her as High Priestess of my own Circle. She is a woman of magnetic presence, sharp intelligence, and deep empathy. She and other members of Circle Atheneum have become my good friends, whose supporting love was invaluable, especially during the very difficult year of my husband's bout with terminal cancer. I still attend as many of Atheneum's activities as my schedule permits.

Atheneum was formed to be a training coven, and Beckett has had a bit of a problem recently with making space for new seekers. She has nearly a full circle of Third Degrees now, with three more "spin-offs," another two pending, and none of these High Priestesses or High Priests want to completely leave, either. Atheneum is evolving into a loosely linked council of leaders who can meet as a peer group to share and support each other in our work with our individual circles.

Beckett has solved her wish to also be available to new seekers by starting a series of open classes, in which she is the primary teacher, assisted by Atheneum's spin-off HPs. The class group is called Dragonstar. It serves as an introduction to Wicca for the curious, a way to meet leaders of circles for those who decide they would like to take the step of joining one, and an additional class schedule for members of Atheneum's daughter circles who wish to participate. We all encourage our members, who want more group study than our own schedules provide for them, to attend Dragonstar.

I can think of no better way to open the discussion of ethics than to give you, with her permission, Lady Beckett's version of:

The Wiccan Way

Recognizing that there is more than one path to spiritual enlightenment, that Wicca is but one of many, and that Wicca holds within itself that belief that there is more than one type of step set to the Spiral Dance, find here listed common denominators of the Craft.

That there is above all the Goddess in Her threefold aspect, and many are Her names. With all Her names we call Her Maiden, Mother, and Crone.

That there is the God, Consort and Sun, giver of strength and most willing of sacrifice.

That an it harm none, do what we will, this be the law.

That each of Her children are bound by the threefold law and whatever we create, be it joy or sorrow, laughter or pain, is brought back to us threefold.

That as She is the Mother of all living things and we are all Her children, we seek to live in harmony not only with each other, but with the planet Earth that is our womb and home.

That death is not an ending of existence but a step in the ongoing process of life.

That there is no sacrifice of blood, for She is the Mother of all living, and from Her all things proceed and unto Her all things must return.

That each and every one of the children who follow this path has no need of another between themselves and the Goddess, but may find Her within themselves.

That there shall not by intent be a desecration of another's symbols or beliefs, for we are all seeking harmony within the One.

That each person's faith is private unto herself or himself, and that another's belief is not to be set out and made public.

That the Wiccan Way is not to seek converts, but that the way be made open to those, who for reasons of their own, seek and find the Craft.

And as it is willed, so mote it be.

—Lady Beckett,
Circle Atheneum, April 1988[1]

Recognizing that there is more than one path ...

We begin with that which is set forth in the first paragraph of The Wiccan Way—that there is more than one way. There are many realities, many paths, and to jump ahead for the moment and include the statement made toward the end, let us also note that "there shall not by intent be a desecration of another's symbols or beliefs, for we are all seeking harmony within the One."

This brings up the very important issues of diversity and autonomy in our Craft. One of the great beauties of Wicca is that there is no central governing authority that creates dogma, no pope whose word is infallible, no official headquarters that sets up rules. Each individual small circle is autonomous, free to choose its own expression. This would provoke in many people the same worries expressed by Ray Buckland's questioner, mentioned before: It's too loose. How does one know how to behave without standards and rules? Well, the standards may be few—and much more strict than one might think at first—but before we get to that, a few more thoughts about the issue of diversity and what I hope we will not do with it.

As I said in Chapter 2, Virgo symbolizes humanity in this Age of Pisces. A common fault of Virgo is to get so hung up on details that she misses the significance of the whole. An example of this can easily be illustrated with the Church, which took the simple, universal idea of "Love thy neighbor as thyself" and proceeded to splinter into hundreds of separate denominations over minor disagreements in procedures such as at what age to baptize, over varying interpretations of the Bible, etc.

But before we criticize such splintering as a Christian problem only, consider Wicca, which varies considerably in regional, traditional, family, feminist, lesbian, gay, mixed, Celtic, Faery ... traditions. Occasionally I hear rumblings of dissent or criticism of one group or another, picking at whether ritual should be done this way or that, or whether it is "right" or "wrong" to emphasize or suppress this or that, and I can only repeat a point made a slightly different way in the previous chapter, and say this:

Peace! If there ever was a religious movement that truly had a chance in this age of being open enough and tolerant enough to live the Piscean concepts of synthesis and Universal Love, it is this one. Let us not fall into the Virgo trap in the same manner as the many Christian denominations have—bickering and criticizing and emphasizing our separateness over doctrinal details. No matter what our basic individual traditions may be, we are much more alike than we are different. Live and let live! May we be serene in our basic concepts of immanence and multiple realities, and trust in the Goddess.

Certainly the need will grow for Pagan religions to band together more, in order to gain the freedom to worship openly and to more easily provide services for members. Jade's book *To Know* describes some councils that have been formed already.[2] Atheneum is well on the way to becoming another one. I believe that it is very possible and desirable to network with and support each other through such central organizations, so long as we keep the focus on our basic similarities, while respecting the autonomy of each circle, the freedom of each individual—and taking delight and creative inspiration from the richness of our diversity.

In discussing each part of The Wiccan Way, I draw some comparisons between Wiccan concepts and Christian ones. This is not done for the benefit of Christians, for I expect that few of them will ever read this book. I do it only to illustrate the idea that a basic common thread runs through all spiritual paths, no matter how much they may seem to differ on the surface. As a Jesuit friend once said to me, "All paths eventually lead to the same Truth." Christianity is the one other religion that I have studied extensively enough to draw close comparisons. I imagine that with a little research I could draw similar comparisons with others, as well.

The comparisons drawn, though they may seem incidental to the main idea of Wiccan ethics, are in fact, in themselves, a model for the expanded understanding of one section of The Wiccan Way that is explained below with one sentence only: "that there should never by intent be a desecration ... " If the primary mainstream religion of the Piscean Age seems "wrong" to you, it is not the fault of the original vision. Beautiful visions can be distorted or spoiled by those who seek control or power over others. In rejecting that misuse of "power over," I believe that it is not only unnecessary, but unwise, to also reject the vision. Rather, may we revere it and make it one more facet of our own inner truth.

That there is above all the Goddess ...

Life issues forth from woman, and from ancient artifacts that can be found, it is evident that it was most natural for people to project that fact onto the unknown realms of the supernatural and call the creator of the universe their Mother. It was only in relatively recent times, to serve the political aims of patriarchal culture, that the creation myths were quite unnaturally altered so that man became the first creature of a Father God, with woman issuing from him! Wicca simply takes—retains—the more logical and common sense point of view, seeing the Goddess as the Mother of all living. She is seen as the original Trinity, three-in-one. As Maiden, she personifies new beginnings, potential, and independence, and her primary symbol is the waxing crescent Moon. As Mother, the Full Moon and Mother Earth, she is fulfillment and consummation. She is nurturing Mother with Child, but is also sensual, sexual, and strong, the ultimate in feminine power. As Crone she is the wise, elder woman, respected for her vast experience and for her ability to discern the time of endings, and to cut the cord when necessary. Her primary symbol is the waning crescent Moon.

The Goddess has been called by hundreds of names in hundreds of places throughout the world. Behind all of her names we find basically the same ideas. To illustrate this fact, and to again call attention to the importance of recognizing and honoring the points of unity among people (Pisces paradigm leading toward Aquarius) rather than emphasizing the differences, I offer as an example one who is not commonly thought of as Goddess, but should be—Mary of the Christian Gospels.

Barbara Walker, in her *Women's Encyclopedia of Myths and Secrets,* says that the pre-Christian Goddess Mari was Goddess of the Sea and the Great Fish.[3] So why choose the very similar and non-Aramaic name of Mary for the mother of this Age of the Fishes? Coincidence? I doubt it. More likely the influence of Gnostic early Gospel writers who knew exactly what they were doing.

Mary represents Pisces. Yet she is first represented to us in the gospels as Virgin. Virgo the Virgin, as was pointed out in Chapter 2, is the opposition sign to Pisces, and the complementary opposite seems always to figure strongly in religious symbolism of a given age. Yet here we also see a similar concept of Virgin to the Maiden aspect of the Threefold Goddess. Mary is a young girl, unmarried, who is chosen to be the future mother of the God-man. That harks back to many earlier mythologies of other virgin Goddesses who give birth. Christian myths (and art) that are not part of the Gospels put Mary as a child who was dedicated from the start to the temple, with Joseph selected as her protector during the birth when his wooden staff bloomed miraculously into a lily. Clergy, interpreting the Gospels, have portrayed Mary as submissive, but a closer reading reveals one who is quite spirited, more in keeping with the Virgin/Maiden aspect of the Threefold. Did she accept the word of God's angel so meekly? She did not! Quite independently she set out by herself on a journey to visit her cousin Elizabeth, obviously because she was unprepared to believe the angel until she had checked to see if the part of the prophecy that applied to Elizabeth was indeed true. The pristine, chaste, too-good-to-be-real version of Virgin Mary is a creation of patriarchal church fathers, not of the original Gospel writers. From what we know of her at her earliest appearance, she could just as easily be the Virgin of the Threefold, and that is how we should now create her, in her Maiden aspect.

Mary is, of course, a familiar figure as the Mother—the Madonna—but in her Christian version, still too one-dimensional, and limited by the distorted definition of Virgin as forever chaste. Again, if we return to the Gospels and think about it, the Mother of the Threefold emerges. Here is a woman of power, who accepts the challenge of journey in her pregnancy, gives birth under difficult conditions, holds court as visitors from afar come to pay homage, takes charge of her adult son and the situation at the wedding at Cana, raises other children (this is implied in Matthew 12:46), and undertakes more journeys to support the ministry of her son. The Christian fathers apparently could not handle the more sensual aspects of Mother so Mary had to be split, and Mary Magdalene became the whore (as preached from pulpits—nowhere in the Gospels is she even remotely identified as such).[4]

For the Crone image, no more beautiful imagery exists than the Michelangelo Pieta, the famous sculpture of Mary holding her dead son across her lap. There, in the Gospels, we have the recreation of the myth of the sacrificed and dying God. Mary (another Mary, sister of Martha, we are told—but why the same name again?) anoints him with oil before the sacrifice. Mary-the-Mother-now-the-Crone stands by with dignity at the cross, in sorrow; but in her wisdom of what must be, accepts the necessity of the sacrifice.

And finally, at the tomb, we see Mary the Crone (Jesus' mother), Mary Magdalene (now the Mother—probably Jesus' wife, as is implied from the Nag Hammadi Gospels and is stated as probable per *Holy Blood, Holy Grail* research[5]), and a new, previously unmentioned, Mary who would be the third aspect, the Virgin/Maiden. And it is to Mary Magdalene, Mother and Lover, that the risen Christ first appears.

It all fits. Nothing new. It's time we reclaimed this myth from its church distortion and call Mary the Goddess she so obviously is.

How should I, as a Wiccan, relate to the three Marys, or to any other Goddess or God persona? I seek and recognize their different aspects within myself and others at different stages of life, in different moods, in various circumstances. To focus on a specific aspect of deity is usually much more personally helpful than to deal with the all-encompassing totality and mystery of the life force.

That there is the God …

The Wiccan God is seen as the divine Son of the Mother and his primary symbol is the Sun—although it is nearly as common for him to be called the Horned God, the Great Stag, personification of pure, masculine energy—strong, wild, and free. Yet this Son/Sun is also the Consort and Lover of the Goddess. He represents the yearly cycle of the seasons, the eightfold cycle of the Sun in relation to the Earth Mother. In the Sun's apparent motion, from the viewpoint of Earth, he seems to increase and decrease in light. From this observation the concept arose that, while the Goddess is eternal, the God must be born, grow to fulfillment, be sacrificed for the salvation of his people, and be born again. In his waxing aspect, from the increase in light that begins at Winter Solstice to the longest days of Midsummer, he is the Oak King, the Bright Lord. At this time of consummation of love with the Goddess, his energy goes into the womb of the Mother, into the grain that will become the harvest that ensures the survival of humanity. He gives his all, and in his ecstasy is struck with the illumination of his responsibility, of the sacrifice that he must make in order to ensure the continuation of life. With his transformation into maturity and wisdom, he faces the full realization of his waning light to come, and becomes the Holly King, the Dark Lord. He will reign in this aspect from the decrease of light that begins after Midsummer to the longest nights of the Winter Solstice, when he will be born once again as the Bright Lord of the Sun.

The God, also, has been called by hundreds of names in hundreds of places, all with basically similar ideas. In keeping with the same example as I offered above, Jesus the Christ can easily be seen as both Bright Lord and Dark Lord. Here is the Sun/Son born of the Virgin Mother, destined to be the deliverer of the people. He reigns brightly for his season, spreading his message, and then becomes a willing sacrifice for the sake of the people (for spiritual nutrients rather than to energize the grain as in the seasonal myths, but the symbolism is similar). He dies, goes into the underworld (cave) for three days (symbolically similar to the three months of the winter quarter), and then is resurrected to "shine" even more brightly.

The church does not deal comfortably with the Dark Lord aspect (or the Crone). Perhaps this is a big reason why the extreme dualistic split came about that created Satan. But if we throw that out and deal only with what we know of Jesus from the Gospels, minus the interpretations of Christian clergy, we can find a persona who is not a lawgiver, not stern at all, except on occasions like his temper over the pollution of the temple. Here is one who is gentle and compassionate, wise and understanding, at home in the outdoors, in command of the elements, always courageous, calm and regal in his acceptance of his own sacrifice. And through it all, asking only that we love each other as ourselves. Is this so different from the Horned God, Sun King/Dark Lord, Oak King/Holly King?

Here, for one last time, I repeat my theme that we must experience the similarities of these mythologies, reclaim them, reinterpret them, and put them in a perspective that will help us understand and heal our age and our heritage. We must feel (water) the Universal Love of Pisces before we think (air) about the Universal Truth of Aquarius. The old habits of Pisces will carry over into the action (Cardinal Ascendant) of Aquarius, just as Aries action put forth the new "Word" of Pisces. The rejection of the Piscean Age before it is understood (escapism, self-delusion: faults of Pisces) could cause the realization of Aquarian ideals to wind up as irrational distortions.

You will hear about the eight phases of the Wheel of the Year in much more detail in later chapters. For now, in summary of the eightfold cycle of the God, and as one more illustration of the unifying thread in only apparently diverse mythologies, I offer this comparison:

God, the Bright Lord, is:

1. Born to the Mother at Yule, Winter Solstice

2. Shows his first light of individuality at Imbolc (Candlemas)

3. Experiences lively youth at Spring Equinox (Eostar)

4. Takes the Maiden Goddess in sacred marriage at Beltane

5. Reaches his full light at Summer Solstice (Midsummer), giving his full energy to the womb of the Mother for the continuance of life, knowing full well that his energy spent, he must now *change* (sacrifice, responsibility). In the maturity of this newly realized wisdom, he becomes:

God, the Dark Lord, who is:

6. He who gives back onto the world what he has been given (teaches) at Lughnasad (Lammas); his energy gone into the grain of life

7. He who is the reaped grain, the fallen stag, must sacrifice himself in order that his people might have life at Fall Equinox (Harvest, Mabon)

8. He, who goes forth into the invisible world at Samhain (Halloween), assists the passing of souls in and out of that realm, and awaits his own resurrection.

And the eightfold cycle of one concept of the Lord of many names, that has been especially significant during the past 2000 years of western civilization:

1. Jesus, the son of the Virgin, the resurrected Lord at Yule

2. Jesus the child, showing his first light in the temple (Candlemas)

3. Jesus the youth (hidden by canonical scripture) (Eostar—Easter now celebrates the resurrection at this season, but retains the Pagan egg customs for the pleasure of the young)

4. Jesus married, according to standard tradition of his culture (hidden by canonical scripture) (Beltane—celebrated by the Catholic Church in honor of Mary, who is crowned as May Queen)

5. Jesus, after his sojourn in the desert, receives illumination and full recognition of his mission (Midsummer)

6. Jesus the teacher (Lammas—disseminating phase)

7. Jesus sacrificed on the cross (Fall Equinox)

8. Jesus in the tomb, awaiting his resurrection (Samhain—celebrated in the Catholic Church as All Soul's Day)

An it harm none ...

When you stop and think about it, is there any real difference in intent between the concept that was introduced at the dawn of this age, "Love thy neighbor as thyself," and "An [means 'as'] it harm none, do as ye will"? Whatever words you choose to phrase it in, if everyone behaved in the spirit of either of the two statements, no laws would be necessary. "Love thy neighbor ... " has, over the nearly 2000 years just past, been detailed into so many laws that no one can possibly keep count, and people still don't seem to "get it." So, do detailed little laws to interpret the big law "work"? Not very well, it would seem. And that, basically, would be my retort to the man who called in to that television interview show and said "As it harms none ... " was too loose and offered no guidelines.

For millennia our various religious denominations have tried to make their points by making hundreds of detailed rules about morality. Yet society as a whole seems still be a long way from "Love thy neighbor as thyself." "As it harm none, do as thou wilt" may be "loose," but behind it is the very important concept of responsibility for distinguishing, in each individual instance, what is "right" and what is "wrong."

I have seen many people in my lifetime who ignore, bend, dismiss, or rationalize around various rules or laws that are set by their religious or other authorities. "Rules are made to be broken," they say. Yet most everyone I have met in the Craft takes "As it harm none ... " very seriously and truly strives to live by it constantly. I am left to conclude that the teaching of personal responsibility rather than rules works better in the long run.

It should be noted that "as it harm none" applies to self-destructive behavior, as well as to harm directed toward another. "None" includes yourself—so take care. (This is also true of the intent of "love thy neighbor," for in order to do that, you must first "love thyself.")

Now, of course, there are times when we can harm another (or ourselves) without knowing we have done so, or without intending to do so. And sometimes a choice must be made that will harm somebody either way, yet there is no choice not to choose. In such cases, you do the best you can—but you are still not completely "off the hook" for you must responsibly accept, without blame, the consequences of your choice.

The most emphatic application of "As it harm none ... " is in regard to the practice of magick. The more adept you become in techniques of mental focus, projecting your will, raising and moving energy, or whatever else you'd like to call it, the greater your responsibility grows. The ultimate ethical "no-no" in the Craft is the intentional use of magickal techniques to harm another, or indeed, to do anything at all to interfere with the free will of another. You may do what you will for yourself, but to bind or manipulate another specific person in the process puts you at grave risk of bringing the Threefold Law upon yourself. This has been known to backfire on people, even when their magickal spells had what they considered to be the most positive of intentions for all concerned. It's like the old adage, "Be careful what you wish for, because you may be so unfortunate as to get it." I'll give you a few specific examples later, in the section on magick.

... whatever we create, be it joy or sorrow, laughter or pain, is brought back to us threefold.

Okay, the number three is pretty arbitrary, but that is not the main issue. The point is—as in another old adage—"What goes around comes around." Without even going into the areas of karma and reincarnation, you can prove the truth of this idea in many small ways in daily life. Try it in any supermarket line. Scowl and be grumpy and impatient and see how you are treated. Then try another line and smile and be gracious and polite, even if others seem grumpy, and see how the atmosphere changes. Most anyone who has ever consciously thought about it, and tried it, will tell you that you do indeed get in your life pretty much what you are willing to put into it and what you expect from it.

The number three means, basically, that if the intentions you put out are carried by the extra energy of magick, what comes around will be much more powerful than in any ordinary circumstance.

Wiccans are keenly aware of the energies that they are creating in their lives, both casually and intentionally, and they take responsibility for their creations. If things are not going as they would like, they examine what they might be doing or projecting or thinking that they could change, rather than looking for someone else to blame.

Timing is not always evident in what "comes around"—the payback could be when you least expect it, or even in another incarnation. Yet from personal stories I've heard related, it would seem that I am far from the only one who has noticed that the more adept one becomes at the focused intents of the Craft, the more immediately and clearly one is struck by "instant karma." The importance of clarity, integrity, and compassion in what you are thinking and doing becomes quite evident.

... we are all Her children ...

Again, "love thy neighbor ... " All people, everywhere, carry within them the spark of interconnectedness with the Life Force, the divine essence that has been called soul. In this we are all one, and should strive to live in harmony with each other. The Earth, from which we all have come, is a living and vital being, with whom we must also seek to live in harmony. Though their extent of group activism may vary, Wiccans tend to be quite concerned about ecology and take some personal actions toward the protection of the environment. And as has been said before, they tend to be quite open and tolerant of people who are different from themselves.

That death is not an ending ... but a ... process of life.

Few things are more universally feared than death. Humans have always alleviated that fear by projecting a belief in some form of afterlife. Who has the "right" answer? No one can know for sure, although cases of verified past-life remembrances and of post-clinical death recall lend evidence to other more psychic perceptions of a continuum of life in an invisible world. Reincarnation is a commonly accepted belief among Wiccans. This seems a quite natural outgrowth of the observation of all nature in an endless cycle of birth, death, and rebirth.

That there is no sacrifice of blood ...

Contrary to some very unfortunate misconceptions born of popular Halloween witchery fed by Christian fundamentalist fears, I have never heard of any Wiccan group anywhere sacrificing anything. The concept of Satan, and any consequent sacrificial practices that may have emerged from Satanic cults, grew out of the reactions of some medieval Catholics against the abuses of the church hierarchy. In the Inquisition and the burning times, fears of Satan were used to feed hysteria against Witches in order to serve the interests of the ruling powers. Myths, historical artifacts, and even sacred scriptures tell us that there were ancient peoples in various places who did offer human or animal sacrifices. No doubt it was from some such ancient myth or practice that Christians originally got the idea of commemorating the blood sacrifice of Jesus by drinking his blood and eating his body in the form of wine and bread—a rather gross symbolism, when you think about it in only that way. (What one perceives as weird depends mostly on whether it is merely different from normal experience. A person experiencing a Wiccan ritual for the first time may find it strange, but a person who had never before seen or heard of a Christian communion service or Eucharist would probably find it just as strange, at first observation.)

In any case, the God of Wicca is most definitely not murdered as a sacrifice. Rather, he is conjoined with the Mother, giving his seed energy most willingly into her womb where it will become the fruits of new life. Life comes forth from the Earth Mother and eventually is recycled back to her, to reemerge in a new form. In this context, the sacrifice or "death" of the God symbolizes that the endless cycle of death/rebirth is only a change of form.

That each ... has no need of another between themselves and the Goddess, but may find Her within themselves.

Though novices may be guided by the High Priest or High Priestess in the traditions and practices that will help to more fully access the Goddess/God within, the High Priest and High Priestess are not intermediaries. How can there be an intermediary between the self and the self? All Wiccan initiates are considered to be priests or priestesses, even though they continue to seek and learn. The God and Goddess within each individual is respected, as is each person's right to seek his/her own path.

That there shall not by intent be a desecration ...

Though we are free to disagree with each other, the religious beliefs and symbols of all are respected and revered as various aspects of the One.

That each person's faith is private ...

It is not the business of any Wiccan to discuss, gossip, or otherwise reveal information about the religious practices or beliefs of other individuals. This could certainly be said to be proper in any case, but here it is included because popular misconceptions about Wicca by the general public make it potentially uncomfortable or even dangerous for some people to be publicly identified as practitioners. Because of this, discretion and respect for the privacy of others is not only polite, but often necessary.

That the Wiccan Way is not to seek converts ...

Wiccans do not proselytize, nor are they missionaries. Seekers are often heard to complain that they can't find a circle, but I've never heard one complain that a Wiccan was chasing after them, trying to win them as a convert! So what is this book, you might say? Well, the philosophy still is "live and let live." If you've read this far, or have even picked up this book at all, I think it's safe to say that you are a seeker. We are of the belief that when the seeker is ready, the teacher(s) will appear, so we make the way open, with love and respect for you, whether or not you choose this path.

And as it is willed, so mote it be!

The Essential Relationship of Goddess and God

In the explanation of The Wiccan Way I discussed the Goddess and the God separately, but it is very important to realize that they can never be truly separated, for they are One. Patriarchal culture has attempted to separate them, and in so doing has stripped the Goddess—and women—of power, and has essentially emasculated the God—and men! The natural polarity of complementary opposites has been suppressed and denied, replaced by a dualism that categorizes everything into good and evil, God and Satan.

It's a wonder that Satan has not been depicted as female, except that doing so would probably have been perceived as giving the feminine too much power! Thus has the ultimate evil been portrayed as also male, as a repository for all male characteristics deemed not suitable for the all-good male God. As for the female, she has been seen as only mortal, not-God. Powerless against the ultimate evil and forever separate from the ultimate good, she has been regarded as suspect, and even dangerous, for the earthy sensuality and intuitive sense that is her basic nature—and that of the denied Goddess she embodies.

Much has been written about the damage to the female psyche under patriarchal dominance. Not as much has been written about the damage to the male, and to the viability of balanced and fulfilling relationships between male and female.

I said earlier that the patriarchy has emasculated God and men. "Emasculated" is defined by Webster as "to deprive of virility, procreative power ... strength, vigor, or spirit." If the full nature of the masculine principle is to have all that, then truly God—and man—has been split in half. Deprived of the Goddess, his very virility and procreative power is reduced to something less than "good," to the shameful desires that are the temptations of Satan and of mortal woman.[6]

In the patriarchal world view, Spirit is separated from matter, alienated and remote from Nature. Man's strength becomes understood not as inner power, but power over his own nature, his environment, and others. He is taught from childhood to suppress his feelings, to deny pain and fear, in order to maintain his power and control. He protects his territory, his place within the "pecking order," and refuses to recognize the irony of his state. The anger that he cannot turn on those with power over him is often turned, instead, on his women, his children, on anyone farther down on that "pecking order," or even on himself through illness, depression, alcoholism, etc.

The Pagan Horned God is not "split in half"—far from it. He is one with Nature, the very energy of Life. He is a gentle protector, but also the hunter and warrior who faces death in the service of the Life Force. He is the divine Son, Lover and Consort, wise Father, Magician and Sage. His virile sexuality is seen as sacred—a deep connecting power with the Goddess.

She, too, is not apart from Nature. She *is* Nature—the form and manifestation of all Life. She is the Wheel, the cycle; he is that which travels on that cycle.[7] She is eternal: Creator, Preserver, Destroyer. He is that which comes into being: born, grows to fulfillment, declines, dies, and is born again. Together they are One, two halves of the same whole, essential to each other. Without energy, form is inert and lifeless; without form, energy has no purpose.

Now, before someone protests, "Cut the flowery, spiritual stuff—I can well live without that other half who has done [insert despicable act] to me," consider the thought that both Goddess and God dwell within. Within each mind and soul are all the potential attributes commonly identified with the masculine and the feminine principles. We tend to project them onto physical beings of the appropriate gender, according to our social conditioning, but it is important to understand how much of such thinking is reality and how much is only projection.

There is no doubt that the reemergence of the Goddess is empowering for women. She inspires them to see their own inner divinity, and to redefine their bodies and their life cycles (that were shamed by patriarchal religion) as holy and sacred. She calls them to reidentify their natural qualities that have been considered weak as strengths, and to claim their own power for the creative action and initiative that was once primarily defined as masculine.

Along the way of the path of self-empowerment, however, it is evident that for many women, a huge and unhealthy amount of anger is still being projected upon men in general. It has been my experience that whenever anyone expresses an extreme dislike for anyone else, nearly always it turns out to be a projection of some inner quality that is being suppressed or denied. If you are still in a man-hating mode, I understand it. I've been there. But ask yourself, are you trying too hard to either express or suppress the God/male within? Women who can acknowledge all the potentials of both their inner female and their inner male, both those that are expressed and unexpressed, with acceptance and comfort, have no need for rage at males. They have no need to demand power; they simply are powerful.

Margaret Thatcher has said, "Having power is like being a lady. If you have to tell people you are, you aren't."[8]

In my experience, most men in the Craft have achieved an inner balance, inspired by the mighty Horned God and his love for the Goddess, that women can truly celebrate. They are free to fully explore their spiritual nature without suppressing their sexuality. They are sexual without coercion, they can express emotion, engage in dramatic play as children, develop close and mutually supportive relationships with powerful women—and with other men of strength and character, as well—without any threat of loss to their masculine dignity. In short, they are free to love.

Although progress is being made to correct the very harmful imbalances of the patriarchy, we still have a long way to go. Creating a matriarchy is not the answer, no matter how much some may reason that women would do it better. The Goddess without the God is no more fulfilled or Whole than the God without the Goddess.

In searching for a concluding thought to this section on the relationship of Goddess and God, I find that I have come to a place where I must directly state my case for advocating a balanced approach to Wicca that includes both women and men—or for groups who prefer to worship only with others of the same sex, to include both Goddess and God.

For we who live in physical bodies of one gender or the other, no matter what our experience of the opposite gender, it isn't going to go away—and in spite of past hurts, I think that very few women would really want to eliminate all men from their lives, or men to eliminate all women. Even for those who think they might, the reality is that we all live together on this planet, and it will be easier and happier if we live in harmony and appreciate the value of ourselves as "complementary opposites."

The best way to learn to live in harmony with others is to first establish harmony and balance within yourself. Learn to love the attributes of both Goddess and God within you, and to discover the balance of those attributes that is right for you.

It can help to think of others whom you meet as mirrors, for they also (no matter how badly you may think they are behaving at the moment) have Goddess and God within. Could it be that their behavior that is hurting or annoying you reflects something hidden and suppressed within yourself that you've been unwilling or unable to look at? If so, is there an appropriate way to express it? Or even if you choose not to overtly express it, consider this: if you own it, you are in charge. It can only have the power over you that you choose to give it.

You are a mirror for that other person who is mirror to you. Reflect the power appropriately, and reflect it with love. This is the way of the positive practitioner of Wicca, this is the way of creative change ... and this is the way of the happiest manifestation of the Threefold Law for yourself. Trust it. Try it. It works!

Endnotes

1. Reprinted with permission of the author.
2. Jade. *To Know: A Guide to Women's Magic and Spirituality.* Oak Park, IL: Delphi Press, Inc., 1991.

3. Walker, Barbara G. *The Woman's Encyclopedia of Myths and Secrets*. San Francisco: Harper & Row, 1983.

4. Preachers have frequently implied that the woman who had been caught in adultery, whom Jesus saved from stoning—"Let he who is without sin cast the first stone"—is Mary Magdalene (John 8). Not true! The woman is identified *only* as "a woman." The only biblical reference to Mary Magdalene that could possible be construed as negative is in Luke 8:2, when in speaking of the women who traveled with Jesus and the disciplines, there is a passing mention of "some women who had been cured of evil spirits or maladies: Mary Magdalene, from whom seven devils had gone out." (*The Holy Bible,* New American Catholic version, Thomas Nelson Publishers.) Other translations say "unclean" spirits. Some occultists have considered this a reference to the seven chakras. In any case, the context more likely refers to a cure of illness. Certainly, this short passing mention can in no way honestly be taken to identify the Magdalene as a whore. No, the "whore" label is clearly derived from the imagination of some ancient clergymen misinterpreting what is actually in the Bible to suit their own purposes. Unfortunately, the idea has been picked up and elaborated on throughout the age, to the point where most people just accept it as "gospel" without ever looking in the Gospels to verify it!

5. Robinson, James M., Ed. *The Nag Hammadi Library*. San Francisco: Harper & Row, 1977.

   Baigent, Michael, Richard Leigh, and Henry Lincoln. *Holy Blood, Holy Grail*. New York: Dell Publishing Co., 1982.

6. Guralnik, David B., Ed. *Webster's New World Dictionary of the American Language*. New York: Fawcett, 1979.

7. This section on the Essential Relationship of Goddess and God came about first because Lady Beckett, in reviewing my interpretation of her The Wiccan Way, said that she thought I needed to say more about the Goddess and God as One, essential to each other. Lady Joy-of-Heart had recently given a class for the Atheneum-sponsored Dragonstar study group. I'd been out of town and missed the class, but she offered me her notes

to read. The four paragraphs previous to this note are based on key concepts from her class, which aided my thinking in writing this section.

8. This quote was flashed on the screen during a Career Track Seminar I attended in San Diego. No specific published source was given.

Magick

Though Wicca is primarily a religion, a common part of the practice is the working of magick (I choose to use the spelling ending with the "k" in order to differentiate the usage of the word from the type of magic that suggests trickery or sleight of hand, or just a "sparkly feeling" without focused intent).

A Theory of Magick

There is a power—an energy source—that is greater than self or a thousand selves. It is an awesome power. Its form is the Universe, and in that, the power can be seen. Yet we call it also "the unseen," because no one can see its totality. We can see and feel the power in any living thing—a leaf, a wave, the wind, a bird, a newborn child—so many things that, in our day-to-day lives, we may take for granted. Yet if we really stop to contemplate these things—or most anything else we could name—each one is an awesome miracle. Each form that comes into being is a part of the Whole. When eventually, to our perception, it ceases to exist, it goes back to the "unseen" and becomes part of a new form.

71

We can see and feel the parts of the Whole—that leaf, or seed, or breeze, or drop of rain, or fellow human being—and we can then know and feel that we carry a portion of the power within. Our own power is very great, and with it we can create many things in our lives, yet in comparison to the power of the Whole, it may sometimes seem not enough. So we seek to augment our own power by calling on that which is larger than self.

Now, a concept of Oneness could seem troublesome or even shocking to some at first, when they consider the full implication of what that means. Consider this: the Whole power that is One power encompasses all. This power, which is both seen and unseen, can be said to be positive, in that it is life-perpetuating and life-affirming. It *survives,* despite the feeble attempts of any individual or group of individuals to thwart it. Forms may be altered—built or destroyed—but the power of the Whole remains.

Destroyed? Think about it—what can be called upon when one seeks to work magick, or to pray, or to take any thought or action that calls upon a power beyond the conscious self. The awesome, all-encompassing power has been called by many names, depending upon who is calling: God, Goddess, the Force, Allah, Jehovah, Jesus—yes, and even Satan.

Claiming Power Within

The responsibility involved in claiming power within must acknowledge that "good" and "evil" are relative, a matter of perception, a matter of intent. Is it not possible that I could seek to call upon power beyond myself in order to facilitate an intent that I might call good (perhaps even Godly), but someone else might call bad (perhaps even Satanic)? Think of it—people have prayed to win sporting events and they have prayed to win wars. Who was the other side praying to? Concepts of what is good and evil are generally relative to one's own desires, expectations, customs, mores, etc. The unseen power can be said to be good ("positive") *only* in that it is basically life perpetuating—in some form the Whole survives.

Sometimes, in order for the whole of life to be affirmed, something must be destroyed. So the life affirming force must also contain within it the capacity for death and destruction. Dualism projected outside the self, which is basic to many religious traditions, sees this capacity as two separate forces: evil in opposition to the forces of good. LIVE reversed is EVIL.

I say that they are not separate, but are both aspects of the same awesome force.

When we seek to learn the arts of magick, it is essential that we acknowledge the darkness within, as well as the light, and accept responsibility for both. If we are not to project our capacity for "good" outside ourselves, but instead claim it within, than how can we reasonably or honestly think we have the right to project all potential for "evil" outside? It is very important for the practitioner of magick to know the self, and to accept all facets of the self as parts of the self, which one can choose or not choose to express.

It is all well and good to "live in the light" and choose to do and think of all sorts of admirable things, but when you deny any part of the self—your capacity for anger, fear, jealousy, pettiness, carelessness, greed, intemperance, intolerance, or whatever other unadmirable thing you might name—you are setting that part up as the Shadow and giving it power over you. Sooner or later, you will probably encounter that Shadow in some situation or person whom you attract into your life. Is it the devil? God punishing you? Bad luck? Bad astrological transits? No—just the mirror that life has a way of holding up to you to show you that very thing you have denied as being an aspect of yourself. When we are not willing to acknowledge such potentials within ourselves, we generally attract into our lives something or someone that forces us to look at them.[1]

When we call upon the unseen force within, or augment its power by calling on the unseen force without, we must remember that what we are calling on is the force of the One which is All. We do not have to choose to activate all of our many potentials. We may choose to express only what in our opinion are the most admirable ones. But when we lack the awareness of the full range of our potentials, or when we deny them, we are being very foolish and treading on dangerous ground.

With that in mind, let's now consider a few more clearly defined examples of the ethics of positive magick.[2]

Positive Magick

We seek to live in harmony within the One. Yet we may sometimes desire that which we do not have. We may seek to empower ourselves, but if we seek in any way to exert power over another, who is also part of the One, how do we know that what we seek is the choice of the other? Because it is "good" for him/her? Can you be sure? For now, or for all time to come? These are important things to consider, from the standpoint of the intent of a magickal act. In the view of the positive practitioner, it is not ethical to direct magick at anyone in a manner that will interfere with free will, unless that person requests it.

So in planning an act of magick—a spell, if you will—it is very important how you formulate your intent. For example:

You Want to Attract (or Keep) a Lover

It is unethical to direct your intent toward a specific individual, for that would interfere with his/her free will. What is it that you really want? Get down through all the layers of superficialities to the bottom line. Isn't it, perhaps, that you want to have a fulfilling relationship in which you can share love? Okay, then. That is your intent. Direct your spell only on what you want for yourself. Perhaps something like this:

> As it bring harm to no one, and according to the free will of all, it is my will and intent to give and receive love with he (she) who is right for me, and me for him (her), in a relationship that is fulfilling in every way.

You Want a Job

Perhaps you are trying to get a particular job. Maybe it is ethical to go for the specific here, but still, let's first examine what you really want. Is it perhaps that you want fulfilling work in which you can feel successful and support yourself financially? Fine. That is your intent, which could perhaps be worded:

> With the intent of harm to no one, and according to the free will of all, it is my will and intent to have work in which I can find success and fulfillment and prosperity.

Aside from ethics, in regard to phrasing intents as shown above, it is significant to note the following: Few of us are so adept at predicting the course of future events that we can know for sure if a closely specified intent is really even best for us, let alone the other people with whose free will we may seek to interfere. Intents directed with manipulation or binding of the will of another can backfire threefold and more. Again, it's the old adage, "Be careful what you wish for, because you may be so unfortunate as to receive it." How do you know for sure that the "perfect" man (woman) you think you love so madly won't turn out to be a bastard (bitch) to live with? How do you know that the specific job you are interviewing for tomorrow is really going to make you happy after you get it? No, whether we are talking ethics or just plain, practical, common sense, it is better to focus your magick on the basic things you want for yourself. Do not attempt to manipulate others.

You Want Money

Aside from love and career, the third most popular personal issue that is likely to be a subject for spell-casting (as it is for the seeking of consultation with astrologers, psychic readers, or mainstream counselors) is the desire for more money.

Money, or more accurately, the lack of it, is probably an issue about which more people have hang-ups than about sex! The issue is not really about money. It is about limitations and insecurity, probably planted in our psyches by early programming (of which no harm was intended) that gave us presumptions about what we could or could not have, and what we did or did not deserve. Our attitudes about prosperity/security stem from all the shoulds and shouldn'ts and fears during growing up that have contributed to our perceptions of our own self-worth. It can involve deeply subconscious feelings that are very difficult to redirect, if indeed they can be, completely.

Yet, in finally emerging from many years (most of my adult life) of constantly worrying about money to a state of not wealth, but certainly comfortable non-worry, I have come to realize that the parable of Jesus about the lilies of the field is really true. (That is one I could never grasp before—it seemed just too idealistic and out of touch with the real world.) The parable (from Matthew 6) tells of

Jesus' teachings in regard to worrying about material things versus seeking the way of the spirit with faith. He said:

> *Consider the lilies of the field. They neither toil nor spin, yet not even Solomon in all his splendor was arrayed as one of these ... If God can clothe in such splendor ... will he not provide much more for you, O weak of faith! Stop worrying then ... seek first his way of holiness ...*

The New Age version of the lilies of the field tale is "prosperity consciousness." It goes:

> *The Universe is infinitely abundant. The only thing that stands between anyone and a full and unlimited share in that abundance is the perception of limitation, or feeling of unworthiness.*

It has not been at all uncommon for people involved in metaphysical disciplines or spiritual paths to feel that it is somehow crass and even unspiritual to make money. Especially psychic healers, but other types of "readers," as well, have hesitated to charge for their services at all, or to undercharge if they do. Somehow there is the perception that spirituality and the material world are in conflict. That, my friends, is yet another bow to the dualistic concepts of the old world view—God is good, Earth is bad; God saves and provides for the humble, but the material world tempts one to sin. I say: drop that attitude now. There is nothing wrong with casting a spell for prosperity. And it can work, if you do not limit yourself through "poverty consciousness"—and if your primary focus is not on mere acquisition, but on the integrity of your chosen spiritual path.

In the manner in which we have already considered the phrasing of intent, ask yourself: What is it that I really want? Do I want money, or something that money can buy? Do I want money, or do I want security? Or do I want self-esteem?

In seeking security and self-worth for yourself, you cannot take on the burden of responsibility (and/or guilt) for the attitudes and condition of everyone else in the world whom you perceive to be even less advantaged than yourself. Certainly charity is admirable— yet no matter how much you give, there will be still more people around with their hands out. For now, let's leave that issue for another time, and limit our consideration to what you deserve.

Consider this: if you are reading this book, the likelihood is that you are seeking a spiritual path—a path toward growth, a path toward Truth. How much can you truly accomplish in following such a path if you are constantly distracted by worry about how to get the next bill paid? How much more might you accomplish if you let go of worry, and simply do whatever you have set yourself to do, be it for mundane job, family, or any other facet of your life, with the honor and integrity of being true to yourself as you walk the path you have chosen. Trust that if you are thus true to yourself—your being—then all that you need, you will have. Thus in being true to yourself, you have the same beauty and abundance as the lilies, who only needed to be lilies.

As for a money-related phrasing of intent, perhaps:

> *As it harm none, and according to the free will of all, it is my will and intent to have all the material abundance that will fully support my path toward spiritual growth as I seek my highest Truth.*

It works, believe me—but I still think it does not come out of the clouds like manna, or on a "silver platter." You have to be responsible for your commitments. Working a mundane job or running a business with honor and integrity, for example, is part of following your path.

Healing Through Magick

The principle of non-manipulation, and respect for the free will of others, means that it is not ethical to do a spell for healing, or any kind of a psychic healing, on someone unless that person requests it. How do you know that the recipient really wants to get well? Perhaps there is some psychological or karmic reason s/he wants to be sick. Who are you to decide for someone else what is best for his or her ultimate growth?

A specifically directed healing can be effectively directed at one who wants it and is cooperating in receiving the healing energy. A few ideas for techniques that can be used are in the next section.

Yet you may be unable to talk to a person you know is ill, and whom you think might like to receive healing energy if you could ask. Still, if you are not absolutely sure of the desire of the one to whom you would like to direct healing energy, you do well to limit your good intentions to merely surrounding that person with healing light/energy which s/he may choose to accept or reject according to his or her own free will.

For a specific example of healing magick directed at one who requested it and was prepared to receive it, see the Healing Ritual in Chapter 10.

Working with Magick

It has been said that "thoughts are things" and "what you believe, is" and "it's all in the mind." It's as simple as those phrases state— and as complex, and as mysterious. There's little difference between various techniques of magick and mental techniques taught by various disciplines that would not be considered to have any connection with magick. A couple of examples of mental training programs are DMA (Dimensional Macrostructural Alignment) and Silva Mind Control. Quite a variety of teachers have taught techniques of "creative visualization." Some of them are metaphysical/occult related, but others might deny any connection—such as health professionals who teach children with cancer how to visualize little "Pac-men" inside their bodies gobbling up all the cancer cells.

No matter what you call it, "it is all in the mind." And it works! I can't tell you exactly how—no one can. There are things in this Universe that just cannot be explained by a strict scientific method. No one can explain all of the workings or the ultimate potential of the brain. Even scientists tell us that we normally use only a small fraction of the brain's potential power. Many people, myself included, have experienced that the power of the focused mind can make things happen that someone else might think to be impossible. Beckett has said that to work magick is to knowingly be cause instead of effect, to charge your desire with will, intent, and purpose.

Although I can't tell you just how magick works, I can tell you about a few of the techniques that apparently help it to work.

First, the importance of belief—of faith—must be emphasized. Mental concentration is not enough. You must also believe that what you intend will manifest. Consider the faith of Jonah, who calmly thanked God for his deliverance, even as he sat in the belly of the whale, with no deliverance in sight!

For a much less colorful, but more ordinary and personal example: Before I got involved with Wicca, but had studied creative visualization, I was living in Connecticut, doing a monthly radio talk show on astrology. The radio station was in a busy downtown area, and the show was in the middle of the day, when parking was just impossible. After a few frustrating and time-consuming searches for a parking space, and long walks to get to the station on time, I decided to try a little magick (although I didn't call it that at the time). When I got within a few blocks of the station I began to visualize, as clearly as I could, a car pulling out of a space in front of the station. From that time on, through over two years of monthly shows, I had no more than one or two occasions of having to walk more than a block. Usually someone would pull out right in front of the station, just as I drove up behind them. Quite often, there was even time left on the meter! (I'm still pretty good at finding parking places—except occasionally when I either forget to focus, or allow myself to question, even for an instant, whether it will work.)

The point that I'm coming to with all this is that making magick work is no big, secret, mystical mystery. It is mental focus. One focused mind can accomplish a great deal. A group of minds focused on the same intent can accomplish even more.

"So why do we need rituals and spells? Why not just think, like you did during the approach to the parking space?" some readers may be asking. It is because thinking alone tends to be done with the conscious mind. The subconscious may have another agenda, and unless you get them together, you are not likely to get what you "think" you want!

Wiccans call the subconscious the "Young Self." Young Self loves all that mystical mystery. Young Self likes to play, just like a child likes to play. Young Self learns best by "going through the motions," and by experiencing with all the senses.

The conscious mind tends to be more logical; the subconscious mind is intuitive. Logic and abstractions can be pretty boring to a Young Self who prefers to play. S/he can dreamily wander off when what the conscious "parent or teacher" directs should be focused upon, and flit after a pretty butterfly, or slip back into an old habit or opinion or assumption that interferes with the directive. Ritual appeals to Young Self, thus helping you keep both sides of your brain centered and focused on your intent.

There are many books that can be explored to help you get ideas for magickal techniques that will help your focus. The Annotated Bibliography includes several of them. For now, here are just a few things you could try.

Candle Magick

Working with candles can be done alone or with a group. Here is a basic ritual you could follow, but before you do, review what I've already said about being clear about what you really want. When you know your intent, phrase it with absolute simplicity, uncluttered by extraneous "stuff" that may interfere. The old "k.i.s.s." rule applies—"Keep it simple, Susie" (or "Sam." Contrary to the usual "k.i.s.s." saying, we do not acknowledge "stupid"):

1. Select a candle of an appropriate color.

2. Set it out on a table with a lighted white candle, anointing oil, some lighted incense, and containers of water and salt and a carving tool.

3. Cleanse the candle with each of the elements in turn:

    Sprinkle salt on it. Say:

    With earth I do cleanse this magical tool.

    Sprinkle water on it. Say:

    With water I do cleanse this magical tool.

    Pass it through the incense smoke. Say:

    With air I do cleanse this magical tool.

    Pass it through the candle flame. Say:

    With fire I do cleanse this magical tool.

4. Carve appropriate symbols (hearts, dollar signs, runes, occult symbols, words—whatever is meaningful to you) in the candle as you meditate on your intent.

5. Rub the candle with oil, from center up and from center down. Take your time. Focus on the intent.

6. Again, sprinkle the candle with salt. Say:

With earth I do charge this magical tool and arm it with my will.

7. Sprinkle the candle with water. Say:

With water I do charge this magical tool and arm it with my will.

8. Pass the candle through the incense smoke. Say:

With air I do charge this magical tool and arm it with my will.

9. Pass the candle through the flame. Say:

With fire I do charge and seal this magical tool and arm it with my will.

After the candle has been prepared, you could light it and burn it all the way down, or you might light it for a set time each night for a set number of days before burning it all the way down.

If you are burning the entire candle all the way on the night you prepare it, and you expect to be able to sleep, then you should put it in a metal candleholder, not glass, and leave it in a fireplace behind the screen, or in the center of a shower stall, or in your bathtub. It usually takes all night for a taper to burn. *Be safe.*

Consider the time of the Moon in working this or any other spell. If what you want is a new beginning, use New Moon. If you want increase, use a waxing Moon. If you want to get rid of something, use a waning Moon. This can be further refined by considering the zodiacal sign of the Moon, aspects to one's own horoscope, etc.

Keyword Correspondences of Colors

White: innocence, prophecy, respect, cleansing, outgoing, expansion, clairvoyance, wholeness, generosity, spirituality, purity, truth, centering

Red: South, fire, blood, life, sex, courage, energy, force, strength, health, impulsiveness, passion, will power, vitality, magnetism

Orange: encouragement, adaptability, stimulation, attraction, enthusiasm, friendship, self-control, receptivity, organization

Yellow: East, air, intelligence, imagination, power of the mind, creativity, charm, confidence, persuasion, unity, success, activity, action, concentration

Green: North, earth, abundance, fertility, luck, generosity, balance, cooperation, success, money, ambition, overcoming greed or envy, health/healing

Blue: West, water, truth, inspiration, wisdom, immortality, loyalty, serenity, sincerity, devotion, fidelity, honesty, peace, deep emotion

Light Blue: tranquillity, understanding, patience, health

Dark Blue: occult power, protection

Purple: psychic ability, dignity, idealism, wisdom, spiritual or occult power, progress, independence, protection, pride, honors

Brown: earthiness, stability, firmness, thrift, concentration, overcoming hesitation, uncertainty, indecision

Pink: honor, love, morality, affection, service, spiritual awakening, unselfishness, leadership, diplomacy, femininity

Black: endings, death, closing of doors, banishing

Silver: removes negative forces, opens astral gates, conducts energy, the Goddess

Gold: attracts higher influences, attracts energy, the God

Astrological Color Associations

Aries: bright red

Taurus: green, brown—sometimes light blue is given

Gemini: bright yellow

Cancer: silver, soft shades of water colors—blue, green, purple

Leo: bright sun yellow, gold or orange

Virgo: rust, olive, brown tones

Libra: lighter blues, aqua, pink

Scorpio: deep reds—burgundy, magenta, black

Sagittarius: every source varies on this one, and not many are fiery—purple, green, deep blue. Let's also say amber or orange

Capricorn: dark browns, dark tones in general

Aquarius: electric blue

Pisces: dark shades of water colors—purple, green, blue

Sun: gold, yellow, amber, white

Moon: silver, white

Mercury: yellow, orange

Mars: red, rust

Venus: pink, rose, violet, soft blue

Jupiter: royal purple, green

Saturn: black, gray, blue-violet, indigo

Uranus: iridescent colors

Neptune: aqua, deep water colors

Pluto: deep reds, black

Poppets

Another way to focus intent is to make a small image of yourself, or someone who asks you to work a spell for them. You could sew together two muslin cutouts of a little doll shape and perhaps stuff meaningful herbs inside before you complete the sewing up. (Herb correspondence books are in the Bibliography.) The doll could be decorated with a face or other personalized markings and appropriate symbols (as for carving the candle).

Or you could tie together muslin strips or dried leaves, into a doll-like form.

Make the poppet according to the same Moon timing suggested for the candles. Cleanse it and charge it in a similar manner.

You might then keep it near you as a reminder until your intent manifests. Or you might make it at New Moon and burn it at Full Moon, thus sending it into spirit that your intent might be fulfilled. There are no rules as to specific methods. The intent is what counts. Creativity in method helps the focus.

Cord Magick

With similar guidelines in regard to color choices, timing, cleansing and charging, and phrasing of intent, the emphatic tying of knots into cords can be very powerful. The number of knots you tie could

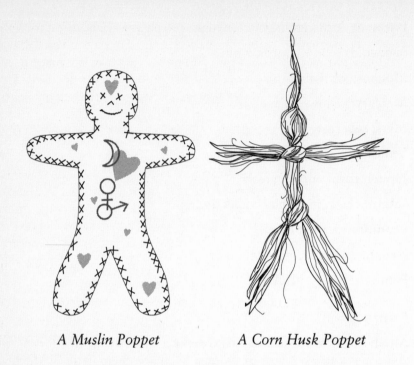

A Muslin Poppet   *A Corn Husk Poppet*

have a symbolic significance in regard to what you want. You could keep the cord as a reminder, or tie it around a candle that you plan to burn.

Another possibility is good for bringing back something you have lost. Write the name of the item on a piece of paper, tie it to a cord, and pull it slowly across the table to you as you visualize the lost item coming back to you.

The possible variations of this, or of most any other technique, are limited only by your imagination!

Other Techniques

Later, in the chapters containing actual rituals, you will read how a number of ideas for magick can be incorporated into group workings. In some of them, techniques are used that have already been suggested, while others utilize group activities that could easily be adapted into an effective solitary spell. The same general techniques of formulating intent and visualization apply in all cases.

Tools, "games," and "toys," such as some of these techniques may seem to be, are not given because I think they have any inherent power in themselves. They are suggested only as stimulation for your creativity, not as set "spells" to be followed. They are given because such things appeal to Young Self and greatly aid the imagination, the vividness of the visualization, and the ability to stay focused. It is important to remember that your primary tool—and the only necessary one—is always your mind.

Here, in alphabetical list format, are some additional basic ideas that were used in the rituals:

Binding and breaking free: Wrap black yarn around your wrists as you meditate on a habit you wish to break or a trait that you know is holding you back from something you want to do. Work up an emotion of anger within yourself, along with a determination be free of the habit or trait. When you feel ready, vigorously and emphatically break free of your bonds. Call on the Goddess and God within to strengthen your resolve. (Spring Equinox, page 174.)

Burning intents: Write your intent on a piece of paper, meditate on it, and then burn it in an iron cauldron, bonfire, metal bowl, or whatever is safe. As it burns, you are sending your intent into Spirit, to manifest according to your will. Use regular paper if your want a slower burn, or magician's flash paper if you want a quick but spectacular flash. Flash paper is not that hard to find in San Diego. There are magic shops in major shopping malls. Check your local yellow pages. (Lughnasad, page 198; Samhain, page 208, and others.)

Burning questions: Formulate a question on paper, meditate on it, perhaps dance (see below), and then cast it in to the fire, trusting that the flash will be a flash of inspiration that will provide an answer. (Sagittarius Moon, page 262.)

Dance: Any intent can be enhanced by dancing, singing or chanting, and rhythm. These things can have a mesmerizing effect that wipes out all background noises or mental static that may interfere with your focus. (Imbolc, page 169, for one. Dance is used in other rituals, too.)

Drums: This is the same principle as above. Steady beating on a drum causes a mesmerizing effect that can greatly aid the focus and the raising of energy. (Sagittarius Moon, page 262.)

Healing: Cast sacred space around the person who has requested the healing. If the person cannot be present, draw an image of him or her. This can be a simple line drawing, or it could be a photo. With felt-tip pens of appropriate colors, draw symbols of health and protection—anything that to you would represent the healing of the afflicted area and the general return to health of the person. Additionally, colored light in appropriate healing colors could be cast on the picture by shining light through colored transparencies or cellophane. Cleanse and charge the image with your salt water, and then send it forth into spirit to be transformed into a manifestation of health by casting it into the fire and air.

If the person can be present, then draw upon the healing energies of Lady and Lord and focus that energy through your hands. Feel heat build up in them, and then lay your hands on the area of the body to be healed. An excellent book for learning how to heal by the laying on of hands is *Hands That Heal* by Echo Bodine Burns.[3]

Incense: Make an incense of herbs and oils that symbolizes your intent. Meditate as you hold the censer, until you can visualize what you desire just ahead of you. Add a pinch of your special incense to the burning charcoal, and then slowly blow the smoke toward your goal, directing the fire of your energy toward it on the winds of air. (Imbolc, page 169.)

Rebirthing: Pass yourself through something, such as the holly wreath at Yule, as you visualize shedding that which is finished and being reborn into a fresh, new beginning. (Yule, page 163.)

Planting seeds: This can symbolize any new beginning. You could plant actual seeds, perhaps flowers in the color of an element you wish to enhance in yourself, or you could add to your New Moon candle magick by planting your anointed and lighted candle in a pot of soil. (Imbolc, page 169; Spring Equinox, page 174.)

Scrying: Gazing into a scrying tool with concentration can stimulate valuable insights that can aid you in creating what you want in your life. You could use a crystal ball, a black mirror, or a black bowl with water in it. Other possibilities for scrying include a pool of water, a fire in the fireplace, a candle flame, cloud formations ...

Stones: Hold a black stone in your hand and will a trait, habit, attitude, etc., that you wish to banish into the stone. Then take the stone and throw it into the sea (an ultimate cleansing tool), or bury it deep in the earth. Or cleanse and charge a small crystal with your positive intent, and then wear it in a small pouch on a cord around your neck, as a talisman and constant reminder of your intent.

Water: Water from the sea, a lake, a stream, the rain ... all represent the womb of the Mother, which gives new life. Take up some water from a natural source and touch it to yourself, as you visualize yourself being bathed and cleansed, safely in the Mother's arms. Feel loved and secure, with your unwanted feelings washed away. Return the water to its source, and thank the Mother for your new life. (Cancer Moon, page 237.)

Writing: Write down an affirmation of what you want. State it clearly and simply and firmly. Write down five little secondary things that you must do to support your choice. These can be little things, such as affirming to get up earlier tomorrow to have extra time. Tonight and every night, until you have what you want, read your affirmation aloud and firmly. As you do each thing, cross it off your list. Young Self will feel very successful as each small step is accomplished, and you will receive the momentum you need to reach the final goal. Each night, after you reread your affirmation, spend five full minutes clearly visualizing your goal as if you already have it. (Virgo Moon, page 247.)

Protective Magick

In Chapter 10 there is a ritual for cleansing and charging a building. This involves an example of defensive or protective magic—to ward or shield your home from unwanted intrusion, bad intents, or even danger from within or without. Does this mean I am suggesting you should do this, and cancel your insurance and urban security system? Hardly. But I have had a couple of experiences that lead me to believe that the effects of intrusion, if any, may be greatly mitigated by protective magick. One of them I'll tell you about.

Somewhat over a year ago, a rock thrown through my living room picture window late one night was scary for a moment. ("Now what? Do I have some neighbors who are spooked by my rituals?") I called the police, who said this type of thing happens so much around the city, even in the nicest of neighborhoods, that if there was no theft or injury, essentially there was not much of anything they could do. ("Okay, no one was close enough to be hurt—I won't assume it was anything but isolated vandalism.") I vacuumed up the glass, resealed (magickally) the window area, and went to bed. The very next morning a friend drove by, saw the window, and called me to offer the assistance of her retired father who had been in the business of fixing such things. He insisted on promptly fixing it for no more than the cost of supplies. Previously, we had just cleansed, charged, and sealed the house. Now, I extended my line of protection out to the edge of the property all the way around. At the next Full Moon, my circle cleansed the rock, sent forgiveness and love to its source, and turned it into a "pet rock" for our garden. All has been peaceful since—in fact, I often have had visitors (who did not know I was in the Craft) who have casually remarked, "How peaceful this house is!"

But I still lock my doors and use the built-in security system that came with the house—for the same reasons I don't leave my laptop computer in my locked car in a public parking lot, nor would I let a small child play in the street—no matter how well I had shielded them. I have seen magick work many times. I expect it to work. However, magick was never touted as a substitute for common sense. Or I could put a slight variation on an oft-quoted phrase: "Goddess helps she who helps herself." Mundane protections were created for our wise use, too.

It is prudent to have a psychic shield you can place around yourself or a child in your care, or some other person who requests it of you. In some ways I feel that I have always instinctively had one, and can be open or closed off at will. Yet it is always better to be aware of what you are doing or not doing. For some people who are particularly sensitive, this can be a major issue. If they do not develop a shield they can be bombarded with negative "vibes" from others around them, and can be vulnerable to being brought down mentally, emotionally, and physically.

The importance of what one believes cannot be underestimated. People have been made ill even to the point of death when they believed in the power of someone directing a psychic attack—Voudoun, black magick—against them. Less dramatically and less consciously, people can become ill through constant exposure to a psychically draining friend, colleague, or even a loved one, who is so needy of attention that no matter how much is given it is never enough. Or they can be "thrown off track" and drained by steady doses of ill will from someone who directs intense dislike or jealousy toward them.

If you feel that you are vulnerable to "bad vibes" or psychic attack, you could build your defenses through a creative visualization in which you place a shield around yourself. Think about something that works for you, that will represent safety. You might start by casting a circle around yourself. Cleanse the area by sprinkling it with water and walking around it with burning incense. Sprinkle salt on the floor in a circle and sit inside it with a lighted dark blue candle. Focus on the flame and slowly, with concentration, visualize a shield forming around you. Design it in a manner that makes you comfortable—anything from a stone wall to space-age metal. If that makes you a bit claustrophobic, design a door that will open and shut at your slightest command. That way you can open up your shield, and instantly snap it shut around you again when you feel the need.

You might also want to add a cloak of invisibility—a way that you can, at will, cover your shield or blend it into the environment. Sometimes safety means standing out and moving with a show of great confidence. Other times safety may mean becoming "invisible"—so nondescript and ordinary that you pass unnoticed. Being alert to these distinctions is the common sense aspect. Adding the ritual protection is a good way to teach Young Self common sense!

When you feel calm and secure about the protection that is now around you, thank the Lady and Lord, after which you can leave your salt circle. Allow the candle to continue burning all the way down.

You can also direct a protective spell to a distant place. Once when a daughter and her family were seriously threatened by a major hurricane approaching their home, I set a spell of protection by placing their pictures on a map of the area beside a burning candle. I drew a ring of salt all around these objects and spoke the intent that the hurricane be deflected out to sea where it could do no serious harm to them, or to the lives of anyone else around them. After completing my little ritual, I thanked the Lady and Lord for their safety and I knew they were safe. I relaxed and went on with my activities for the evening.

That my act had anything at all to do with the fact that a little later that day the hurricane changed direction, moving away from them, would be derisively denied by scientific types. And perhaps accepted by those who preach that "all is an illusion" and "we create our own reality" and "thoughts are things." All I know for sure is that doing it made me feel a whole lot better! (And is that not a value in itself? Certainly it was better than worrying and wringing my hands. What good did worry ever do?)

Sex Magick

A couple can create powerful energy to direct toward a mutual intent through sexual intercourse. Such a ritual, normally done by two alone, in privacy, can be the ultimate cumulative working for a full ritual experience, beginning with the formal casting of the circle, and continuing to the invocations of God and Goddess. Lovemaking in this manner is a truly sacred act, creating a strong psychic bond between the priest and priestess, and facilitating a powerful projection of energy. When done with an attitude of balance and mutual love and respect, the balance of God and Goddess within is intuitively understood and enhanced. Such a ritual could be used to set out a beacon to attract a child, or to attract like-minded people to their circle, or for any number of other mutual intents. It is ethically essential that the act be totally non-coercive, with mutual awareness and consent. Because of the potential for strong and permanent bonding between the two, this type of ritual should not be undertaken lightly or casually. It is best reserved for working couples who are married or who are previously established and compatible lovers.

Raising Energy

To summarize, whatever method you might use to focus your intent, your mind is your major tool and the only necessary one. Meditation and creative visualization are very effective. But they are not the only way, nor the most effective for some. You may find that the addition of various sensual effects work better. Music and burning incense may add to your focus. Other possibilities, for either solitary or group work, include chanting, singing, drumming, swaying, and dancing. You will find examples of all of these in the rituals to come.

Wiccan imagery often involves a repetitive sound or action that builds energy to a "cone of power" which is then released and directed toward the intent. Magick can be done alone, and the more focused you are the stronger you will be. Yet whatever a solitary mind can do, two strongly focused minds, or a cohesive group mind focused on the same intent, can do more powerfully. This, of course, is one reason for incorporating group magick into our rituals of worship—we share energy for the benefit of one who requests special assistance, or for the benefit of all.

Endnotes

1. For further study on the Shadow, projection or mirroring, you could find many books that discuss the psychology of Jung. Among the books I've listed in my Bibliography, I suggest Liz Greene's *Relating* and Shakti Gawain's *Living in the Light*.

2. Influenced, of course, by Marion Weinstein's *Positive Magic,* in addition to the oral teaching of Lady Beckett, Lord Landerthorn, and Habondia, Crone of Circle Atheneum.

3. Burns, Echo Bodine. *Hands That Heal*. San Diego: ACS Publications, Inc., 1985.

Circle of the
Cosmic Muse

(Note: For short, in the remainder of this book, HP means High Priest, HPS means High Priestess, and HPs means both of them.)

Background and Formation

I have already told you about some of the thoughts, experiences, and events that lead me to seek out Wiccan ritual as a form of worship that honored the divine feminine aspect, the Goddess.

Shortly after I came to San Diego in 1987, Terry Lamb asked me if I would care to accompany her to a Sabbat ritual. I was already acquainted with Terry since she was president of the local chapter of the National Council for Geocosmic Research, an astrology organization for which I've served on the national board of directors for many years. She was writing an astrology column for the newsletter of a local metaphysical book shop, Mystic Moon, which specializes in Wicca. The shop's owners, Wiccan HPs Judith Wise-Rhoads and

Scot Rhoads, were conducting a ritual which was open to guests. It was held in a lovely canyon backyard, overlooking the city. The circle was outlined with candles in glasses embedded in the ground, with a central altar—a permanent set-up. It was a large crowd, a bit too large to "connect" with very many individuals, but I thoroughly enjoyed the ritual, the outdoor setting, the singing.

After that I attended three or four other open Sabbat rituals that I heard about through Terry, but didn't seek out any classes or closer contact. Perhaps I just wasn't ready yet; perhaps my particular taste was for something a bit more formally structured than I had experienced so far. For Beltane of 1988 I attended a ritual at a public park that was a joint Sabbat of at least three or four circles plus guests. There I met Lady Beckett and others from Circle Atheneum. I felt a strong, immediate "connection" with her, and we talked for some time. She offered me the opportunity to attend their next Full Moon ritual, and I accepted. I was characteristically cautious about "opening up" too soon, but I felt a real affinity for the way in which they conducted ritual, and I felt comfortable with the people in the group. They offered attendance at their classes, and I accepted. At the August Full Moon I formally dedicated and began studying for my degrees.

Meanwhile, Terry and I began to do Sabbat rituals together. At that time she was interested in doing ritual, but not ready to join a group. We would schedule our rituals on a different night than Atheneum's (so I could keep up with my degree program). Sometimes just the two of us would work, but more often another woman friend or two would join us. Since I was the one actively training to become a priestess, I fell into the role of primary planner, and we held most of our rituals in my home.

By the last half of 1989 my home rituals had grown considerably, with irregular attendance by other astrologer friends, guests from Atheneum, friends of friends. Terry and I had always preferred to have a group of both men and women (for balance), even though we started out with all women because that's all we knew who were interested. Now a few men began to attend, too, and I had begun to ask friends from Circle Atheneum to act as High Priest for me at these Sabbats. By now I had completed my Second Degree from Circle Atheneum, and knew for certain that I wanted eventually to form my own circle. But I wanted to complete my Third Degree first.

In February of 1990, I was initiated into the Third Degree, but did not consider spinning off then because my husband had become quite ill. He died in May, and that whole year became much too extensive a transition period for me to take on any more than I was already required to handle, in dealing with my grief, and in learning how to manage the business that my husband had left me to administrate. (I had been the Art Director, but managing the entire operation required considerable skill-stretching!) As I have mentioned before, the support of the members of Circle Atheneum, along with knowledge of the eternal cycle and some specific transformations of my Third Degree initiation, were of enormous help to me in getting through that year with inner serenity.

By the next February I felt "together" enough to be ready to take on the commitment of a circle, so at my home 1991 Imbolc ritual I announced to the people attending that I wanted to form an "official" circle, that I would call it Circle of the Cosmic Muse because of my intent to develop rituals with the inspiration of astrology, and that those who wanted to participate in an ongoing program should talk to me. We scheduled a formation meeting, and held our first Full Moon ritual later that month. And so it continued, with my formal "spin-off" from Circle Atheneum at Spring Equinox. (A spin-off is a ritual where a fully-trained member of a circle is formally acknowledged as being HP or HPS of a new circle.)

Our "Way"

Structure of the Circle

As of this writing there are sixteen regular members of the group—seven men, nine women—plus a few others who come sometimes. I now work with a High Priest, Mark Adams (Lord Willow), who is an extremely helpful and supportive co-leader. He is also a Third Degree from Circle Atheneum, as is Greraven, who is not a member of our circle but has helped us whenever we need a Crone, since no one in our group is yet ready to take on that role. One additional Third Degree, Ibis, serves us as a circle Elder. The others are quite a mixed group. Ages range from the 20s to the 60s, not counting a few children of members who attend sometimes. Some people are married, others are single. Some are astrologers, a couple of them well-known;

most others have no previous astrological background at all. How did we find each other? Who knows—it happened, it works.

We generally meet twice each month. If there is both a Sabbat and a Moon that month, those will usually be the only two meetings. If there is only a Moon, then we have a class. The classes are on a variety of subjects, some designed as orientations to ritual form and symbolism, others to teach basic astrology to the non-astrologers. Some classes have covered such topics as the history of Wicca, ethics, comparative traditions, forms of magic, correspondences of herbs and oils, etc. Sometimes Mark or I conduct the class, other times another circle member does because s/he has particular expertise on the topic, and occasionally we invite a guest teacher. Always the classes are participatory, with lively discussions encouraged. Usually classes are held in the evening, but sometimes we've held an all-day weekend workshop for the purpose of making robes or ritual tools.

We publish a schedule at least six months in advance so that circle members can reserve the dates. We expect attendance (unless with a good excuse and a call in advance) of those who consider themselves to be regular members of the circle.

No collection plate is passed; no fees are involved. This is "traditional" in most circles. There's no church building to support, no salaries to pay, and groups are small. While Wiccan priests or priestesses might accept a fee to teach at a book shop or to give a public lecture, most do not charge any fee whatsoever to train the people they accept into their circle. In some cases a collection might be taken up in order to make group purchases of something, such as study material to be shared. Often people "bring something to share" when coming to class or ritual—usually munchies or beverages. For Sabbats we generally have a full potluck supper. Volunteers to offer cakes, beverages, or flowers for the ritual altar are gratefully accepted.

About Hierarchy

Some all-female groups, especially, make a major point of being non-hierarchical, in reaction to the association of hierarchy with patriarchy. This is understandable, and I do not dispute that with a small group of women friends meeting to do ritual, general consensus decision-making and a shifting of ritual planning responsibilities to a different person each time might work quite well. In actual practice, though, I'll bet that in many cases, the result is somewhat disorganized and not especially effective. I have attended rituals that lacked a strong leader or a basic structure, and they didn't work very well. Usually "spontaneity" takes pre-planning on the part of someone who knows how to facilitate a group!

The fact is, some people handle leadership better than others, and with a certain amount of demonstrable structure, often people who are not "natural leaders" develop the self-confidence and ability to lead far beyond their own expectations. Even though I had extensive past public speaking ability before I began my Wiccan training, I was not at first anywhere near ready to handle the energies of conducting an effective ritual. The process of training brought about tremendous growth for me, and I have observed that to be the case in many others. People who were at first very shy and uncertain have blossomed into powerful priests and priestesses. I have seen numerous examples of Wiccan trainees where the individual transforms not just the ability to lead effective ritual, but indeed the entire experience of leading a successful and productive life.

Of course much of this rests on two things: the will of the individual student, and the willingness of the HPs to guide and then step aside (minus any interfering egos) and let the student shine. In the latter, Mark and I had marvelous role models in Lady Beckett and Lord Landerthorn.

One might think that dealing with a small group of people is easy, and consensus should be easy, too. Perhaps if you are just dabbling in ritual this could be the case. For us, Wicca is our religion, a constant and serious philosophy and practice of life. For those who choose this path, the High Priestess and High Priest are, indeed, clergy. Even though all initiated Wiccans are considered also to be priests or priestesses, and no one stands between them and the Goddess/God, the fact remains that the HPs are looked upon as teachers, and sometimes as counselors, as well as spiritual leaders. I doubt very much if it would be possible to start a circle, continue it for any time at all, and escape those roles.

Responsibilities and Privileges of Leadership

The members of our circle, although a small group, some of whom come and go, are seekers who become as family. It is true that we generally only see each other at scheduled meetings; everyone has his or her own life. Yet if you think you can become involved with a group such as this without ever becoming involved in their personal issues or their interactions with others in the group, think again. Within a circle, a "group mind" develops that greatly contributes to the general rapport and to the building of energy. When one is "out of sync," others feel it. "Pastoral" or "parental" counseling needs occur, and you may also find yourself in the role of mediator of dissents or misunderstandings. The role of High Priestess or High Priest is not a role that anyone should ever take on lightly, without serious thought and preparation for the commitment in time and energy and understanding that one is making.

Considerable work and time is also involved in just the mechanics of running a circle—scheduling, planning rituals, getting together what is needed to do them, coordinating participants, keeping everyone informed, etc. When I started my circle, I actually thought I was prepared to take this on myself! Since then I have come to deeply appreciate the fact that I have acquired a "working partner" to share the load!

Following the example of Circle Atheneum, we also designate two assistants, who accept for a limited time of about one year, the responsibility of helping us. These two, the Maiden and the Red Priest, are chosen among those who have completed at least the First Degree, and have indicated the will and the potential to add to their training in this way, and perhaps eventually become HPs.

The Maiden comes early and sets up the altar for ritual, and takes it down, and does whatever else is needed to assist the High Priestess. The Red Priest assists the High Priest, networks with other circles and acts as "sergeant at arms" at public rituals—entering circle last, and handling any questions/interference from bystanders so that ritual will not be disturbed. Both have roles in initiation rituals, and sometimes in seasonal Sabbats. (Terry, who took me to my first ritual in San Diego and has worked with me ever since, eventually deciding to commit to the training when her personal life (small children) permitted the time, became my first Maiden, and went on to become our first Third Degree and first spin-off! She is now Lady Terra of Circle of the Cosmic Dance.)

Another significant leader is the Crone, an honored Elder woman of Third Degree who shares the wisdom of her experience. She has an important role in initiations. Our circle is still a bit too young to have our own Crone emerge, so we are grateful for the continued assistance of Greraven, even though she has now become

Lady Shelayne (see Circle Names), started her own circle, and cannot attend ours regularly.

The privileges? You learn constantly from the people you teach. Growth and wonder never cease.

Traditionally, a circle or coven belongs to the High Priestess who starts it, along with her High Priest, if she has one. One does not ethically attempt to usurp that role. If a person feels s/he would rather do things a different way, and be the primary leader, the thing to do is "spin off" and start a new group. (The term "hive" is also often used to refer to the same process.) Sometimes this has been known to happen not too pleasantly, because the HPs, prone to laxity, too much ego, or whatever other human faults you might name, do not do an effective job, and dissension ensues.

Ideally, new leaders are born and form new circles in the positive manner that I have been fortunate enough to experience—sent forth with the blessings and good wishes of their Mother circle, and a continued, interested, but non-authoritative and non interfering networking link.

Circle Atheneum now has four "daughter" circles, with two more pending, plus the Dragonstar study group. The HPs all stay in fairly close touch with each other, helping each other when requested. We share some of our Sabbats. Last Midsummer, Atheneum's fifth birthday, had over 70 people participating in the ritual, including Atheneum's own "Mother," Circle of the Soaring Spirit.

Degrees

We are not primarily a training circle, as is Circle Atheneum, but we do offer Dedication and three degrees for those who wish to take that route. If a member prefers to just participate in the rituals but not do the formal degree work, that's okay. Our stated purposes are these:

1. To provide a nurturing environment of mutual support of those who seek spiritual growth and inner balance, through group worship of the immanent Life Force of the Universe, personified as Goddess and God.

2. To develop the use of astrological symbolism as a basis for sacred ritual.

3. To offer, to those who wish it, training through Dedication and the three degrees of Wiccan tradition.

4. Last, but not least—to relax in the enjoyment of congenial companions and in the creation of good energy.

For those who choose the degree program, we require a set of questions to be answered in writing. This is in addition to more subjective interactions that let us know when the person is ready to move to the next step. The questions for Dedication and First Degree are, for the most part, thought-provoking rather than demonstrations of rote learning. There are no "textbook answers." They force the candidate to carefully think through all the aspects and ethics of the path s/he is choosing. First Degree, of course, is considerably more complex than Dedication and requires a demonstration of understanding of what it means to be a priest/ess. The questions for the Second and Third Degrees require more thoughtfulness, plus a detailed demonstration of knowledge of the traditions and symbols of the circle, of how to do rituals, and in the case of Third Degree, how to facilitate a group and conduct training of new seekers. (Our lists of questions appear in Chapter 10.)

Dedication is not considered to be an initiation, but rather is a statement of intent to follow the path of the Goddess, the God, and the Craft. At this point the person does not commit to the circle itself, but only to the path. Dedication ceremonies take place during Full Moon rituals, and the candidate is given the complete wording of the ceremony ahead of time so s/he can read it and think about what it means. Since there is no reason to keep this ritual secret, it is printed in the Special Rituals chapter. It is essentially the same as that which was handed down to Circle Atheneum from Circle of the Soaring Spirit, and is similar to others I've seen in various books—I cannot identify an original source.

I am not including our initiation rituals in this book, because to do so would destroy a large measure of their effectiveness. If the initiates knew exactly what to expect, it just wouldn't be the same! (Publicly opening my "Book of Shadows" has some limitations.) For each of the three degrees, an entire evening is set aside, just for the ritual of initiation. Only people who have already been initiated at that level are permitted to attend.

At the First Degree the initiate becomes a priest or priestess, so the initiation is akin to an ordination. It is also a rebirthing experience, for one makes a commitment to Goddess, God, and the Craft in a way that can never be broken, even if one ceases to practice. So in a sense, life begins anew from this point—"born again Pagan!"

Yet, at this point the new priest/ess is still a novice in the tradition of that particular circle. Here, we (my High Priest and I) accept responsibility for the continued training of the initiate, a commitment which may well require considerable time and empathy. At this point the initiate also makes a commitment to the circle. This means that s/he agrees to strive to learn and use our methods until they are thoroughly mastered, and to give our circle activities a high level of priority in his or her life. It is okay and even encouraged that the novice attend other rituals and classes when s/he gets the chance, so long as such visits do not prevent participation in ours.

As a symbol of the First Degree, the initiate is given a nine foot long red cord, which is usually worn around the waist or elsewhere on his/her ritual robe. Red symbolizes the color of the Great Mother, and the courage that it took the initiate to take this very significant step.

For the Second Degree the initiate must plan, write, and do an entire Full Moon ritual alone, in order to demonstrate the ability to do so. Later, the initiate will be scheduled to do a Moon for the entire circle. The Second Degree initiate is considered by us to have progressed to the point of being fully responsible for him or herself, including ethical standards, ability to continue studying on his/her own if that is the choice, and able to handle the energies of a ritual. Two cords are given, a gold one symbolizing the link with God, and a silver one symbolizing the link with the Goddess.

One of the several requirements for the Third Degree is the writing and planning, and usually working center for, one of our Sabbat rituals. The cord is black, symbolizing the initiate's mature knowledge of the whole of the implications in choosing this path, of the full cycle of human experience, and perhaps most importantly, that one never stops growing and learning. We now consider the initiate to be responsible not only for self, but for the training of others. If, at this time, s/he chooses to form a circle of his/her own, we will provide a joyful sendoff and many blessings. If s/he chooses to stay within our group, we will consider him/her to be a respected elder, whose advice, feedback, and participation is especially valuable.

The Altar Set-up and Tools of Ritual

Our altar set-up varies with the season, but there are some things that remain constant. A major goal is to make it beautiful and balanced, with necessary tools easy to reach and use.

Altar

At home, both our indoor and outdoor altars are circular. Indoors we use a low, round coffee table, and outdoors we use a wooden circle atop a birdbath. The table is first draped with a cloth. I have a white, circular tablecloth for the indoor table that is cut to exactly touch the floor, and over it I usually, but not always, use a rectangular white cloth on which I have embroidered pentagrams at each corner in one of the element colors. This cloth is arranged so that the pentagrams face the appropriate directions. Sometimes, instead of using that cloth, I use a colored tablecloth in the element color that corresponds to the sign the Full Moon is in, or one that is appropriate to the season for a Sabbat, such as black for Samhain.

On the altar are the following:

Symbols of Goddess and God: Usually I use a statuette of a lady for the Goddess, and a piece of deer antler for the God.

Flowers: Or leaves for fall, or other appropriate decorations.

A pentagram: My altar has a sea theme, because that is my particular affinity. My pentagram is a large starfish.

Spirit and God/Goddess candles: In the center of the altar is a white candle, representing the spirit of the eternal One, the Whole. This is flanked by a silver candle on the left, for the Goddess, and a gold candle on the right, for the God.

Extra light source to work by (lighted before ritual begins): Indoors we usually use two fat, white altar candles on either side of the altar flower arrangement. Outdoors we have a ceramic oil lamp hanging from a branch above the altar. During the ritual a pre-selected "Light-bearer" takes one of these extra candles around to hold for the callers of the Watchtowers to see by, if the callers are reading from cards.

Censer: I use an abalone shell filled with rock salt, on which rests a charcoal briquette on which the incense is burned (fire). Next to it is placed a small sea shell containing incense, and a large feather (representing air).The incense smoke is directed by waving the feather, and the censer and its use represents the elements of both fire and air.

Water container: I use a large white seashell. Obviously, this symbolizes the water element.

Salt container: For me, this is a small ceramic bowl with a lid on which a star has been carved. It contains coarse sea salt, and represents earth.

Vial of anointing oil: This is mixed from essential oils according to correspondences that fit the theme of the ritual we will be doing.

Bell: A brass Tibetan bell, in our case, with the clapper removed. We sound it by tapping it with the handle of an athame.

Chalice: Mine is pewter, with a mermaid stem. Represents water and the feminine aspect; filled with a beverage to drink during the ritual. Wine is probably most commonly used. We use non-alcoholic beverages, such as cider, so as not to exclude anyone in attendance who cannot drink alcohol. I have heard of some circles using milk or water in their chalices. We put the bottle under the altar, to refill the chalice later. After it is served once around by the HPs, we sit on the floor/ground casually for the announcements and sharing, and continue passing the chalice and extra cakes.

Plate: Represents earth; used to serve the cakes (or cookies, sweet-bread, etc.) Mine is hand-crafted ceramic, carved with stars and a landscape motif. One could certainly put together most of the things needed for an altar from standard kitchen items; in ancient times, this was probably the usual way. I have improvised on occasion, too. But I—and most of my priestess friends—prefer to have special things that are set aside only for ritual use.

Boline (bow-LEEN): This is a white-handled sharp knife, conse-crated for magical use only. It is the only tool actually used for phys-ically cutting things. It is used outside of ritual, for example, for cutting herbs or for making ritual tools. Within ritual it might be used for such things as to cut cords, to repair a candle that has become clogged with wax, to carve symbols in a candle, to cut fruit, or to stoke the charcoal if it is being stubborn about burning properly.

Athames (pronounced a-THA-me, with short vowels on the first two syllables): With HPs working together, the HPS' athame is on the left and the HP's on the right. The athame is a double-edged dagger, usu-ally personalized in some way. Mine is black with a pewter mermaid on the handle. Mark's is brass, with a dragon claw handle. The athame is strictly a ceremonial tool. It is used to cut and direct energy, but it is never used to physically cut anything. The athame is a very personal tool, usually used only by the owner. We have sheaths so that when we are attending rituals for which we are not working center, we can wear our athames. Usually a Wiccan acquires an athame about the time of First Degree initiation. It is consecrated during the initiation. In our tradition, it is only correct to wear an athame to ritual after one has completed First Degree.

Wands: Again, the HPS' wand is on the left, the HP's on the right. Wands are used to invoke spiritual energy. They are usually hand-made by the owner, and again, are highly personalized—although one often sees beautifully crafted glass and crystal ones on sale in metaphysical shops. Mine is a piece of very beautiful driftwood, that was rescued from the surf near my home. It is the length of my arm from hand to elbow, and has been sanded and oiled. It has a laser-point quartz crystal set into the end, and an assortment of other crys-tals and stones set in natural curves and hollows of the wood.

Broom: This is placed under the altar. It is a "country-style" broom, with a shorter handle than the usual kitchen broom.

Sword: This is also placed under the altar (no room on top!). I bought it from an import shop in downtown San Diego.

Circle staff: This is propped within easy reach of the altar. Ours is two tall intertwined poles, with a quartz crystal mounted at the top, point up, surrounded by small sea shells and a small starfish. A leather thong tied at the top holds a blue macaw feather. The staff and crystal are fire, the star is earth, the feather is air, the seashells are water. The staff is passed to whoever wishes to speak during sharing.

The ritual "Bic": You could also use a book of matches. In any case, something to start the fire with. We use those propane "guns" that are available at any hardware store. These save smudged and singed fingers trying to get the incense charcoal going. The spirit candle is lit with the propane "wand," and the Goddess/God candles are lit from the spirit candle. A propane wand is sent around the circle with the Lightbearer, for the callers of the Watchtowers to use to light the Watchtower candles.

Will, Intent, and Purpose: Last, but most certainly not least, this is indeed the most important tool—and the only one that is absolutely necessary. If you don't have it, no fancy tools will compensate. If you do have it, you can do an effective ritual with no tools at all. The only necessary tool is your *mind*.

Watchtowers: Something is needed to designate the four corners of your space. When we work inside, our altar is in the center of the living room, facing East. For the first year and a half we used television tables draped with appropriately colored cloths for the Watchtowers. They were placed at the outside edge of the circle, one at each of the four compass point directions. East had a yellow cloth and yellow candle, South had red cloth and candle, West had blue cloth and candle, North had green cloth and candle. Now I have acquired a special set-up for each corner (in my living room the compass point directions are in the four corners) that stays there all the time. East is a wall candelabra that holds three fat, round yellow candles and casts an intricate shadow on the wall. South is a floor candelabra with three tall, narrow spires holding red, twisted candles that burn in fiery spikes. West is a beautiful mermaid painting (a gift from my daughter Molly). On the shelf below the painting are three candles in various shades of blue in holders of three different heights, with a seaweed-like weed arrangement and an assortment of shells. In the North corner, on the baby grand piano, is a striking metal sculpture of a stag, whose rack of antlers holds three green candles. Over the piano hangs a large macramé plant holder that was made by my mother, designed with the motif of the rings of Saturn. From it grows a lush, green vine that falls down behind the stag.

Outdoors we use bamboo pole tiki torches, festooned with colored ribbons, at each direction. Because my garden is arranged with a slightly raised brick platform under a trellis in the East, we use a birdbath there for the altar, topped during rituals with a wooden round and draped with an altar cloth. The East torch stands just beyond the altar, and a winged Goddess figure is permanently mounted in a tree branch that extends slightly behind and over the altar. Recently we enhanced the West quarter by installing, right beside the tiki torch, and surrounded by flowers, a working stone fountain with a mermaid perched on top. Everyone likes the sound of the water in the background during ritual.

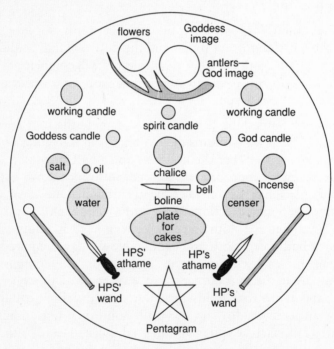

The broom and the sword are under
the front of the table within easy reach.

Basic Altar Diagram

Generally, that's all of it, except for extra tools that might be added according to the plans for a specific ritual, such as the cauldron, paper and pencils, individual candles, etc. When you read the rituals later in the book, you will find a note about any special preparations needed at the beginning of each one. Otherwise, assume that all of the things listed above will be used and arranged approximately in the order that you see them on the diagram of an altar table, and in the photograph of our outdoor altar.

A priest or priestess working alone might arrange things differently. For example I might put my athame and wand on the right, both because I am right handed and because the right side is traditionally said to be masculine, and the athame and wand are both tools of the masculine aspect. Whatever I decide, I would arrange my tools in a pleasing balance.

A priest working alone, of course, has his own tools and handles them in the manner that pleases him, but when he is working with a priestess, the altar and its arrangement are her province. With the exception of the HP's own athame and wand, which he handles, the HPS hands all tools to the HP or whoever else is to use them during ritual, and they hand them back to her when they are finished for her to replace where she wants them.

The Order and Parts of Ritual

This section explains the procedures followed in the rituals of the Circle of the Cosmic Muse, and the symbols and/or intent of each action. Other circles will do some things in a similar way and other things quite differently. Because all circles are autonomous, you will find, if you are able to visit various groups, that there are a wide variety of ways to work ritual. However, most any Wiccan circle that you may visit, and many other Pagan ritual groups as well, will do at least a few of the same things that we do.

The most common procedures are moving clockwise to build energy, cleansing the ritual area, followed by doing some specific action intended to create a sacred space, and calling the elements to the four directions. Aside from those common actions, the formality of procedure varies greatly from one group to another.

Spontaneity is probably most pronounced in some of the feminist Wicca groups, who may have little or no plan for what will happen until they start, and may rotate the leadership (priestess) at every circle. Formality is probably the greatest in older traditionalist groups, who may do the Esbat (Full Moon) ceremony exactly the same way every time, with the same Charge of the Goddess that has been handed down through generations.

Our method is somewhere in the middle of those two extremes. It is formally structured in that we build the circle the same way every time, and we have the same basic parts of the ritual, with a few responses worded the same way. Within that structure, we are as creative as possible, using different words and workings at every ritual, sometimes planned ahead, and sometimes improvised on the spot.

We are creative and spontaneous (within our structure) because frankly, it is more fun to do something different every time, and also because we find it more personally meaningful to vary the words and the theme according to the seasons and cycles and to the varying personal needs of the group. We are formal and structured in our procedural outline because maintaining some elements of repetition and familiarity help a great deal toward making ritual participatory for the entire group, rather than a performance of those working center, with everyone else being left to merely observe.

My High Priest and I have made a few changes in the way we do ritual as contrasted with the specific methods in which we were trained by Circle Atheneum. We expect that when members of our circle do rituals somewhere else, they might do it differently than we do. That's fine. We are not "stuck" on any one form as being superior to another. There is great value, however, in first learning one way, so that you can become comfortable enough with the procedure to transcend the logistics of trying to keep track of what comes next in order to more strongly focus on the heart and spirit of what you are creating. Therefore we expect our members, as they begin to write their own rituals for our circle, in working toward degrees, to follow the basic format as it is given here. They must include each section heading listed as follows in bold type, but are encouraged to use their individual creativity in the writing of the various parts under each heading. They are not required or expected to use an astrological theme just because I do, but can use any theme or concept that appeals to them. Rowena, for her Second Degree Moon, chose ecology for a theme; Otter is using dream stories as his theme. We do ask that they incorporate our usual endings for the

Watchtower calls and other expected responses, so that other members of the circle can more easily participate.

Casting the Circle

This is a process of creating sacred space, or, you could say, of constructing the temple. We do not have a special building set aside only for worship, as a church, but we create our sacred sphere around us wherever we are, outdoors or in.

Casting the circle is usually done by the priest and priestess who are working center, before the others enter. I have cast circles with everyone in, but in most locations it is easier to move freely around the space and bring the others in after the circle is cast. In order to work with everyone already in, you really need enough space to circle around outside the group to define the perimeters, as well as to move within the circle. This is usually only possible at a large, public ritual. When the majority are new to what we are doing, and the ritual is modified or simplified to accommodate that, it works fine to build the circle with everyone already standing at the perimeter. But when we are building a full circle, I still find (having done it both ways) that the focus, the flow, and the dance of building the circle works better in open space. From the viewpoint of one not working center I have found that I can more easily see and focus on the casting of the circle when watching from the outside edge, than by standing within and trying to keep track of where the HPs are moving around among and behind the participants. Besides, the special greeting on entrance feels good whether you are the one who is greeting or the one being greeted.

In the instructions below (because it is less complicated and because this, after all, is my method, which may not be exactly preferred by someone else), I will usually refer to what the HPS does as what "I" do.

Greeting of HP and HPS

Standing before the altar and facing each other, me on the left, he on the right, we hold hands and center ourselves, at the same time that either our Crone or our Maiden is leading everyone else in a centering meditation (examples of meditations are given at the end of

Chapter 10). We do this because when we begin to cast the circle we want everyone to be centered, observing and visualizing with us. This helps build the energy. We greet each other with the same words and motions that we will use to greet everyone else when we bring them into circle.

The words and motions of greeting for both HPs and for others, later, when they are brought into circle, are:

> *(Name), I do greet thee as we enter into this magickal rite. Blessed Be.*

As this is said, we draw an active, invoking spirit pentagram (see pentagram illustrations on page 119) on the person's forehead with oil. We then draw a solar cross from his/her head to solar plexus area to right shoulder to left shoulder as we say:

> *In the name of the God and Goddess who within thee dwell.*

The vertical bar of the cross represents the God, and the horizontal bar represents the Goddess. Gathering energy from above, we then bring our hands downward in front of your body, through your aura and central meridian. This is a cleansing motion. Then we gather earth energy from below and bring it up through your aura and central meridian. This is a charging motion. Then we hug and kiss in welcome, which greatly contributes to rapport and to the building of energy.

Sweeping

I hand the broom to my HP who takes it deocil (means clockwise, pronounced JES-sill) to the East. (All motions of building energy within circle are deocil.) He salutes, silently going through the same motions of "as above, so below" as he will later do and say aloud with the sword, then he proceeds to sweep all around the circle on three levels: physical—ground, mental—shoulder to head height, and spiritual—above the head. He is firmly visualizing all negativity being swept out of the area. Everyone else, as with all the actions of casting the circle, will help us if they visualize with us. When he finishes, he returns to the altar and gives the broom back to me.

Consecration of Altar Instruments

At the same time as the sweeping is being done, I prepare the altar. If any tools are being used for the first time, I cleanse and charge them. Otherwise, only the earth/water, fire, and air elements are cleansed and charged, since in some respect they always involve previously unconsecrated materials. To do this, I first take up the container of water, salute (hold it up toward the East and toward our altar images of Goddess and God), place it on the pentacle, and form a banishing earth pentagram across it with my athame, saying:

> *O element of Water, I do banish and cast from thee all that is impure and unclean, that thou may be a fitting tool for our magickal use.*

I lift the athame in the air, casting off any impurities, and then circle it in the air, gathering charging energy, and then form the solar cross over the water, saying:

> *And I do charge thee in the names of God and Goddess.*

I replace the water and then take up the container of salt and repeat the same words and motions, except that now I say:

> *O element of Earth …*

Next the same words and motions are used to cleanse and charge the censer, which represents two elements:

> *O elements of Fire and Air …*

Finally, I salute with water in one hand and salt in the other. I place the water on the pentacle and take a pinch of salt, mixing it into the water, saying:

> *I now do blend this salt of the earth with this water to form the sweet elixir of the Mother's womb, from which we have all come and onto which we must one day return.*

At this point my HP has usually just finished sweeping and has returned to stand beside me.

Cleansing of the Circle with the Elements

I now give my HP the censer, and I take the water container. I go first to the East, with him following. I salute the East, saying:

Cleansing of the Circle

With Earth and Water I cleanse the East.

I stand slightly aside and wait while he salutes with the censer, saying:

With Fire and Air I cleanse the East.

We then proceed to the South, me sprinkling water around the edges of the circle and he directing incense smoke as we go ... and so on, returning full circle back to the East, where we again salute once, and then return to the altar.

Banishing Pentagrams

To me the drawing of the banishing earth pentagrams with my athame is the ultimate, final, and firm act of banishing any unwanted energies from the area and beginning to replace them with my own will and intent for a protected and secure circle. (Although Wiccan books are divided on whether athame and sword are air or fire, and my Atheneum training originally taught fire, I associate these tools primarily with air—power of mind—because that is how I use them. With them I direct my mental focus and energy, to define my intent and purpose, to define space and to establish boundaries. I am admittedly also influenced by long association of the Tarot suit of swords with air, but primarily my choice is based on my reason for using the tools. Lady Beckett has recently been teaching a more comprehensive interpretation of this most personal of the Witch's tools. She is saying that the athame is all elements, for it is made from ores of the Earth, forged in fire, cooled in water, and used to direct energy through the air.)

To return to my specific pentagram rite, I go to the East, pause, draw in a deep breath, and focus. I draw a large banishing Earth pentagram, visualizing it in bright green light and firmly commanding with my mind that all unwanted energies within the entire defined area shall be gone. I do not circle the pentagram because I do not want to contain this intent in the East only, but rather to encompass the entire sphere. I point the athame firmly through the center, exhaling and drawing a small circle of spirit which I visualize expanding in green light. As I move the athame deocil, arm extended at shoulder height, I visualize an electric blue line being drawn around the entire circle, as I walk to the next quarter. I repeat the banishing pentagram at each quarter, completing the circle to the east, where I pause, kiss the athame, and then return to the altar.

While I do this, my HP circles opposite me, sharing my visualization. As I draw the pentagrams, he stands in the pentagram position, arms extended, legs apart.

Defining the Sphere with the Sword

Now that the area is fully cleansed, it is time to build the sphere or temple. I give the sword to my HP, who takes it to the East. Now he salutes by lifting the sword high, saying:

> *As above;*
>
> (sword to the ground)
>
> *So below.*
>
> (sword held in front of his body)
>
> *As within;*
>
> (sword held at arms length)
>
> *So without.*
>
> (sword and other arm sweeping outward)
>
> *As the Universe;*
>
> (return to center)
>
> *So the Soul.*

While he does this, I, standing in the West, go through the same motions, ending with my hands crossed over my breast. Then we circle opposite each other three times, I mirroring his motions by my outstretched arms toward each of the three levels. He defines the boundaries of the sphere at ground level (physical), head height (mental), and above the head (spiritual). We are (and everyone else should be, too) visualizing electric blue light issuing from the point of the sword.

Invoking Spirit

With the sword, the boundaries of the sphere have been defined, the space created. But in order to make this truly a sacred space, a temple, we need to fill it with spiritual light. I now take up my wand and from the center of the circle I face the area between the air and fire quarters. These are the elements associated with active, kinetic

Presentation of the Sword to the High Priest

energy. I draw a large active, invoking spirit pentagram in the air, ending with a broad, encompassing sweep, and visualizing white light. I then turn deocil to face the area between the Water and Earth quarters. These are the elements associated with responsive, magnetic energy. I draw a large passive, invoking spirit pentagram in the air, again ending with a broad, encompassing sweep and visualizing white light. I turn to the altar and point the wand toward it, saying:

> *May the Spirit flow within.*

Mark lights the center white candle, symbolizing the presence of the spirit of the One that we have invited to fill our sphere. I then turn toward those who are waiting to enter and draw a solar cross in the air, saying:

> *With perfect love and perfect trust I do welcome you within.*

I see my wand as primarily a tool of fire—like a torch, a beacon, or a lightening rod with which spiritual energy is invited and conducted into the circle.

The Form of Ritual

Entrance and Greeting of Participants

My HP and I move to the edge of the circle, bringing oil. One of us (it varies on who gets there first) cuts a door by drawing one in the air counterclockwise (widdershins, because we are temporarily banishing a portion of the energy field that we have built around the circle). I greet the men, he greets the women (cross-polarities are used whenever possible; it helps to build energy). Words and motions are the same as given before. After everyone is in, one of us will close the circle by drawing the door-shape deocil—clockwise. When we have a designated Red Priest, it is his job to enter last and close the circle by drawing the door in the air deocil.

Dedication and Consecration

These are usually thought of as just "Consecration" because it's all done consecutively by the High Priestess, but there are really two parts in one. The Dedication is an announcement of the intention for the circle. I always briefly state the purpose and main theme of our meeting. The major theme will be much more fully defined during the Charge. I then go right into the Consecration, which is to be delivered with love but also with authority, and should include in some form or other (with a wide range of possibilities for creative writing), the intent that the circle shall be protected, that it shall be a meeting place where desirable energies such as love, power, truth, etc., shall flourish, that it shall focus and contain the energies that we shall raise within it, that new growth or insight into the mysteries might be gained or a defined purpose be fulfilled (such as celebration of an event, a healing, a specific intent, etc.).

Charging and Strengthening the Circle with the Elements

I next call forth two people who, previous to beginning the circle, have been assigned to earth and water, fire and air. (It is the Red Priest's job to elicit volunteers for the element charging and for calling the directions.) I hand the two the tools and they go to the East, just as the HP and I did at the initial cleansing, but say instead:

> *With Earth and Water I charge the East ... [etc.]*

As they move around the circle from quarter to quarter, the person with the earth and water will dip fingers in the salt water and then touch each person on the forehead with it. This is not a cleansing act. Everyone was centered and cleansed when they entered the circle, and the circle has been thoroughly cleansed. It is an act of blessing (similar to holy water in a church). The person who has the censer is to direct the incense toward each person with the feather. Again, this is an act of blessing and charging.

Passing the Kiss

This strengthens the rapport among all participants and helps to build the energy. I kiss and hug my HP, saying:

> *In Perfect Love and Perfect Trust.*

He kisses and hugs someone else in the circle, saying the same thing. That person passes the kiss to whomever stands deocil, and so on around the circle. The last person comes to center and returns the kiss to me, completing the circle. (That person then returns to his or her place by walking deocil.)

Watchtowers

The illustration on page 119 shows the motion of the various pentagrams. They are the same as those used in the Golden Dawn. Some Wiccan circles use these as we do, others use only the earth pentagrams.

Before the circle started, four people were assigned to call the Watchtowers. Sometimes the calls are prewritten on cards for them to read, and sometimes we improvise, with each person making up his or her own call. In either case, so that everyone can participate, we nearly always end the calls with the same words:

> *Guardian of the Eastern Sphere, now we seek your presence here. Come, East [or South, West, North, as the case may be], come. Be here this night.*

To call the Watchtowers, first the HP rings the bell three times and then I say:

> *All Hail the Watchtower of the East.*

At that point I am saluting the direction to be called by holding my athame in the air pointing toward it. Everyone else in the circle also turns in that direction and salutes with one raised hand, or the hand holding the athame. The caller speaks, and then everyone simultaneously draws the appropriate invoking pentagram in the air, circles it, points at the center, and then draws their hand/athame back into the center, motioning the elemental energy inward. The color visualization is the color of the corresponding element: yellow for East, red for South, blue for West, green for North. The caller lights the torch or candle. The bell is rung again, and everyone turns to the next quarter, and the whole procedure is repeated.

Watchtowers are *evoked*. Evocation suggests an "evocative" stirring up or summoning the elemental energies to stand as guardians of the directional points. It is done authoritatively, but with respect, for the elementals are powerful aspects of Nature, and we are asking them to come and assist us.

Power Chant

This helps to build and focus the energy for the invocations. We may use other power chants later for workings, but here, I feel there is no more appropriate chant than:

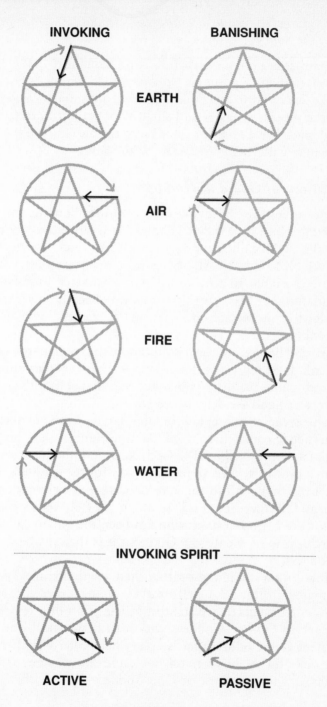

Pentagrams

> *As above, so below; as within, so without; as the Universe,*
> *so the Soul.*

And again, it is a point of repetition and familiarity that helps every-one feel unified. *As above, so below; as within, so without* is repeated over and over again. We hold hands and sway. I generally move the repetition faster and slightly louder until I feel that it has peaked, and then I raise the hands into the air (still held) as a signal to conclude with *As the Universe, so the Soul.*

Invocations of God and Goddess

In some circles the HP invokes the God into himself, and the HPS the Goddess into herself. My HP and I generally prefer to invoke for each other, HPS calling the God and HP drawing down the Moon upon the HPS. Why? Partly because in every way possible we are trying in our circle to achieve balance, and the cross-polarity seems to help with that. Also, we do it this way because it seems to us to be easier to concentrate on receiving the energy flow when we are not speaking.

As said before, we use a gold candle to represent the God and a silver candle to represent the Goddess. These candles are lit by the one onto whom the deity is invoked as a signal that the energy has been received and the deity is present.

The order of calling and bidding farewell to God and Goddess is admittedly somewhat based on traditional roles, but feminist though I am, it feels right. The God, consort of the Goddess, is called first, in a protective role, to pave the way for the Goddess. The God-dess leaves first for the same reason, also in deference to her as Queen and Mother—or "Lady first," if you will. Also, we could note that it is the High Priestess, who has been the one to call spirit into the circle, who now calls the God, but it is then the God who calls the Goddess.

Invocation is a request rather than a summoning. The energies are invited within the self, rather than projected, as in the Guardians/elements to a Watchtower. The priest or priestess calls for the spark of God or Goddess within to build and blend with the immanent God/Goddess that is everywhere. S/he asks that the force of the deity fill the body, mind, soul, and spirit and expand, touch, and share with the spark of God/Goddess of all within the circle.

Having been thus filled, the HPs speak and act as God/Goddess for the remainder of the ritual.

The magic and mystery of invocation varies—sometimes it works more strongly than others. During classes we who have worked center have shared our experiences of the wonderful rush that happens when it really works, and the common experience that, especially when first beginning to work center and unsure about what comes next, all initial nervousness can truly and magically vanish when the God or Goddess is invoked and felt within.

The Charge

In many circles, especially at a Moon, which is primarily a ritual of Goddess worship, the Charge is only the Charge of the Goddess. She says it all. The God typically has a bigger role within Sabbat rituals, which celebrate the seasonal cycle of Sun and Earth. In our Moons we strive to create a dialogue between God and Goddess. Though she usually has the more extensive message (after all, it is a Moon ritual), we are attempting to distinguish each Moon according to the zodiacal signs that the Sun and Full Moon are in at the time.

The Full Moon is the opposition aspect to the Sun. The Moon reflects the light of the Sun in a manner that clarifies and gives substance (form) to that light, and which, unlike the blinding light of the Sun, can be easily approached and seen. The Moon is a form of mental energy, but her wisdom is that of intuitive insight and flow of feeling rather than the conscious logic that is more associated with the Sun rising into the light of day, or the Sun's messenger, Mercury. The Moon, at Full Moon lunation, is in the complementary opposite sign to the Sun. Therefore the dialogue between priest and priestess, as well as the charge and any working that evolves out of the charge, attempts to balance the polarities in a way that will touch some chord in the lives of the participants, and help them to understand and use the universal, archetypal energies that have been invoked.

During the course of a year of Moon rituals, all signs will be at one time the Sun and at another time the Moon, and it is our intent that everyone will come to an intuitive understanding of issues symbolized by the signs that at some time or place will be useful to each of them in their lives, regardless of their individual astrological identities. Everyone has every sign someplace in his or her chart.

The Charge is to Wiccan ritual much as the homily or sermon is to a church service. We do try to make it more fun, and to get participants involved, too.

The Working

This is not an automatic part of the typical Moon ritual tradition. Often I have participated in other groups where they go from Charge to Great Rite, and special intents are reserved for the sharing time. I feel strongly, however, that if magick is to be performed, it should happen when the energy is high. Sharing cakes and wine tends to ground the energy. Therefore my charges usually flow right into some kind of directed working that involves everyone—a guided meditation, flash paper intents, binding and breaking cords, circle dancing and chanting are a few of the things we have done. This type of thing works most strongly at Moon circles where all those present are "family" and accustomed to working together. Magickal working is for Moons. Sabbats, especially when guests are present, are more for enactment of mythology, revealing the mystery behind that mythology, and for pageantry—although the seasonal cycles of Earth and Sun are certainly to be related to life cycles of individuals. That relationship, indeed, is the mystery!

The pageantry feeds the group mind and identity, and our relationship to all that has gone before, what is and what will be. For our Full Moon rituals, the workings are directed more toward the personal intents of each individual. For our Sabbats, the charge is generally extended by some form of mythological enactment or group energy raising, rather than toward a working of individual intents. When you read the rituals later in this book, you will see much more clearly what I mean.

Great Rite

This is a symbolic act of union between God and Goddess. But to consider it to be merely sexual—a fertility rite—is to sell it short. What is happening is a balance of polarities, a merging of the God and Goddess within into One Whole. The Great Rite, done with the proper intent, should be just as effective whether it is done by priest and priestess, by oneself alone, or by people of the same sex.

The chalice symbolizes the feminine, and the athame the masculine. Other circles vary as to whether HPS holds the chalice, HP

The Great Rite

the athame, or whether they reverse the polarities with HPS holding athame, HP the chalice, with him kneeling to her. Mark and I decided that we don't like either one in regard to the intent of balance within. Sex is a way of reaching out for and learning about wholeness and completion through merging with another person, but the only true wholeness and completion must ultimately be found within. We both hold the chalice, and both hold the athame, one's hand over the other's. We both stand and look into each other's eyes as equals. We speak:

HP: Athame to Chalice.

HPS: Spirit to Flesh.

HP: Man to Woman.

HPS: As the God and Goddess within.

All: Conjoined they bring blessedness to life.

The response is said as we thrust the athame into the chalice. We then withdraw the athame and I hold it for him to take a small drink from it, after which he offers it to me and then I replace it on the altar.

Ibis, Elder of my circle, has been in Wicca since his teens and he is now in his 60s. He has told us, with considerable wit and twinkle in his eye, of a couple of instances he knew of from the past in which the Great Rite was enacted in full during a group ritual, rather than symbolically. You can also find this written in some of the older, more traditional books on Gardnerian Wicca, particularly in regard to their Third Degree initiation ritual.

Of course, actual sex magick does happen, and it can be very powerful, but in all of my contacts with quite a number of circles (other than the stories related by the friend already mentioned), I have not heard of it happening in any context other than in private rituals for two between couples who are working partners within a committed relationship. (See also Sex Magick, page 90.)

Any rumors you may have heard about orgies at Witches' rituals are vastly overexaggerated! I can't say it never happens, any more than one could say orgies have never happened at a "yuppie" party, either. But it is not common. Most of the Wiccans I know are monogamous. They do honor sexuality as natural and sacred to the Goddess —"All acts of love and pleasure are my rituals."

Blessing of the Cakes and Beverage

This is usually done silently by the HPs, using their wands. They simultaneously lift their wands into the air to gather energy, and then touch them to the chalice and the plate. They then serve everyone deocil around the circle. The HP takes the chalice and offers it, saying:

> *May you never thirst.*

The HPS offers the cakes, saying:

> *May you never hunger.*

The recipient responds with various responses such as *Blessed Be,* or *Nor you my Lady* (or Lord/Sister/Brother, as the case may be) as they choose. One cake and a small amount of whatever is in the chalice are reserved as offerings to the Goddess.

Sharing

Right after the cakes and beverage are offered, we signal everyone to sit down and relax. This is a time when announcements may be made, when special requests are made, and/or when anyone may share whatever they feel like saying to the group. To encourage open sharing we have borrowed from the Native American traditions the concept of a talking stick, our consecrated Circle Staff, which is passed to anyone who requests it. Whoever holds it has the attention of everyone and is charged to speak articulately with the power of all of the elements. Sometimes, if requests for help have been given, we will raise energy again for a healing circle. Generally, for the raising of energy at this time, or earlier, as part of the working, we incorporate various methods of chanting, dance, drumming, song, guided meditation, etc.

Closing the Circle

As was stated before, the Goddess leaves first, usually for us by being bid farewell by the HP. She is thanked and kissed goodbye, and the HPS extinguishes the silver candle. She then thanks and bids farewell to the God, and the HP extinguishes the gold candle.

In bidding farewell to the Guardians, the HP rings the bell and I call out:

All hail the Watchtower of the East ... [etc.]

As we did when the Watchtowers were called. The caller of each quarter then thanks and bids farewell to the Guardian and then extinguishes the torch or candle. The dismissals end with *Blessed Be,* said by everyone. The banishing pentagram for that element is drawn in the air by everyone, circled, with the hand pushed through the center as if waving the guardian away.

All then join hands to repeat together the conclusion:

May all beings and elementals attracted to this rite be on their way, harming none. The circle is open but unbroken. Merry meet, merry part and merry meet again, Blessed Be!

If we are not "at home" the dismissal is varied as follows: Before the concluding statement is said together, the HPS will formally banish the circle, moving widdershins. The concluding statement will then leave out the part about the circle being open but unbroken. This is because it is not appropriate for us to leave our circle, our temple, in a place that will be soon occupied by many other people who may be of different energies, convictions, faiths, and may not be comfortable within the energies we have created there. You will find our usual ceremony for banishing the circle on page 179.

Offering to the Goddess

After the ritual has ended, and the circle is open, the HPs take the cake reserved for the Goddess, and the chalice, and pause for a moment of meditation, outside (if we are not already outside). We salute the Moon, offer our thanks, and then pour out the remaining beverage and crumble the cake onto the ground.

Astrology and Ritual

The "A" Word

The "A" word isn't quite as scary to the public (excepting some Christian fundamentalists, of course) as the "W" word, but it has caused its problems. The National Council for Geocosmic Research has tried to skirt the issue by calling it "geocosmic correspondences," and Reinhold Ebertin tried, with some success, to rename it "Cosmobiology," but still, the title "astrology" prevails. With it, we continue to experience the media derision, and refusal, in a penchant for quick and easy sound bites, to probe beyond the "pop" astrology of tabloid fortune tellers.

It is not my purpose in this particular book to defend astrology. My bibliography refers you to several good books if you are interested in probing its validity on a more mundane level. I'll offer here only a few personal observations and opinions.

Astronomy and astrology were essentially the same discipline until the time of Kepler, who was one of the last great astronomer/astrologers. During his time the world view that became dominant was one of mechanistic science, a philosophy that cannot allow for the intangibles of astrology, and so the study of the stars was split in two, for the first time in history. Up until that point *astra-nomos* (the numbers—measuring—of the stars) was a discipline that served *astra-logos* (the word of the stars). Methods of investigating the movements in the cosmos were perfected primarily in order to increase the ability to judge the correspondence of those movements with life on earth. Now, while a few astronomers have come to new respect and interest in investigating the "word of the stars," most of them are still, among contemporary scientists, the most reluctant to even look at the possibility that the cosmos could have any but the most remote connection with human life.

Meanwhile, the astrologers, most of us renegades to one degree or another, demand the most precise calculations of the planets' places and then apply them to a myriad of methods, traditions, and flights of fancy of which little is agreed upon by all, except the general conviction that "it works," and therefore, let's use it! In that, astrologers are primarily technicians, rather than scientists. (Electricians can't explain why electricity works, either, but they know how to harness it and make it work.)

My technical specialty, from the first year I studied astrology, has been the Cosmobiology and Uranian methods, originally developed in Germany. My second book, *Dial Detective*,[1] is a highly technical, step-by-step, precisely illustrated instruction book for these methods—a 180-degree turn-around from the philosophical approach of *Twelve Wings*. I am completely baffled by why this purely mundane astrology works so well—amazed and delighted with it. Admittedly, in the past, I was also sometimes a little afraid of it. In more recent years I've left fear behind in a greater acceptance of living in the "now," and also in the knowledge and experience that no matter how skilled one gets at prediction, one can never be sure. Life quite often takes rather unexpected twists, and the astrological factors still "work" in hindsight, with one of their perfectly logical alternative interpretations that you just didn't think about ahead of time.

One thing is certain, you can't live in the future until you get there. Thinking that you know what is going to happen becomes a part of your experience of now, for good or ill. It doesn't save you at all from making decisions about what you are going to do or think or not do or worry about ... just as if you had the total free will to create the future according to your own best choice. Do you have that free will, or do you not? Does it matter, since you have to act as though you do, anyhow?

Perhaps we will know, someday, beyond the veil. Meanwhile, I find astrology most useful at times. It is a good tool for thinking through alternative decisions, gaining understanding of self and others, planning when to take action or when to hold back, and learning to accept with serenity that which is beyond my power to change. It is my tool of choice; it may not be right for you. Each must seek and discover the right path for herself or himself.

For the purposes of my rituals and of this book I am not interested in personal horoscopes or mundane astrology, but instead, in astrology as a universal language of symbolism. Everyone has every sign, every planet, somewhere in his or her chart. Everyone, at one time or another, experiences every issue associated with the various astrological factors, either within the self or in interaction with others. Everyone experiences every phase of the cycles of life that reflect the yearly seasonal cycle of Earth and Sun, and the monthly cycles of the Moon. You may not experience your personal cycles with the same timing as the seasons, or the Moon, but understanding the cycles of Earth and Cosmos can lead you to a new depth of awareness of the ebb and flow of your own life. The symbolism helps to touch a personal chord for people who participate.

Astrology—A Divine Science?

Certainly astrology can be used in purely secular ways. It is used by financial analysts to play the stock market, by therapists to help analyze and work with clients, by business people to help select employees or plan presentations, by countless people for self-help or better understanding of relationships or speculating on the future ... even by politicians and presidents planning moves. Some have said, however, that astrology is "the divine science."

Search to the roots of any religion, and astrology can be found. Truly it was probably the mother of all religions, for it was only natural for ancient people to look at the mysterious lights moving in the sky and think of them as gods. Ancient religious art and scripture abound with references that attest to astrological correspondences.

Although astrology can be a tool of many things—psychology, finance, politics, business, gambling, self-help, religion, psychic phenomena—it belongs to none of them. It is a discipline unique in itself, a language of symbolism, the study of time. Yet if our highest purpose in life is to grow in spirit and in harmony with the Life Force and our place within its flow (as I believe it is), then surely the highest purpose of astrology is as a tool of the spiritual and as a sign of Divine Order.

Basic Keys to Astrological Symbolism

The following section is to identify the basic astrological symbolism that is used as a framework for the rituals in this book. It is intended both to orient non-astrologers toward a simple keyword understanding of basic astrology, and to orient astrologically-knowledgeable readers to the correspondences used within the Craft.

The Elements

The four basic elements of the ancients are so entrenched in our idiom in regard to personality type that most people take them for granted, even if they'd never think of them as being astrological. We speak of a "fiery" temperament, of "air-heads," of being "all wet," or "down to earth," and on and on we could go with many other examples. The elements are important in astrological interpretation, and they are highly significant in the Craft, having correspondences to the four directions and to the tools of the altar. Some of the major correspondences to astrology and to the Craft are as follows:

Fire	Earth	Air	Water
Aries	Taurus	Gemini	Cancer
Leo	Virgo	Libra	Scorpio
Sagittarius	Capricorn	Aquarius	Pisces
Mars	Venus	Mercury	Moon
Sun	Ceres	Pallas	Pluto
Jupiter	Saturn	Uranus	Neptune
South	North	East	West
Summer	Winter	Spring	Fall

Fire	Earth	Air	Water
Spirit	Body	Mind	Soul
energy	form	consciousness	subconciousness
impulsive	stable	logical	intuitive
red	green	yellow	blue
intuitive (Jung)	sensation (Jung)	thinking (Jung)	feeling (Jung)
wands (Tarot)	pentacles (Tarot)	swords (Tarot)	cups (Tarot)
wand	pentacle	athame	chalice/cauldron
candle	salt, sand, soil	incense	liquid
south declination	north declination	sunrise	sunset
hot, dry	cold, moist	cool, dry	warm, moist
The Lion (Leo)	The Ox (Taurus)	The Man (Aquarius)	The Eagle (Scorpio)
masculine	feminine	masculine	feminine
positive	negative	positive	negative
yang	yin	yang	yin
kinetic	magnetic	kinetic	magnetic
salamanders	gnomes	sylphs	undines

The Elements and the Four Directions

An important factor in Wiccan ritual form is the orientation to the four directions and the calling of the elements. We stand in a circle, but within that circle is an equal-armed cross. Those familiar with astrology will immediately recognize the cross within a circle as the glyph for Earth.

As has already been given, each of the four directions is associated with a long list of correspondences, with the four elements heading the list. Although various magickal traditions vary, the tradition in which I was trained is typical of the apparent majority in that east corresponds with air, south with fire, west with water, and north with earth. To build the circle, one walks around the circle from east to south to west to north. The clockwise motion is called deocil or sunwise. This is the same direction in which the Sun and the planets seem (from an earthly vantage point) to rise in the east, culminate in the southern sky, and set in the west, and it is also the pattern by which an astrological chart is drawn. Those of you who are astrologers will immediately think, as I did, "but the correspondences are wrong!"

If the circle is like a chart-model, and it's so important to walk in the direction of planetary rising, then the directions should be the same as the Ascendant and Midheaven axis of the chart, or the cardinal points of the zodiac. East should be fire/Aries, south should be earth/Capricorn, west should be air/Libra, and north should be water/Cancer.

Yet the Wiccan directions are not the same as the zodiacal directions. Why?

I asked why. With my extensive astrological background, this issue bothered me a great deal when I first began studying Wicca. I asked everyone I thought might know and I looked through a lot of books on Wicca. Nobody could give me an answer other than to suppose that in the geographical location where the tradition started the ocean was probably to the west, south was the direction of warmer weather (heat/fire), north was the direction where it got colder, etc. Or ... "it's just traditional. That's the way it was handed down." I was not satisfied with that rationale. It just didn't seem to make sense. Great importance was given to the idea of a circle, and that whenever possible males and females should stand alternately around that circle so that energy would pass from masculine to feminine to masculine polarity. Yet when we moved from Watchtower to Watchtower we passed from masculine/air to masculine/fire to feminine/water to feminine/earth. The zodiacal model seemed more meaningful to me, so that is what I used when I first began to do circles on my own. I was reinforced in this decision when I attended a class on Egyptian magick and found that the zodiacal cardinal points were used in that ritual, and when I later heard of a local Celtic tradition coven that also used the cardinal points (although justifying them by the geography of the area where the tradition started rather than by knowledge of the zodiac).

In spite of my logic, however, I could feel a strong energy associated with the directions according to the more predominant tradition. Then I discovered through reading that ritual magick according to the Golden Dawn and the Masonic traditions also used those same non-zodiacal directions ... and the whole subject continued to nag at me, so I continued to search for a rationale. It somehow seems very important to me to balance my feelings (water) with my thinking (air), and my common sense (earth) with my flashes of insight (fire)—and there I go, with the polarities of magick tradition!

I don't have all the answers yet. A more thorough study of the history of the occult might yield more pieces for the puzzle, and when I find them I'll let you know—and if you find anything pertinent, please tell me. So far it has been pretty hard to trace down what came first, because Wiccan, Masonic, and magickal authors so often seem to think their own beliefs go way back before recorded history—maybe even to Atlantis or alien visitors from another planet! The interesting thing is that there are so many similarities in various branches of the ancient mysteries that certainly a common source is probable.

No Wiccan source that I could read or ask could give me a reason for the directions or correspondences other than "must have corresponded with the geographical directions where the tradition started." Two non-Wiccan sources gave a rationale based on the four winds.

The first of these sources, The Hermetic Order of the Golden Dawn, began only a bit over a 100 years ago (1887), yet Carl Llewellyn Weschcke's forward to his publication of Israel Regardie's teachings and rituals claims that the order provided the foundation for much of the current occult revival and resource material for contemporary Wicca. Maybe including the directions? I don't know. So far I haven't found a Wiccan book that claims any rationale—or history—for the directions that predates Golden Dawn.

In the chapter on pentagram ritual Regardie says:

The elements vibrate between the Cardinal points for they have not an unchangeable abode therein, though they are allotted to the Four Quarters in their invocation in the Ceremonies of the First Order. This attribution is derived from the nature of the winds. For the easterly wind is of the Nature of Air more especially. The South Wind bringeth into action the nature of Fire. West winds bring with them moisture and rain. North winds are cold and dry like Earth. The SW wind is violent and explosive—the mingling of the contrary elements of Fire and Water. The

NW and SE winds are more harmonious, uniting the influence of the two active and passive elements.

Yet their natural position in the Zodiac is: Fire in the East, Earth in South, Air in West, and Water in the North. Therefore they vibrate: Air between West and East, Fire between East and South, Water between North and West, Earth between South and North.

Spirit also vibrateth between Height and Depth.

So that, if thou invokest, it is better to look towards the position of the winds, since the Earth, ever whirling on her poles, is more subject to their influence. But if thou wilt go in the Spirit Vision unto their abode, it is better for thee to take their position in the Zodiac.

Air and Water have much in common, and because one is the container of the other, therefore have their symbols been at all times transferred, and the Eagle [Scorpio] assigned to Air and Aquarius to Water. Nevertheless, it is better that they should be attributed as before stated and for the foregoing reason is it that the invoking sign of the one and the banishing sign of the other counterchange in the Pentagram ... If thou wilt use the Pentagram to invoke or banish the Zodiacal forces, thou shalt use the Pentagram of the Element unto which the sign is referred ... Whenever thou invokest the forces of the Zodiacal Signs as distinct from the Elements, thou shalt erect an astrological scheme of the Heavens for the time of working so that thou mayest know toward what quarter or direction thou shouldest face in working. For the same sign may be in the East at one time of day and in the West at another.

So according to Regardie, it's okay under some circumstances to use the zodiacal directions, if you orient them according to the time of working, and you use the pentagram that belongs to the element, not the direction. For most rituals, however, he uses the directional correspondence to the winds.[2]

This idea of the four winds can also be found in Elisabeth Haich's *Initiation*, a fictionalized autobiography in which she deals at length with her memories of a past life in Egypt in which she was initiated as a priestess of the temple. In one of her lessons from the high priest she was told of the Four Faces of God that never change their position. The north face of God is fiery, while the south is cold. This is related to the face of a person which radiates expression, whereas to turn one's back emits cold. Since God is everywhere, no matter where this north face radiates heat, that which receives it is south, and therefore hot! (I know this sounds a little confusing—I leave it to you to read the book and puzzle it out. It's a very interesting book.) The Egyptian high priest of the story goes on to say that any child knows the difference between the winds from the four directions because if one stands out in the wind one can feel it. (I can't say that I've caught that specific distinction yet—we might try playing child and go out in the breeze to test it!) No matter where on earth a wind arises (says the book), if it comes from the south it will be perceived as warm (fire); from the north, cold (earth); from the west, moist (water); and from the east, dry (air).[3]

After giving that elemental correspondence, the priest goes right on to explain the cardinal points of the zodiac with their elemental and directional correspondences without one single word of why one cardinal cross is completely different from the other! Why hasn't this bothered some of these authors?

In a Brotherhood of Light book on ancient Masonry by C.C. Zain, I found a rationale for the directions based on two different sets of astrological measurements. East and west are based on sunrise and sunset, the east being active/masculine because the Sun comes up and it's the beginning of day, and the west being feminine because the Sun sets and the Moon reigns by night. The Sun is, by daily motion, moving in the plane of the ecliptic (celestial longitude). This measurement is indicated in the Masonic emblem by the Euclid's square. But because the Sun, Moon, and planets do not move in the same plane, but rather describe orbits that are inclined to one another, the Compass (another major part of the Masonic emblem) is also required. The inclination of the planets' orbits causes them to form different angles to the Celestial Equator, and these angles are called the planet's declination. Aspects of declination are called Parallels. Many astrologers consider Parallels of Declination to be very important and intense aspects.

So the Masons accounted for declination in their assignment of north and south. As they accounted for the cycle of daily motion (sunrise and sunset) for the assignment of east and west, they also accounted for the cycle of yearly motion in their assignment of north and south. This yearly north/south motion can be seen as the seasons change: each day from Autumn Equinox until Winter Solstice the Sun apparently rises a little further south. After Winter Solstice it slowly "returns" to the east for Spring Equinox, and from then until Summer Solstice it rises each day a little further to the north, then returning to the east again, and so on.

The Masons saw their lodge as dimensional in both time and space, not a flat plane on the floor. Perhaps this idea is also at the root of magick traditions and has to do with why the plane of the zodiac alone is not used for Circle. When we include the plane of the equator, too, along with both daily and yearly motion, we perceive a spherical model, rather than a flat circle, and a better image of the Whole.

One reason, then, for the assignment of south to the masculine Sun and north to the feminine Earth is given: *as the south is the region from which the sun comes to overcome the evil powers of winter in the spring of the year, and as the blighting cold comes from the north as the sun moves southward in autumn, those Masons sitting in the south represent benefic influences, and those sitting in the north represent malefic influences.* This, of course, places the Masons in a very out-of-date patriarchal category—but it is a rationale for the directions!

The reasoning behind the assignment of south as masculine/Sun and north as feminine/Moon/Earth is also explained in the two pillars of the temple. (Golden Dawn also has the two pillars.) Because the ancient Masons believed that life depends on sex, they erected two pillars in the temple, one on either side of the great eastern gateway. The pillar on the right is called in Hebrew, *Jachin;* meaning, "He that Strengthens." And it is the Royal Sun returning from the right, or southern declination, and rising through the eastern horizon that brings renewed strength after the winter season.

The pillar on the left is called *Boaz;* "Source of Strength." It represents the passive and inert north. It is the left side of the Gateway of the rising Sun, which attracts the Sun northward. Truly, the feminine in nature by its attractive power is the Source of Strength, *Boaz;* and the ever-active masculine, *Jachin,* seeking that source of strength becomes the Strengthener.[4]

A suggestion of the traditional directions can also be found in the Bible, in the four living creatures of the Old Testament prophet Ezekiel:

> *Their faces were like this: each of the four had the face of a man, but on the right side was the face of a lion, and on the left side the face of an ox, and finally each had the face of an eagle. Their faces looked out on all their four sides; they did not turn when they moved, but each went straight forward.*
>
> —Ezekiel 1: 8-9[5]

This suggests the same idea as in *Initiation,* in that the faces are fixed and never changing like the winds and the Four Faces of God. Also, in the same arrangement as the Wicca/Golden Dawn/Masonry directions, the face of the man (Aquarius/air) has the lion (Leo/fire) to the right and the ox (Taurus/earth) to the left, leaving the eagle (Scorpio/water) opposite.

It should be understood that in biblical times the Cardinal Cross (due to precession) was Taurus, Leo, Scorpio, and Aquarius, the Guardians of East, South, West, and North, respectively—the Four Corners of the World. These signs are also prominently associated with the directions in Golden Dawn. Elsewhere in Ezekiel:

> *Each had four faces: the first face was that of an ox, the second that of a man, the third that of a lion, and the fourth that of an eagle.*
>
> —Ezekiel 10:14[6]

Here we have the signs given with the Taurus Cardinal East of that time first, yet if we go deocil around the creature, we still have earth to air to fire to water!

Finally, we have a contemporary rationale in psychologist/ astrologer Liz Greene's book *Relating* in which she correlates the elements with the four Jungian archetypes. She does not discuss zodiacal polarities, magick, or anything of that nature. She does describe at length the personality types associated with the elements, and she casts air versus water and earth versus fire as the most completely opposite types. Air is assigned correspondence with Jung's archetype of thinking, while water is feeling. Earth is sensation, while fire is intuition.[7] So Liz Greene, too, sets up a cross of polarities that place element and sign correspondences in opposition to each other that are not in opposition in the zodiac.

A problem in reconciling the issue of the order of the elemental correspondences is in the misperception of walking "sunwise" as meaning that one must also be walking in zodiacal order. It's true that the Sun and the planets rise and set daily, in the direction that we call "clockwise," but the direction in which they pass through the signs of the zodiac (in yearly motion) is opposite—counterclockwise. In the tradition of magick circles we are, in fact, dealing with more than one system of measurement and symbolism.

It is helpful to think of movement within the circle as being simply forward and backward rather than as planetary motion, e.g. "sunwise." Deocil, like the clock, moves forward (in time), and thus adds or builds energy. Widdershins, or counterclockwise, a backward movement (in time), subtracts, takes away, or banishes the energy.

To think of movement within the circle as an imitation of planetary motion definitely muddies the symbolism, because anyone with any astronomical bent knows perfectly well that this "sunwise" movement is only apparent. The Earth is going around the Sun, not vice versa, and the planets are actually moving forward through the zodiac when they go counterclockwise!

The zodiacal polarities are not true opposites in the sense of being really different. They are complementary opposites, each pair being of the same active/masculine or receptive/feminine polarity. Someplace maybe there is a reason why they were assigned that way, and maybe someday I'll find it! They do require balance, and I think it makes sense to consider this, especially as a basis for ritual dialogue between the Sun of a month and the Full Moon. But they also reconcile with each other much more easily than do the polarities of air/water and fire/earth.

Earth contains and limits water, water wears away earth, or they can each nurture the other—or turn into a muddy rut. But usually they get along quite well.

Fire and air usually get along great, too. One feeds the other— or they can just go up in smoke and dissipate.

But with air and water there's quite a bit more tension. They are alike (as, in another sense, Regardie pointed out) in that they are both related to mind. But, to use contemporary jargon, air is like the left brain and water is like the right brain. Too much air (cool logic) can whip water into waves of stubborn emotionalism. Or water feelings can drown out the airy abstraction and reason.

Earth and fire are an even more difficult pair. Fire is spirited—romantic instincts do not wish to be contained or limited by earthly realities. Earth can smother fire, or fire can wreak havoc on the earth. The air/water and fire/earth polarities are more difficult to balance, and personalities heavily oriented toward one often find it difficult to get along well with the other. Yet with understanding they can be mutually stimulating, and they usually have a strong attraction for each other.

(Only Golden Dawn, of the sources I've researched, deals at all with the conflict of fire and water: southwest winds are violent and explosive. That is perhaps the toughest pair to balance. Water emotionalism can douse the spirit of fire; fire can turn water to steam.)[8]

I conclude that there is definitely a place and a need for the system of polarities used in the cross within the circle of magick tradition. The energy charge or tension of bringing conflict (opposition polarities) into balance is, I think, not quite so strong when the Watchtowers are assigned according to the zodiac—and we are in the business of building energy. Although I've led some quite successful rituals with zodiacal Watchtowers, and I think there's a place for both systems, I do now think as well as feel that it does make sense to place the active/masculine and receptive/feminine energies in opposition to each other across the circle, as well as, when possible, to alternate males and females around the circle. The more energy, the better!

The Signs and their Complementary Opposite Polarities

The sign polarities are an important part of the basis for my Moon rituals, for at the time of each month's Full Moon lunation, the Moon is in the opposite sign of the zodiac from the Sun. In order that each Full Moon ritual be distinct and special, "touching the chord" for participants in a new way, we "play" the Moon as a balance point for the seasonal symbolism of the Sun sign. Everyone has every sign in their chart and therefore in their character somewhere, and must deal with the issues of every sign sometime, even though one or more of these issues may be more emphasized than others in the individual's life experiences.

A short dialogue between the Sun (God) and the Moon (Goddess) role-plays the two signs and leads into the Charge of the Goddess, in which her special perspective on the season, from the viewpoint of the opposite sign, provides the complement and balance. This, then, provides the theme and lead-in for the special participatory working for the group.

The following keyword interpretations of the sign polarities are provided as a reference to which you might wish to refer as background for better understanding of the rituals, and perhaps for writing new ones of your own.

Aries opposite Libra

Aries: cardinal, positive, yang, fire
Libra: cardinal, positive, yang, air

> I, my own interests vs. you, your interests
> self-identity vs. relating
> selfishness vs. sharing
> war vs. peace
> charging forth vs. maintaining harmony, balance
> assertion vs. compromise

Key issue in common: identity
   Aries asserts self; Libra seeks identity through relating to others.

Duality within each:
   The Aries impulse to be always first is strong in initiative and courageous leadership—or it is headstrong selfishness that demands its own way.
   Libra compromise keeps the peace with tact, diplomacy, moderation, and balance—or anxiously vacillates in a constant search for approval.

Taurus opposite Scorpio

Taurus: fixed, negative, yin, earth
Scorpio: fixed, negative, yin, water

> mastery of the physical world vs. mastery of inner self
> ease vs. conflict
> holding on vs. letting go
> acquisition vs. elimination
> personal resources/values vs. joint resources/values
> generation vs. death/regeneration

Key issue in common: mastery
> Taurus finds security in mastery of the material world; Scorpio finds power through mastery of the inner self.

Duality within each:
> Taurus stubbornness gives the perseverance to achieve mastery—or obstinate resistance to necessary change.
> Scorpio power to control can be turned inward for self-discipline and revitalizing strength—or outward to manipulate others.

Gemini opposite Sagittarius

Gemini: mutable, positive, yang, air
Sagittarius: mutable, positive, yang, fire

> reason vs. revelation/faith
> logic vs. impulse
> knowledge vs. wisdom
> near vs. far
> science vs. religion

Key issue in common: wisdom
> Gemini sees truth through reason and logic; Sagittarius sees truth through revelation and faith.

Duality within each:
> The Gemini duality is versatile and adaptable, able to see new possibilities in a situation, from different points of view—or duality can also mean scattered, fickle irresponsibility.
> Sagittarius enthusiastically inspires others with idealism—or dogmatically insists what everyone must believe.

Cancer opposite Capricorn

Cancer: cardinal, negative, yin, water
Capricorn: cardinal, negative, yin, earth

> home vs. state
> mother vs. father
> unconditional love vs. conditional love
> nurturing vs. self-sufficiency

Key issue in common: community
Cancer protects and nurtures the home and family life; Capricorn advances and protects the professional and public life.

Duality within each:
The Cancer maternal instinct is nurturing and caring, warm and protective—or possessive, anxious, and smothering.
The Capricorn ability to concentrate on reality is responsible, practical, and just—or opportunistic and unscrupulous.

Leo opposite Aquarius

Leo: fixed, positive, yang, fire
Aquarius: fixed, positive, yang, air

individuality vs. group identity
attachment vs. detachment
creative self-expression vs. group expression

Key issue in common: leadership
Magnanimously and generously, Leo rules; egalitarian Aquarius rebels against the rule of any individual.

Duality within each:
The Leo confidence radiates warmth, strength, and generosity—or is domineering, authoritarian, and pompous.
The Aquarian nonconformist can be the humanitarian who strives for needed reform in society—or the radical who rebels against everything that restricts personal freedom.

Virgo opposite Pisces

Virgo: mutable, negative, yin, earth
Pisces: mutable, negative, yin, water

reality vs. vision
discrimination vs. synthesis
practicality vs. impracticality
organization vs. chaos
facts vs. fantasy
details vs. the whole

Key issue in common: service

Virgo, the realist, is unselfishly dedicated to fulfill earthly human needs; Pisces, the visionary, is selflessly devoted to the needs of the spirit.

Duality within each:

The Virgo ability to discriminate is highly ethical and very efficient—or narrow-minded, petty, and nit-picking.

Self-sacrificing Pisces serves with loving compassion and great empathy—or wallows in the self-pity of the suffering martyr. [9]

The Uncomplementary Opposite Polarities

Some readers may have noted that I did not designate the signs as "masculine" or "feminine," even though it is traditional to do so. Tradition has it that all the positive signs are masculine and all the negative signs are feminine. If we could truly consider positive and negative to be like opposite poles of a battery, both equally necessary to make the thing work, the association with masculine and feminine would be just fine. Unfortunately, that is not the case. I looked up positive and negative in the dictionary, just to make my point:[10]

positive: explicit, dogmatic, affirmative, constructive, having real existence, based on fact, electric: having a deficiency of electrons, math: greater than zero

negative: expressing denial or refusal, lacking that which is positive, math: quantity less than zero, electric: having an excess of electrons

So, we have a pretty obvious "good" connotation for positive and a "bad" one for negative, except for the issue of deficiency or excess of electrons. What does that mean?

electron: any of the negatively charged particles that form a part of all atoms (see **electric**)

Okay ...

electric: of or charged with electricity; producing or produced by electricity

This is not telling us much yet. To go on:

electricity: a property of certain fundamental particles of all matter, as electrons (negative charges) and protons (positive charges)

And on ...

protons: an elementary particle in the nucleus of all atoms

And on around in circles? Let's try "charge" ...

charge: to add an electrical charge to (battery); the chemical energy stored in a battery

battery: a cell or group of cells storing an electrical charge and able to furnish a current

current: the flow or rate of flow of energy in a conductor

Are we having fun yet?

conductor: a thing that conducts electricity

Goddess help me! Circles again.

energy: force of expression; an inherent power, capacity for action

force: strength; physical coercion; power to control, persuade; energy that causes or alters motion

Hm-m-m. Are we getting somewhere?

persuade: to urge or cause to do

Not yet. Or ... I sense a connection. What is another way of causing motion? Yes!

magnetic: anything that attracts

magnetism: the quality of being magnetic; the force to which this is due

magnate: a very influential person

attract: to draw to oneself

attraction: anything that attracts; the mutual action by which bodies tend to draw together

Yes! And what is another word for motion?

kinetic: 1. of or relating to the motion of material bodies and the forces or energy associated therewith 2. a: active, lively b: dynamic, energizing

Other traditional word-associations with negative/feminine are "passive" and "responding," while positive/masculine are "active" and "initiating." Let's do a new table:

Negative/Feminine/Yin	Positive/Masculine/Yang
I want, I need, I require ...	I'll get it for you!

The above two phrases are used by Shakti Gawain in her book *Living in the Light,* to describe the inner female and the inner male.[11] So, I now ask you, who is really doing the motivating, the initiating? The "passive" element, that's who! And who is acting in response? He who says, "I'll get it for you."

Remember the following from the section on the directions?

source of strength (Masonic)	he who strengthens (Masonic)

Another way to look at it, is that the motivator/reason to act leads to the action/energy, which leads to the response/form.

I propose two new words to describe the masculine and the feminine:

magnetic	*kinetic*

I like those better than positive and negative, but I do not kid myself that it will "take." Changing word associations in the popular idiom is very difficult—just like Witch and astrology.

In any case, the main thing I would like to change is the fixed association of the earth and water signs with feminine and the fire and air signs with masculine. Males and females come with dominant personalities in all 12 signs, and everyone expresses so-called feminine or masculine traits in various degrees at various times. Our challenge is to honor both the inner male and the inner female, and to become comfortable with them both, allowing each of them to freely express when appropriate. It is important to always keep in mind that masculine does not necessarily mean male, and feminine does not necessarily mean female. It would probably be best if we could just drop the words masculine and feminine and characterize the signs as primarily:

negative charge, yin, magnetic
earth: Taurus, Virgo, Capricorn
water: Cancer, Scorpio, Pisces

positive charge, yang, kinetic
air: Gemini, Libra, Aquarius
fire: Aries, Leo, Sagittarius

The Planets

So far, I have not extensively used the symbolism of the planets in ritual, other than Sun and Moon (which are not really planets, of course, but which are referred to as such in astrology, just for convenience of categorizing parts of the horoscope). I have used the other planets in some of the calls to the Watchtowers, and those that I consider to clearly "belong" to one of the four elements are listed under that element in the table of correspondences already given.

Planets are the most important factor to consider in the interpretation of an individual horoscope, but they are not as easily useful, in my opinion, for group ritual—at least not in their Roman names, primarily Gods. I consider some of the planets that bear the names of Gods to be more feminine in nature than masculine, particularly those that rule the feminine signs, so if I call attention to those planetary energies, I am likely to substitute an appropriate Goddess name.

Planets represent basic energies of the personality. As an analogy, they could be described as the light. A light shining through a stained glass window takes on different colors. The signs are like the stained glass window. It colors the light/energy that shines through it, but does not really change the basic principle. For example, Mars represents how one acts or asserts oneself. Mars in Aries may act quickly and impulsively, while Mars in Taurus may act slowly with deliberation, but we are still talking about how one acts.

Here are a few of my favorite keywords for the planets, as they are symbolic of functions or energies of the personality:

Sun: how you shine—vitality, self-esteem

Moon: how you feel—memories, subconscious/intuitive thought

Mercury: how you think and communicate—intellect, logical thought

Venus: how you love—expressing affection, desire

Mars: how you act—assertiveness, work energy

Jupiter: how you grow—expansion, wisdom

Saturn: how you accept responsibility—discipline, limitation

Uranus: how you change—innovation, rebellion, tension

Neptune: how you escape—dreams, fantasy, vision

Pluto: how you express your power—transformation, destruction, regeneration

Asteroids

Four major asteroids are increasingly being used by astrologers. In part, their popularity comes from the quest for additional feminine planetary symbolism.

Ceres: the Great Mother, shows how you nurture, both self and others; unconditional love

Pallas: the Goddess of Wisdom, shows how you gain wisdom and create from it, your acceptance or fear of success, balance of career with relationships

Vesta: the Temple Priestess, shows how you handle commitments, find meaningful work, integrate spiritual and sexual energies

Juno: Goddess of Marriage, shows how you relate—issues of compatibility, sharing, trust, meeting intimacy

For detailed information on the mythology and the use of the asteroids in astrology, I highly recommend *Asteroid Goddesses*, by Demetra George with Douglas Bloch (from which I derived the above interpretations).[12]

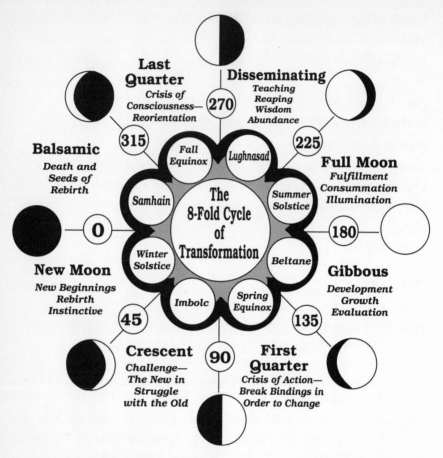

The Eightfold Cycle of Transformation and the Wheel of the Year

The eight Sabbat rituals are based upon an ancient eightfold cycle that has roots in several cultures. I have been unable to discover just where or how long ago it was defined that the number eight represents rebirth and transformative experience, but the most recent clear definition of an eight-phase cycle was given by the great astrological philosopher Dane Rudhyar.

I wrote an article called "The 8-Fold Cycle of Transformation" to accompany the lunar phases tables in my late husband's final book, *Tables of Planetary Phenomena*, ACS, 1990.[13] It covers the symbolism of the cycle and its correspondences with the Wiccan

Wheel of the Year. So, with permission from the publisher (me), here is an adaptation of that article (minimizing or eliminating the material applying to personal horoscopes) which will serve to provide a background for understanding the basis on which the Sabbat rituals in this book were written.

The Eightfold Cycle of Transformation

The only constant in life is change. Nothing is static. From the tiniest cell to the most complex organism, the cycle continues—life, growth, deterioration, death, and life, again. In planetary symbolism we associate the Moon with change, in reflection of her constantly changing faces in the waxing and waning of her cycle.

Four of the Moon's faces are well known, and many calendars mark those lunar phases: New Moon, First Quarter, Full Moon, and Last Quarter. Not as familiar are the four cross-quarter phases, as described by the great astrologer-philosopher Dane Rudhyar in his 1967 book *The Lunation Cycle*. These four are Crescent, Gibbous, Disseminating, and Balsamic.[14] All together, then, we have a cycle of eight—a cycle of transformation that we can see reflected in our lives.

Eight: Transformation, Rebirth, and Power

Eight has a long history of association with transformation and rebirth. In astrology we say the 8th house of the horoscope is the house of death and rebirth. The baptismal fonts in many churches—symbols of rebirth—are shaped like an octagon. Before Christianity, eight was a symbol of the Egyptian god Thoth, who poured water of purification on the heads of new initiates. Ritual circumcision, as a mark of the covenant with God, is traditionally performed on the eighth day of life.

Rudhyar briefly links ancient Hindu, Chinese, and Christian Gnostic symbolism of the number eight with release of power in the dynamic interplay between two moving factors, but gives no specific reference. Numerologists consider eight to be a power number, and so do astrologers. Consider the eightfold aspect series on which the lunar cycle is based. These hard aspects—conjunction, square and opposition, semi-square and sesquiquadrate—are considered to be the most powerful of all aspects in regard to physical manifestation.

A Cycle of Relationship

It is important to note that in discussing the lunar cycle, we are not just talking about the Moon in your chart. We are talking about the Moon in relation to the Sun. The lunar cycle is a cycle of relationship. Rudhyar says, "Relationship generates power; without relationship there is no power available for release."

Rudhyar says that the point of basic crisis in the relationship between two polar factors are the squares—thus the fourfold cross which is the foundation of both the eightfold and the twelvefold divisions of the circle. "But four more points, bisecting the four quarters, are necessary to mark the positions (or the moments) of greatest momentum and most critical release."

An Eightfold Solar Cycle

It is interesting that in the eight ancient Pagan holidays, which are the cycle of transformation through the seasons of the year, the Greater Sabbats are Imbolc, Beltane, Lughnasad, and Samhain. These four fall at the cross-quarters (semi-squares) between the fourfold cross of the equinoxes and solstices that mark the beginning of each season. These solar holidays, based on the eightfold aspect series of the Sun to the vernal equinox, celebrate the cycle of nature. Yet their mythology is such a close match in meaning to Rudhyar's interpretations of the lunar phases that I have wondered if he might have used them as a framework for his interpretations—although I could find nothing in his book to suggest a connection. They do connect in symbolism, however, and the meaning of one cycle contributes much to the understanding of the other.

The cycle of the eight seasonal Sabbats—the Wheel of the Year—is the interplay of relationship between the Sun and Earth. Earthly forms change in response to the energy of the Sun. Seeds germinate, sprout, grow, mature, wither, die, are dormant, are warmed by the Sun, and then the cycle begins again. The lunar cycle is the interplay of relationship between Sun and Moon, as the Moon reflects the light of the Sun through her constantly changing faces. Here, however, it is important to realize the true partner in this relationship—Earth! The phases of the Moon as we know them exist only in reference to our vantage point on Earth. The phases tell us nothing about the Moon herself, but only about the state of the relationship between her, the satellite of Earth, and the Sun.

The Moon, then, serves us earthlings by telling us about relationship—but what relationship? Not our relationships with other people—although certainly many of our life events and accompanying development are worked out through our interactions with others. The true relationship at issue here is our relationship with ourselves, the inner relationship of form and energy (spirit).

It seems that some concept of dualism is necessary for our perception within the universe. For our purpose here, let's symbolically assign the Sun the role of spirit, of divine energy, while Earth represents matter, or form. Let's not assign either one to an arbitrary category of "good" or "bad," but rather, perceive them as equally important. Without form, energy is pointless, has no purpose. Without energy, form is inert and lifeless.

Now, what does all this symbolically mean to us in terms of understanding our birth charts and consequently, our lives? Let's imagine the Sun saying, "I am light and vitality. Receive my energy that together we might have life and purpose for being." Our earthly forms might answer, "But you are too bright! I can't even look at you directly without hurting my eyes. If I try to take in all your energy all the time, I'll burn out. Give it to me in measured doses that I can handle and give me some time to rest!"

And what, then, says the Moon? She might say, "Let me serve you. I will mediate for you by reflecting the light of the Sun in softer hues. I am approachable—you can easily gaze on me, and I will show you the light in progressive stages and help you understand the flow of the life energies within you. Let me show you the seasons of your life!"

Moon and Mother Earth have long been linked with feminine characteristics and the Goddess, while Sun has been associated with masculine characteristics and God. (This is not a universal idea. Some mythologies include Sun goddesses, and the "man in the Moon" idea came from somewhere!) The concept of the Goddess as the more approachable mediator is not new, either—even within patriarchal Christianity which denies her divinity. Countless prayers have been offered to Mary as intermediary.

The Moon as mediator, reflecting or making objective the message of the Sun, is an intellectual concept. Now, in astrology we think of Mercury (a "masculine" planet) as intellect, and by that we mean the rational, logical thought processes of mind. But this is only one aspect of mind. Even the most logical, scientific procedures begin with a hunch—an intuitive thought. This is the realm of the Moon! Our first thoughts of the Moon usually emphasize her nurturing qualities, her changeableness—but we must not overlook her importance as a symbol of mind. Our culture has devalued the aspect of mind which is more closely associated with the Moon by the very words used to describe the intuitive aspect of intellect—*sub*conscious or *un*conscious—as if this function was inferior.

We have also associated the principle of action with the masculine and responsiveness with the feminine, yet if conscious actions tend to proceed in response to intuitive motivations, then who is acting and who is responding? Which aspect of mind, then, is more powerful?

The value of intuitive qualities and of the feminine principle in general are fortunately being reevaluated as the old world view of patriarchy begins to lose its hold on our culture. In any case, the relationship symbolized by the lunar cycle is the relationship within self, and we all carry our own "male" and "female" within. We might think of our Sun (and Mercury, his messenger) as a symbol of the basic, vital energy with which we are to act in order to fulfill the purposes of this lifetime. We can then look to our Moon in her relationship to our Sun for the intuitive wisdom to act in harmony with the seasons of our lives. So mark well—and never underestimate—the power of your Moon as she shows you her changing faces in reflection of the bright vitality of your Sun.

A brief commentary on each of the eight phases in the cycle of transformation follows:

Yule—The "New Moon" Phase of the Cycle

This is the dark of the Moon. Conjunct the Sun, she is, of course, not visible in the night sky. In the cycle of the seasons, Yule or Winter Solstice represents the rebirth of the light. Here, during the longest night of the year, the Goddess gives birth to the Sun Child, and hope for new light is reborn, in joy and celebration. This mythology has been carried out in many religious traditions, including Christianity, in the choice of Winter Solstice for the birth of the son—Jesus. Also, Lucina the Sun Goddess, who rekindles the Sun and brings new light, is known today as Santa Lucia with the wreath of candles on her head.

At this stage of the cycle we have a sense of creative new beginning brought forth largely through instinct or sheer impulse. We meet the challenge of the moment dynamically, often dramatically, and move forward with the urge to get things going—but we may not yet have the process well thought through.

Here, new creative energy is released that marks the beginning of a new cycle. But it is not yet firmly established, and it is not yet certain just how it will develop. Often, when an event occurs that "marks" a new cycle of experience in your life, you may not even be aware of its importance until you look back on it later. This phase is a time of gradual awakening to new goals. It is not yet a definite break with the past, but it is a time when old familiar patterns seem to lack vitality and you instinctively feel a sense of creative new beginnings.

Imbolc—The Crescent Phase

In the monthly lunar cycle this is the time when the first silvery crescent of light appears in the night sky—the newborn light begins to manifest. At the time of the yearly seasonal holiday known as Imbolc or Candlemas, the newborn Sun God is seen as a small child nursing at the breast of the Mother. A newborn, in symbolic correspondence to Yule, cannot as yet be clearly seen as an individual, unique personality. The newborn is definitely a new beginning, full of potential—but what form will that potential take? We wait to see. The baby Son/Sun of Imbolc has become an individual. His light is growing in brightness and we can begin to see the potentials for this new year take shape, and we are full of hope.

At this phase of the cycle, new beginnings are nurtured, seeds stir beneath the earth, and it is time to think of spring cleaning as winter and death are swept away. The energy is directed toward blessing and empowering new beginnings. Some Wiccan groups favor this time of year for initiations into the Craft.

At the Crescent phase of any cycle of experience, you feel a strong impulse toward action, yet seem forever to be involved in intense challenges. In one way or another you are trying to break with traditions or habits of thinking that belong to the past. The new beginnings that were released at the New Moon phase now crystallize and take form. You are challenged to carry forward, but in order to do so, you may have to pull away from something in the past.

Eostar, or Spring Equinox—The First Quarter Phase

In the lunar phases, half of the Moon is now visible at night, a balance between dark and light. In the yearly solar cycle this corresponds to Spring Equinox or Eostar, when days and nights are of equal length. It is the point of equilibrium just before life bursts forth, the chains of winter are broken, and light will reign as the days grow longer. Rituals of this holiday might involve the action of breaking bindings in order to symbolically empower self-change. The God and Goddess are young children at play, and holiday festivals affirm the child within and celebrate new birth with brightly colored eggs.

This phase has been called the "crisis of action." You are attracted to action, noise, and movement because you sense in yourself a constant urge to get going—to progress—even if the end goal you are moving toward is still just a bit hazy. You feel that you have to clear away old forms or structures that you perceive as obstacles, so that you can create new ones. This phase brings a crisis of action in any new direction that you are establishing in your life. This is the time to make it happen—to be aggressive in pursuing your goals. If there is anything from your past that is holding you back, this is the time to resolve that issue and clear it away once and for all.

Beltane—The Gibbous Phase

The Moon in the sky is increasing in light, but not yet full. The seasonal correspondence is to Beltane or May Eve, the time of sacred marriage which honors the life-giving fertility of the blooming earth. The maiden Goddess now comes of age, blooming with self-discovery, and is pursued by the God in fun and courtship. Celebrations include weaving the web of life around a Maypole and leaping the Beltane fires for luck and future fulfillment of wishes. Wiccan handfastings are often held at this festival.

The Gibbous phase is a time of self-discovery. You are developing your capacity for personal growth in your desire to make your life something of value. You constantly evaluate—constantly ask "why"—where you are going, how you are growing, and what you are doing that has significance. Nothing is taken for granted. It is important to you to make things clear, to discover better ways of doing things. Now you are challenged to perfect the methods of your new direction in life. You could call this the period of apprenticeship.

Your new direction is established but not yet fulfilled. This is a stage of development in which you must analyze and evaluate your growth and reorganize or improve your techniques so that you can grow beyond the technique and reach out for true fulfillment.

Midsummer—The "Full" Phase of the Cycle

In the lunar cycle, the Moon now shines opposite in the zodiac from the Sun, reflecting his light in all her fullness. In correspondence with the seasonal cycle it is now Midsummer, or Summer Solstice. At the longest day light triumphs, yet at the same time, begins its decline into the dark. From here on the light will wane. This is the symbolic sacrifice of the Sun King who embraces the Queen of Summer in fulfillment of love that is also death, for in his maturity he realizes that his energy must go into the form of the harvest grain, which will die in order to feed new life. It is a season of fulfillment, consummation, abundance—and yet, at the same time, a recognition of the other side, the ending that approaches but is not yet real.

In many Wiccan celebrations this is the time when the Oak King, who represents the waxing year, is supplanted by the Holly King, who represents the waning year. The two are one, but the Oak King or Bright Lord is the growing youth, and the Holly King or Dark Lord is the mature male archetype who fully recognizes his responsibility to his people and the sacrifices he must make to provide for them.

The Full Moon is opposite the Sun in the zodiac, reflecting his light from the "other side." At the Full phase of a cycle you have reached the fulfillment of the "light" that was only an unformed idea in the darkness of its initial beginning. You have achieved your goal. But what next? And, even more importantly, what for?

Though we may intellectually know that true completion is within self, the achievement of most any goal has little significance for most people without somehow relating it to others. The events and experiences of this phase often involve relationships, for it is through feedback from others that you gain objectivity and clarity about what you have achieved, and for what purpose. Now that you have it, what will you do with it? How does that affect others? Who will you share it with? Who cares? It is the discovery of purpose that is the paramount experience of this phase. Just like the Bright Lord at Midsummer, you must come to the realization that fulfillment, consummation—even abundance—is not enough. You have climbed to the top of your mountain ... but now what? Is there nothing left but to go down? Is further growth possible? A bit scary, isn't it? At this phase, then, you must find illumination, a worthwhile reason, meaning, or purpose for what you are doing. You must integrate any opposing issues from within or without. And then you become as the Dark Lord, aware of your future responsibility and your full mission.

Lughnasad—The Disseminating Phase

In the lunar cycle, the round Moon is now a bit flat on one side, but still very bright in the sky. This phase corresponds to the solar festival of Lughnasad which, in the beginning of August, celebrates the first fruits of the fertile harvest that assures life's survival.

The full harvest is nearly ready, but it is not yet completely certain—still vulnerable to weather and change. It is a time of waiting and maturing, with energy directed toward prosperity, growth in wisdom, and the reaping of plenty. The Sun King, now Dark Lord, gives his energy into the corn and grain, knowing full well that the time of harvest is at hand. The body of the Earth Mother is full with the ripening harvest. The Mother will soon give way to her aspect as Crone, the reaper, that the people may feed on the energy of life, in order that new life may grow. We bless the coming harvest, and think about what we must give back to the Earth and to others.

At this phase of any cycle of experience, the illumination of purpose that is at the Full phase must be disseminated—spread. This is the time for you to share with the world the fruits of your achievements, and more importantly, the wisdom of your illumination. This is the time to teach what you've learned. It is the time to communicate ideas that are meaningful to you—to share your wisdom, your beliefs, your interests, with others.

Mabon, or Fall Equinox—The Last Quarter Phase

In the lunar phase, we come again to the Moon that is half light and half dark. In the solar cycle at Autumn Equinox, the days and nights are equal. It is a time of balance. At this balance point, however, it is light that must give way to increased darkness. It is harvest and as such, it is time of joy and thanksgiving, yet it is also a time of leave-taking and sorrow for the approaching decline of life. The Goddess mourns her fallen consort, yet the festival emphasis is on the message of rebirth in the harvest seeds and plenty.

The Last Quarter phase has been called the "crisis in consciousness." Deep down inside you begin to realize that you are ready to move towards something new. What you have been doing, thinking, being, somehow doesn't seem to serve you anymore. The new direction that you once began and brought to fulfillment has been done, and no longer excites you. On the surface, the way you are feeling may not show at all. On the surface, you may stick to established structures and patterns because you really do not know "what's next" yet—you just know that you want something else. At this point, a "crisis in consciousness" will begin to lead you away from the dominant activities of your current cycle and begin to prepare you for a future new direction.

Samhain—The Balsamic Phase

At this phase of the Moon, only a sliver of light now remains in the night sky—the waning crescent. The Balsamic Moon corresponds to Samhain in the solar cycle, the Sabbat that is more popularly known as Halloween. This is said to be the time when the veil between the visible and invisible worlds is thin, when souls who are leaving this physical plane pass out, and souls who are reincarnating pass in. Darkness is increasing, the Goddess reigns as the elder Wise Woman or Crone (model for the secular Halloween witch), and the God, the Dark Lord, has passed into the underworld to become the seed of his own rebirth. Winter approaches, but it is understood that death or rest is a natural and necessary part of the cycle, in order that life may continue.

During the Balsamic phase of any cycle, you are likely to feel and/or seem to others to be somehow out-of-sync with the majority. You are there, but you are not really "there" anymore. You are "listening to the beat of a different drummer," one could say. You are beginning to have a sense of what you are going to do or where you are going to go next, but you are still keeping it to yourself.

Sometimes you might experience this phase as a true "dark-of-the-Moon," a fallow period when nothing much gets accomplished. You may try several new starts in your attempt to reach out for your new cycle. Some of them fall by the wayside, and you may become discouraged. But finally something will work. The seed is planted—the conception of your new cycle! Understanding the true meaning of this phase is very important. At this time of death, we should not dwell on mourning for what has ended, for it has served its purpose. Rather we must know that every ending is the seed of a new beginning. The wheel keeps turning.

The Eightfold Cycle can be seen in the seasons—Sabbats—but also in our own entire lifetime, viewed by astrologers through the Progressed Moon cycle, in each month through the changes of the Moon, and indeed within the cycle of progress of every idea and project that you initiate and eventually release, to go on to something new.[15]

A Concluding Comment of Variance in Traditions

Some Pagan resources that you might read will differ as to the symbolism or mythology of some of the Sabbats. This comes from traditions handed down from various cultures. For example: Imbolc is a word of Celtic origin which means "in the belly." So in that tradition, the Goddess would be pregnant, and the myth celebrates the Earth as being pregnant with the new life that will be born at Spring Equinox. To make this work within the sequence of the Sabbats, would one then consider Yule to be the conception? Or the discovery of pregnancy? Yet most groups do indeed consider it to be the birth of the Sun, or the Oak King. And then the same groups might deal with pregnancy in the mythology that they celebrate at Imbolc, because "it means 'in the belly'"—which seems somehow to be a slightly different myth. If the Sun returns at Yule, beginning a new solar cycle, then it is cannot be the Sun that is being carried by the pregnant Goddess at Imbolc. Apparently she is pregnant with the fruits of the eventual harvest. Yet her impregnation is celebrated at Beltane and/or Midsummer.

Although there is really nothing wrong with dealing with varying myths at different Sabbats that are not clearly sequential, I think the totality of the Wheel of the Year as a meaningful cycle that can be related not only to seasonal mythology, but to all of the many cycles of life experience, is much stronger when it is defined in eight clearly sequential phases.

From Winter Solstice, the longest night of the year, on until Summer Solstice, the longest day, the Sun will rise a bit earlier each day and set a bit later. The light increases—the waxing half of the yearly solar cycle. Clearly this is the birth of the Sun, and works best as Number One of the eightfold cycle.

In my opinion, the Rudhyar definitions of the eight lunar phases fit in exceedingly well with the eight solar phases, applied in sequence as given here, beginning with Yule. It lends the entire concept of the Wheel of the Year a much more significant framework from which to design rituals that the participants will be able to relate to their life experience.

You will see this framework "in action" in the next chapter.

Endnotes

1. Simms, Maria Kay. *Dial Detective.* San Diego: ACS Publications, 1989.

2. Regardie, Israel. *The Golden Dawn.* St. Paul, MN: Llewellyn Publications, 1971, 1986.

3. Haich, Elisabeth. *Initiation.* Garberville, CA: Seed Center, 1965.

4. Zain, C.C. *Ancient Masonry.* Brotherhood of Light.

5. *The New American Bible,* Catholic Edition. New York: Thomas Nelson Publishers, 1971.

6. Ibid.

7. Greene, Liz. *Relating: An Astrological Guide to Living with Others on a Small Planet.* New York: Samuel Weiser, Inc., 1978.

8. Regardie, *The Golden Dawn.*

9. Most of the preceeding material on the complementary opposite sign polarities is from *Twelve Wings of the Eagle,* and is reprinted with the permission of ACS Publications.

10. I first looked up this sequence of words in *Webster's New World Dictionary,* previously cited, and then compared it with *Webster's New Collegiate Dictionary* that I have in my office. The resulting definitions are a paraphrased composite of the two dictionaries.

11. Gawain, Shakti. *Living in the Light.* San Rafael, CA: New World Library, 1986.

12. George, Demetra with Douglas Bloch. *Asteroid Goddesses.* ACS Publications.

13. Simms, Maria Kay. "The Lunar Cycle: An 8-Fold Cycle of Transformation" in *Tables of Planetary Phenomena,* by Michelsen, Neil F. ACS Publications, 1990.

    The illustration of the eightfold cycle, as well as some of the text in this section, is reprinted from *Tables of Planetary Phenomena,* with permission of the publisher.

14. Rudhyar, Dane. *The Lunation Cycle.* Boulder: Shambala, 1971.

15. "Progressed Moon cycle" refers to secondary progressions, a symbolic system by which astrologers move a natal horoscope forward in time, in order to interpret the progression of the individual's life. The symbolism is approximately (it takes a mathematical procedure to be exact) one day equals one year. For example, the planetary positions on the 35th day after birth would tell the astrologer something about the individual's 35th year of life. Since the Moon moves 12 to 15° of the zodiac in one day, the Progressed Moon correspondingly moves a degree or more in each month of the progressed year. Because of that, the movement of the Progressed Moon is especially important for the timing of events.

    The Progressed Moon position in relation to the position of the Progressed Sun forms eight distinct phases as defined by Rudhyar in *The Lunation Cycle.* He interprets the birth phase according to characteristics of the basic personality. He goes on to interpret each progressed phase according to the types of challenges, growth, decline, fulfillment, etc., which may be happening in the individual's life during the time of each phase.

    I can relate very well to the accuracy of Rudhyar's interpretations in regard to my own life developments, and I have found that most everyone else I've discussed it with has found them to "work" in their lives, as well.

The Wheel of the Year—
Rituals for Eight Sabbats

About Dates and "Energy Points"

It should be noted that at the beginning of the fifth century AD, December 25 was chosen as the birthday of the Son by a Christian church council. It was a deliberate choice to "Christianize" the very popular Pagan holiday of the Winter Solstice. It has been said that at that time December 25 actually coincided more closely with the actual solstice day than it does on current calendars. Since our calendars conveniently give us the astronomically correct days for the solstices and the equinoxes, Pagans tend to celebrate these Sabbats on the days that the Sun enters the four cardinal signs: Capricorn, Aries, Cancer, and Libra.

The Greater Sabbats, however, have not been of sufficient concern to the general public and to astronomers to be shown on calendars at the astronomically correct cross-quarter date (halfway between the solstices and the equinoxes). This is probably why Pagans continue to celebrate them at the old fixed dates, which no longer coincide with the actual cross-quarter points.

If the equinoxes and solstices are considered to be significant "energy points," then there is all the more reason why the Greater Sabbats, at the cross-quarter "points of dynamic release of energy" (Rudhyar), should be celebrated at the actual astronomical cross-quarters, which are 15° of each of the fixed signs: Aquarius, Taurus, Leo, and Scorpio. Sometimes the "bigger party" nature of a Sabbat means that the nearest weekend gets picked rather than the actual day, but aside from that concern, my circle tries, as closely as possible, to schedule Sabbats on the actual cross-quarter days, or as close to them as weekend days allow. In keeping with that, I will give both the traditional dates and the cross-quarter dates as each Sabbat ritual is presented.

About Varying Mythologies

Some of the confusion over whether the myth of the birth of the God should belong to Yule or to Spring Equinox probably stems from the fact that in a number of cultures Spring Equinox was considered to be the beginning of the year. The classical Greeks invented the still-used system of numbering the degrees of the zodiac of signs according to the beginning of the seasons, and decided that the fiducial of that zodiac should be 0° Aries on March 21, Spring Equinox. In the ancient Roman calendar March was the first month, and this is still reflected in the numerical names for some of the months: September (7), October (8), November (9), December (10). January 1 was officially adopted as the beginning of the year in 153 BC to coincide with the date of entry into office of the Roman consuls.[1] But it was not until sometime after the adoption of the Gregorian calendar that the church settled on January 1 (the circumcision of Jesus) to be the beginning of its year. One source I remember reading (and can no longer identify) said that it was not until the mid-eighteenth century that January 1 superseded the Annunciation (March 25) as the beginning of the church year in England.

About the Rituals

It is assumed that before you read these rituals you will have already read the chapter on the order and form of ritual. Here you will not see the details of casting the circle unless they differ in some way from the usual form, and you will not see the parts of the ritual that are generally always the same (such as casting the circle, charging with the elements, passing the kiss, the preliminaries of calling Watchtowers—ringing the bell, HPS' "all hail ... "—the power chant, the serving of cakes and beverage, the formal closing of "may all beings and elements ... merry meet ... ") unless for some special reason we have altered them. What will be given here are the parts that are unique to each particular ritual.

Yule (Winter Solstice)

Correspondence to Lunar Phase: New Moon.

Keywords: Rebirth, New Beginnings.

Time: When the Sun enters 0° of Capricorn, usually December 21. (Depending on the time zone you live in, it is possible that on some years the Sun's ingress into the sign could fall on December 20 or 22.)

Special note: At this ritual we usually have a few guests, some of whom are not Pagan. This Sabbat, more than any other, is an ideal "bridge" ritual since the basic symbolism of Yule and Christmas are so similar. I've found it effective for both my circle members, and for their family or close friends who may come as guests, to weave the Christian myth into our own mythology. The symbolism works, and it makes a valid point of universality.

Special preparations for the altar: In the center is a Yule Log decorated with evergreen and three candles: one white for the Maiden, one red for the Mother, and one black for the Crone. Around the rim of the altar is our holly wreath, which is a hula hoop with noise-maker removed, and covered with silk holly and glitter. This will be lifted up later in the ritual for participants to step through.

Yule 1991

Greetings, Centering

HPS and HP greet each other as usual, then HP greets Crone and Maiden, and withdraws to the edge of the circle to lead the group in a centering meditation:

> *We gather tonight to await new light. In ancient times it is said that a maiden prepared to become a mother, to bring forth a special Son who would bring in a new age. On this night the Maiden, who is also Mother and Crone, prepares to welcome the Sun, the light of a new year. Let us now prepare ourselves to welcome the new light within ...*

Continue with usual centering meditation calling energy from the Cosmos above and the Earth below into the chakras. (See Centering Meditations, at the end of Chapter 10.)

HPS is dressed in red as Mother, Maiden in white, and Crone in black. The three cast circle according to the following sequence:

Sweeping on three levels: Maiden
Cleansing the circle: Maiden—earth and water; Crone—fire and air
Banishing pentagrams: HPS
Defining circle on three levels with sword: Crone
Invoking Spirit with wand: HPS

All three alternate in greeting and bringing in each participant, as everyone sings first two verses of "Silent Night, Solstice Night" (See Music, Chapter 11).

Consecration

> **HPS:** *Once again the wheel has turned full circle. It is Winter Solstice—night of the longest darkness, as our Lord Sun waits in the shadows. We meet to call him back. Return, O Lord of Light! Be reborn this night, as the great wheel of life must ever turn.*
>
> *As we wait in darkness, we are surrounded by the great Celestial Sphere, where we may look upon the faces of the Mighty Ones and see in them a reflection of our own eternal souls. I now do call upon their energies to shine within*

us as I proclaim this to be a circle of power, truth, love, and light reborn. I call the bright initiative of Aries, the steady stability of Taurus, the versatility of Gemini, the warm caring of Cancer, the sparkle and splendor of Leo, the diligence of Virgo, the harmony of Libra, the passion of Scorpio, the enthusiasm of Sagittarius, the wise humor of Capricorn, the free-thinking spirit of Aquarius, the mystic intuitiveness of Pisces—as we now seek to turn the wheel of our lives, in perfect love and perfect trust. And as it is willed, so mote it be.

Passing the Kiss

HPS to Maiden to Crone to circle.

Watchtowers

East: First I call to guard the East
Place of rising light
Air, the breath of clarity
Of mental powers bright
Guardian of the Eastern sphere
Now I call your presence here
Come, East, come. Be here this night.

South: To the South I call the fires
As beacon for the birth
Send back the Sun and increase light
To energize the Earth
Guardian of the Southern sphere
Now I call your presence here
Come, South, come. Be here this night.

West: Now I call to guard the West
Gateway to the night
Water, flow of life, now bring
Intuitive insight
Guardian of the Western sphere
Now I call your presence here
Come, West, come. Be here this night.

North: To the North I call the Earth
So cold in winter's dark

Thy seed now waits for Sun's new warmth
And life-renewing spark.
Guardian of the Northern sphere
Now I call your presence here
Come, North, come. Be here this night.

HPS: *About 2000 years ago, three astrologers from the East followed the stars to witness the birth of the avatar of this age, and since then, in many lands all over the world, that birth is celebrated in this season. Tonight we, too, pay honor to that child as the symbol of all bright, new beginnings of growth and light. As the astrologers followed the starry night westward, so, too, we follow the stars on this solstice night, knowing that as they set in the west, they will also symbolize the journey of the Star Goddess into the invisible world, where she will once again give birth to the Sun and the new yearly cycle, bringing new light and hope to all on Earth. Let us now follow that star.*

All sing "We Three Kings" (See Music, Chapter 11).

Invocation of the Goddess

Sung to tune of Schubert's *Ave Maria*[2]:

HPS, Maiden, and Crone:
Maiden of Beauty, hear us as we call to thee
Come forth and take thy place as Mother
Reborn the child of light must be.
Queen of Night, O Lady of Wisdom we call
Weave thy magick tonight
Here we stand and humbly wait to serve thee
Come within and fill our souls with love
As thy sphere of stars is slowly turning
Bring us new light, the light of your glorious Son
Ave Maria ...

As each speaks the following she lights her candle on the Yule Log:

Maiden: *I come to you as Maiden, young and free, fresh as springtime, belonging to no one, happy with the sheer joy of life. Yet within me a yearning stirs ... to create and to share, and so I become ...*

Mother: The Mother—full rich, abundant. I bring forth the fruit of my creativity, and I nurture, preserve, love and am fulfilled ... and yet an ancient prophet once told me, as I stood with my son, Jesus, in a temple, "Yea, a sword shall pierce through thy own heart, also," and I knew that I must also be ...

Crone: The Crone, ancient wise one, Lady of Darkness, Pieta, Mother of Sorrows. We Three-in-One who brought forth that special child so long ago, also anointed him for burial—a bright light that grew and was sacrificed to be reborn as a new light—a whole new age.

HPS/Mother: We honor that special birth this night as we meet to greet the yearly rebirth of the Sun. The never-ending cycle of birth, death, rebirth—light to dark and dark to light again—reminds us that all things have their time and season—of beginnings, fulfillment, and ending, of letting go to make way for new beginnings ...

Invocation of the God

HPS: I call the God. Return from the shadows, O Lord of Light. The wheel has turned. We call you back to warm us, to charge the seeds of spring within us, within the hearts of all.

HP standing in the East, holds unlighted gold candle toward the altar to light it from the white candle held forward by HPS.

HP: I hear you, Lady. I greet you with joy and with the first light of new possibilities that were only dreams when last we met to turn the wheel.

Maiden [with breathless anticipation]: Yes, at Samhain you said that all things are possible in the future. Is the future now?

HP: It is nearly dawn, my Lady. It is the time to begin.

Crone [solemnly]: But yet too soon to know what the future will truly hold.

HPS/Mother: So we must warm and nurture the new seeds within, that they might grow.

HP: Come to me. I bring you new light.

HPS/Mother: This is a wreath of holly, eternal circle. As tonight a Son is born, as the Holly King gives way to rebirth as the Oak King, so should we now let go of all fears, all doubts, all outworn ideas, all projects finished— anything in our lives that holds us away from the new beginnings that will lead to new growth. As you step through the holly, let go of the past, walk toward the light, and be as the Sun reborn.

Crone directs people to move clockwise toward the East. As each one passes to the west of the altar, she passes the holly wreath over him/her. Maiden helps each one step out, and hands them a small white candle. As each person passes the HP they are to light the candle from the God candle.

During this all sing the third verse of "Silent Night, Solstice Night," followed by "Joy to the World." (See Chapter 11.)

After all are again standing in the circle, still holding the white candles, HP brings his candle to the altar, and greets the three ladies.

Great Rite

All four touch chalice and athame, as they speak the traditional affirmation of life:

Athame to Chalice, Spirit to Flesh, Man to Woman, As the God and Goddess within, Conjoined they bring blessedness to life.

HP: Let the time of celebration begin. Behold the fruits of the Earth Mother. May you never hunger; may you never thirst. Blessed be!

All sing "Deck the Halls" while cakes are passed. Use the traditional words here—they are Pagan!

Closing

HP: Instead of our usual sharing here, we will open the circle and carry out the old tradition by burning our Yule Log in the fireplace. Bring your candles, too.

HPS: Thank you, Bright Lord, for the light that you have brought to us this night. May we carry it within throughout the coming year.

HP: And thank you, most gracious Lady [bowing slightly to each of the three aspects in turn], for your freshness of spirit, your nurturing care, your infinite wisdom. Live within us throughout the coming year.

HPS: All hail ... [to each Watchtower, in turn]

East: For fresh new breezes, we thank you. Hail, farewell and Blessed Be.

South: For new fires of spirit, we thank you. Hail, farewell and Blessed Be.

West: For new waves of insight, we thank you. Hail, farewell and Blessed Be.

North: For the promise of growth, we thank you. Hail, farewell and Blessed Be.

HPS: The circle is open but unbroken.

HP: Let us carry it with us in spirit as we proceed to the Yule fire.

At the fireplace everyone places their small candles around the Yule Log. As it burns, we have our grab bag gift exchange and sharing, and end with "merry meet."

Imbolc (Candlemas)

Correspondence to Lunar Phase: Crescent.

Keywords: Emergence, First Light, Challenge.

Time: This Sabbat is traditionally celebrated on February 2. The actual cross-quarter takes place when the Sun is at 15° of Aquarius, most likely about February 4.

Altar Preparation: The cauldron is on the altar, packed with sand, with a white candle in the center. Additional white candles lie beside it, to be given to each participant.

Imbolc 1992

Consecration

HPS: We meet to turn the wheel. At Yule, winter solstice, the Sun-child was born—the infant year—heralding the end of the darkness of the old year's cycle, and the coming of the light of the new. The promise of light was born, but it was then only potential. What was born now begins to manifest. The days grow visibly longer. This is the feast of waxing light, called Imbolc in Celtic tradition, sacred to Brigid, Goddess of fire and of inspiration. It is the second phase of the eightfold solar cycle, cross quarter of Aquarius the innovator, reformer, seer of the future.

And what does that mean to each of us? This is a time of initiation and of individuation. Here we experience the phase of any personal cycle when an unformed potential begins to take shape. The spark of inspiration takes flame as we mold our new beginning with a will and purpose that is uniquely our own. To do that, we must often sweep away that which no longer serves us, in order that we may focus our energy toward the increase of the new light that glows within.

I do conjure that this shall be a circle of power, of inspiration where within the bonds of the supportive, protective love of brothers and sisters, we may raise, contain, and release the energy of increased light. By the love of the Threefold Goddess and her mighty Consort, I do bless and consecrate this circle, and as it is willed, so mote it be.

Watchtowers

East: O Air, I call to the Eastern tower
Stir fresh new winds of mental power.
Sweep clear our minds of past debris
Blow forth new thoughts of clarity.
Guardian of the Eastern sphere
Now we seek your presence here.
Come, East, come! Be here this night!

South: O Fire, I call to the Southern tower
Burn bright the flames of spirit power.
Charge us with your energy
Inspired will, intensity.
Guardian of the Southern sphere
Now we seek your presence here.
Come, South, come! Be here this night!

West: O Water, I call to the Western tower
Wash into our souls with waves of power
Cleanse and heal us, help us know
Our path of truth within your flow.
Guardian of the Western sphere
Now we seek your presence here.
Come, West, come! Be here this night!

North: O Earth, I call to the Northern tower,
Protect us with your strength and power.
As your seedlings sprout, we see and know
How our new plans must form and grow.
Guardian of the Northern sphere
Now we seek your presence here.
Come, North, come! Be here this night!

Invocation of the God

HPS: Lord of Light, you who embody the vibrant energy
of God within—I call your spirit to this rite. You who
were Sun reborn at Yule, now come forth in the bright
hopes of youth. Fill this your priest with light, and
through him shine, to touch your light and kindle hope
within us all. As it is willed, so mote it be.

Invocation of the Goddess

HP: O bright Goddess of Fire and of inspiration, hopes
are high in this season, but incomplete without you. O
Mother of Life, who called me forth from the darkness, I
now call you to this celebration of increased light. Fill this
your priestess with the wisdom of your spirit, and through
her touch the Goddess within us all. As it is willed, so
mote it be.

Dialogue/Charge

> *HPS: So here we are once again my Son, in the earliest months of your new cycle of growth. Quite a difference I see already. Your youthful energy already begins to warm me with the promise of spring. Your light grows stronger with each passing day ...*
>
> *HP: Yes, I've been having fun since Yule, shining brightly every day, but try as I might, I don't see anything happening yet. I thought I'd set the world on fire and I can't even make winter go away.*
>
> *HPS: Patience, my Son. The wheel turns slowly. Spring will come soon enough. I can see you grow with each passing day, even if you're not so sure just yet. Wonder what you'll be when you grow up this time?*
>
> *HP: I'll be lots of things! I'm going to be something special for everyone here, the energy charge that helps their plans take form. Tell her, everybody. What are you going to do this year, (name), ... how about you?*

This is completely improvised. HP asks for plans, HPS expresses doubts about possible challenges that could get in the way of them, until HP interrupts:

> *We're never going to get anything moving if we keep worrying about old stuff. Let's just build the light!*
>
> *HPS: You are right, my Son, this is the time to build the light. It is the time when the darkness, the past must be banished, let go, when visions of our new ideals and goals may now crystallize into visible form—individual and uniquely, for each of you, your own—a bright new light within you, that with our love and inspiration, you will nurture into healthy growth that you will eventually share with others.*

HPs take God/Goddess candles, and with them, light the green candle in the center of the cauldron.

> *HPS: As we share our light with you [HP passes out candles] and lead you in the spiral dance, take this light and*

add it to your own. Raise the cone of your own power to create your life and to inspire the new growth that now begins. When you feel inner readiness, plant your candle-seed within the earth. When I call out "Now," focus the energy into My cauldron for a new burst of growth for all the seeds of new life sown.

Song for raising energy as we dance around the altar:

Turn, turn, wheel of the year
Winter be gone, let spring be here
Fire bright, Sun's new light
Turn, turn around.

After all candles are planted, HPS continues:

Now ... keep the energy flowing. Join hands and let's refocus our thoughts on sharing our hopes and our light with others and with the Earth, our Mother. Feel heat and light flow from hand to hand and visualize it filling the circle and expanding beyond, wherever our intent shall carry it. We will bring the censer around the circle. Each of you put a pinch of incense, along with your intent, on the fire and direct the energy of our circle, sending it forth on the winds of air.

Great Rite

Sharing

Farewells

HP: *Mother of Life, of fire and inspiration, we do thank you for your love and vision, and bid you hail, farewell and Blessed Be.*

HPS: *Young Lord of Light and vibrant energy, we do thank you for the renewal of all our bright hopes within, and bid you hail, farewell and Blessed Be.*

East: *You've swept away our past debris*
And brought fresh winds of clarity
Power of Air, our thanks to thee
Now hail, farewell and Blessed Be.

South: You've charged us with your energy
Inspired will, intensity
Power of Fire, our thanks to thee
Now hail, farewell and Blessed Be.

West: You've cleansed us, healed us, helped us know
Our path of truth within your flow.
Power of Water, our thanks to thee
Now hail, farewell and Blessed Be.

North: As your seedlings sprout, we'll see and know
How our new plans must form and grow.
Power of Earth, our thanks to thee
Now hail, farewell and Blessed Be.

Spring Equinox (Eostar)

Correspondence to Lunar Phase: First Quarter.

Keywords: Balance, but crisis of action—time to "spring forth."

Time: Usually March 21.

Special Note: For this you get a bonus—two rituals. The first one was written by my High Priest Mark Adams, as part of the requirement for his third degree from Circle Atheneum. We shared this Sabbat with Circle Atheneum and with Dragonstar, the Wiccan study group sponsored by Atheneum. Mark and I worked center. He and I had been working together a year previous to this. I had acknowledged him as my High Priest at his third degree initiation in October 1991, but it was at this Spring Equinox ritual, the first "birthday" of our circle, that he was acknowledged by Lady Beckett and Lord Landerthorn of Circle Atheneum as an official "spin-off." They interrupted the ritual just after the Great Rite to conduct a ceremonial presentation to him of a special cord linking him to the Mother Circle and a blue-handled athame which is made by Landerthorn to present to each new High Priest to spin off from their circle.

My spin-off to start Circle of the Cosmic Muse took place during Circle Atheneum's Spring Equinox 1991, which members of my circle attended. It also involved a cord, in a moving ceremony in which the cord linking Lady Beckett and I was cut, each of us retaining half, and I was presented with the circle Book of Shadows (on a Macintosh disk, of course!) and other gifts, and I presented Lady Beckett with her traditional black garter (as her first spin-off) and silver buckle. Wiccan tradition has it that when a High Priestess has accumulated three silver buckles from spin-offs, she is a "Witch Queen."

The second ritual is one that I conducted with the assistance of Rob Hand as High Priest, at the 1992 United Astrology Congress in Washington, DC. UAC is the largest astrology conference held in the United States, and is held once every three years. This ritual was held in one of my faculty lecture slots and was billed as an experiential astrology "Spring Ritual."

The ritual by Mark which was used in San Diego is more characteristically Wiccan. The ritual used at UAC, which I wrote with editing and suggestions from Rob, was presented for an all-astrologer group, and is therefore much more closely tied to the astrological motif and the Rudhyar First Quarter phase.

Preparation: Our circle Maiden had a basket in which we had prepared little packets of flower seeds in those plastic eggs that break apart in the middle. Flowers and colors of eggs were coordinated with the four element colors. Also, the plates of cakes included an assortment of foil-wrapped chocolate eggs in the colors of the four elements.

Spring Equinox 1992[3]

Consecration

HPS: We gather today to celebrate the Spring Equinox, the third spoke on the ever-turning wheel of the year. It is a time of balance, of equal days and nights, yet soon shall the light spring forth, as the growing Sun reaches for the fulfillment of his power. I do conjure that this be a Circle of Power and of Love ... a Circle that will be a barrier of protection and a meeting place between the world of humanity and the realm of the Mighty Ones, a sacred space where we may share the joy, peace, and energy of this season. And this Circle shall contain and protect the Power we shall raise within it. By the Power of the Lady and the Lord, in all their many names, do I bless and consecrate this Circle. As it is willed, so mote it be.

Watchtowers

> **East:** *To the East I call the spirits of Air*
> *Let your fresh breeze blow through this circle.*
> *Come sylphs, bring your gift of communication*
> *To aid our celebration.*
> *Guardian of the Eastern sphere*
> *Now we seek your presence here.*
> *Come, East, come, be here this rite.*

> **South:** *To the South I call the power of Fire*
> *Let your passion flow throughout this circle.*
> *Come salamanders, lend us your energy*
> *To aid our celebration.*
> *Guardian of the Southern sphere*
> *Now we seek your presence here.*
> *Come, South, come, be here this rite.*

> **West:** *To the West I call the spirits of Water*
> *Let your emotion and intuition permeate this circle.*
> *Come undines, bring your deep well of understanding*
> *To aid our celebration.*
> *Guardian of the Western sphere*
> *Now we seek your presence here.*
> *Come, West, come, be here this rite.*

> **North:** *To the North I call the power of Earth*
> *Let your compassion and bounty nurture this circle.*
> *Come gnomes, lend us your strength*
> *To aid our celebration.*
> *Guardian of the Northern sphere*
> *Now we seek your presence here.*
> *Come, North, come, be here this rite.*

Invocation of the God

> **HPS:** *I call now on the young Lord of Day, reborn at Winter Solstice. Come! Join us, bring us your light and joy and energy as we celebrate the Spring Equinox, that magick time when light and dark are in balance. Descend upon this your servant and priest and through him touch the God within us all.*

Invocation of the Goddess

HP: I call to the Earth Mother, the ever-constant yet ever-changing Goddess. Come! Join us, bring your love and knowledge and understanding, as we celebrate the Spring Equinox, when the land is just beginning to show that which was promised at Imbolc. Descend on this your servant and priestess and through her touch the Goddess that dwells within us all.

Charge

HPS: So ... it is Spring ... look about, my young Lord, tell me what you see.

HP: I see fresh growth on all of the plants. Flowers are springing up everywhere, and their blossoms ... oh, they are so beautiful ... in your hair, my Lady. Their fragrance is almost overwhelming ... [seeks to embrace her]

HPS [she dodges away]: Not so fast, my young love! What else do you see?

HP: The woods are teeming with new life. There are young creatures all over the place. They are so entertaining, so busy living ... loving ... [tries again to kiss her]

HPS [again escaping, laughing]: Your light has grown strong, my love, but 'tis not yet quite the time for you to overtake me. This is the time to keep balance!

HP: Yet you feel my warmth ...

HPS: Yes! I have been rather busy, haven't I? The warmth of your increasing sunlight makes me feel fresh and new after the cold of winter, and I feel like making new things of beauty to bring spring to this beautiful world. I have such fun creating all this ... the delicate blooms on the apple tree, the bees that flit from flower to flower, that first hatching robin, each and every flower that blankets the country, and all my creatures both great and small. I enjoy so watching their young as they cavort and play. Everything is a new discovery to them, they love life as much as I do. And soon ... don't doubt that I look forward to our Maypole dance as much as you do.

Yes, my children, much has already been accomplished in this season of Spring, but I am still bursting with zest and life, and I want to give each of you my special gifts. As the Maiden passes among you, take from her basket an egg of Spring, choosing an element color that symbolizes what you most want to create in your life. Within each egg there are seeds from specially selected flowers. Take these seeds and plant them at home, but before you plant them, meditate on your goals and your desires that you wish to flourish and grow by summer. Be sure to plant them where you can see them each day, because as the flowers grow and bloom they will serve as a constant symbol and inspiration for the completion of your goals.

And now let us celebrate and reaffirm life.

Great Rite

(This was Mark's "official" spin-off. Ritual in Chapter 10.)

Bless cakes, candy eggs, and beverage; quarters serve.

At a large public ritual, in order to speed up the process, we generally have four chalices and four plates. The guardians of the four directions come forward, the HPs bless the offerings, and then the guardians serve to the quarter of the circle clockwise from them.

Announcements

Farewells

HP: Gracious Goddess, Mother of our beautiful Earth, we do thank you for your gifts of Spring and for your presence within our celebration. Until once again we call, we bid you hail, farewell and Blessed Be.

HPS: Young Lord of Day, we do thank you for the bright energy you have brought to our celebration, and we look forward with delight to your increased light. Until once again we call, we bid you hail, farewell and Blessed Be.

East: O spirits of Air, for the fresh breezes you have brought to our celebration, we thank you and bid you hail, farewell and Blessed Be.

South: O powers of Fire, for the energy of passion that we have felt in our rite, we thank you and bid you hail, farewell and Blessed Be.

West: O spirits of Water, for the flow of good feelings you have brought to our celebration, we thank you and bid you hail, farewell and Blessed Be.

North: O powers of Earth, for the promise of bounty that we have felt in our rite, we thank you and bid you hail, farewell and Blessed Be.

Note: When we hold rituals at our usual place, my living room or back yard, we open the circle but do not banish it: "The circle is open, but unbroken." When we meet in a public place, as we did for this ritual, because the group is too large for a private home, we do banish the circle, in deference to those who come after us in that place who may not feel comfortable with the energies we have created there. Following is our method of banishing the circle. It is an old, traditional farewell that was given to Mark by Peter the Owl of Ring of Bright Water.

HPS: As we are about to separate and leave this sacred place of friendship and love, remember that the whole world has a claim on our kind works.

HP: Be ye of one mind. Do good unto all. And, may the Gods of love and peace delight to dwell within thee and bless thee.

HPS takes spirit candle and goes to the East, salutes, and walks the circle widdershins, chanting Gregorian-style:

By this holy flame, this circle disappears and can be found no more.

Participants, lead by HP, chant in response:

All things be as they were from the beginning of time.

HP: May all beings and elementals attracted to this rite depart on their way harming none. Merry meet, merry part and merry meet again. Blessed Be.

A Ritual for Spring:
United Astrology Congress 1992

Preparation: Lengths of black yarn, enough to wrap around the wrists of each participant, were on the altar. We don't do the Great Rite at a public ritual such as this where most participants are not Wiccans. We just have a plate of goodies to share; in this case, candy eggs in the colors of the elements. Since we weren't robed, I had a stole in each element color to designate the guardians of the directions, a red one with a gold Sun on it for Rob, and a black one with the triple Moons in silver for me. Fire laws and potential danger for a large group prevented candles at the quarters, so we used colored wands (painted dowel rods with glitter stars) instead. For background music and accompaniment for the chants, we were fortunate to have the assistance of our good friend Ken Negus, who played classical guitar.

Consecration

> *HPS: We gather to greet the Spring. Life bursts forth from Earth, breaking the bonds of winter. In the eightfold seasonal cycle of Earth and Sun, this is the third phase. Just as in the first quarter of the lunar cycle, this third phase is the crisis of action. Winter—the past—is left behind. No longer must we allow it to hold us back.*
>
> *As light and dark are equal, so too, is this a time when all elements within us must be brought into a new balance, in preparation for the season when light will surge forth. Be it a time of joy! Let your hearts be as one with the Maid of Spring and the Sun Prince as they dance through the fields, flowers spring forth at their feet, and new hope is born throughout the land.*
>
> *Be this a circle of unity, of friendship, and of love, a sacred space where each one of you may kindle the increasing light of Spring within yourself. To give us aid I now do call upon the energies of twelve cosmic aspects of the eternal One ...*

Eleven participants were pre-designated to give the following responses as I called out the sign.

Aries: Charge forth with initiative, for Spring has come ...

Taurus: Let earthy sensuality flow throughout our bodies ...

Gemini: Fresh breezes now blow, to stimulate new thoughts ...

Cancer: With loving care may we nurture our budding creations ...

Leo: As our hearts swell with pride in our progress ...

Virgo: May we work toward our future harvest with diligence and care ...

Libra: Let there be harmony and balance of all polarities within, that we may truly appreciate the wholeness of life.

Scorpio: With intensity of purpose, let us banish that which binds us to the past, that our spirits may soar with the Eagles ...

Sagittarius: And look toward the future with enthusiastic idealism...

Capricorn: Yet grounded with realism and practicality.

Aquarius: Keep us mindful of personal goals in harmony with the well-being of the whole of humanity.

HPS: As with the mystic vision of Pisces we now merge with our Lady and Lord in perfect love and perfect trust. As it is willed, so mote it be!

Watchtowers

East: O spirits of Air, to the Eastern tower
With Gemini's quickness, send your power.
With the graceful dance of Libra's light
And Aquarian idealism, join our rite.
Guardian of the Eastern sphere
Now we seek your presence here.
Come East, come, be here this night.

South: O spirits of fire, to the Southern tower
Leap high, bright flames of Aries' power

Glow proud and bright with Leo's light
May the Archer's truth inspire our rite.
Guardian of the Southern sphere
Now we seek your presence here.
Come, South, come, be here this night.

West: *O spirits of Water, to the Western tower*
Protect us with Cancerian power
With Scorpio's waves of deep insight
And Pisces' dreams, infuse our rite.
Guardian of the Western sphere
Now we seek your presence here.
Come, West, come, be here this night.

North: *O spirits of Earth, to the Northern tower*
Send sensual, strong Taurean power
May Virgo's care and healing light
And Capricorn's will, enhance our rite.
Guardian of the Northern sphere
Now we seek your presence here.
Come, North, come, be here this night.

Power Chant

As above, so below; as within, so without; as the Universe,
so the soul ...

Invocation of the God

HPS: *I call the Lord of Day, bright and fiery Sun, Father*
of Life, symbol of the eternal God. You who have returned
from the shadows and are now poised to charge forth
toward your full brilliance, be with us now. Live within
the body of this your priest, and through him touch the
God within us all. As it is willed, so mote it be.

Invocation of the Goddess

HP: *I call the Lady of Night, eternal Threefold Goddess,*
soul of Nature, Mother of all Living. We see you in the
beautiful waxing Moon, O Maid of Spring, and in the
blooming of Mother Earth, and as the Crone of the
retreating darkness. Be with us now! Live within the body

of this your priestess, and through her touch the Goddess within us all.

Charge/Dialogue

HP: *I greet you with joy, my Lady. I feel great in this season. All kinds of new energy flows within and I am ready to go. Soon I'll overtake you—you'd better run!* [starts after her]

HPS [ducks under his arm and runs away laughing]: *Not so fast, my Lord. I love your dance and the feelings of warmth you stir within me, but I'm not so sure just yet that I'm ready to yield to your light. I need a moment to think about what I might be giving up if I embrace you.*

HP: *Think! What's to think? You can't just stay where you are. You're the one who's always saying "the only constant in life is change." [reaches out arms] Trust me!*

HPS [coyly]: *Oh, I don't know. It's cool and comfortable in the twilight, too, and I know all about where I've been. How do I know you won't burn me?*

HP: *You're flirting, you wench! You know perfectly well you're looking forward to the Maypole dance as much as I am! But you make your point, as always. Our people may need some encouragement to move ahead with their new growth cycles.*

HPS: *Whenever we move forward into the light of spring in any new cycle of activity, thoughts, or feelings, we often find that old baggage from the past draws us back and may even threaten what we are trying to create. The third phase of the eightfold cycle symbolizes the time that we must take action. We stand at a point of equilibrium between past and future, but life can never stand still. The only constant is change. If we do not spring forward, we will surely slip back. Within your own mind many detailed explanations—excuses?—may exist why you think you cannot move forward. Let's reduce them all into symbols of the four ancient elements. We ask that you hold your hands forward and together so that we may symbolically bind you to help you meditate on what holds you back.*

Please trust and do not fear, and I think you'll find the total experience to be a pleasantly positive release. As a group, please help raise the energy that will help us "let go" by chanting with us, changing the element as we pass each quarter.

The Working

At the East Watchtower:

HP: *Your thoughts are too scattered, you can't make up your mind, you're too dogmatic.*

East: *My mind binds me ...*

HPS binds hands of the person, repeats the response to start chant. As the chant continues the HPs continue around the circle , binding the hands of each participant with the lengths of black yarn. Just wrap the yarn around their wrists two or three times. Don't knot it!

At the South Watchtower:

HP: *You act on impulse, you're too willful, your will is unfocused.*

South: *Self-concern binds me ...*

At the West Watchtower:

HP: *You suffer from sensitivity, you hold on to feelings, you are confused.*

West: *Emotion binds me ...*

At the North Watchtower:

HP: *You're stuck in the mud, nothing is ever good enough for you, life is just too grim.*

North: *Necessity binds me ...*

After all are bound:

HPS: *What do you need to be free?*

Depending on size of room and how many participants, people will either be directed to circle clockwise and approach each of the quarters, or to stay in place and gesture to each one in turn. Chant:

> *All will change, all will change*
> *All She touches grows with change*[4]

HP rings bell.

> **HPS:** *Now! To the East! With conscious mental focus, release your bonds!*

HP rings bell.

> **HPS:** *To the South! With clearly focused will, release your bonds!*

HP rings bell.

> **HPS:** *To the West! From the power of unconditional love, release your bonds!*

HP rings bell.

> **HPS:** *To the North! With persistence, precision, and purpose, release your bonds!*

HP rings bell.

> **HPS:** *To the Center! With all the love of God and Goddess within and without, release and be free!*

> **HP:** *The bonds of winter are broken! The new life of spring go with you all! Blessed Be!*

> **HPS:** *As a symbol of new life and new beginnings, I offer you the eggs of spring. As you eat of these you shall ground the energy we have raised, taking it within you, making it part of you. If there is one particular elemental color that symbolizes the energy you most need to assimilate, choose it.*

Baskets of multi-colored candy eggs are passed around. Chant:

> *Earth and Air and Fire and Water*
> *Return, return, return, return*
> *Be-e-e within us, be-e-e within us.*

At this point:

> **HP:** *And now, gracious Lady, we do thank you for your presence within our circle and within our souls. Until once again we call, hail, farewell and Blessed Be.*

HPS: Bright Lord, we do thank you, too, for your presence within our circle and within our souls. Until once again we call, hail, farewell and Blessed Be.

HP rings bell before each Watchtower call.

HPS: All hail ...

East: O Guardians of the East, spirits of Air
For clarity, harmony, and freedom of thought,
We do thank you and bid you
Hail, farewell and Blessed Be.

South: O Guardians of the South, spirits of Fire
For initiative, vitality, and enthusiasm
We do thank you and bid you
Hail, farewell and Blessed Be.

West: O Guardians of the West, spirits of Water
For cleansing, healing mystic insight
We do thank you and bid you
Hail, farewell and Blessed Be.

North: O Guardians of the North, spirits of Earth
For healing strength and stabilizing power
We do thank you and bid you
Hail, farewell and Blessed Be.

HPS: Normally, at the end of such a ritual in my home, we open the circle, but leave it in place. In such a public place as this, it is well to banish the circle, carrying it with us in our hearts, if we will, but leaving this place free of energies that may not be welcome to others who shall come after us. Yet before we separate and leave this sacred sphere of friendship, remember that the whole world has a claim on our kind works.

At this point we proceeded with exactly the same banishing ritual as was given in the Spring Equinox ritual just before this one.

At Spring Equinox 1993, we adapted this ritual for Circle of the Cosmic Muse. In order to utilize our Maiden and Crone, we had the Crone do the binding part. She was the one to admonish each Guardian as she bound him or her, and she bound each person in the circle. I went along with her to hold the extra pieces of yarn for her. The Maiden was the one to say the words beginning, "As a symbol of new beginnings ... " and to pass out the colored eggs.

Beltane (May Eve)

Correspondence to Lunar Phase: Gibbous.

Keywords: Development, growth.

Time: This ritual is traditionally celebrated on either April 30 (May Eve) or May 1 (May Day). It is, however, the Taurus cross-quarter. Usually the Sun gets to 15° of Taurus on about May 5.

Preparation: This ritual has been especially fun. In both '91 and '92 we did it in essentially the same way, at the public beach near my home, right next to a fire ring at which we have a picnic. We erected a huge Maypole with ribbons in the element colors right in the center of our circle. The bonfire was at the South quarter. A simple portable altar with only minimal tools was put at the foot of the Maypole and moved to the edge of the circle before the Maypole dance. We don't robe at the beach, nor do we use sword or athame, so as not to unduly rattle bystanders, to whose curious questions we have just responded with "We're having a May Day picnic." We've had no problems.

Beltane 1992

Consecration

> *HPS: Tis the lusty month of May! It is the Taurus cross-quarter of the eight spokes of power in the Wheel of the Year! This is the fullness of springtime—time of the sacred marriage when we honor the life-giving fertility of the blooming earth. The lovely Maiden Goddess has reached her menarche, come of age, and now discovers her sexuality as she dances in courtship with the young Sun God. As the fourth or Gibbous phase of the eightfold cycle, this is a time of development, of evaluating the growth of our plans for the year, of honing our skills and building*

toward the culmination of light that comes with Midsummer. As we weave our ribbons around the Maypole we will weave into our lives new clarity of purpose. With the focus of our energy and will, we fertilize our intents that they may grow to fulfillment.

And now, I call upon the assistance of the Mighty Ones of the stars that surround us as I conjure this to be a circle where we may all be infused with the bright initiative of Aries, the strong will of Taurus, the versatility of Gemini, the protectiveness of Cancer, the creativity of Leo, and diligence of Virgo. Let the harmony and balance of Libra prevail within this space. May our spirits soar with the eagle of Scorpio, with the swiftness of the Archer's arrow, as with Capricorn's drive we dare to climb whatever mountains may lie in our path. In the spirit of Aquarius, let us fearlessly seek new truths, as here by the surging waves of the Mother's womb, our souls reach out with the mysticism of Pisces in union with our Lady and our Lord, in perfect love and perfect trust. And as it is willed, so mote it be!

Watchtowers

East: *Soft spring breezes blow now forth*
Greetings be onto thee
In the name of the Maid of Spring I call
Your presence, Blessed Be!

South: *Fiery Beltane fires come forth*
Greetings be onto thee
In the name of the Maid of Spring I call
Your presence, Blessed Be!

West: *Cool waters of stream and lake and sea*
Greetings be onto thee
In the name of the Maid of Spring I call
Your presence, Blessed Be!

North: *Earth of green and flowers wild*
Greetings be onto thee
In the name of the Maid of Spring I call
Your presence, Blessed Be!

Invocation of the God

> **HPS:** *Young Sun King, Horned One, Stag*
> *Spirit wild and free*
> *Come dance and sing with the Maid of Spring*
> *Come forth, we welcome thee!*
> *Thy priest awaits thee*
> *Fill him now, with all thy magic light*
> *Come, young king, to our Beltane fire*
> *Come share our joy this night.*

Invocation of the Goddess

> **HP:** *Lovely Maiden, Mother, Wise One*
> *Threefold Goddess be*
> *A flame within our hearts tonight*
> *That grows in energy*
> *Thy priestess seeks thee*
> *Fill her now, with all thy magic light*
> *Come, my Queen, to the Beltane fire*
> *Come share our joy this night.*

Charge

> **HPS:** *Do any of you remember Maydays from your child-hood—when you made a pretty basket, put flowers in it, left it on the doorstep of someone very special, rang the doorbell—and then prepared to run ... and pretend that you didn't want to be kissed?*
>
> *"For I am the secret door that opens onto the land of youth, and I am the cup of the wine of life, the cauldron of Cerridwen, and the holy grail of immortality ..."*

She puts on Maidenly flower wreath, changing demeanor as she does so. The HP comes up behind HPS, places a flower at her feet, rings a bell and darts away:

> **HP:** *Bet you'll never catch me!*

They chase/dance around circle, HP almost letting HPS catch him two more times, but each time getting away before she can kiss him.

The participants keep a rhythm with clapping, drums, or tambourine.

HPS: But why do you evade me? I know you really don't want to run away.

She holds out her arms to him, but just as he comes to her, she laughs and darts away, saying:

Keep running, young stag, I think you have just a bit more to learn before you get what you want.

They dance once more around the circle, this time he almost catches her two more times, as each time she says:

No, no, it's not quite time yet! Soon, my Prince, soon shall you reach the fullness of your light, but not yet!

She then takes up the chalice, and invites him to take her hand, saying:

Tonight feel the brightness and enthusiasm and the joy of life of the Maiden and the young Horned One. Think of the time of youth when you are old enough to think you know a lot and can taste an anticipated fulfillment just a little ways ahead. It is a time of development, of apprenticeship—for there's a bit more to learn, a bit more that you must do ... but then! No wonder this phase of the cycle is so much fun. Time enough later to consider what happens after you get what you are working and yearning for. For now, enjoy! Remember—"All acts of love and pleasure are my rituals."

In affirmation of fulfillment to come, and in celebration of the balance and union of the life force within.

Great Rite

Bless cakes and share.

Move altar instruments to the edge of the circle, leaving only the Maypole in center. Instructions are then given for the Maypole dance and Beltane fire. There is music in background for dancing, and fire in the cauldron.

Begin by jumping the fire for luck and the fulfillment of personal intents. Then each takes a ribbon and begins dancing around the Maypole, weaving intentions and building a cone of energy, softly chanting in a sing-song manner. Everyone grabs a ribbon, and counts off by twos. Ones go deocil, twos go widdershins, each person alternating going over and under each person s/he passes. When ribbons are woven to the bottom, all kneel around the Maypole and visualize the cone of energy grounded into the flowers at its base. Each person will then select a flower to take home and keep as a symbol of the new growth of his/her intent. Chant:

> *Weave, weave, it is our fate we weave*
> *By choice, not chance*
> *With love and will*
> *It is our fate we weave.*

Farewells

> **HP:** *Maid of Spring, Mother, Wise One*
> *Thanks we offer thee*
> *Honor and love go with you, Hail!*
> *Farewell and Blessed Be!*

> **HPS:** *Young Sun King, Horned One, Stag*
> *Spirit wild and free*
> *We loved your dance, we bid you Hail!*
> *Farewell and Blessed Be!*

> **Air:** *Soft warm winds, now fly away*
> *Our blessings go with thee*
> *Till next your magic forth we call*
> *Farewell and Blessed Be!*

> **Fire:** *Fires of Beltane, embers now*
> *Our blessings go with thee*
> *Till next your magic forth we call*
> *Farewell and Blessed Be!*

> **Water:** *Cool waters of lake and spring and sea*
> *Our blessings go with thee*
> *Till next your magic forth we call*
> *Farewell and Blessed Be!*

> **Earth:** *Earth of green and flowers of spring*
> *Our blessings go with thee*
> *Till next your magic forth we call*
> *Farewell and Blessed Be!*

Since this is a public place, the banishing of the circle closes.

Midsummer (Summer Solstice)

Correspondence to Lunar Phase: Full Moon.

Keywords: Fulfillment, illumination, necessary recognition of responsibility.

Time: usually June 21.

Preparation: A large pentacle is drawn with colored ribbon on the altar. Lady figure in center of pentacle. Red candle at top, yellow candle at top right, white candle at top left, purple candle at bottom right, black candle at bottom left. Cauldron in front of Lady. Masks at East Watchtower. Separate masks are needed to denote Maiden, Mother, Crone, Sun God, and Dark Lord. Before ritual starts each person should write an intention on a piece of paper. The intention should be of something that is yet to be released or done in order that fulfillment on a matter might be attained, or it could be a question that needs illumination.

Midsummer 1993

Consecration

> **HPS:** *Tonight the Wheel once again turns. The days are long in this, the full triumphant power of the energy of the Sun. It is a time of fulfillment, a time of festival and of rejoicing, as the Earth Mother who receives that energy blooms with the beauty that will become the fruit of the harvest. Shall this joy go on? Shall the light increase forever? No! The time of waxing is at an end, the time of waning is at hand. The energy of the mighty Bright Lord must go into the form of the Mother—the corn, the grain—and die—in order to feed Earth's children, to become the seed of a new cycle. And so we must pause to reflect, even in our triumph of Midsummer. We must look for an inner illumination of the profound meaning of our times of fulfillment. For without meaning—and growth and purpose—fulfillment is emptiness.*
>
> *In the symbolism of the twelve mighty faces of the eternal One, I conjure this a circle of power and enlightenment:*

May the surging energy of Aries be with us ...

Supported by Taurean persistence, determination and will.

Let the quick and sharp mental powers of Gemini guide the projection of our thought ...

As we children of the Moon are protected in this sacred place between the worlds by the warmth of the Mother's love.

Let our circle shine with the vitality of the Sun and the strength of the Lion ...

Directing the energy we shall raise with Virgoan precision and purpose.

Bring Libran balance to all polarities that we may truly appreciate the wholeness of life.

Here in the light of Scorpio's Moon I proclaim death to all blindness, all blocks, that keep us away from our inner light. Born within us be ...

All the faith and inspiration of the Archer ...

And the practical sense of Capricorn to help us achieve our goal.

May we be washed in the waves of spirit poured forth from the urn of the Waterbearer ...

As with deep Piscean mysticism we merge with Lord and Lady in perfect love and perfect trust!

And as it is willed, so mote it be!

Watchtowers

East: *To the Watchtowers of the East*
I call forth the Air, power of mind.
Increase the focus and projection of thought.
Blow forth, winds of change! Come East, come. Be here this night!

South: *To the Watchtowers of the South*
I call forth the Fire, power of spirit.

With passion I greet thee ... your inspiration, your energy, your vitality.
Charge forth! Come, South, come. Be here this night!

West: *To the Watchtowers of the West*
I call forth the Waters, power of soul.
Wash over this circle in purity, reveal thy mysteries, charge us with thy deepest knowing.
Flow Waters! Come, West, come. Be here this night!

North: *To the Watchtowers of the North*
I call forth the Earth, power of body.
Charge this circle with thy nurturing strength, that we grow toward the light
Come forth! Come, North, come. Be here this night!

Note: Contrary to our usual practice, for this ritual the High Priest invokes the God and the High Priestess invokes the Goddess.

God Invocation

HP: *Hearty and powerful Lord of the Sun, I ask your vibrant presence now. I exalt in the fullness of your strength, now may I share in your energy. Flow through this your priest and charge this circle with light and vitality and power. As it is willed, so mote it be.*

Light gold candle. HP moves to the East and dons bright mask, continuing round the circle back to the altar.

HP: *I come to you as Lord of the Sun, brightly shining, full of power and life. For this first half of the year I have reigned, ever growing in strength and increasing in light. In my light and my desire the seeds are planted, nurtured in her body, and in their season will bear fruit. Tonight is the climax of my desire. Come to me, my love. I rejoice in your beauty ... even though I know the sacrifice that will be required of me!*

Accent words with drum. Light yellow candle on pentacle.

Goddess Invocation

HPS: *Threefold Goddess, Mother of the Earth, Lady of the Moon, I feel your presence all around me ... you who*

*create, preserve, destroy—and yet create again. I find you
in all the forms of Earth, I see you shine forth from the
eyes of my brothers and sisters, and I feel the warmth of
your love that lives always within me. Let now that love
grow and build—fill this priestess and through me flow,
that I may give clarity and form to the message of the Sun
in the fullness of his cycle.*

Light silver candle. HPS moves to the East and takes white mask,
continuing round to the altar.

Charge of the Goddess

*HPS: I come to you as the Maiden, beauty of the crescent
Moon, of fresh new beginnings, of seedlings swelling to
sprout, of cool spring breezes, of refreshing rain, of glowing embers soon to burst into flame, of new ideas born in
your mind, of new hopes that soar on your spirit, of new
intuitions that emerge from your soul, of new desires that
rise up in your body. Rejoice with me! Tonight fulfillment
is mine! Dance with me in joy!*

Light white candle on pentacle. HPS plays tambourine or bells and
leads HP in graceful and happy dance around the circle three times.
Encourage group to clap. On the last time around, she allows the
priest to catch her. They kiss, then she breaks away and raises hands
for all to stop clapping. She proceeds around to the East, removes
white mask and dons the red, continuing around to the altar.

Light red candle in pentacle.

*HPS: I come to you as Mother, beauty and power of the
full Moon, of desires, hopes, and dreams fulfilled, of flowers in glorious bloom, of vines and lush growth laden with
new life, of lusty winds, of mysterious and surging waves,
of flames of passion, of mature and responsible use of
mind, of strength and intensity of spirit, of deep love and
connection of all souls, of body ripe with life and growth.
Tonight I reign supreme. I am filled with his passion, his
vitality. Our dance is the dance of life!*

Great Rite

HPS now returns chalice to the altar and then proceeds to the East, removes red mask and dons the black one. Light black candle in pentacle.

> **HPS:** *I come to you as Crone, beauty of the waning crescent, of desires past and awareness of ending, of crops harvested and fields now bare to lie in rest until a new time for sowing, of thundering storms or still air, of deep, dark, mysterious pools, of dying embers, of the true wisdom of experience, of spiritual peace, of deep, quiet knowing within the soul, of body weary and declining in strength— but with sure awareness of the eternal cycle, of death that brings new life, of endings that lead to new beginnings. The time has come, my Lord. Are you ready for your sacrifice?*

HP hands HPS bright mask; she cradles it and puts it aside.

> **HP:** *My light must now decrease that fruits may be brought to harvest, that the endless cycle of seasons may proceed in accordance with the order of the Universe.*

> **HPS:** *Just as the Sun must set, before it can rise again, know that all that increases must eventually decrease, that which is fulfilled will lead to another matter which is unfulfilled.*

> *Nothing is static [give HP the dark mask], all must change that you can grow in mind, body, soul, and spirit.*

> *Come with us now, all of you, three times around the circle, as you meditate on your intent. On the third time around touch your intent with the flame of spirit and cast it into my cauldron, asking that now, or in your dreams this night, you might find illumination and growth in awareness. And as it is willed, so mote it be!*

HPS leads all in a stately manner around the circle three times, followed by HP. On third pass light intention from one of the candles and place it in cauldron to burn. When HP comes to the East for the third time, he moves forward to light purple candle and speaks:

I come to you as the Dark King. My bright aspect must now be sacrificed to the corn, to the fulfillment of the harvest. My light will slowly decline as the days grow shorter and the dark nights longer, and as her body swells with the bounty of the Earth that I have helped her create. Soon the harvest time will come, and that which has grown will die. She will follow me into the dark world where, all in proper season, She will bring me forth once again as the Sun Child—new life, new hopes, new dreams. Know, then, that all things have a season and a purpose. I go gladly into the darkness, without doubt or fear, for as surely as the Sun sets, the Sun shall rise again!

HPS removes her black mask, and smiles as she removes the dark mask of the HP, saying:

HPS: Let us not go into the darkness too soon, my Lord. We understand and accept what will come, but this night my body is full of your vitality, and I delight in your brightness. This is the season of light and warmth and joy. Let's make the most of it while it is here. [kiss] Let the feast begin!

Bless the cakes and wine for sharing.

Farewells

HP: Threefold Goddess, Maiden, Mother, Crone, you are the cycle of our lives. We live in you and you live within us. Though we bid you now farewell, we know that your love dwells always within. May we ever radiate that love. Hail, farewell and Blessed Be!

HPS: Mighty Father of our vitality and fire of our spirit, thy truth and wisdom has brought us illumination. Your strength in sacrifice inspires us to meet all aspects of the cycle of life in emulation of your courage. We thank you for your presence in this rite. Hail, farewell and Blessed Be!

East: Airy Guardians of the East, Power of Mind I do thank thee for thy participation in this rite. Hail, farewell and Blessed Be!

South: Fiery Guardians of the South, Power of Spirit
I do thank thee for thy participation in this rite.
Hail, farewell and Blessed Be!

West: Watery Guardians of the West, Power of Soul
I do thank thee for thy participation in this rite.
Hail, farewell and Blessed Be!

North: Earthy Guardians of the North, Power of Body
I do thank thee for thy participation in this rite.
Hail, farewell and Blessed Be!

Lughnasad (Lammas)

Correspondence to Lunar Phase: Disseminating.

Keywords: Reaping, teaching, abundance.

Time: Traditionally August 1, but actually the Leo cross-quarter. 15° of Leo usually comes about August 7.

Preparation: Element symbols are available to pass around during the working: a feather for air, a red candle in a glass for fire, a seashell full of water for water, and a rock and a flower for earth.

Lughnasad 1991

Consecration

> *HPS: Once again it is time to turn the wheel. This is the sixth phase of the eightfold solar cycle, the cross-quarter of Leo, which is called Lughnasad. It is the wake of Lugh, the Sun King, who having reached the consummation of his power at Midsummer—at Solstice—began his season of decline. Now he goes into the corn and grain, his energy poured forth into the body of Earth Mother, whose fruitful bounty will nourish life.*
>
> *I now do conjure this a circle of power, of energy, of truth, and of vision—a sacred space between the visible and invisible worlds. In the symbolism of twelve mighty faces of the Eternal One ...*

May the dynamic spirit of Aries be with us ...

Grounded by Taurean persistance and stability.

May the quick mental powers of Gemini aid the projection of our thought ...

As we children of the Moon stand surrounded and protected by the warmth of our Mother's love.

Let our circle sparkle with the creativity and splendor of Leo ...

Yet direct its energy with Virgoan precision and purpose.

Bring Libran balance to all polarities within this space, that we may truly appreciate the wholeness of life.

Let the sting of the Scorpion bring death to all attitudes that hold us away from our highest purpose. May our spirits soar as the Eagle ...

With all the inspiration and enthusiasm of the Archer ...

Yet with the practical ability of Capricorn to help us achieve our goals.

In the spirit of Aquarius, may we ever seek Universal Truth ...

As with true Piscean mysticism we now merge with our Lord and Lady in Perfect Love and Perfect Trust.

And as it is willed, so mote it be!

Watchtowers

East [caller standing at West quarter]:
To the East I call the Air
Guardian of the Eastern Sphere
Now we seek your presence here.
Come, East, come! Be here this night!

East [standing in the East—light torch and then speak facing into circle]: I come quickly on the winged feet of Mercury and the winds of change. Uranian innovation I bring. May rational yet creative thought be yours, for I am Consciousness. I live in all of you and you in me.

South [caller standing at North quarter]:
To the South I call the Fire
Guardian of the Eastern Sphere
Now we seek your presence here.
Come, South, come! Be here this night!

South [standing South—light torch and speak facing into circle]: With the passion of Mars I charge forth to greet you! Jupiterian expansion and enthusiasm I bring. May your spirits shine like the Sun's light and be always free, for I am Vitality. I live in all of you and you in me.

West [caller standing at East quarter]:
To the West I call the Water
Guardian of the Western Sphere
Now we seek your presence here.
Come, West, come! Be here this night!

West [standing West—light torch and then speak facing into circle]: I flow forth with all the mystery of the depths of Pluto, the ethereal mysticism of Neptune, and the ever-changing emotions of the Moon. I am Un-consciousness, but do not underestimate my power because of that archaic word ... I live in all of you and you in me.

North [caller standing at South quarter]:
To the North I call Earth
Guardian of the Northern Sphere
Now we seek your presence here.
Come, North, come! Be here this night!

North [standing North—light torch and then speak facing into circle]: Like a great stone I stand solidly and responsibly here at the limits of your space. I bring the discipline of Saturn, yet also I bring the lush, green beauty and brilliant flowering of Venus. I am growth and stability, and I live in you and you in me.

Invocation of the God

HPS: Mighty Lord of Day, now gone into the dying corn, Lord of Deepening Shadows, still I call you forth, in our need for your brilliance, strength and vitality ... and I call *you Father, Son, Lover, Husband, Brother, but most of all, vital half of that life force within that brings completeness. Even though the season of waning light approaches, may we carry your brightness always within. Let that energy now flow through this your priest and throughout this circle. As it is willed, so mote it be.*

Invocation of the Goddess

HP: Lady of the Moon, of Earth and of mysterious Waters from which life began and to which all must one day return, I call you forth in the need of our people for your nurturing care, your compassion ... and I call you Mother, Daughter, Lover, Wife, Sister, but most of all, vital half of that life force within that brings completeness. Darkness approaches, Lady. May your intuitive wisdom be with us. Let your love now flow through this your priestess and throughout this circle. And as it is willed, so mote it be.

Charge

HPS: The Disseminating Moon corresponds to this sixth phase of your cycle, my Lord. It is a time of sharing.

HP: Yes, at Midsummer, in the Fullness of my cycle, illumination was mine. Yet having reached the heights, I now must wane, my energy gone into the ripening grain.

HPS: And the grain shall be harvested and feed the people, sharing your energy for life and growth. Then winter and darkness and death will come, but I will call you forth once again, my Sun, to a new cycle of light and spring.

HP: But what does this mean to the inner lives of our people?

HPS [to participants]: Know you that all phases of the cycle, each turn of the Wheel is necessary and vital to life. This phase brings the lesson of sharing. Having reached the fulfillment of any goal, what then will come? Having reached the top of a mountain, can you climb still higher? Shall you stay always in that place? Hardly likely, my children. Surely you know that the only constant in life is change. No, eventually you must come down, and there will be other mountains yet to climb ... but this is not yet the time of darkness; much time of sunlight still remains before the winter. Doubt not and fear not, be not anxious for the future, but live fully in the Now. You have been given much. The harvest is abundant. What shall you share with the Universe, with your brothers and sisters, and with the God and Goddess within?

Meditate now upon on the elements of Life. As you receive them, answer aloud or silently, as you choose, with love and sharing.

This was a larger group, with guests, so to speed up the process HP and HPs and two Elders ("Elder" refers to a circle member of Third Degree) each started with the person at the appropriate quarter to the element s/he was holding, and took it completely around the circle, giving it to each person to hold while asking them the question and waiting a moment for an answer.

Priest (HP): You are Goddess. You hold the air, power of thought, in your hands. What will you do to direct him? [pass feather]

Priestess (HPS): You are God. You hold the sea, mysterious power of feeling and soul, in your hands. What will you do to protect her? [pass seashell with water]

Priest (Circle Elder): You are Goddess. You hold the fire, the energy and power of spirit, in your hands. What will you do to rouse him? [pass candle]

Priestess (Circle Elder): You are God. You hold the earth, power of body, in your hands. What will you do to heal her? [pass rock and flower][5]

Dedication

HPs: Two of our circle have chosen this night to dedicate themselves to our Lady and Lord. Will the Crone bring forth the candidates?

This is not a usual part of the Lughnasad ritual. A Dedication can take place at any ritual. Since one was scheduled as part of this particular 1991 ritual, we have inserted it here, to show at what point during the ritual something such as this is normally inserted. The full Dedication ritual is found in Chapter 10 on Special Rituals.

Great Rite

Sharing

> **HP:** *Behold the bounty of the Mother ...*
>
> **HPS:** *Formed with energy from the Father ...*
>
> **Both:** *The fruit and grain of life. May you never hunger.* [pass chalice and cookies]

Farewells

> **HP:** *Eternal Mother, Lady of Earth and Moon, thank you for the special awareness we have received from your intuitive wisdom within. Hail, farewell and Blessed Be.*
>
> **HPs:** *Eternal Father, Mighty Lord of Day, thank you illuminating this, our sacred space, and for your vital energy within. Hail, farewell and Blessed Be.*
>
> **East:** *To the powers of Air I bid thee thanks*
> *Our blessings go with thee*
> *Till next your magic forth we call*
> *Farewell and Blessed Be!*

Guardian in the East bows and then turns to blow out torch.

> **South:** *To the powers of Fire I bid thee thanks*
> *Our blessings go with thee*
> *Till next your magic forth we call*
> *Farewell and Blessed Be!*

Guardian in the South bows and then turns to blow out torch.

> **West:** *To the powers of Water I bid thee thanks*
> *Our blessings go with thee*
> *Till next your magic forth we call*
> *Farewell and Blessed Be!*

Guardian in the West bows and then turns to blow out torch.

> **North:** *To the powers of Earth I bid thee thanks*
> *Our blessings go with thee*

Till next your magic forth we call
Farewell and Blessed Be!

Guardian in the North bows and then turns to blow out torch.

Autumn Equinox (Harvest, Mabon)

Correspondence to Lunar Phase: Last Quarter.

Keywords: Harvest, reorientation, crisis of consciousness.

Time: Usually September 21.

Preparation: Have ear of corn in small basket with enough kernels broken off to pass out. Before the ritual starts, have participants write on flash paper something for which they are thankful and put it in the cauldron.

This ritual was held on the beach. The cauldron was in the center of the altar. A large bonfire in the beach fire ring was at the South. Candles atop poles with element color streamers marked each quarter. In order to make the candles stay lit in the ocean breezes at the beach, we replaced the wicks with two wicks of much thicker weight.

Autumn Equinox 1992

Consecration

> **HPS:** *We meet this night to celebrate the Autumnal Equinox. It is the ancient festival of Harvest, and truly it is a time of joy and thanksgiving for the abundance in which we have all shared. It is a time of balance, equal day and equal night. Yet unlike the Vernal Equinox when we poised ready to spring forth toward action, new growth, and increased light, now instead, we stand at the brink of darkness—and, quite likely, uncertainty and anxiousness for what is to come. At this seventh spoke of the eightfold Wheel of the Year we acknowledge the crisis of consciousness that comes to all when any cycle of life is nearly over.*
>
> *Here within this sacred space that we have created, may we link our hands, our minds, and our hearts together as*

we rejoice in our bounty—and look toward the endless continuum of the turning of the wheel. I conjure this circle to be a force of unity and love, a sphere of light that shall contain, preserve, and direct the energy that we shall raise within. In all the names of the Goddess and her Mighty Consort, I do bless and consecrate this circle of power. As it is willed, so mote it be.

Watchtowers

East: To the East I call the power of Air
In Libran Balance we now share
Light of day and dark of night
Mind that blends with deep insight.
Guardian of the Eastern sphere
Now we seek your presence here.
Come, East, come, be here this night.

South: To the South I call the energy
Of flames of life and spirit free
Yet grounded, balanced, given form
Sun that wanes, in spring reborn.
Guardian of the Southern sphere
Now we seek your presence here.
Come, South, come, be here this night.

West: To the West I call the Waters deep
Mysterious force, all souls do keep
Sun that sets, be Child of Moonlight
Balance truth with mystic sight.
Guardian of the Western sphere
Now we seek your presence here.
Come, West, come, be here this night.

North: To the North I call the power of Earth
Harvest's death gives seeds of birth
Though Sun far South means winter cold
His sparks of life, Earth's womb enfold.
Guardian of the Northern sphere
Now we seek your presence here.
Come, North, come, be here this night.

Invocation of the God

> *HPS: I now do call the presence of the eternal God and I call him in the ancient ways as Lord of Day, the bright and fiery Sun whose energy brings warmth and light to Earth Mother. Flow now within your priest and through him touch and be the God within us all. As it is willed, so mote it be.*

Invocation of the Goddess

> *HP: I now do call upon the eternal Goddess and I call her in the ancient ways as Lady of the Night, ever-changing Moon, Mother Earth, and Crone who reigns as light declines. Flow now within your priestess and through her touch and be the Goddess within us all. And as it is willed, so mote it be.*

Speak to the people, and while doing so, gradually spiral out from center, HP moving toward the West, HPS toward the East, carrying covered basket of corn.

> *HP: I am light and energy ...*

> *HPS: And I am darkness that gathers that light-energy and weaves it into form. I am the body of the Universe, and I am the Earth, your Mother ...*

> *HP: Without her, my energy has no purpose, no reason to be ...*

> *HPS: And without him, my world is dark, my body cold ...*

> *HP: Together we are One ...*

> *HPS: In the dance of life ... One we may be, yet never are we the same, for nothing ever remains without change in the endless cycles of the turning of the wheel.*

> *HP: This is a time of joy, the season of balance, of equal day and night. The harvest is complete and is bountiful, and we are fulfilled. Yet, now I must move to the west, for all that rises must also set.*

HPS: My body, too, must rest and renew. And so we do bid thee farewell, O Sun, O Dark Lord of Shadows. Yet we know that you, whose light now wanes, is ever with us. Behold the grain of life, into which your energy has been transformed. [hand seeds to Maiden to pass around] Behold the seed that shall rest in the Earth and be born anew. Receive now a seed of life, and know that in the silence of the darkness, new wisdom may be gained. The light shall wane, but the wise shall weep not, but rejoice. What sets must also rise again! Let us dance the dance of life.

All circle around and sing "Lord of the Dance."

HP: All have received much from the bounty of the harvest. You have written that for which you are personally grateful and placed it in the cauldron. Into the invisible world it shall go, in the spirit of thanksgiving. As it is willed, so mote it be!

At this point, ignite papers that participants placed into the cauldron.

Great Rite

Spin-off Ritual for Terra

Again, this special event title is inserted here because at this particular 1992 ritual we had our first spin-off. See page 303 in Chapter 10 for the full wording of a Spin-off Ritual.

Sharing

Farewells

HP: Lady of the Moon, through you we have seen that in dark and change, enlightenment may be found. We thank you for your presence here and bid you hail, farewell and Blessed Be.

HPS: Mighty Lord of Day, from this point of balance light recedes, yet your brightness remains always within. We thank you for your presence here and bid you hail, farewell and Blessed Be.

East: *Guardian of the East, Spirit of Air, we thank you for your presence in our circle this night. Hail, farewell and Blessed Be.*

South: *Guardian of the South, Spirit of Fire, we thank you for your presence in our circle this night. Hail, farewell and Blessed Be.*

West: *Guardian of the West, Spirit of Water, we thank you for your presence in our circle this night. Hail, farewell and Blessed Be.*

North: *Guardian of the North, Spirit of Earth, we thank you for your presence in our circle this night. Hail, farewell and Blessed Be.*

This ritual was held at the beach, so we closed with the banishing ritual, as it has been previously given.

Samhain (Hallows, Halloween)

Correspondence to Lunar Phase: Balsamic.

Keywords: Death and seeds of rebirth.

Time: Traditionally celebrated October 31, actually Scorpio cross-quarter. 15° of Scorpio usually occurs about November 7.

Special Note: Again you get a bonus—two rituals. In San Diego, Circle Atheneum has for a number of years sponsored a large public Samhain, called "Witches Night Out." It usually draws at least one hundred people from various circles around the area, and is getting bigger every year. This is the one time of year when Pagans can be very public about having their party because everyone else is having Halloween parties, too. Everyone comes in costume, and the admission is canned or packaged food or other donations, usually given to a shelter for women in downtown San Diego. There's a big potluck supper, music, and fun, with the central event of the evening a Samhain ritual in which we add a bit more "theater" than we do for our private rituals. Every year a different set of HPs work center, several other people are designated to play various roles, and the ritual is rehearsed ahead of time.

The first ritual is the one for which Mark and I served as HPs in November, 1990. This was the first time that he and I "worked center" together. We were then both members of Circle Atheneum.

Preparation: The altar was draped in black cloth with iridescent glitter. A statue of the Crone was surrounded by white glittered sticks and autumn leaves. Since this was for a large group, four chalices and plates of cakes were prepared so the guardians could each serve one-fourth of the circle. A bit in front of the altar a silver pedestal stood, with a cast iron cauldron on top, in which several charcoals burned.

On the wall behind each of the four quarters, pentacles were drawn with miniature Christmas tree lights in the appropriate color. Each quarter had a couple, one to call the opposite quarter, and one to be the element called. The ones who were the elements had head drapes in the appropriate color, white eye masks, and a flashlight held at their chest pointing upwards that had been covered with cellophane in the appropriate color. The caller had a battery-operated candle with a Christmas tree light in it in the color of the element to be called.

Before the ritual started each participant was asked to write on a piece of magicians' flash paper (available at various magic shops) the name of a person who had passed over whom they wished to remember, and also to take a piece of black thread and tie knots in it, focusing on their intention for a personal issue in which they needed to let go of something or someone.

I chose to invoke the Crone for this ritual, rather than the traditional HPS invocation of Mother, so I wore a black robe.

Public Samhain 1990

Consecration

> **HPS:** *We meet this night to celebrate Samhain, the eighth phase of the eightfold solar cycle that is the Wheel of the Year. It is the final phase, the time of death—a time to honor the memory of those who have gone from our visible world ... a time to acknowledge and release that which is finished within our own lives ... and a time to reflect upon the mystery of what may lie beyond.*

I now do conjure this to be a circle of protection, of power and truth and love. Be it a sacred space between the visible and invisible worlds where we may fearlessly look upon the faces of our Gods and see in them a reflection of our own eternal light. From our home with Earth Mother we see the mighty Sun pass around us in his yearly cycle, and the phases of his relationship to the Mother are eight, but the number of his faces are twelve. Twelve aspects of the mighty One, each like a mirror in which we see ourselves.

May the dynamic spirit of Aries give us courage ...

Grounded by Taurean persistance and stability.

May the quick mental powers of Gemini aid the projection of our thought ...

As we children of the Moon stand surrounded and protected by the warmth of our Mother's love.

Let our circle sparkle with the creativity and splendor of Leo ...

Yet direct its energy with Virgoan precision and purpose.

Bring Libran balance to all polarities within this space, that we may truly appreciate the wholeness of life.

And now as we gaze at the eighth reflection, we see the countenance of the Scorpion—the face of death. Give us the faith to accept and release that which has finished that our spirits be reborn as the Phoenix ...

With all the inspiration and enthusiasm of the Archer ...

Yet with the practical ability of Capricorn to help us achieve our highest purpose.

In the spirit of Aquarius, may we ever seek Universal Truth ...

As with true Piscean mysticism we now merge with our Lord and Lady in Perfect Love and Perfect Trust.

And as it is willed, so mote it be!

Watchtowers

East [standing West]: To the East I call the Air. Blow forth, O winds! Come quickly as the winged feet of Mercury. Bring us refreshing breezes to clear our thoughts, and carry our spirits aloft with new understanding of your swift winds of change as the Wheel must turn. Guardian of the Eastern sphere, now we seek your presence here. Come, East, come. Be here this night.

Caller draws invoking pentagram in the air with the candle wand turned on. As s/he completes this, the pentagram on the wall behind that quarter is turned on, and the Guardian standing there illuminates his/her face mask with the cellophane covered flashlight. This procedure is repeated for each caller/receiver.

South [standing North]: To the South I call the Fire. Charge forth, O flames! Bring us the passion of Mars, the enthusiasm of Jupiter. Warm our spirits with your energy and vitality. Charge us with the courage to turn the Wheel! Guardian of the Southern sphere, now we seek your presence here. Come, South, come. Be here this night.

West [standing East]: To the West I call the Water. Flow forth, O mysterious Neptunian waves! O tides of emotions that ebb and flow with the ever-changing Moon, let us look into your depths and learn your mystic secrets as we seek to turn the Wheel. Guardian of the Western sphere, now we seek your presence here. Come, West, come. Be here this night.

North [standing South]: To the North I call the Earth. Come forth, O dependable one. Like the rings of Saturn, define our limitations, and then help us see beyond the death of winter's cold to Spring's rebirth—O help us turn the Wheel. Guardian of the Northern sphere, now we seek your presence here. Come, North, come. Be here this night.

HP: And so the Guardians are here. Can you feel their presence? Can you hear them? Listen ... Listen, O listen to the Autumn Wind:[6]

East: Hear the leaves rustle in the trees—see them blow free in swirling gusts about your head. And think of the *leaves of memory of this year in your lives. Feel the cool, brisk winds of change as they whisk the dust out of the corners of your mind and blow debris from your lives.*

HPS: Listen ... Listen, O listen to Autumn's fires:

South: *For passion you call? For energy and courage, as winter's chill settles into your very soul? Gather round my flames and listen to them crackle—smell the burning leaves of your memories and feel the warmth of those that you would hold within your heart. Yet know that they are gone—gone to the realm of spirit. Let them go ... let them go.*

HP: Listen ... Listen, O listen to Autumn's waters:

West: *So you seek to know my secrets? Stand in my waves and listen to the sound of surf. Feel how I pull the sand from beneath your feet, just as your emotions pull at the foundations of your reality and speak to your soul of change. Depths of insight lie within you—let them flow.*

HPS: Listen ... Listen, O listen to the Autumn land:

North: *Hear the dry crackle of leaves beneath your feet, the sounds of change and death. Yet listen to the silence of the seeds that slumber in the depths of my body. Like a great standing stone I mark your boundaries, yet like a warm blanket I protect and nurture your new beginnings as yet unborn. Seek for them in the silence of your soul.*

Invocations of the God and Goddess

HPS: *I now do call upon the Eternal God and I call him in the ancient way as Lord of Day, the fiery Sun who in this season has become the Lord of Deepening Shadows. Though it be night and you have passed into the invisible realms, we ask the presence here of your ever-constant spirit. Let your light now flow through this your priest and through him touch the light of God within us all.*

HP: *So you call upon my light in this season of darkness. The nights grow long. Earth Mother takes on the garb of winter, her fruitful bounty once warmed into growth through my energy now withers and dies. Do you fear the darkness, my people? Do you sometimes wonder why good things must come to an end?*

HPS: *It is truly a mystery, my Lord.*

HP: *I shall call upon She who unveils all mystery, ancient Crone who reigns as darkness falls and winter comes. Eternal Goddess, Lady of the Night, Waning Moon, your people need your wisdom and compassion. Cycles are ending, dreams have been lost, goals abandoned, loved ones have passed beyond. They seek answers, my Lady. Let your love now flow through this your priestess and through her touch the mystic depths of the Goddess within us all.*

Charge and Dialogue

HPS: *So we have come to the time of endings, my children. Yet if you know not the darkness, how can you see the light? Death is but the other side of life, you see. The stag and the corn must die that you might live. The grain must die to make new seed, and sometimes that which you have created or loved or counted upon must die in order that you might learn and grow. I am the Grandmother of Time[7] and I bring to you the growth that comes from maturity though the satisfaction of tasks completed, the sorrow of losses that must be accepted, the wisdom gained when problems are solved. I live within you when you recognize that a cycle of your life is finished and willingly let it go. Fear not the darkness, my children, for it is within the dark womb of the loving mother that new life begins. In the darkness you shall dream and I shall come to you and give you insight. I bring you rest to renew both body and spirit ... just as the Earth Mother now wears the cloak of winter that she may rest her body in preparation for return of the Sun's energy that will bring forth the new life of spring.*

HP: *All things are good within their proper season, and so the mystery has been revealed.*

HPS: Focus now upon that which you have bound within your black threads, upon that which you know deep within your souls must now come to an end. Let them be cast into the cleansing fires of my cauldron. Release them—let them go!

At this point I dumped the basket of black threads, to which Mark had previously added a small packet of flash powder, treated with chemicals to give it a reddish cast, onto the burning charcoals in the cauldron, with a flourishing and very "witchy" gesture. I must say that in the darkened room, lit only by candles and the wall pentagrams, the resulting flash was impressive!

HP: Focus now upon the souls whose names you have inscribed on paper, and forever in your hearts. Let the flames carry them forth into the realm of spirit in loving tribute to shared memories.

At this point he cast the flash papers into the cauldron with a flourish and another impressive white flash.

HPS/Crone: The Wheel has turned! In this time of death, a new cycle now begins. Let us join in the reaffirmation of life.

Great Rite

HP: Will the Guardians come forth?

HPS: Behold the death that brings you life.

Just as the cakes and wine are blessed, the Maiden and Mother approach the altar, from northeast and southeast, carrying baskets of acorns.

HP: The Maid and Mother have come.

Maiden: Grandmother, we bring a token of new life to come.

Mother: Let the people take and keep these acorns as a talisman and symbol of that which they shall create in the year to come.

HPS: Go forth and pass among our people.

Song: "We all come from the Goddess" (See Music, Chapter 11).

Sharing

The couples at each quarter come forward to have the cakes and wine blessed and then they pass it deocil from their quarter.

Farewells

> *HP: Lady of the Night, through your wisdom we have seen that in the darkness enlightenment may be found. We thank you for your presence here and bid you hail, farewell and Blessed Be.*

> *HPS: Lord of Day, though your light recedes into the shadows, we carry your brightness always within. We thank you for your presence here and bid you hail, farewell and Blessed Be.*

> *East [standing West]: We do thank the Guardian of the East, spirit of Air, for his presence here this night. Hail, farewell and Blessed Be.*

Receiving Guardian turns off flashlight, pentagram behind is also turned off. This procedure repeated for each dismissal.

> *South [standing North]: We do thank the Guardian of the South, spirit of Fire, for his presence here this night. Hail, farewell and Blessed Be.*

> *West [standing East]: We do thank the Guardian of the West, spirit of Water, for her presence here this night. Hail, farewell and Blessed Be.*

> *North [standing South]: We do thank the Guardian of the North, spirit of Earth, for her presence here this night. Hail, farewell and Blessed Be.*

Closing ritual of banishing circle in a public place follows, as has been previously given.

Samhain 1991

The second ritual is our private Samhain, for our own circle in my home. We repeated it in 1992.[8]

Preparation: The altar was draped in black with iridescent glitter. It was decorated with a bunch of black candles in all sizes and heights, and a variety of scrying tools—a large black mirror, crystal balls, black bowls of water. In the West a drape of black fabric was hung. The HPS, dressed in red as the Mother, is shadowed during the casting of the circle by another priestess dressed in black with hood, as the Crone. In all that the HPS does, the Crone is right behind her. The HP wears a cloak with a black hood, but at the beginning of the ritual the hood is down. The Crone has a small cauldron containing black stones. The HP has a small cloth bag containing small crystals. On the altar are an apple and a pomegranate, each in a small bowl.

Consecration

> *HPS: One again we meet to turn the Wheel. It is the festival of Samhain, the eighth and final spoke of the Wheel of the Year. It is the cross-quarter of Scorpio, Lord of the 8th House of the celestial sphere, the realm of death. On this night, as we form our sacred sphere, out of time and space, we perceive that the boundaries between the visible and invisible worlds are thin, less defined—that souls of either realm might look beyond the veil, glimpse the other side, and perhaps pass through. Our Lord Sun has become the Lord of Shadows—the days grow short. We rise in darkness, return home from our daily work in darkness, and the nights are cold. Even our Lady Moon is dark on this night, which this year is not only the cross-quarter of Scorpio, but also New Moon.*
>
> *Fear not, I say! I conjure this to be a circle of power and protection. As we stand in the shadows of the heart of the Scorpion, I do call upon the energies of that mighty image of the One for the courage to face the darkness. Give us the faith to accept and release that which is finished. Let our spirits be reborn as the Phoenix and soar with the Eagle to seek and find a new dawn of light. In all the names of the Threefold Goddess and her mighty Consort I do bless and consecrate this circle as a beacon of light and love between the worlds. As it is willed, so mote it be!*

Watchtowers

East: Power of mind and clarity
We seek you now, your truths to see.
Guardian of the Eastern sphere
Now I call your presence here.
Come, East, come, be here this night.

South: At Southern Watchtower, fiery bright
Now form a beacon, spirit's light.
Guardian of the Southern sphere
Now I call your presence here.
Come, South, come, be here this night.

West: Western portal, watery deep
Place of mystery, souls do keep.
Guardian of the Western sphere
Now I call your presence here.
Come, West, come, be here this night.

North: Stable earth, a rampart form
Protect this circle from all harm.
Guardian of the Northern sphere
Now I call your presence here.
Come, North, come, be here this night.

Invocation of the God

HPS: *I now do call the eternal God and I call him in the ancient way, as Lord of Day, who in this season has become the Lord of Shadows. Send thy spirit forth through the darkness of this night, O Lord. Return from the Summerland. Pierce our sacred sphere with thy vibrant presence. Flow through the body of this thy servant and priest, and through him touch the light of God within us all. As it is willed, so mote it be.*

God Charge

HP lights gold candle and puts on black hood before speaking:

HP: *This is the time of the eighth and final turn of your earthly Wheel of the Year, the death of the seasonal cycle. Your Great Mother has given forth of her bounty in the* *harvest of the grain. The plants that bore her fruits now brown and wither, and the Great Stag has fallen, too—all facts of life in your reality, life that must die so you may eat and continue on to another day. For truly you must know that no ending is forever. The final spoke of completion of one cycle becomes the emptiness, the zero, that contains all potential—the thought-seeds of new beginnings—the turn of the Wheel that never ceases. Tonight you must celebrate the darkness, for without it, how can you know the light? On this night you shall seek a new understanding. I call my Lady for her assistance in revealing this mystery ...*

Invocation of the Goddess

HP invokes the Goddess into both HPS and Crone.

HP: *I call the eternal Goddess, Mother, who brings forth and nurtures life, who is also Crone—she who cuts the cord, she of wisdom and mystery. Be with us now, my Mother, my love, my Lady. Thy priestesses await you. Fill them now, and through them touch the Goddess within us all.*

Goddess Charge/Dialogue

HPS and Crone together pick up silver candle and light it from the white one. Crone removes hood.

HPS: *Tonight we speak of death and honor the darkness. From your perspective, the Day Lord has passed into the Shadows, his light grows dim, the nights grow cold, and once lush growth now dies. Has he abandoned me—has he abandoned you? Or is there yet another deeper truth? I tell you now to beware of looking toward the Cosmos as if the cause for what happens within your life lies there! It is I, the Earth Mother, who changes the seasons, as I move away from his constant heat and passion to have my time of rest! The Sun appears to rise, appears to set—appears to set ever more in the direction of his fiery southern home as the days grow ever shorter. Yet it is I who turn my wheel! It is I who set the times of beginnings, of growth, of fulfillment, of waning, of endings. Do not be deceived by appearances, my children.*

Crone [takes up black mirror and holds it toward the people as she circles]: The Cosmos provides a mirror of your soul, reflecting the cycles of your life that you create. On this night of darkness I charge that you shall look within my scrying mirror, or within these other tools of mystery—deep pools of water, candle flames, the crystal—windows into your soul. In this season of release of that which has been completed, you must look at and acknowledge that which has come to an ending within your own life, and bid it a final farewell, even though this may bring you pain. It must be done! [take up the cauldron of black stones] Each of you, take a stone from my cauldron, a stone of darkness into which you may focus your intent. Gather more closely around the altar, sit comfortably and gaze into the scrying tool that is before you. When you have clearly seen that which you must release, direct its energy into your stone.

HPS: If a loved one has passed out of your world this year, it is time to release that soul that it may peacefully pass into the invisible realms unburdened by your pain. Yet death is not always physical and certainly not final, as surely you know. Each of you will experience many little deaths within your lifetime. Some may be sad, or challenging, or fearful—yet necessary for your continued growth. If habits, attitudes, relationships hold you back, you must learn to let them go. Yet remember that every ending carries within itself the seed of a new beginning. This is the way of life and death and life again. Be not afraid!

Scrying (about five minutes is given for this).

Crone: Does anyone wish to share an insight of release or name a soul who is passing into the invisible realm that we all may add our loving farewells? [verbal sharing—random saying of names—Crone then takes up the pomegranate and boline] When the maiden Persephone dwelt in the Dark World, she ate of the seeds of this fruit and so was bound always to return. [cut the pomegranate in a small bowl with the boline and pass it around] Behold the fruit of life, which is death. Taste the fruit of death.

HP: I go now to the western portal of the setting Sun. There I shall welcome the souls who wish to pass through and guide them safely. There also I shall await all that which you choose to release. From this point the darkness shall increase even more, for a time. Be not afraid!

Crone: Follow me widdershins onto the western portal. Dance the dirge of death and banish whatever in your life that you know has reached the time of passing. Feel the presence of the Dark Lord, bid farewell to souls who are passing into his realm ... and give unto him your stone of darkness.

HPS takes a black stone, too, and joins the circle moving toward the Dark Lord. She somewhat hesitantly drops her stone in his bag and moves on around the circle to the eastern side of the center altar.

HPS [interrupting music just as the last person reaches HP and he moves behind the veil, speaks dramatically]: Grandmother! I am no longer sure. I thought I could accept my choice—but I miss his warmth. How can I go on without his touch? I'll turn back the Wheel—take back my stone. My love, return to me!

Crone [lifts arms to form a barrier in front of HP]: NO! It is finished. You must let him go. Even we cannot turn back the hands of time. It is time for you to rest and sleep and dream.

HP [from behind the veil]: My Lady, my people—look beyond appearances to the truth. I am the constant, burning energy of the Life Force. Even in the forms of night and winter I am never really gone from you, for in times of darkness I watch over your dreams.

HPS: But what is a dream ... it is intangible—nothing. What can a dream hold?

HP: A dream may be nothing, but all is nothing without a dream. Within the dream one can be young and old, wise and foolish, one can be all that one is not.

HPS: You confuse our children, those are opposites, contradictions.

HP: That is the nature of the dream.

HPS: To bring contradictions?

HP: No, to bring all possibilities. For the dream holds the promise of the future.

HPS: Do you hear this, my children? All things are possible in the future![9] Let us dance deocil back to the altar and its tools of mystery—and dream of the future. Lead us in the dream, O Lord of the Dance!

HP, still hooded, comes out from behind the veil and leads people deocil around the circle as "The Lord of the Dance" is played. (See Music, Chapter 11.) As each person sits near the scrying tools he gives him or her a quartz crystal.

Crone: Again I charge you to look within the mirror of your soul and this time, look not to what is passing away, but instead search for insights into the future as yet unknown. Just as the western portal stands open on this night of transformation, that new souls may pass into incarnation, so must you be open to new possibilities. When the dream comes to you, focus it into your crystal and save it there. Hold it close to you as you return to the world, as the symbol of the seed of your new beginning.

Scrying (again, allow about five minutes).

HPS: Does anyone wish to share a new possibility or welcome a new soul who is returning or has recently returned? [after allowing a little time for anyone who wishes to share thoughts, she takes up the apple and boline] Behold the apple, which has been said in some traditions to be the fruit of man's fall. Again I say to you, do not be deceived by appearances. Behold this so-called fruit of death … [cut apple crosswise, show its center, which contains a five-pointed star with a seed at each point] which is life—the fivefold star of rebirth! Taste the fruit of rebirth!

All things must die, yet all are born again. Everything passes, changes. Seed becomes fruit, fruit becomes seed. In birth we die, on death we feed. Know me in the endless cycle and be free of all fear. Join us in an affirmation of life.

Great Rite

Crone joins HP and HPS.

> **HP:** *Athame to chalice …*
>
> **HPS:** *Spirit to Flesh …*
>
> **Crone:** *Man to Woman …*
>
> **All:** *As the God and Goddess within*
> *Conjoined they bring blessedness to life.*

Blessing of Cakes

> **Crone:** *Behold the bounty of the Mother. Feed on life that new life within you may be born.*

She hands chalice to HP and cakes to HPS, which they proceed to pass to each person in the circle in the usual manner.

Sharing

Farewells

> **HP:** *Lady of Light [bows to HPS] and of Darkness [bows to Crone], of love and of wisdom, we thank you for within our circle and within our souls. Hail, farewell and Blessed Be.*
>
> **HPS:** *Lord of Darkness and of bright, new possibilities, we thank you for your presence in our dance and in our souls. Hail, farewell and Blessed Be.*
>
> **East:** *Guardian of the East, power of air, we thank you for clarity gained this night. Hail, farewell and Blessed Be.*
>
> **South:** *Guardian of the South, power of fire, we thank you for your beacon of spirit light. Hail, farewell and Blessed Be.*
>
> **West:** *Guardian of the West, power of water, we thank you for mysteries revealed at your portals. Hail, farewell and Blessed Be.*
>
> **North:** *Guardian of the North, power of earth, we thank you for your strength and protection. Hail, farewell and Blessed Be.*

Endnotes

1. My calendar information comes from notes from the "Master Class on Spherical Astronomy" presented by Cape Cod Chapter of NCGR in September of 1980.

2. Classic *Ave Maria*, by Franz Schubert, available in many sheet music arrangements, and on countless recordings.

3. Ritual by Mark Adams, and published with his permission.

4. This chant is printed in Starhawk's *Spiral Dance*, San Francisco: Harper & Row, 1979.

5. I got the idea for the above question/answer sequence with each person holding the elements from Diane Stein's *The Women's Spirituality Book*, St. Paul, MN: Llewellyn Publications, 1987.

6. Vespertia of Circle Atheneum suggested this very poetic idea of calling for the answers from the Guardians with "Listen, O listen to the Autumn Wind ... " etc.

7. This title for the Crone, which I obviously like very much, was taken from the title of one of Z. Budapest's books: *The Grandmother of Time*, San Francisco: Harper & Row, 1989.

8. The writing of this ritual was, to a large extent, assisted by my HP, Mark Adams, and Greraven, who worked as Crone. The three of us spent a long evening together planning it.

9. The preceding dialogue from the first voice of the Dark Lord from beyond the veil, was gratefully and with their consent adapted from a November Full Moon ritual by Lady Aanja and Lord Falkan of The Circle of the Wildewood. (Anything any of us do that is especially effective is likely to be gleefully stolen to show up in the rituals of another circle!)

Full Moon Rituals for a Full Year

The Significance of the Sign Polarities at Full Moon

All of us have every sign in our chart, and therefore in our character somewhere, and must deal with the issues of every sign sometime, even though one or more of these issues may be emphasized more than others in our individual life experiences.

In our astrological Moon rituals we seek to understand the sign archetypes not only just in our own charts, but in a universal sense, as anyone might express each one at some phase or cycle of experience.

At each Full Moon the Sun and the Moon are in opposite signs of the zodiac. Sometimes on a Full Moon day, if you are looking at an astrological calendar, you might see that by the time you would

225

do a ritual that same evening, the Moon will have moved into the next sign. But the Full Moon lunation degree, thought by astrologers to be a significator of the time period (particularly the two weeks until the next New Moon), will be in the exact opposite degree to that occupied by the Sun at the exact time of Full Moon. Full Moon is an opposition aspect between Sun and Moon.

Most everyone is at least somewhat familiar with Sun signs. In Full Moon ritual, we attempt to show the complement and balance that is offered by the sign of the Moon. Opposition signs are said to be complementary opposites. Although the pairs are quite different from each other, they share common qualities—cardinal, fixed, or mutable; a positive or negative charge—and they share similar issues and faults. They are of different elements, but the element pairs in each case are those with the most affinity for each other.

The interpretive meanings of the sign polarities were covered in much greater detail in Chapter 7. These basic points are mentioned again only in preface to the Moon rituals to come.

A Traditional Drawing Down the Moon Ritual

The first Moon (we tend to refer to a Full Moon Esbat as just "Moon") to be presented here is not one in which astrology is emphasized, but rather is a traditionally worded "drawing down the Moon" ritual.

When I started my circle, with the plan to write rituals with a strongly emphasized astrological framework, I decided that my group (most of whom were completely new to Wicca) should first know what a traditional Wiccan ritual was like before we started rewriting the traditions.

With the help of our circle elder Ibis, who has been a Wiccan most of his life, extensively studying the Gardnerian and Alexandrian traditions, as well as Egyptian magic, I adapted a ritual that contains a close approximation of the almost universally known (among Wiccans) Charge of the Goddess, which is printed in many Wiccan books, usually uncredited. According to the Farrars, the original version was written by Doreen Valiente, Gardner's High Priestess. According to Guiley's *The Encyclopedia of Witches and*

Witchcraft, a Charge in verse was written by Gardner and later revised by Valiente. Later she wrote the prose version of the now famous Charge. Similar rituals to this one (somewhat more formal yet), or the Charge alone, can be found in many published books on Wicca. For this one, I use the style and most of the wording from the Farrars.[1]

Some Wiccan circles use a ritual similar to this one, with the traditional Charge, at every Full Moon. The Charge has a very special beauty that encapsulates the very heart of the Wiccan world view. I love it, although I choose not to use it every time, preferring to speak more spontaneously according to my specific theme for that ritual. I do the Charge occasionally though (at least often enough so that I can be sure to always be able to deliver it expressively and from memory). It is always meaningful and special for those in attendance.

Drawing Down the Moon

This was the first Moon ritual for Circle of the Cosmic Muse. It differs slightly from the ritual form that we later settled upon, so it is reprinted here exactly as we planned and performed it.

Preparation: Pillar candles on each side of the altar are lighted, and also the incense, and soft music begins. Greraven shall lead everyone in a centering meditation just beyond the area where the circle shall be cast. Mari, kneeling at the altar, shall center at the same time. She will then call Ibis forth to assist in the preparation of the circle, as the others watch and support with their focus.

Cleansing and Definition of the Circle

First, Mari shall draw the banishing earth pentagram, large, at the altar facing East, once only, circling it, to contain and banish any negative energy. She will then give Ibis the sword and take up the broom. She will sweep the area, while Ibis stands watch with the sword. She will then ask him to define the perimeter of the sphere with the sword, which he will do, after first saluting at the East with "As above, so below … "

Mari will then cleanse and charge the elements, giving each to Ibis to hold as she does this. She will then give Ibis the censer, take up the salt water, and they will walk the circle deocil, cleansing its perimeter with the elements. This shall be done silently, with only the music in the background.

Mari will then cut a door in the circle with her athame, Ibis will leave to guard the door from outside, and she will seal the door. Mari will charge the circle by drawing the active invoking spirit pentagram to the southeast, and the passive invoking spirit pentagram to the northwest. She will light the center white candle and then walk the circle deocil with her wand, saying:

> *I conjure thee, O Circle of Power, that thou beest a meeting place of love and joy and truth; a shield against all wickedness and evil; a boundary between the world of humanity and the realms of the Mighty Ones; a rampart and protection that shall preserve and contain the power that we shall raise within thee. Wherefore do I call upon the spirit and energy of the Universe to bless thee and consecrate thee, in the all the names of the Goddess and the God.*

She will then sound the bell.

The Greeting

Mari will first cut the door and admit Ibis to the circle, greeting him by drawing the solar cross, head to chest to right shoulder to left shoulder, saying:

> *Ibis, I do greet thee, in the name of the Goddess and God who within thee dwell.*

She passes her hands down the central meridian of his body to cleanse, and then upwards to charge.

She touch the center of his forehead with oil, saying:

> *Let the third eye now be opened.*

Then she draws a deocil circle followed by an invoking fire pentagram. End by saying:

> *Blessed Be.*

Then she kisses him and spins him in.

Ibis will then admit a woman to the circle, and so on. When all are in, Ibis closes the door with his athame.

Strengthening the Circle

Mari will call forth two people to charge the circle with the elements. They will salute and charge at each directional altar, saying:

> *With earth and water I do charge the East ... [etc.]*

Mari will then start the passing of the kiss, in perfect love and perfect trust. As this is done all may sing "The River is Flowing" (See Music, Chapter 11).

Watchtowers

Ibis rings bell three times, and says:

> *All Hail the Watchtower of the East.*

> **Mari:** *Ye Guardians of the Watchtower of the East, Powers of Air; I do summon, stir and call you up, to witness our rites and to guard the circle.*

She then draws the invoking pentagram with her athame. A designated person standing at that quarter will light the candle.

Repeat for each direction, naming appropriate element.

Invocation of the God

Mari and Ibis face each other at the altar. He crosses his hands across his chest, and she holds her hands high in horned salute, and says:

> *I invoke thee and call upon thee, Mighty Father, Sun, and Consort of the Mother, who brings Her light and warmth. Charge forth, O Great Stag, of energy and spirit free. Live now within the body of this thy servant and priest.*

She then touches Ibis on the shoulders. He raises the horned salute, and then lights the gold candle.

Drawing Down the Moon

Mari stands with her back to the altar, arms crossed on breast. Ibis kneels before her and gives her the five-fold kiss: kiss right foot, then left, saying:

> *Blessed be thy feet that have brought thee in these ways.*

Then right knee, left knee, saying:

>*Blessed be thy knees, that shall kneel at the sacred altar.*

Then the womb, saying:

>*Blessed be thy womb, without which we could not be.*

Mari now assumes the "open" position, hands cupped upward like the Moon. Then Ibis kisses the right breast and then the left breast, saying,

>*Blessed be thy breasts, formed in beauty.*

Finally, he kisses her lips, saying

>*Blessed be thy lips, that shall utter the Sacred Names.*

>*I invoke thee and call upon thee, Mighty Mother of us all, bringer of all fruitfulness; by seed and root, by bud and stem, by leaf and flower and fruit, in the fullness of the Moon, do I invoke thee to descend upon the body of this thy servant and priestess.*

He touches Mari on forehead. She lights the silver candle.

>**Ibis** *[kneeling before her]: Hail, Aradia! Pour forth thy store of love; I lowly bend before thee, I adore thee to the end. O Mighty One, descend to aid me, who without thee am forlorn.*

Stands up, taking a pace backwards, still facing Mari.

>**Mari** *[draws invoking earth pentagram before him]: Of the Mother darksome and divine, mine the scourge and mine the kiss. The five-point star of love and bliss, here I charge you in this sign.*

Charge

>**Ibis:** *Listen to the words of the Great Mother; she who of old was also called among men Artemis, Astarte, Athena, Diana, Aphrodite, Cerridwen, Dana, Arianrhod, Brigid, Isis, Mary, and by many other names.*

>**Mari:** *Whenever ye have need of anything, once in the month, and better it be when the Moon is full, then shall ye assemble in some secret place and adore the spirit of*

Me, *who am Queen of the Craft of the Wise. There shall ye assemble, ye who are fain to learn all sorcery, yet have not yet won its deepest secrets; to these will I teach things that are yet unknown. And ye shall be free from slavery; and ye shall dance, sing, feast, make music and love, all in my praise. For mine is the ecstasy of the spirit, and mine also is joy on Earth; for my law is love unto all beings. Keep pure your highest ideal; strive ever towards it; let naught stop you or turn you aside. For mine is the secret door which opens upon the Land of Youth, and mine is the cup of the wine of life, and the Cauldron of Cerridwen, which is the Holy Grail of immortality. I am the gracious Goddess, who gives the gift of joy unto the hearts of humanity. Upon Earth, I give the knowledge of the spirit eternal; and beyond death, I give peace, and freedom, and reunion with those who have gone before. Nor do I demand sacrifice; for behold, I am the Mother of all living, and my love is poured out upon the Earth.*

Ibis: *Hear the words of the Star Goddess; she in the dust of whose feet are the hosts of heaven, and whose body encircles the Universe.*

Mari: *I who am the beauty of the green Earth, and the white Moon among the stars, and the mystery of the waters, and the desire in your hearts, I do call upon your souls to rise up and come to me. For I am the soul of nature, who gives life to the Universe. From me all things proceed, and unto me they must return. Let my worship be in the heart that rejoices, for behold, all acts of love and pleasure are my rituals. Let there be beauty and strength, power and compassion, honor and humility, mirth and reverence within you. And for you who seek to know me, know that all your seeking and all of your yearning are of no avail, unless you know the mystery; that if that which you seek you find not within yourself, you will never find it without. For behold, I have been with you from the beginning, and I am that which you shall find at the end of desire.*

Let us now raise a bright cone of energy that will charge and direct the new beginning that is this Circle of *the Cosmic Muse. Follow my lead, we will build in speed, and then when the energy is at its peak, I will charge you to ground the energy in this space that we have created, by dropping to the floor to sit in the circle.*

All: As above so below, as within so without ... [repeated, then:] Down!

As the Universe, so the Soul.

Great Rite and Blessing of Cakes

Ibis kneels before Mari with chalice. Mari places athame in chalice.

Mari: Athame to Chalice ...

Ibis: Man to Woman ...

Mari: As God and Goddess within ...

Both: Conjoined they are One in the blessedness of life.

Mari sips the wine, passes it to Ibis, returns it to the altar. She gives Ibis the cakes to hold, while she draws an invoking earth pentagram over them, saying:

May this food be blessed into our bodies; bestowing health, abundance, joy, and fulfillment. [take cake for the Lady]

One cake is always reserved to give back to the Earth after ritual is over.

Ibis takes chalice and Mari the cakes and serve the circle, saying:

May you never thirst; may you never hunger.

Sharing

Introduction of the Circle Staff, and how it will be used as a "talking stick." Discussion/reactions regarding tonight's ritual. Explanation of the banishing and invoking pentagrams with handout of diagrams.

Announcements

Thanks to Goddess and God

> **Ibis:** *O Mother of us all, bright and full Moon and beauty and abundance of the Earth, we have been truly blessed by your presence in our circle this night. Hail, farewell and Blessed Be.*

Mari snuffs silver candle.

> **Mari:** *Great Sun and Stag, spirit strong and free. Thank you for sharing your energy with us this night. Hail, farewell and Blessed Be.*

Ibis snuffs gold candle.

> **East:** *Ye Guardians of the East, Powers of Air, we do thank you for attending our rites, and bid you hail, farewell and Blessed Be.*

Repeat for others, drawing banishing pentagram each time.

> **Mari:** *May all beings and elementals attracted to this rite be on their way, harming none. The circle is open but unbroken. Merry meet, merry part and merry meet again! Blessed Be!*

The Astrological Moons

Now that I have paid honor to the formal tradition, I will present the remainder of a year's worth of Full Moon rituals from my circle—one for the Moon in each of the twelve signs of the zodiac. (There are normally 13 Full Moons in one year—12 lunar cycles of about 29 days each falls short of the 365 days in our calendar year. Each Full Moon occurs in the sign of the zodiac following the one before.)

Circle of the Cosmic Muse has actually done all of these rituals—some in '91, some in '92—although not necessarily using exactly the words given here. Which brings us to an opinion I should give you on pre-written rituals, memorization or the lack of it, and such.

Nothing bogs down a ritual so much as having the eyes and minds of the people who are speaking constantly focused on their notes. It is better to improvise a ritual completely than to read it word-for-word from a paper. Yet notes are not all bad, and they are, in fact, necessary for many people who are just starting out. I used them at first, too, until my confidence grew—at the least I had 3 x 5 cards with the main points and the order of ritual on them.

I don't mind having the callers of the Watchtowers read from cards. They usually don't have any preparation time, and may be new to ritual. But I do think that the priest and priestess who are working center should strive to do as little reading as possible. If they have prewritten the ritual, and want it to be said word-for-word, they should memorize it, or at the very least confine themselves to small, unobtrusive "crib cards" with key words to jog the memory. From my observation, it is rare for a person to be able to read expressively enough to be effective, and at the same time, manage all the props and actions that are part of ritual. Being stuck trying to remember and then shuffling for notes is even worse—one can easily lose the focus on the energies being created.

The best idea for most people, I think, is to not even try to memorize word-for-word. Write the rituals, if you wish. (I did, because I wanted them for this book!) But then memorize only the concepts on which you plan to speak, and the order in which you plan to do things. That way, the most you will need is a card with a few words to key the order of what comes next, placed on the altar, to refer to if necessary. Then, say things in your own words, based on the concept. That way, what you say will be more natural, more expressive, and most importantly, more meaningful.

Trust in the Goddess and the God. If you can get through your ritual plan prior to the invocations with a reasonable building of energy, you will grow to find that once you have invoked the deity, you are home free ... if you trust the flow. Truly something comes over you, through you, builds up within—however you may want to express it—and you are no longer your mundane self. You are the Goddess/God! You will say exactly what is the right thing to say at that moment, whether it is what you planned to say beforehand, some variation of it, or something you hadn't even thought of before.

So use these rituals as a framework, but don't get "stuck" in them. Take pieces or ideas from one or another and patch them together with ideas of your own, or those you might get from someone else's book. We may have come close, but we didn't say the words exactly as they are given here when we did these rituals, so why should you?

When you are doing a formal ritual such as the traditional one given first in this chapter, you should memorize it, and know it sufficiently well so that you can get past the form and concentrate on the energy—in much the same manner as a good Catholic priest says the mass. (That, too, is a magickal ritual, whether it is acknowledged as such or not.) "Paper shuffling" is distracting to both you and those watching, and does not help the magick.

In the traditional forms, the repeated words and specific actions take on a power of their own, and should not be altered. For the most part, our initiations are in that context, repeated the same way every time.

Most of our rituals, however, are varied in theme, partly spontaneous—and we sincerely try to make them relevant to human experience in a way that will touch everyone present. Don't memorize that type of ritual. Plan, and then improvise.

Since I've completed one ritual for each sign, often with Mark's feedback and/or assistance, we have, for the most part, quit writing our Moons. Instead, we talk over the basic symbolism of the sign polarities and any issues that we think might be particularly relevant to our group, decide on something to do for the working, and then we "wing it." It has worked great. (Although I have to say I've wished a couple of times that we had written down an especially effective dialogue or Charge, so I could remember it later!) On some occasions we've also asked people to make up their own calls to the Watchtowers "on the spot"—and everyone (including the caller) has been pleasantly surprised at how relevant and effective they were.

So you see, there are different ways—and no one "right" way. Sometimes the traditional forms are just what is needed. Sometimes a carefully pre-written ritual is "right," and other times an unwritten improvisation works best. These rituals are offered to help you get started, or get new ideas, or find the way that is best for you.

Before each ritual you will find the "astrological polarity concept," which is a statement of the sign characteristics of Sun and Moon on which the ritual was based. Following that will be a note about any special preparation or tools that will be needed, in addition to all the usual ones. In these rituals only the parts that are variations are given. Assume that we cast the circle and did all of the standard parts the same way as they are explained in detail in Chapter 6.

In review, the basic order of our entire ritual is:

1. Greeting of High Priest and High Priestess, and simultaneously, centering meditation for group lead by Maiden or Crone

2. High Priestess consecrates altar elements, while High Priest sweeps circle on three levels

3. HPs cleanse circle with earth and water, fire and air

4. HPS draws banishing pentagrams at each quarter and connects them

5. HP defines circle on three levels with sword

6. HPS invokes spirit into circle with wand

7. HPs cut door and greet each participant

8. HPS speaks Consecration

9. Circle is charged with earth and water, fire and air by two pre-chosen people

10. Kiss is passed around circle

11. Calling of the Watchtowers

12. Power chant: *As above, so below ...*

13. Invocation of the God by HPS

14. Invocation of the Goddess by HP

15. Dialogue between God and Goddess

16. Charge of the Goddess

17. Working

18. Great Rite

19. Blessing of cakes, chalice

20. Sharing, passing the Circle Staff

21. Farewell to the Goddess by HP

22. Farewell to the God by HPS

23. Dismissal of the Watchtowers

24. Opening of the circle

Because reading these words, alone, may not convey the same nuance as if you saw us actually do the rituals, I'll make one final point in regard to the attitude with which we "play" the dialogues between God and Goddess. These are Moon rituals, primarily Goddess worship. The words, alone, could perhaps in a few cases lead you to think that the God is the "fall guy," showing a less than completely admirable aspect of his sign so that the Goddess can correct him by showing the other side. Other times she may seem frivolous, or ask questions as if she did not know the answer. In the way that we enact the rituals, however, it is clear that we are only playing. In our concept, the God and Goddess know what they are doing, and they know all sides of the issue, but they "play" to make their point, to teach a message of balance. The role-playing conveys a truth that people feel inside more meaningfully than they might receive the same idea if it was merely straightforwardly stated in the Charge. And ... we often elicit a chuckle or two in the process, which we think is desirable and adds to the energy, which will ultimately culminate in a serious working.

Cancer Full Moon

January 19, 1992

Astrological Polarity Concept: Capricorn (the Sun at this time) tends to be formal and traditional, and down-to-earth. He deals with reality, prefers structure and the practical approach. Cancer (the Moon) is a water sign, full of emotion, inclined to be moody. She deals with feelings and takes a nurturing approach, in balance to the practical realities of his message.

Preparation: The cauldron was on the altar, filled with sea water. Beside it were little seashells that could hold water, enough for every participant. For background music we played an environmental tape of ocean waves.

Consecration

> *HPS: Listen to the sounds of the sea, the waves that break into foam and wash up on the sand—soothing, gentle—or crash against the rocks—powerful, persuasive. All life on*

Earth once came forth from the sea, womb of the Mother. High above, the bright Full Moon—the lunation this month in the watery sign of Cancer, symbol of the Mother and her timeless, never-ceasing love. Would that we could drift and dream with her ebb and flow ...

Yet at this first Moon of 1992 we are very aware that a new year has begun—Sun reborn in Capricorn, sign of Saturn/Kronos, Father Time, "laying down his laws" that structure the practical realities of our lives.

Here in this time and place may we create a timeless and sacred space between the visible and invisible worlds, where we may call upon the unseen energies to flow ever more strongly within us. I charge that this shall be a circle of unity, of love and of trust, where we may seek and share and grow from the insights that our gracious Lady may reveal to us. By the love of the Threefold Goddess and her mighty Consort, I do bless and consecrate this circle of power. As it is willed, so mote it be.

Watchtowers

East: O Air, I call to the Eastern tower
Now quickly, lightly, send your power.
Dance with grace and golden light
Inspire our thoughts, come join our rite.
Guardian of the Eastern sphere
Now we seek your presence here.
Come, East, come, be here this night.

South: O Fire, I call to the Southern tower
With bright vitality, send your power.
Dance brightly with your flame-red light
Inspire our spirits, join our rite.
Guardian of the Southern sphere
Now we seek your presence here.
Come, South, come, be here this night.

West: O Water, I call to the Western tower
With waves of feeling, send your power
Dance through our dreams with deep blue light
With mystic insight, join our rite.
Guardian of the Western sphere

Now we seek your presence here.
Come, West, come, be here this night.

North: *O Earth, I call to the Western tower*
With sensual strength, now send your power.
Dance through glades of green-glow light
With care and purpose, join our rite.
Guardian of the Northern sphere
Now we seek your presence here.
Come, North, come, be here this night.

Invocation of the God

HPS: *I invoke thee and call upon thee O Great Father, Sun and Consort of the Mother, who brings her light and warmth. Come forth, Mighty Horned One. Live now within the body of this thy servant and priest and through him touch the spark of God within us all. As it is willed, so mote it be.*

HP: *I greet thee, Lady Mari, and all ye who are gathered here. It is time to draw down the Moon, as thy gracious Mother has directed shall be done once in each month. Are you ready then, priestess?*

HPS: *Yes, my Lord.*

Invocation of the Goddess

HP: *Then let us do it properly, according to tradition.*

With her showing some mild sighs of resignation, he helps her to stand center back to altar, arms crossed over breast, then kneels before her to give the fivefold kiss.

Blessed be thy feet that have led thee in these ways.

Blessed be thy knees that kneel at the sacred altars.

Blessed be thy womb, without which we could not be.

Blessed be thy breasts, formed in beauty.

Blessed be thy lips that shall utter the sacred words.

I invoke thee and call upon thee, Mighty Mother of us all, bringer of all fruitfulness, by seed and root, by bud and stem, by leaf and flower and fruit, in the fullness of the Moon, do I invoke thee to descend upon the body of this thy servant and priestess that through her all here may feel the presence of Goddess within. As it is willed, so mote it be.

Charge and Working

HPS *[a bit petulantly]: Must we be so formal and traditional? I'm really not in the mood tonight.*

HP: *That is one of your most frustrating and yet fascinating aspects, my love—that you are so changeable. Tell me, what are you in the mood for tonight?*

HPS *[with happy emotion and appropriate gestures]: First I'd like to run into the waves, feel them wash over me, cleansing all my cares away, and then float on them, feeling lifted and softly rocked like a child, safe in her mother's arms ...*

HP: *Not too practical tonight. It's pretty cold down there at the beach.*

HPS: *(sigh) I suppose it is your role in this season to see that we face the realities of life. All right then, I'll bring the sea here. In our imagination we can always be wherever we wish. [with HP assisting, pass small shells for people to dip full of ocean water from the cauldron] I bring you the sea which has the magical power to cleanse even the most impure and polluted things. Give to her your feelings, those things that worry you, the emotions that pollute your spirit and keep you from feeling secure. Close your eyes and feel yourself floating and drifting on the waves, rocked and safe, as you bathe yourself in my waters. Touch the water to yourself and return the touch to the water in your shell as you visualize all those unwanted feelings being washed away, cleansed and changed. Be safe, my children, be at peace; you are loved.*

Now, pour that water back into my cauldron, symbol of the womb, the eternal sea, container of power to cleanse or consecrate, destroy or create, and it shall be returned to the sea to be recycled and reborn, perhaps in your dreams this night, but soon, as new feelings that will support you and give you comfort. You may take the little shell and keep it nearby as you sleep, as a reminder.

Dedication Ritual

A person was dedicated on this night. See Chapter 10 for the format.

HPS: And now, my Lord, it's time that we fed these people, don't you think? They must be hungry after all that work.

HP: Of course! On that we can always agree.

Great Rite

Sharing

Farewells

HP: Lady of the Moon, protective Mother, thank you once again for your caring warmth that surrounds and fills our circle. Till once again we call, we bid you hail, farewell and Blessed Be.

HPS: Father of our Souls, Mighty Sun and Consort of the Mother, thank you once again for your strong and shining presence within our rites. Till once again we call, we bid you hail, farewell and Blessed Be.

East: O Guardians of the East, spirits of Air
Dance on your way with grace and flair!
Take our grateful love, and be now free
Hail, farewell and Blessed Be.

South: O Guardians of the South, spirits of Fire
Dance to the world, your gifts inspire!
Take our grateful love, and be now free
Hail, farewell and Blessed Be.

West: O Guardians of the West, O Water sprite
Dance on to the sea, with magickal sight!
Take our grateful love, and be now free
Hail, farewell and Blessed Be.

North: O Guardians of the North, spirits of Earth
Dance on to the world, with strength and mirth.
Take our grateful love, and be now free
Hail, farewell and Blessed Be.

Leo Full Moon

February 16, 1992

Astrological Polarity Concept: Aquarius (the Sun) is more concerned with the needs of the collective than those of the individual. He has a vision of the way things ought to be and seeks reform. Leo (the Moon) is concerned that the creative expression of the individual not be suppressed in the process. His is a more intellectual approach (air sign); hers is passionate and romantic (fire).

Preparation: At the previous meeting everyone was told to bring with them to Moon something that expressed creativity that they could share with the group. It could be a poem, music, a reading, art, handicraft, etc.

Consecration

HPS: Once again we meet, as the gracious Goddess has so charged us to do, in the fullness of the Moon. Here do we gather, we who seek to know her mysteries. It is the season of Aquarius, and our Lord the Sun pours out his electric waves of energy, seeking to charge us to look ahead of our troubled times to an age yet to come when freedom and equality shall exist for all. And as we have come to expect of her, our Lady Moon, in reflecting his full light, will show us her own perspective and point of balance.

Therefore I do proclaim, in the glowing light of the Leo Moon of the Queen of Heaven, that this shall be a circle of drama and excitement, of mystery and of dreams, and of truth and love. Around this sacred space between the worlds, may we cast a spellbinding aura of magickal light, that shall preserve and contain the energy that we shall raise within. In all the names of our Lady and her Lord, I do bless and consecrate this circle. As it is willed, so mote it be.

Watchtowers

East: *To the East, O winds of Air I call*
Cast golden light on one and all.
We seek your wit, your quick delight
May free expression grace this night.
Guardian of the Eastern sphere
Now we seek your presence here.
Come, East, come! Be here this night!

South: *To the South, O sparkling Fires arise*
Cast bright red light o'er Southern skies.
Bring passion, flair, excitement bright
Let magick sparks inspire our rite.
Guardian of the Southern sphere
Now we seek your presence here.
Come, South, come! Be here this night!

West: *To the West, O lovely waters flow*
Cast luminous lights of deep, blue glow.
Infuse us with your mystic sight
Let waves of mystery grace this rite.
Guardian of the Western sphere
Now we seek your presence here.
Come, West, come! Be here this night!

North: *To the North, O Earth, abundant, fair*
Cast soft, green light and loving care.
Let sensual warmth pervade this night
Support our growth within this rite.
Guardian of the Northern sphere
Now we seek your presence here.
Come, North, come! Be here this night!

Invocation of the God

HPS: *I call to thee, O bearer of Lightwaves, O youthful innovator who directs our thoughts into the future. Come forth, Lord Sun, of energy and spirit free. We seek thy presence within our circle and within our lives. Shine now through this thy priest and through him touch the light of God within us all. As it is willed, so mote it be.*

HP [to the people]: I see that you have all gathered. That is good, for we have much to do together. But the circle cannot be complete without our Lady ...

Invocation of the Goddess

HP: I call to thee, gracious Lady of the Silver Moon, gentle benefactor, teacher of the mysteries. The people gather in your light—they wait to hear your message. Shine now through this thy priestess and through her touch the light of Goddess within us all. As it is willed, so mote it be.

Charge and Working

HP: Now that everyone is present, we'd better join hands around the circle right away and get our thoughts focused on a few of the ways this world needs to be reformed. I have an agenda right here ... [produces list, a long piece of rolled paper from a calculator]

HPS: Hey, just a minute. This is my night to shine!

HP: But your light only reflects mine, my love ... my agenda ...

HPS: Reflects your light? Moi? You are suggesting that a Leo is only reflecting light? We shall have to see about that! Let's reform the world later. First, I want to have some fun, cast a little spell, create a little fantasy ...

HP: But what will that accomplish? A waste of time, when people are still not equal, not free—

HPS: Sometimes freedom is not of the mind, but of the heart, my Lord. And a light that is big enough to change the world is made up of many little individual ones—like this candle flame of mine. Listen ... I will demonstrate the value of my own—and other's—individual and special lights.

I then sang the following words to a sans voce cassette tape of "The Music of the Night" from *Phantom of the Opera* by Andrew Lloyd Webber. A few of the phrases are Webber's; most are changed. We used the accompaniment that was provided for the theme song from that same tape in the background for the rest of the ritual. It has a very rhythmic beat. For those who might wish to try this "Charge" in the same manner that I did it, the tape information is in the Annotated Bibliography.

Night time comes and heightens each sensation
In the dark, I wake imagination
Silently your senses abandon their defenses
Helpless to resist my soft moonlight
For I bring you the magick of the night.
Softly, slowly … night unfurls her splendor
Can you sense it? Tremulous and tender.
Feeling is believing, sight alone can be deceiving,
Trust this spell I weave by candlelight
Join me in the magick of the night.
Come closer and gaze into my candle light
In the flame see the dreams you wish to be
In the darkness it's easy to create
A dream that can become reality.
Softly, let my silver Moon caress you
Feel it, sense it, let it now possess you.
Open up your mind, let your fantasies unwind,
As you dream into my flame of candlelight,
Glowing in the mystery of the night.
Come with me, I'll take you to another world
Leave all thoughts of the life you've lived before
Let your soul take you where you long to be
There you'll know that you belong to me.
Floating, dreaming, sweet intoxication,
Touch me, trust me, savor each sensation.
Now our spell is cast, let all doubts and fears be past,
Know the power of your dreams by candlelight,
The power of the Full Moon on this night!

(musical interlude)

Only you can truly be my light …
Help me make the magick of the night.

Spoken, as music-only tape continues in background:

Help me each of you, I can only shine through you … you
are my light, now share it with the others … who will be

first? Come join me ... increase the spell! Build the energy of it ...

Individual sharing of creativity. HP passes staff to each person as he or she presents (this was really fun! There were poems, readings, various crafts, a painting); when all had finished:

HP: *These are all individual points of energy ... join now your hands, minds, and hearts and link this energy. Feel the power as it flows around the circle. Let this force be harnessed for the common good of this planet and the people who dwell here. What can be accomplished when like minds join energies together? Speak your intents my people, as the energy builds and flows. Visualize and hold our planet in the light of our energy sphere. Focus and build the energy. Hold it and feel it glow ... [individuals speak intents at random] Return now to the circle, remembering that when you go forth into the world that you carry its light with you, and remember that anything can be accomplished when individuals link their energies together for a common purpose.*

HPS: *Isn't it wonderful? The magick that we can create together.*

Great Rite

Sharing

Farewells

HP: *My Lady, we do thank you for your wisdom, your magick and your presence within our circle and our lives. Hail, farewell and Blessed Be.*

HPS: *My Lord, we do thank you for your bright vitality, your vision and your energy within our circle and our lives. Hail, farewell and Blessed Be.*

East: *From Watchtower East we send the Air*
Go forth with winds so free
We thank you for your presence here
Farewell and Blessed Be!

South: *From Watchtower South we send the Fire*
Charged with vitality
Thank you for your presence here
Farewell and Blessed Be!

West: *From Watchtower West we send the Waters*
Return now to the sea.
Thank you for your presence here
Farewell and Blessed Be!

North: *From Watchtower North we send the Earth*
In glad serenity
Thank you for your presence here
Farewell and Blessed Be!

Virgo Full Moon

March 17, 1992

Astrological Polarity Concept: Pisces (the Sun) is a romantic and a dreamer, an inspirer of fantasy. Virgo (the Moon), while respecting the value of dreams, believes that in order to make them manifest, you have to work, have a system.

Preparation: A basket of little paper scrolls (rolled paper with a bit of red yarn around them tied in a bow) and small pencils are placed on the altar before the ritual begins.

Consecration

> **HPS:** *Our Lady Moon is full this night ... within the beauty of our circle, let feelings flow and swell, like the tides of the sea. Listen ... beneath the music that you hear ... the waves break into foam, and we may sense the presence of our Lord Sun as Neptune, ruler of the Fishes of the Cosmos, who inspires our fantasies and our dreams. Shall the cares of this day be washed away in his music? Or shall we focus now upon the center of our circle, where the single light of the candle is like the flame of Vesta the Virgin, keeper of the hearth, who reminds us of the personal satisfaction and, yes, even the spiritual peace that*

can come through orderly and down-to-earth attention to our daily tasks?

Feel the flow of love pass from hand to hand, my brothers and sisters, as I do conjure this to be a circle of power and balance, of truth and of compassion. In this sacred space between the worlds, protected by our sphere of light that shall preserve and contain the energy that we shall raise within, with the love of our Lady and our Lord, I do bless and consecrate this circle. As it is willed, so mote it be.

Watchtowers

East: *To the East I call the Air to come quickly on the winged feet of Mercury, and bring us your refreshing breezes to clear our thoughts and carry our spirits aloft with new ideas. Guardian of the Eastern sphere, now we seek your presence here. Come, East, come. Be here this night.*

South: *To the South I call the Fire. Charge forth, O flames! Bring us the passion of Mars, the enthusiasm of Jupiter, and warm our spirits with your energy and vitality. Guardian of the Southern sphere, now we seek your presence here. Come, South, come. Be here this night.*

West: *To the West I call the Water. Flow forth, O mysterious Neptunian waves! O tides of emotions that ebb and flow with the ever-changing Moon, let us look into your depths and learn your mystic secrets. Guardian of the Western sphere, now we seek your presence here. Come, West, come. Be here this night.*

North: *To the North I call the Earth. Come forth, O dependable one. Bring us the discipline of Saturn, and yet also the beauty of Venus, that we may bloom and grow with the flowers of Spring. Guardian of the Northern sphere, now we seek your presence here. Come, North, come. Be here this night.*

Power Chant

Invocation of the God

HPS: King Neptune, Lord of Day, you who cast your shimmering gold on the waves of the sea and warm the body of the Mother as she nurtures the new growth of Spring, you who bring energy to our dreams of new possibilities, I do call your bright presence to our circle. Flow now through the body of this your priest and through him shine to touch the light of God within us all.

Invocation of the Goddess

HP: Vesta, Virgin Goddess and Lady of the Night, Mother of growth and of wisdom, the people gather to celebrate the fullness of your silver Moon, and they wait to learn your mysteries. Come within this circle, my love. Flow now through the body of this your priestess and through her shine to touch the light of Goddess within us all.

Charge

HP: Have you a dream, my people? Tell me about it. What do you wish could happen in the world? In your life? Even if you think your dreams are out of your reach, still ... tell me.

HPS: Yes, tell him—tell us both. I, too, would like to hear this. My charge to you this night can wait a bit ... and perhaps, then, even serve your dreams this night. Tell us. Who will be first?

Wait for response; some probably will, some won't.

Good! But the rest of you, I know you all have dreams, but perhaps wish to keep them to yourselves? I understand.

One reason why you may not wish to be too open about your dreams, is because you are not sure if you can make them come true. How about it, my Lord, can they?

HP: All things are possible.

HPS: That may be true, yet will only dreaming make what you want into reality?

HP: It can, sometimes ...

HPS: *It works for some people, sometimes, but not always. Most of the time, I think, it takes more than that. It takes a plan, focus ... a system. My gift to you tonight is a system. Everyone take a scroll and pen.*

HP: *So efficient! Where's all the romance of last Moon?*

HPS: *It was fun—but sometimes we must be practical. Surely you can feel that, my Lord, especially from within this priest who has called you! [Mark is a Sun in Virgo!] Yet we shall strive to achieve balance with their dreams. [to the circle] I'll give you a five-step plan to turn a dream into reality.[3]*

Step one is to be clear about what you want. Everyone, quickly, write down five things that you want. Let these things be what you really want, independent of whether or not you think they are possible. Your dreams are possibilities—not "impossible dreams!" The things can be material or non-material, but define them clearly ... "I want a better job, a new car, a love relationship, to lose weight" ... I will give you only one limitation. Choose only for yourself—do not phrase your choices so that they require the action of another person. Remember, we do not use our magick to manipulate others.

Step two: Ask yourself, of each thing you have chosen to list, "If I could have this right now, would I accept it?" If you can immediately say "Yes," you do want it. But, did any of you have any contradictory thoughts? The Young Self, the subconscious, tends to accept everything you tell it, and you all know the tremendous influence it has. For example, you say, "I want a better job." Young Self says, "Yes!" You say, "I don't have time to look." Young Self says, "Yes!" You say, "Jobs are hard to get in this economy." Young Self says, "Yes!" You say, "Learning something new is difficult." Young Self says, "Yes!" Get the picture? One more example, to be sure. You say, "I want to lose 20 pounds." Young Self says, "Yes!" You say, "Diets are hard." Young Self says, "Yes." You say, "When I get hungry I get headaches." Young Self says, "Yes." You say, "I get such a craving for chocolate." Young Self says,

"YES!" If any such dialogue goes on in your head about one or more of your choices, you don't really want it at this time. Cross that one off.

Step three: Hopefully, you have at least one thing left that you really want! Let's make a project of that one thing. Write a formal affirmative statement about it, such as "I choose to have a better job ... or to lose 20 pounds."

Step four: Think about what you have written. Is there a more basic choice upon which it rests? Your results depend upon the basic underlying choice. For example, a basic choice underlying getting a better job may be "to be successful," and underlying losing 20 pounds is "to be thin." If you have contradictions about the basic choice, you are unlikely to get the results you want. Also, think about the secondary choices you must make to support what you have written as your primary choice—"I choose a better job" could be supported by looking for ways to be more efficient where you are, looking at want ads, making calls, going to an employment agency, taking a course, writing a new resumé, and so on. These choices will be easy to make if you really want your results.

Step five: Take this scroll home with you. Every night this month, before you sleep, read your affirmation, and restate it, preferably aloud and firmly. Now, when Young Self, who does your feeling for you, feels successful—even in small ways—momentum is created and larger successes will come. So acknowledge and support Young Self by writing down five successes of the day. A success is the accomplishment of anything you intended to accomplish toward your goal, however small. "I intended to make that call today and I did—success! I intended to pass up chocolate today and I did—success!" Now, spend five minutes clearly visualizing what you have chosen as if you already have it.

HP: *Yes, and in your dreams, Young Self will remember. It will work. Next Moon they'll have progress to share! My dreams and your realism will support each other, my Lady.*

HPS: *Perfectly balanced as always, my Lord!*

Dedication

Great Rite

Investiture of Maiden and Red Priest

HP and HPS present two new tools of the circle: the Maiden's crown and the Red Priest's staff. Cleanse and charge the tools and seal them with the candles of Lady and Lord. Announce that a Maiden and Red Priest have been chosen for our first appointments, then call forth Terra and Tear. HP states duties of Maiden, then asks:

> *Terra, do you accept these responsibilities?*

After she answers, crown her.

HPS states duties of Red Priest, then asks:

> *Tear, do you accept these responsibilities?*

After he answers, present staff.

We made a special staff, with small antlers mounted at the top, for the Red Priest, and a crown of white silk flowers similar to a bridal headdress, with ribbons down the back rather than a veil, for the Maiden. These things belong to the circle and are used by the Maiden and Red Priest during their term of service. Each adds to crown/staff a small token of his or her own at the end of the approximate one year term of office, before passing the tools on to the new Maiden and Red Priest.

Sharing

Farewells

> **HPS:** *Bright Lord, who this night has inspired us with possible dreams, we do thank you for your presence within our rite and bid you hail, farewell and Blessed Be.*

> **HP:** *Gracious Lady, who this night has shown a way to turn our dreams into reality, we do thank you for your presence within our rite and bid you hail, farewell and Blessed Be.*

> **East:** *Guardian of the East, spirit of Air, we do thank you for your stimulation of our thoughts and bid you hail, farewell and Blessed Be.*

South: Guardian of the South, power of fire, we do thank you for your energy and enthusiasm, and bid you hail, farewell and Blessed Be.

West: Guardian of the West, spirit of Water, we do thank you for your depth of feeling and insight, and bid you hail, farewell and Blessed Be.

North: Guardian of the North, power of Earth, we do thank you for your dependability and strength, and bid you hail, farewell and Blessed Be.

Libra Full Moon

April 14, 1992

Astrological Polarity Concept: Aries (the Sun) is full of energy and wants to charge ahead and get going on things. He is self-centered and self-confident, primarily seeing what *he* wants. Libra (the Moon) represents the scales of balance. She prefers to relate, to work with the "other." She wants very much to keep the peace and is willing to compromise, but is also concerned with what is fair.

Preparation: A light blue candle will need to be on or near the altar before starting.

Consecration

HPS: We meet this night to celebrate the first Full Moon of springtime. Our Lord Sun is fiery and full of all the zest of the Ram, ready to charge toward his full power and light. Our Mother Earth, already responding to his warmth and energy, blooms with new color and life. Her Moon reflects his light this night, yet she holds the scales of Balance, and the mystery of her own special counterpoint of wisdom to this season of the Ram. I now do conjure this to be a circle of protection, of power and truth and love. Be it a sacred space between the visible and invisible worlds, a sphere of light that shall contain and preserve the energy that we shall raise within. In all the names of our Lady and her mighty Consort I do bless and consecrate this circle. As it is willed, so mote it be.

Watchtowers

East: *Soft, spring breezes blowing free*
Through golden, glowing light.
By the love of Lady and of Lord
We call you to our rite.
Guardian of the Eastern sphere
Now we seek your presence here.
Come, East, come. Be here this night.

South: *Sparkling fires leap high and bright*
Red flames of glowing light.
By the love of Lady and of Lord
We call you to our rite.
Guardian of the Southern sphere
Now we seek your presence here.
Come, South, come. Be here this night.

West: *Cool waters of stream and lake and sea*
Soothing, soft, blue light.
By the love of Lady and of Lord
We call you to our rite.
Guardian of the Western sphere
Now we seek your presence here.
Come, West, come. Be here this night.

North: *Earth of green and flowers wild*
So colorful and bright.
By the love of Lady and of Lord
We call you to our rite.
Guardian of the Northern sphere
Now we seek your presence here.
Come, North, come. Be here this night.

Invocation of the God

HPS: *Charge forth, Bright Lord of Day. Though it be night and your fire can only be seen reflected in the Moonlight, still I call you to send your fiery energy to charge our circle. Shine through this your servant and priest to touch the light of God within us all.*

Invocation of the Goddess

HP: *Hail, my Lady Mari. So it is once again the time of Full Moon, when my lovely Queen of Heaven shines in all her fullness, reflecting my light, clarifying its message—and at the same time, exerting her often saucy independence by standing opposite me in the heavens. So be it! We shall hear what she has to say. My Queen, I call thee to grace this circle with your presence and shine with love and wisdom through this your servant and priestess to touch the light of Goddess within us all.*

Charge

HPS: *Saucy, you call me? And just what name might you use to describe yourself, strutting about as the great Horned One?*

HP: *Well, what do you expect? It is spring and I feel a great burst of energy. I want to charge forth like a ram. Watch out, world! Here I come! [put hands to head like horns and charge at Goddess]*

HPS *[laughs, moves slightly away, holding hands out to his chest]: Not so quickly, my Lord! My "saucy" message—as you put it—I heard you well—my message this night is one of balance …*

   Life is full of opposites—light and dark, hot and cold, wet and dry, noise and silence, left and right. This night the Sun shines opposite the Moon. He is Aries and she is Libra, and all of these are opposites. Now shall opposites be but sub-categories under the opposite headings of "good" or "bad"? Some would have it so, yet I would challenge you to name any that would remain under the same heading throughout the cycles of your life. Hot and cold, wet and dry—it is easy to see with such as these why all of one cannot work without the balance of the other, and thus their goodness or badness varies according to circumstance. Perhaps this is why Libra is so known for sitting on the fence and not being able to decide which of two alternatives to choose!

Other opposites are not so easy to reconcile—war versus peace, for example, and there are no easy answers, nor any that are absolutely "right" for all—and what are right and wrong but opposite opinions? Your Lord and I are both light and darkness, and we are here within each of you and within the earth on which you stand, and I say to you that the answer is balance. Assert yourself, when you must, to restore harmony. Compromise, when you must, to restore harmony. Yet to fight to destroy the spirit of your opponent, or to compromise to the point where your own spirit is subdued—these things only tip the scales to the other extreme. And no one else can truly tell you what is right or wrong for you—the answer lies within. One thing I can tell you—when you are in balance, in equilibrium, life flows easily, so if you are experiencing great effort or difficulty, ask yourself: what in my life is out of balance? Then fix it! Need help? Look within. He is there, within you, spurring you on with his fiery energy to charge forth and do what you must do. And I am there, too, loving you, and helping you think through the ways in which compromise and diplomacy might help to smooth your path.

As you all have learned, sometimes your individual intentions are greatly helped by drawing upon the energies of your brothers and sisters within the power of your magick circle. Each of you no doubt has some area of your life in which you feel the need of greater balance—in how you relate to someone in your life, perhaps; in managing your work versus your personal life, perhaps, or in reconciling your desires with that which you know is appropriate in the current situation.

This light blue candle shall symbolize the harmony of balance. Pass it around your circle and each one anoint it with oil and with your intent. All of you, focus on the one who holds the candle. Send your energy and all of your focused attention to the one who holds the candle, that each personal need be charged by the group mind. Later we will burn the candle all the way down, sending the power of its magic into spirit that our will and purpose may become reality.

The Great Rite celebrates true balance as God and Goddess within are One.

Great Rite

Sharing

Farewells

HP: *My Lady, we thank you for showing us the value of harmony and balance in all things, and for your gracious presence within our circle and within our lives. Hail, farewell and Blessed Be.*

HPS: *My Lord, we thank you for showing us the value of energy and initiative, and for your lively and vital presence within our circle and within our lives. Hail, farewell and Blessed Be.*

East: *Soft, spring breezes gently blow*
So light and cool and free.
We thank you, now and bid you hail
Farewell and Blessed Be.

South: *Sparkling fires, red glowing flames*
So high and bright and free.
We thank you now, and bid you hail
Farewell and Blessed Be.

West: *Soothing, soft blue waters*
Of stream and lake and sea.
We thank you now, and bid you hail
Farewell and Blessed Be.

North: *Earth of green and flowers wild*
So colorful to see.
We thank you now, and bid you hail
Farewell and Blessed Be.

Scorpio Full Moon

April 28, 1991

Astrological Polarity Concept: Taurus (the Sun) is growth and springtime; Scorpio (the Moon) faces the darkness that is the other side. Taurus symbolizes holding on; Scorpio symbolizes letting go. Both are concerned with power and security. Taurus seeks power and security through building, acquiring—mastery of the material world. Scorpio seeks power and security through mastery of the inner self.

Preparation: No special tools are needed, but a drumbeat will enhance the chant and dance. We often use drums to raise energy.

Consecration

> *HPS: Once again we meet in the fullness of the Moon. It is the month of Taurus, the season of growth, as new life takes root in Mother Earth, as our new thoughts take on form and substance. Feel her strength beneath your feet, savor her beauty ... as I do dedicate and consecrate this circle to be a sacred place where we may renew our connection with the source of beauty and power within earth and cosmos, and within ourselves, in the name of Gaia, Earth Mother, and her great Horned Bull. Within the love and protection of this circle, may we feel and sense the truths that will guide us steadily upon our paths of growth, as we direct the energies we shall raise according to our will. So mote it be.*

Watchtowers

> *East: Hail, East Wind, to you we call.*
> *Her breath bring now to one and all.*
> *Breeze refreshing, winds so free*
> *Blow forth in light and purity.*
> *Guardians of the Eastern sphere*
> *Now we seek your presence here.*
> *Come, East, come! Be here this night!*
>
> *South: Fiery South, burning bright*
> *Tower of warmth and brilliant light*

Bring red flame to light this night.
Encircle us with energy, passion, and intensity!
Guardians of the Southern sphere
Now we seek your presence here.
Come, South, come! Be here this night!

West: *From Watchtower West flow waves of power*
Bring mystic vision to this hour.
Lakes of blue, streams so clear
Mysterious waters, be now here!
Guardians of the Western sphere
Now we seek your presence here.
Come, West, come! Be here this night!

North: *To Watchtower North, from glades of green*
We call our Mother Earth, serene.
Bring safety and security
Protected may our circle be.
Guardians of the Northern sphere
Now we seek your presence here.
Come, North, come! Be here this night!

Invocation of the God

HPS: *Father of the Universe and father of our souls, we feel strength and security in your increased light and we feel your vitality in the growth of spring. Expand now your energy within this your priest and through him shine to touch the hearts of all.*

Invocation of the Goddess

HP: *Mother of all living, Queen of Earth and sky, we see your beauty this night in the bright full Moon above us. I invoke thee and call thee, O Lady of the Moon. Descend now upon the body of this your priestess. Fill her with your wisdom that we may share a special meaning for this night.*

Charge

HPS: *My bright orb above reflects the strong and steady light of the Lord of Day, and the words of your ritual celebrate the virtues of the Taurean aspect of the mighty life* *force that dwells within you all. Yet this is night—a lovely spring night—and I must gently remind you that you call me forth from the sign of Scorpio, which means that my message may sting just a bit, if you are too complacent in your needs for security. Tell us who you are, O great Horned Bull of springtime ...*

HP: *I am a plant that has firmly taken root and grows with strength ...*

HPS: *And I am the hoe that uproots you and throws you aside.*

HP: *I am blue speckled eggs warm in a nest ...*

HPS: *And I am a storm that dislodges that nest and causes the eggs to fall and break.*

HP: *I am a carefully worked out plan ...*

HPS: *And I demand a revision.*

HP: *I am persistent work in progress ...*

HPS: *And I am the circumstance that necessitates change ... and what then?*

HP *[addressed to everyone]: You have the power to the begin anew when you must ...*

HPS: *And you have the power to build on that renewal. Sometimes you must hold on, and sometimes you must let go. The challenge is in knowing which will serve you best at any given time. Have I an easy answer for you? No, it is for you to experience, for that is how you grow. I can tell you that when you feel great fear, your choice may be the wrong one, but if you feel the power and the flow, your choice is right for you.*

Feel now the power of holding on: Plant your feet firmly on the ground and tense your muscles. Feel the tension and the strength of the Mother move up through your body, take a deep breath, make a fist, hold yourself like a solid rock, and feel the power!

Now let go! Relax, let out the breath, lift up, be free, soar like an eagle—and feel the power!

*Let us dance the energies of the Great Mother within—
dance the power into our souls.*

Chant:

*Mother, I feel you under my feet
Mother I hear your heartbeat
Mother, I see you as the eagles fly
Mother take me higher.*

*HPS: Now in the warmth of the energy we have raised I
pass the Staff to any of you who would like to share an
experience of holding on or of letting go. Share that your
experience might touch a similar chord in the life of
another and help them, or share that you might, with the
support of the circle, find new insight or heal yourself.*

Great Rite

Sharing

Farewells

*HP: Lovely Moon, Goddess fair
Womb of Earth and sea
We thank you for your presence, Hail!
Farewell and Blessed Be!*

*HPS: Mighty Sun, Consort, Horned One
Spirit bright and free
We thank you for your presence, Hail!
Farewell and Blessed Be!*

*East: From Watchtower East we send the Air
Go forth with winds so free
We thank you for your presence here
Farewell and Blessed Be!*

*South: From Watchtower South we send the Fire
Charged with vitality
Thank you for your presence here
Farewell and Blessed Be!*

*West: From Watchtower West we send the Waters
Lakes and pool and sea*

Thank you for your presence here
Farewell and Blessed Be!

North: *From Watchtower North we send the Earth*
In glad serenity
Thank you for your presence here
Farewell and Blessed Be!

Sagittarius Full Moon

Lunar Eclipse (June 14, 1992)

Astrological Polarity Concept: Gemini (the Sun) symbolizes reason; Sagittarius (the Moon) symbolizes faith/revelation. Gemini deals in conscious, logical thought; Sagittarius deals in inspiration and flashes of insight.

Preparation: Ask participants to write on flash paper a question that they have for which they have not been able to find an answer, a problem for which they have no solution, or a decision they've been unable to make. All should be things about which they've thought a lot, but so far reasonable answers evade. The cauldron should be in the center of the circle. Participants put their questions in the cauldron as they enter.

Note: This circle was held during a Lunar Eclipse, and that fact is incorporated into the Consecration and the dialogue between Goddess and God. The same ritual could easily be used for a normal Full Moon, with only minor alternations of the wording.

Consecration

HPS: This is the month when the eastern rising of the Sun is in the air sign, Gemini. Let the east winds blow with the changes we know must come as spring's cool breezes prepare to give way to summer's warmth. Our days are bright, as our Lord nears the fulfillment of his power. Yet on this night our Lady Moon—Sagittarius Full Moon, Diana! Huntress!—who normally would be full of fire, leading us on to new inspiration, is eclipsed. We meet in darkness. The Huntress stalks, in the shadow of Earth Mother, through the mystery of the night. What do you seek, Diana? Send your flaming arrows forth like a shoot-ing star. Illuminate this night, that new truths may be revealed within our spirits.

I do conjure this to be a circle of power, of truth, and of love. Be it a sacred space between the visible and invisible worlds. Be it a rampart of protection, secured by the love of brothers and sisters, a silver sphere of spiritual light that shall preserve and contain the energy that we shall raise within. In all the names of our gracious Goddess and her mighty Consort, I do bless and consecrate this circle. And as it is willed, so mote it be.

Watchtowers

East: To the Watchtowers of the East I call the spirits of Air, in the name of Minerva the wise. Bring us the fresh-ness and clarity of your essence. Sharpen our perception. We welcome you, winds of change. Blow forth! Come, East, come! Be here this night!

South: To the Watchtowers of the South I call forth the Fire, in the name of Vesta, keeper of the flame. With pas-sion we welcome thee, your inspiration, your energy, your sparkle. We await thee—charge forth! Come, South, come! Be here this night!

West: To the Watchtowers of the West I call the Waves of the seas, in the name of lovely Venus-Aphrodite who was born of thy depths. Wash over us in purity, clear our vision, that we may know thy deepest mysteries. Flow Waters! Come, West, come! Be here this night!

North: To the Watchtowers of the North I call the spirits of Earth in the name of Ceres, Earth Mother and Goddess of the grain. Surround us, protect us, feed now our souls! We welcome thee. We desire thee. Come forth! Come, North, come! Be here this night!

Invocation of the God

HPS: I call the God, Lord of Day, Apollo of the Sun, who in this season of the Twins is both two and one, king of *oak and king of holly, bringer of truth and the winds of change. Send your vibrant presence among us. Fill the body of this your priest and shine through him to touch the light of God within us all. As it is willed, so mote it be!*

Invocation of the Goddess

HP: I call the Goddess, Lady of Night, Mother whose names are many. I call to thee tonight as Diana of the Archer's Moon! Lovely huntress, poised to send your fiery arrows straight on their paths. We seek you tonight in the mystery of the shadowed Moon. We seek the illumination of your wisdom. Fill the body of this your priestess and through her shine to touch the light of Goddess within us all. As it is willed, so mote it be!

Charge

HPS [to HP]: There you are! I've been looking for you, but the shadows are very deep tonight. Now I've got you. A little flaming arrow ought to help shed light on what our people seek this night.

HP: You're teasing, my Lady. It is not I who denies the fullness of light this night. You have created the shadow. I challenge you to give the people a reasonable explanation why.

HPS: The shadows symbolize the darkness that blocks your minds and hearts when you have a problem with no solution, a question with no answer. We know that you seek the truth this night, that which is true for each of you. Some of you have questions that need answers; others have decisions that you must make. The winds of change blow constantly, fanning the flames of your spirits to seek beyond.

HP: Most questions have logical answers, and decisions are best made through a reasonable analysis of the alternatives.

HPS: I see doubt on some faces here. A bit of indecision, perhaps?

HP: *Well, it's true that there are at least two sides to many questions, and sometimes both seem equally logical. How, then, my Lady, will you suggest they step out of the shadows?*

HPS: *Faith ... have faith! This is the message I bring to you this night. Rational thinking—yes, this is an important way to know. Yet winds can dissipate—go nowhere—be indecisive—without inspiration, without the revelation of spirit. When reason alone will not your answer bring, quiet your thinking mind and listen also to your heart. Let the winds fan the flames of intuition, each feeding on the other, until that magic moment when you know! Walk the path of the Craft, as you have chosen, and know that you need only seek within, to find our breath of mind and inspiration of spirit, in the perfect balance that you need to find the answers that are right for you.*

You have written out the question for which you seek an answer, and have thought it through with logic, yet still have doubts. We shall now seek also the insight of spirit. Thinking only of the question, in an attitude of openness, call upon the Goddess and God, raising the energy of their power within you.

Now chant with me, let your mind be free!
Till in a flash of sudden light your answer you may see!

All chant (with drums—music for the chant is on page 388):

Live within us now, Apollo ...
Live within us now, Diana ...

At the climatic point, HPS calles a halt with a drum roll and HP sets aflame the papers in the cauldron, which has been placed at the center of the circle.

Dedication Ritual

Great Rite

Sharing

Farewells

> **HP:** *Diana-of-the-Hunt, Lady Moon, we thank you for your wisdom and love in our circle and in our lives. Hail, farewell and Blessed Be!*
>
> **HPS:** *Mighty Apollo, Sun and Lord, we thank you for your bright energy in our circle and in our lives. Hail, farewell and Blessed Be!*
>
> **East:** *Swift winds of the East*
> *Our thanks to thee*
> *Hail, farewell and Blessed Be!*
>
> **South:** *Bright flames of South*
> *Our thanks to thee*
> *Hail, farewell and Blessed Be!*
>
> **West:** *Deep waves of the West*
> *Our thanks to thee*
> *Hail, farewell and Blessed Be!*
>
> **North:** *Strong Earth of the North*
> *Our thanks to thee*
> *Hail, farewell and Blessed Be!*

Capricorn Full Moon

July 14, 1992

Astrological Polarity Concept: Cancer (the Sun) is concerned with his home, his garden, his family, and the warmth and nurturing given and found within. He is casually comfortable with feelings and emotional flow. Capricorn (the Moon) prefers tradition and structure in her approach. She is concerned with the realities of life, and the protection of the larger home, the Earth, herself.

Preparation: We hid behind the altar one of those inflatable Earth balls (beachball size). Music playing through the circle casting and early part of ritual is rhythmic and sensual, but another tape of softer meditation music is ready for immediate use. On the altar is a parchment scroll containing the formal Charge of the Goddess.

Consecration

> **HPS:** *Once again we meet in the fullness of the Moon. It is the height of summer, the season of our Lord's brightness. Though his waning time has begun, the days are still long, and even though night has come, we feel his Cancerian warmth in this beautiful garden full of flowers, surrounded by the nurturing love we share. Yet tonight we meet to call our Lady, from her more austere perspective in Capricorn. What mystery will she reveal to us this night? What message will she bring? I do conjure that this shall be a circle of power and of understanding, where we may meet to seek the true realities of our inner and outer lives. Be it a sacred place, between the worlds, a shimmering sphere of light that shall contain and preserve the energy that we shall raise within. In all the names of our Lady and our Lord, I do bless and consecrate this circle. As it is willed, so mote it be!*

Watchtowers

> **East:** *Cool breeze blow forth to the Eastern tower*
> *Bring focused thought and magic power*
> *Aid us as we strive to know*
> *Help us as we seek to grow.*
> *Guardian of the Eastern sphere*
> *Now we seek your presence here.*
> *Come, East, come, be here this night.*

> **South:** *Bright flames rise up at the Southern tower*
> *Charge us with light and magic power*
> *Inspire us as we strive to be*
> *Vibrant, bright, with spirits free.*
> *Guardian of the Southern sphere*
> *Now we seek your presence here.*
> *Come, South, come, be here this night.*

> **West:** *Let the tides now flow to the Western tower*
> *Wash over us with your cleansing power*
> *Bring mystic sight that we may see*
> *The path to true serenity.*
> *Guardian of the Western sphere*

Now we seek your presence here.
Come, West, come, be here this night.

North: *O Earth, stand firm at the Northern tower*
Protect us with your strength and power
Teach us your ways that we may see
How best to live in harmony.
Guardian of the Northern sphere
Now we seek your presence here.
Come, North, come, be here this night.

Invocation of the God

HPS: *I call the great Father, Lord of Day, bright Sun who brings warmth and energy to the Mother. Your children seek your presence and protection. Live now within the body of this your priest and through him shine to touch the light of God within us all. As it is willed, so mote it be.*

HP: *I greet you, my Lady Mari.*

HPS: *Welcome, my Lord.*

HP: *Isn't it beautiful here in the garden? It is so good to be among family [moves out into circle, hugging people all around], so good to relax within our circle. Ah, yes, but our family is not complete without the Mother, and considering from where she travels this night, I suppose I'd better do it according to tradition.*

HPS: *I think you are very wise, my Lord.*

Invocation of the Goddess

HP: *I invoke thee and call upon thee, Mighty Mother of us all, bringer of all fruitfulness; by seed and root, by bud and stem, by leaf and flower and fruit, in the fullness of the Moon, do I invoke thee to descend upon the body of this thy servant and priestess, that through her we may touch and know the Goddess within us all.*

Charge

After she lights the candle, she pauses, and looks at him meaningfully, as if waiting for something. He at first is "blank," but then "catches on," and says:

> *HP: I suppose this means you want to continue exactly according to tradition?*

HPS nods assent with dignity.

> *HP: It seems that I remember once when it was the other way around and you wanted to go off to "float in the waves." This night, unlike that one, is more than warm enough. Well ... ?*

> *HPS: Perhaps later, my Lord. There is a time and place for everything. I feel that in this time and place, the wholeness of my message may be best expressed with a bit more formality. May we have some slightly more dignified music, please? [tape is changed, she hands him a scroll]*

> *HP: Very well.*

He takes the scroll, on which is the formal introduction to the Goddess charge. He unrolls it and formally reads:

> *HP: Listen to the words of the Great Mother ...*

From this point on the traditional Charge of the Goddess through the Charge of the Star Goddess continued with the exactly the same words as are given in the first ritual in this chapter. The Charge creates a mood of peace and beauty, which was allowed to continue for a small pause at the end, after which we changed the music back to rhythm, and lightened the approach.

> *HPS: Now I'm ready to play!*

> *HP: The beach?*

> *HPS: Not quite my theme this night. I have another game in mind. You spoke earlier of the relaxing feeling of being among family, of nurturing each other. That is good, but what of our larger family, outside this circle? If you think only of those close to home, my children, perhaps home might not be so safe and protected in the future. The Earth*

*is your home, and all of its people are your family. Catch
the Earth in your embrace for a moment, and as you do,
tell me what you will do to protect and nurture her and
her people.*

HPS brings out the earth ball (an inflated beachball that looks like
planet Earth) and throws it to the first person who responds to her
question:

Who will be the first to tell me?

From then on the ball is tossed and passed from one participant to
another, until everyone offers a response.

HPS: Let us now reaffirm life.

Great Rite

Sharing

Farewells

*HP: Gracious Lady of the Night, Mother and wise teacher,
we do thank you for your loving presence in our circle and
in our lives, and bid you hail, farewell and Blessed Be.*

*HPS: Bright Lord of Day, Father and loving protector, we
do thank you for your warm presence in our circle and in
our lives, and bid you hail, farewell and Blessed Be.*

*East: Guardian of the East, airy breezes and clear
thoughts, we thank you, and bid you hail, farewell and
Blessed Be.*

*South: Guardian of the South, fiery light and passionate
vitality, we thank you, and bid you hail, farewell and
Blessed Be.*

*West: Guardian of the West, deep waves of feeling and
mystic sight, we thank you, and bid you hail, farewell and
Blessed Be.*

*North: Guardian of the North, stable earth of abundant
growth, we thank you, and bid you hail, farewell and
Blessed Be.*

Aquarius Full Moon

August 12, 1992

Astrological Polarity Concept: Leo (the Sun) is very much the king, regal and confident, but very much the center of his own universe. He symbolizes the creative expression of the individual. Aquarius (the Moon) is a rebel, who challenges authority and seeks to bring about change. She symbolizes the creative expression of the group working together for the benefit of humanity.

Preparation: On the altar, have a small ball of bright blue yarn, of a light enough weight so that it can be broken by yanking it between your hands.[4]

Consecration

> **HPS:** *Again we gather, as we have been charged, at the time of Full Moon, to worship She who is Queen of the Craft of the Wise, and is Mother of the Universe. The Full Moon rises high above this night in the sign of Aquarius, a symbol that caught the imagination of millions for their hopes of a future age "where peace will rule the planet and love will rule the stars." An "impossible dream"? Well, perhaps, if we only dream. But this night, may our Lady grant a new perspective upon how our dreams may manifest into reality.*
>
> *O Lady of Aquarius, sparkling energy of electric blue that we have cast around our sacred space, be with us this night. Pour forth your waves of light to charge this circle, to contain and direct the power that we shall raise within. Let us join our hands in this circle of sisterhood and brotherhood, in perfect love and perfect trust. Let this be a circle where minds may meet and seek to discover the truths that bind us in unity, the truths that we shall live. As it is willed, so mote it be!*

Watchtowers

> **East:** *Uranus, symbol of change we call*
> *Charge us with freedom, one and all!*
> *Blow to the East and circle round*

Help us see that truth be found.
Guardian of the Eastern sphere
Now we seek your presence here.
Come, East, come. Be here this night!

South: *Fire bright, Sun's full light*
Grandeur of Jupiter, Mars so bright
Flame to the South, bring passion's heat
With energy warm us, merry meet!
Guardian of the Southern sphere
Now we seek your presence here.
Come, South, come. Be here this night!

West: *From Plutonian depths now rise*
Lift Neptune's trident to the skies
As silver Moon on waves of night
Flow forth and bathe us with your light!
Guardian of the Western sphere
Now we seek your presence here.
Come West, come. Be here this night!

North: *Saturn, symbol of that which stands*
Solid and firm, throughout these lands
Though change we seek, we call on you
For time and strength to build anew.
Guardian of the Northern sphere
Now we seek your presence here.
Come, North, come. Be here this night!

Invocation of the God

HPS: *In this season of the splendor of the Sun, of long, bright days and warm summer nights, I call the God in his magnificent Leonine garb, regal but generous, warm and true. My Lord, your people seek thee on this night. Descend upon this your priest. Fill him with light and shine through him and throughout our circle, that all may share in your radiance. As it is willed, so mote it be.*

HP: *Lady Mari [bow to her, she curtsies], my people, I greet you with great joy. [stride forward, gesture broadly] Isn't it a perfectly glorious night! What a wonderful sea-*

son to be alive, creative, have fun ... I want to give you
light and warmth and ...

HPS [*taps him on shoulder*]: My Lord, I don't mean to
upstage you, but it is time ...

HP: Ah, yes, so it is. And this is an Esbat celebration, after
all.

Invocation of the Goddess

HP: *Lady Moon, I reach out to thee across the sky—
though why you should want to stand opposite to me is ...
well (sigh), I suppose only one of the charming mysteries
of your cycles. Come forth to join your people who await
thee, O Queen of the Night. Descend upon this your servant and priestess and through her pour forth, from your
starry urn, waves of illumination to radiate throughout
our circle, that all be inspired to seek your truth. As it is
willed, so mote it be.*

Charge

HPS: *Ah yes, my King! It is the Full Moon, and though I
love you for all your dramatic enthusiasm, it is my role to
illuminate how your wondrous generosity might be chan-
neled beyond our circle.*

*My children, my sisters and brothers, my friends ... my
bright Moon in the sky above is only my satellite. The
larger reality is your Great Mother, who cries out for her
people who suffer, and for her body which must feed the
people—but is being damaged by those who see only their
personal interests and not the needs of the whole.*

*The Aquarian spirit rebels, and seeks to break through
the bonds of limited vision. I call out to you now to think
of the things which wrongfully bind us, things which keep
us from being free, things that threaten to damage our
future and that of future generations, things that keep us
separate from true sisterhood and brotherhood. As I move
counterclockwise to bind you with my cord of blue, think
of all the things that need to be changed, all of the bonds
that need breaking, and call them out.*

Now, think of the power of people coming together to bring about change, to break harmful bonds. Let the Goddess within be free, and break the bonds! [all break the blue yarn in pieces]

Turn now to the one who is clockwise from you, and retie all the pieces again. As we so rebuild a circle of Aquarian blue, let us tie a bond of strength, of our power as brothers and sisters, God and Goddess within, to heal the earth and heal ourselves. Build our circle of energy and as you do, speak out. What bonds shall we affirm?

All retie yarn into complete circle and then stand holding it.

By this symbol of breaking our bonds of fear and anger and injustice, and of retying our bonds of friendship, we reaffirm our lives in goals of peace and love and the power and responsibility to join with others to effect healing change. Carry forth this symbol in your hearts as you return to the world.

And now in the balance and wholeness of the Life Force within ...

Great Rite

Sharing

Farewells

HP: *My Lady, once more we thank you for the illumination that you have given us this night. Hail, farewell and Blessed Be.*

HPS: *My Lord, truly your bright presence is ever a joy. We do thank you for being with us and bid you hail, farewell and Blessed Be.*

East: *Blow free, O winds of Uranian rebellion. For your power to change, we thank you. Hail, farewell and Blessed Be.*

South: *Recede onto the realms of spirit, bright flames. For passion and vitality, we thank you. Hail, farewell and Blessed Be.*

West: Into the depths now ebb, O waters. For mystic insight, we thank you. Hail, farewell and Blessed Be.

North: Rest peacefully in the night, O earth. For your abundance and strength, we thank you. Hail, farewell and Blessed Be.

Pisces Full Moon

August 25, 1991

Astrological Polarity Concept: Virgo (the Sun) is efficient, work-oriented, and practical. Pisces (the Moon) is a mystic, who provides the message of the dreams that are necessary to make work worthwhile.

Preparation: Song sheets were passed out for this ritual. The poetry contained in consecration and invocation needs to be thoroughly memorized by the HPs in order for the mood to flow. This ritual was written for my Second Degree requirement for Circle Atheneum, and repeated on the date above for my own circle. For Circle Atheneum I accompanied myself on an autoharp; this time I was fortunate enough to have a member of the circle who could accompany the music on guitar. For the musical part of the Charge, I wrote new words based on the traditional Charge of the Star Goddess, and set them to the tune of "The Rose" by Amanda McBroom. Sheet music with guitar chords is easily available at most music stores, for those who would like to use this adaptation. The music section of Chapter 11 includes the melody line for the passing kiss song and the cakes and chalice song, and also words for the Rose Charge adapted for group singing about the Goddess.

Consecration

> **HPS:** *The Sun, our Lord of Day, has now entered the sign of Virgo, marking this as a time of industry and busyness, a time to bid farewell to the idle days of summer, to get in the harvest, to prepare for the new school year, to attend to all the practical details that are the realities of our lives in the season of Autumn that all too quickly flies by to Winter's festivals. Yet tonight, as our Lady Moon reflects and clarifies the Sunlight in all Her fullness, a new*

message shall be revealed—a message of complement and of balance.

In the beauty of the Mother
Pisces Moon so full and bright
I conjure mystic power
All around be shimmering light!
Let love and vision flow throughout
Let energy be raised
As the Goddess and her Consort
In all their names be praised.
Beyond the world of space and time
Let 's set our spirits free
In the magic of our circle, as
It is willed, so mote it be!

Special Song for Passing the Kiss

Her breasts are the mountains
Her womb is the sea
Her breath is the cool breeze
Refreshing and free.
Her light is the bright Moon
And the stars up above
And the flame in our own hearts
As we share perfect love.

Watchtowers

East: To Watchtower East I call the Air
Vivacious, light and free
Bring Libran peace, Aquarian truth, the Twins vitality
Come quickly as the birds in flight
Come, East, come! Be here this night!

South: To Watchtower South I call the Fire
Surround us with your flames
Of Arian energy, Leo's pride and Sagittarian aims
Inspire our spirits with your light
Come, South, come! Be here this night!

West: To Watchtower West I call the Water
Mysterious, deep, and strong

Cancerian womb, Scorpio depths, and Pisces siren song
Infuse us with your mystic sight
Come, West, come! Be here this night!

North: *To Watchtower North I call the Earth*
So green, abundant, fair
Bring Capricorn power, Taurus growth, Virgo's loving care
Come protect us with your might
Come, North, come! Be here this night!

Invocation of the God

HPS: *Mighty Sun, we see thy face*
Reflected in Her light
Though night has come, thy spirit still
Is honored in Her sight.
Thy priest now waits to serve you, Lord
His flame within grows bright
Charge him with your energy
To share within this rite!

Charge of the God

HP: *I rise in this season in the sign of Virgo—rather serious business for all this sing-song poetry I've been hearing tonight. Well and good—but my special charge to you is that it is time to get busy! The practical affairs of earth demand your attention. Summer is over, the harvest must be brought in. The new school year starts for some, and it's time for new work and new projects for others. It is important to sort out your priorities, to be responsible, to be of service to others and to guard well the health of your body and of the body of our Mother Earth. That is the energy and message of my reality in this season.*

HPS: *So be it, my Lord. So long has my life and my reality been timed by Autumn's call. Yet ... sometimes the brightness of your vitality is almost too much to bear. Sometimes it would be nice to escape ... and dance and sing and dream ...*

HP: *Well, the Moon is full tonight, and She does reflect My light in softer hues. We shall draw down the Moon,* *priestess—and even in the style that you have chosen. My Lady has a way of adding Her own special wisdom to My message.*

Invocation of the Goddess

HP: *Lovely Moon of silver light*
Fulfillment now is found.
I call the muse, illuminate
Thy secrecies profound.
Thy priestess waits to share your light
Your mystic music be
The song that in her heart tonight
Unveils your mystery.

Charge

HPS: *Busy is the time. Ah, yes, that is true. My body is filled with the harvest, and much work must be done to prepare for the winter. So many things to do ... so many details to which you must give attention. Truly it is important to be dutiful, responsible ... to develop your skills. All this I charge you in my full reflection of Virgo's solar light. And yet, this is the night of Full Moon ... the time when harvest must also bring illumination. What is the meaning of all your busy-ness? To what purpose do you serve your earthly concerns?*

Take a few moments now to go with me to the sea, within the realm of your imagination. Sit, if you like, relax and be comfortable. Let's stand on the sand, right at the water's edge. The water flows gently around your feet and it feels good. But now a bigger wave comes in, and as it recedes, what happens? That sand that felt so solidly packed only a moment ago now flows right out from under your feet, and you have to dig in your toes to hold your balance. How like the solid structures of your life that can dissolve like the sand sometimes when your watery emotions take over.

Now, let's climb up on the rocks nearby and view the scene from a different perspective. Look down from the cliffs and see how the water flows into pools among the rocks. *See how the rocks contain the waters of emotion, of soul? At the same time, watch how those waters flow around the rocks, into every little crevice, reaching out for the earth to nurture the body of the Mother. The waters of feeling must be contained by the forms of earth—for it is by accepting responsibility for that which you have built that you will grow.*

Yet, too much containment, too much suppression can hold back the soul ... for a time. Did I ever promise that balance was easy to maintain? Eventually the water will wear away even the most solid rocks—and new forms and structures will be created. Such is the relationship of body and soul.

With the mystic vision of Pisces, I do charge you now to strive to balance the needs of body with nourishment for the soul. Temper duty and responsibility with compassion ... both for others, and for yourself. Allow time and space for reflection. Know that it is my special Piscean gift of inspiration and dreams that make all your work worthwhile! What say you to that, My Lord?

HP: *As always, Lady, you are my true complement and balance! But you are so mysterious and changeable ... soon only your waning crescent will be seen, and then the darkness, before you again return. Where shall our people find You when they seek inspiration?*

HPS: *Listen ... and I'll sing to you a mystery.*
Some say you'll find me in the bright Moon that shines to light this night.
And some say I am the cool breeze that lifts the birds in flight
And they say I am the ocean, the tides that ebb and flow
And they say I am the green Earth and the beauty of a rose.
I am called the soul of nature, the source of all there is
All return to me at dyin' and new life is mine to give
Yet you honor me with pleasure, in all acts of joy and love
As you gather in your circle, as the Full Moon shines above.
Let there be among you beauty, honor, strength, humility

*Reverence, power and compassion, mirth and joy and
spirit free
Now, where am I, where can you find me, you who truly
seek to know?
Stop your searchin' through the wide world and look deep
within your soul.
Yes, nowhere will you find me, if this you cannot see,
Behold, I am the truth within you that unveils the mystery.
And I have been with you always, for I am your love that
grows.
I am the seed that gives your spirit the beauty of a rose.*

Wiccaning

We repeated essentially this same Pisces Moon ritual in 1992, but
this time, at this point in the ritual, we did our very first Wiccaning
for a new baby boy that had been born just a few weeks before to a
couple in our circle. See the full Wiccaning ritual in Chapter 10.

Great Rite

Special Song for Passing of Cakes and Wine

*May you not hunger, may you not thirst
May you be rich in her bounty
May you be joyful, may you be free
In light and love, Blessed Be!*

Sharing

Farewells

*HP: Lovely Moon, Goddess fair
Womb of Earth and sea
We thank you for your presence, hail
Farewell and Blessed Be!*

*HPS: Mighty Sun, Consort, Horned One
Spirit bright and free
We thank you for your presence, hail
Farewell and Blessed Be!*

*East: From Eastern tower we send the Air
Go forth with winds so free*

Thank you for your presence here
Farewell and Blessed Be!

South: *From Southern tower we send the Fire*
Charged with vitality
Thank you for your presence here
Farewell and Blessed Be!

West: *From Western tower we send the Waters*
Lakes and pool and sea
Thank you for your presence here
Farewell and Blessed Be!

North: *From Northern tower we send the Earth*
In glad serenity
Thank you for your presence here
Farewell and Blessed Be!

Aries Full Moon

October 11, 1992

Astrological Polarity Concept: Libra (the Sun) is the diplomat and the mediator—favors harmony, balance, moderation, and fairness in all things. But he can also be the general who will lead the fight if the injustice is great enough. Aries (the Moon) is the warrior and the pioneer—favors action, initiative, and getting there first at all costs.

Preparation: Cauldron in center of circle, containing enough red candles for everyone, carving tools (toothpicks will do), pencils, and pieces of flash paper. Drum(s) will be needed for the chant.

Consecration

HPS: Once again the Moon is full, my brothers and sisters! A Hunter's Moon, sometimes called the Blood Moon, and we will call our Lady this night as the Warrior Goddess—Aries Full Moon—powerful, wild, and free. In this season, our Lord still holds the scales of Balance—yet the dark has begun to overtake the light. What then? What mystery may be revealed on this moonlit night? We gather to await our Lady and our Lord. I do conjure this to be a circle of excitement and anticipation, where we may seek the presence and the truths of the Mighty Ones. Out of time and space, between the worlds, protected by our silver sphere of light, by the power of the Threefold Goddess and her mighty Consort, I do bless and consecrate this circle of power. As it is willed, so mote it be.

Watchtowers

East: *I call to the Air, power of Mind*
New truth we hope to seek and find
Make clear our thoughts that we may share
With one and all, O power of Air!
Guardian of the Eastern sphere
Now we seek your presence here.
Come, East, come, be here this night.

South: *I call to the Fire, Spirit's power*
Send flames of faith from South's great tower
Swirl cones of energy brightly higher
Enhance our will, O power of fire!
Guardian of the Southern sphere
Now we seek your presence here.
Come, South, come, be here this night.

West: *I call to the Water, Soul's great power*
Send magickal tides from Western tower
Bathe us in love and feelings true
O power of Water, we call to you.
Guardian of the Western sphere
Now we seek your presence here.
Come, West, come, be here this night.

North: *I call to the Earth, our Body's power*
Send strength and will from North's great tower
Though winter's cold must come, we know
O power of Earth, still help us grow.
Guardian of the Northern sphere
Now we seek your presence here.
Come, North, come, be here this night.

Invocation of the God

HPS: I call the God, Great Stag of the forest, who in this season of waning light, becomes the Lord of Shadows. O Father of wisdom and maturity, your people seek your presence in this rite. Fill now the body of this thy priest and through him flow to touch the light of God within us all. As it is willed, so mote it be.

Charge of the God

HP: My people, the scales of Balance seem equal still, and harmony flows throughout this sacred place. Would that such beauty always surround us! Yet soon the darkness will become visible, and what will you do, if you, too, must face a darkness within your lives? You may need to seek a compromise, a point of balance between the light of what you desire and the darkness of denial. Yes, this is the preferred way of Balance, of moderation—and often, the way of love.

HPS: But what if the injustice is very great, my Lord? What if the darkness is harmful? What if all efforts at diplomacy fail?

HP: Then the time may come, Lady, when you must fight—if only to restore harmony. [to the group] For though I am the peacemaker, who seeks to relate in harmony, be you all well aware that no relationship can be balanced when one must suppress the Truth that is within. I call to my other half, who is my complement and balance.

Invocation of the Goddess

HP: I call the Warrior Goddess, Threefold Lady of Wisdom—come to us this night and inflame your people with your power. O Lady of life and vitality, your people seek your presence in this rite. Fill now the body of this thy priestess and through her flow to touch the light of Goddess within us all. As it is willed, so mote it be.

HPS: My Lord, you have called me from the Blood Moon—full with the power and flow of life I shine, ready to go forth and fight as I am needed, that our people might live and relate to each other in freedom, truth, and joy.

Charge of the Goddess

HPS [to the group]: You have heard our Lord speak wisely, my people. Truly do we all wish to live in peace and harmony, to love and be loved. Six Moons ago, when we gathered, I stood where he now stands and taught you of the art of compromise. Now I am here to tell you what deep inside you already know—on some issues there can be no compromise! In many areas of your life you can honor the desires of others and still remain true to your- self—but on some things you must not give in to the will of others, for to do so would stifle your very spirit, quench its flame, and with it, the vitality of your being. A life lived in denial of your own inner Truth is no life at all.

Does this strike a chord for any of you? If, in any part of your life, you are anxious, repressed—holding back out of fear, you may be denying a part of yourself that needs to be expressed, that needs to be more assertive. Tonight we shall work on building your inner power to recognize your own Truth, to stand up for it, and if necessary, to fight for your right to express it.

In my cauldron are red candles and pieces of paper, with carving tools and pencils. Carve the symbols of your Truth on your candle, and as you do you will begin to realize what you must do to express it. Write what you must do on the paper. Put the paper in the cauldron, and we will pass among you to collect the tools and offer you oil of the Aries warrior to anoint your candle. Until next we meet I bid you burn it a few moments every day, that you may strengthen your resolve to express the all-impor- tant inner Truth which it symbolizes.

Traditions of our culture have long taught that the fem- inine aspect is one of compromise and submission. Not tonight! Now, let us build the cone of power to charge our intents by calling upon the Goddess within to stand with her Mighty Consort as Warrior.

Dance around cauldron to drumbeat. Chant (music, page 384):

Isis, Astarte, Diana, Hecate, Demeter, Kali, Inanna ...

At the height of energy, burn the papers in the cauldron.

Great Rite

Sharing

Farewells

> **HP:** *My Warrior Queen, we do thank you for the power and energy you bring to our circle and to our lives. Hail, farewell and Blessed Be.*
>
> **HPS:** *My compassionate Lord of peace and justice, we do thank you for the wise perspective you bring to our circle and to our lives. Hail, farewell and Blessed Be.*
>
> **East:** *For clarity of communication that leads to truth, O power of Air, we do thank you, and bid you hail, farewell and Blessed Be.*
>
> **South:** *For energized faith that enflames our will, O power of Fire, we do thank you, and bid you hail, farewell and Blessed Be.*
>
> **West:** *For mystical love that feeds our Souls, O power of Water, we do thank you, and bid you hail, farewell and Blessed Be.*
>
> **North:** *For strength and growth of purpose, O power of Earth, we do thank you, and bid you hail, farewell and Blessed Be.*

October 23, 1991

Bonus Ritual: This one differs from the usual polarity concept of complementary opposite signs. The actual Full Moon Lunation, was, of course, with Sun in Libra and Moon in Aries, but in the 29th degree on the morning of the day we held the ritual. By the time we met, the Sun had moved into Scorpio (and of course, the Moon into Taurus), but the Lunation (which has symbolism for the two week period after its occurrence) was nevertheless in Aries. At this time we knew that a few people within our group had been dealing with various issues, so we decided to use the Aries lunation/Sun in Scorpio symbolism to offer some insight.

Astrological Polarity Concept: Scorpio (the Sun) is a water sign (emotion), but very strong, powerful, and fixed. His is the seasonal sign of the Dark Lord. Aries (the Moon) is fiery, initiating, impatient, impulsive, and "me first"—also a very strong sign. Obviously there will be a challenge here, to see whether he "puts her out" or she sets him "steaming."

Preparation: In the cauldron, on the altar, were cords about eight inches in length, in the colors of the four elements, enough so that if nearly everyone chose the same color, we wouldn't run out. For music during casting of the circle and behind the Consecration we played "Totem," a tape of emphatic and sensual drum rhythms.

Consecration

> *HPS: Feel the passion? The energy? The Sun has this day entered the realm of Scorpio—of deep, dark waters, of surging waves, of liquid, molten fire! Yet the Full Moon lunation, that defines the nature of this time occurred in Aries—forceful, charging, fiery bright. Two strong elemental forces—water and fire—challenging, conflicting, yet brought to balance in the mystery of this night.*
>
> *I do conjure this to be a circle of power, of brilliant energy and fiery light. Let it be surrounded and protected by the power of our love and the intensity of our vision. Within the sacred place, out of time and space, may we receive the courage to face also the darkness and transform it into the power to change. Let us join our hands and hearts together to form a cauldron of spirit, that shall preserve and contain the energy that we shall raise within. And so I do call upon the energies of the Universe to bless this circle, in all the names of the Goddess and the God. As it is willed, so mote it be.*

Watchtowers

> *East: To the Watchtower of the East I call forth the Air, power of mind. Increase the focus and projection of our*

thoughts. Bring understanding of the winds of change that always blow. Guardian of the Eastern sphere, now we seek your presence here. Come, East, come. Be here this night.

South: *To the Watchtower of the South I call forth the Fire, power of spirit. With passion we greet you! Charge forth with vitality. Bring us inspiration! Guardian of the Southern sphere, now we seek your presence here. Come, South, come. Be here this night.*

West: *To the Watchtower of the West I call forth the Water, power of soul. Secretive, deep, mysterious wisdom that lies deep beneath our consciousness, reveal your power! Guardian of the Western sphere, now we seek your presence here. Come, West, come. Be here this night!*

North: *To the Watchtower of the North I call forth the Earth, power of body. Ground us with strength and stability. Fortify our inner security Guardian of the Northern sphere, now we seek your presence here. Come, North, come. Be here this night!*

Invocation of the God

HPS: *I call the God, fiery energy of Life, Lord of Day who in this season becomes the Lord of Shadows. Come forth through the depths of night. We seek thy vitality, thy energy. Fill now the body of this thy priest and through him touch the God within us all.*

HP: *You've called me from my rest and solitude? On the night of the Full Moon? When it's her job to talk to you? This had better be good.*

Invocation of the Goddess

HP: *Lady Moon, you have seen fit to inspire our people to gather. They call for energy, for courage and wisdom to change. Come forth—this is your night. Fill now the body of this thy priestess and through her touch the Goddess within us all.*

Charge

HPS [with spirit]: Greetings, my Lord. It's about time you called me. It was all I could do to restrain myself from getting here first. Tradition! What a drag. Well, let's get some action into this gathering.

HP: Hold on a minute. You are far too rash, always jumping into things before you've probed the possible consequences.

HPS: You're always holding me back. You don't even ask what I've got planned. Trust me! If I waited for you to get things started ...

HP: Selfish witch!

HPS: Compulsive stick-in-the-mud!

HP [pause ... change tone]: Wait a minute ...

HPS [pause]: What are we doing ... [embrace]

HP: Please understand that I get pretty steamed when you burn so brightly. I need to feel my own way before I act. Give me time to understand you.

HPS: And I want to understand you, too, but sometimes my fiery spirit feels completely doused when you try to slow me down.

HP: Well, I'll admit that sometimes you've led me into a new adventure that I might not have tried without you.

HPS: And many of my bright ideas might have fizzled if not for your strong will and persistence to carry them through to completion.

HP: So it seems that our powers both conflict and support. What does this mean for our people? It's your lead, on this night of Full Moon, my Lady.

HPS: Know you that all forms of power dwell within each of you and your challenge is to discover the wisdom and the balance to use each of them as needed, and yet to bring no intent of harm or infringement upon the free will of another. This night you have seen the interaction of fire and water—confrontation handled both destructively and constructively and then balanced. Tonight our work will be the balance of the elements within—the fire and the water, and also the air, power of mind, of logic or of rationalization, of communication or of misunderstanding, of refreshing breezes or of raging storms, and the earth—power of body, of stability or of shifting sands, of security or of domination, of green growth or of parched desert. Within my cauldron you will find cord in the colors of the four elements, the red of fire, the blue of water, the yellow of air, the green of earth. Choose those which you feel you most need to bring into balance in your life at this time. Look carefully into your inner self. Choose not that which you have in overabundance; instead, choose what you lack. Hold the cords and firmly visualize what you need. Approach the altar deocil and pass your cords through the elements and the flames of Lord and Lady that your intent may be charged with the energy of this circle. As you return to your place within the circle, build your emotion within and when you feel it peak, tie a knot into the cord. Pull it tightly, binding your intent into your life and releasing the energy to do your will. Know that the power is not in the cord, it is in your own intent that has been released into spirit that it may manifest. Keep the cord as a reminder of that which you have willed.

Acknowledgment of HP; Presentation of Staff

This was the Moon at which Mark, who had recently completed Third Degree with Circle Atheneum, was formally designated by me as High Priest of Circle of the Cosmic Muse, and presented with custody of our Circle Staff as a symbol of office.

Great Rite

Sharing

Farewells

HP: Bright Lady, tonight you have shown a new facet of your own nature and of ours, inspiring all with the courage to look within and change what must be changed. We thank you. Hail, farewell and Blessed Be.

HPS: My strong and most supportive Lord, as always your presence provides true balance to the Goddess within. We do thank you for being with us and bid you hail, farewell and Blessed Be.

East: O element of Air, Guardian of the East, for your aid to clear thinking, we thank you. Hail, farewell and Blessed Be.

South: O element of Fire, Guardian of the South, for vitality of spirit, we thank you. Hail, farewell and Blessed Be.

West: O element of Water, Guardian of the West, for depth of inner knowing, we thank you. Hail, farewell and Blessed Be.

North: O element of Earth, Guardian of the North, for strength and inner security, we thank you. Hail, farewell and Blessed Be.

Taurus Full Moon

November 20, 1991

Astrological Polarity Concept: Scorpio (the Sun) is passionately and deeply involved in whatever he is doing. He can be quite compulsive about it, in fact. He is a skeptic, not at all afraid to look at the dark side, but is sometimes too intense. Taurus (the Moon) is persistent and intense, too, in her way. She gets things done, but above all, she wants to be comfortable and secure, and she prefers to see only the best side of life.

Preparation: No special tools were needed for this ritual.

Consecration

HPS: The Full Moon this night illuminates the season of darkness. Our Lord has gone into the invisible world, the days grow short, the nights are long. Yet we do not rest, like our wise Earth Mother rests between the seasons of harvest and planting. We seem caught up in more activities each day, as our businesses, our families, our entire culture prepares for holidays to come. Signs of stress are all around us. What wisdom can our Lady bring to us this night? We look forward to her presence. I do conjure this to be a circle of power and of love, a sacred space between the worlds, out of time and space, where we may pause from our busy lives to reflect and to communicate with each other and with the realm of the mighty ones, that we might gain a new perspective and a further glimpse of Truth. Protected may we be, within this sphere of light, surrounded by the presence of our gracious Goddess and her mighty Consort. In all their many names, do I bless and consecrate this circle. As it is willed, so mote it be.

Watchtowers

East: We call to the East, O power of Air
Clear our thoughts, and help us see
How as we gather here to share
We gain the truth that sets us free.
Guardian of the Eastern sphere
Now we seek your presence here.
Come, East, come, be here this night.

South: We call to the South, O power of Fire
Enflame our spirits, help us see
That as each other we inspire
We grow in strength and energy.
Guardian of the Southern sphere
Now we seek your presence here.
Come, South, come, be here this night.

West: We call to the West, O Watery power
Emotions flow like the tides of sea
Show us in this sacred hour
The magic of your mystery.
Guardian of the Western sphere
Now we seek your presence here.
Come, West, come, be here this night.

North: We call to the North, O power of Earth
Bring us strength and help us know

The endless cycle, death to birth
Plant seeds within that we may grow.
Guardian of the Northern sphere
Now we seek your presence here.
Come, North, come, be here this night.

Invocation of the God

HPS: *I call to the Lord of Day—in this season, Lord of Shadows. Return from your realm in the Summerland, O Father of Life. Your people gather, in need of your strength and energy. Return, Great Stag, send your vibrant presence through this your servant and priest, that through him the light of God be shared by all.*

Invocation of the Goddess

HP: *I call to my Lady Moon, gracious Goddess, Mother of Life. Your people gather, in need of your compassion and wisdom. Come, my love, infuse this your servant and priestess with all your nurturing power, that through her the light of Goddess be shared by all.*

Charge

HP: *I greet you, my Lady, and all who gather here, though I am reluctant to remain here long, for much work is yet to be done within my realm, my concerns are deep.*

HPS: *I welcome you, my Lord. Too long is this season without you by my side. Surely you can enjoy this peaceful interlude with us for an evening?*

HP: *How can you speak of enjoyment? Your realm, too, is full of concerns, of tension, of people suffering. How can anyone think of rest with so much to be done?*

HPS: *So intensely you speak, my Lord. And how gallantly you lead me into the lesson of balance for this season. [moves around to massage his shoulders and back] What do you gain, my people, from so much worry and stress over things that are yet undone? Yes, we must build and do what we must do, yet how well can you do any of these*

things if you allow no time for your own comfort? I come
to you this night from the memories of springtime, and bid
you take a break to rest and "smell the roses."

Come, sit around the circle facing deocil, and each one
of you reach out and stroke the shoulders and back of
your sister or brother in front of you, just as I am soothing
our Lord from the tensions and concerns he has expressed.
See, doesn't it feel wonderful?[5]

At this point the group could continue for a while, with soft meditation music in the background and perhaps a guided meditation. For
this particular ritual, since several had asked to hear the "Rose
Charge" again, I got my autoharp and sang it softly to them, while
they massaged each others' backs. Then everyone relaxed, continuing to sit in the circle, and we all sang it together with the alternate
words for singing about the Goddess (see Chapter 11). They stayed
seated, as we quietly continued with the Great Rite, blessing and
sharing. A main purpose of this ritual had been accomplished—
everyone had a peaceful break and felt restored.

Great Rite

Sharing

Farewells

HP: Thank you, gracious Lady, for the peace and comfort
you have brought tonight, and for the wisdom contained
within your serenity. Until we meet again, we bid you hail,
farewell and Blessed Be.

HPS: Thank you, my wise and mighty Lord, for bringing
us your light from beyond the shadowy veil. We are
strengthened by your presence. Until we meet again, we
bid you hail, farewell and Blessed Be.

East: O Guardian of Air, from the Eastern tower
We thank you for your magic power.
Till your light again we see
Hail, farewell and Blessed Be.

South: O Guardian of Fire, from the Southern tower
We thank you for your magic power.

Till your light again we see
Hail, farewell and Blessed Be.

West: *O Guardian of Water, from the Western tower*
We thank you for your magic power.
Till your light again we see
Hail, farewell and Blessed Be.

North: *O Guardian of Earth, from the Northern tower*
We thank you for your magic power.
Till your light again we see
Hail, farewell and Blessed Be.

Gemini Full Moon

December 9, 1992

Astrological Polarity Concept: Sagittarius (the Sun) is inspired and enthusiastic, a seeker of knowledge, but inclined to take a leap of faith without checking all the facts. Gemini (the Moon) is also a seeker of knowledge, curious and bright, but she wants to know why, where, and how, and is not satisfied without a rational explanation.

Preparation: No special tools are needed.

Consecration

> *HPS: How quickly moves this season. The days go by so fast we hardly know which way to turn. All around us we see energies that are scattered, and yet at the same time sharply focused toward the year's end holidays that are soon to come. Our Lord the Sun is in Sagittarius, sign of the revelation and faith that originated the flurry of activities that we see—a faith that knows the entire Truth! Tonight our Lady shines opposite—Full Moon in Gemini—with, as always, a different point of view! I do conjure this to be a circle of inspiration, a protected haven of friendship and love, where we may seek the truth in openness and in fun. Let us link our hands together in this crystal sphere between the worlds, as we share with each other, for the illumination and growth of all. In all the many names of*

our gracious Lady and her Consort, I do bless and conse-crate this circle. As it is willed, so mote it be.

Watchtowers

East: *O East, come quickly on winds of Air*
Your mental power we seek to share
Guardian of the Eastern sphere
Now we seek your presence here.
Come, East, come, be here this rite.

South: *O South, charge forth with flames so bright*
Your vital spirit lights the night
Guardian of the Southern sphere
Now we seek your presence here.
Come, South, come, be here this rite.

West: *O West, tides swell with mystic power*
Waves of love flow 'round your tower
Guardian of the Western sphere
Now we seek your presence here.
Come, West, come, be here this rite.

North: *O North, strong Earth, in you we see*
Abundance, growth, security
Guardian of the Northern sphere
Now we seek your presence here.
Come, North, come, be here this night.

Invocation of the God

HPS: *I call the God, eternal Father, energy of life. We ask your mighty presence within our rite. Fill the body of this your servant and priest and through him touch the God within us all.*

Invocation of the Goddess

HP: *I call the Goddess, eternal Mother, source of life. We ask your mighty presence within our rite. Fill the body of this your servant and priestess and through her touch the Goddess within us all.*

Charge

> HP: *My children, you gather here to seek the ultimate Truth. How fortunate you are that I know it all, and am here to tell you!*
>
> HPS: *Whoa! All? Are you sure?*
>
> HP: *Well, I AM God!*
>
> HPS: *Good point. [laughs] My Lord, how gallantly you play our game and allow me to provide both opposition and balance. But even if in our Oneness, we do have it all, is it right for us to just **tell** these seekers? Will we not spoil the fun if we give them all the answers? Would you who are wild and free bind them from the freedom of seeking their own Truth?*
>
> HP: *So logically and reasonably you speak, my Lady. So be it. How, then, shall we play our game this night?*
>
> HPS: *I think we should take a break from all the busy-ness of this month. Let's relax on the floor and tell ourselves a story. Let's not plan where we'll go. We'll just put thoughts out at random, explore, be creative, ask questions, and see where our minds take us. Everyone lie down on the floor with your head in the center of the circle. East, start a story, and then let's go around the circle, each one adding to what was said before. No rules. You are free. Be as logical or as fantastic as you like—or just say the first thing that pops into your head in response to what was said before you. Who knows? Maybe we'll discover a new twist on our Truth—and maybe not. But even if we don't, we can still have fun—and maybe that's a Truth in itself!*[6]

HPs should let the story continue, till it reaches a resolution point, or the energy peaks—but before it wanes—then call a halt, have everyone sit up, and ask for words of wisdom gained from the experience. You might have to offer a "wind up" yourself, but with most groups, someone or several someones will do it for you. Remember, sometimes even "unwisdom" is "wisdom"—the point is free-thinking exploration of ideas.

Great Rite

Sharing

Farewells

> **HP:** *Beloved Lady, again you have blessed us with your wisdom and your love. Thank you for inspiring our rite. Until once again we call, we bid you hail, farewell and Blessed Be.*

> **HPS:** *Beloved Lord, again you have blessed us with your wisdom and your love. Thank you for inspiring our rite. Until once again we call, we bid you hail, farewell and Blessed Be.*

> **East:** *O East, our thanks for winds of Air*
> *And mental power all could share.*
> *Till once again your light we see*
> *Hail, farewell and Blessed Be.*

> **South:** *O South, our thanks for flames so bright*
> *Your vital spirit sparked our rite.*
> *Till once again your light we see*
> *Hail, farewell and Blessed Be.*

> **West:** *O West, our thanks for mystic sight*
> *And waves of love we felt tonight.*
> *Till once again your light we see*
> *Hail, farewell and Blessed Be.*

> **North:** *O North, our thanks for strength of Earth*
> *Abundance, growth, and sense of worth.*
> *Till once again your light we see*
> *Hail, farewell and Blessed Be.*

Endnotes

1. Farrar, Stewart and Janet. *Eight Sabbats for Witches*. Custer, WA: Phoenix Publishing, Inc., 1981.

    Guiley, Rosemary Ellen. *The Encyclopedia of Witches and Witchcraft*. New York: Facts on File, Inc., 1989.

3. The basic concept for this working is an adaptation of Wiccan philosophy of Young Self and the formulation of magickal intent, combined with the methods of a workshop I attended back in the early 80s called DMA, or Dimensional Macrostructural Alignment.

4. The idea for the working for this ritual was adapted from a ritual described in the "Introduction" of Diane Stein's *The Women's Spirituality Book*, St. Paul, MN: Llewellyn Publications, 1987.

5. This idea came from Maritha Pottenger's *Encounter Astrology*, Los Angeles: TIA Publications, 1978.

6. A group-talk exercise suggested in Barbara Schermer's *Astrology Alive!*, Wellingborough, England: The Aquarian Press, 1989, triggered my idea for this working.

Special Rituals

This group of rituals celebrates the special occasions and life passages that are part of every family and community, and a few of the ceremonies that are specific to the Wiccan religion.

Dedication

When a new seeker comes into my circle, or into any of the other circles with which I am affiliated, s/he is offered the opportunity to formalize certain steps along the path of the Craft, if s/he so desires. The first of those steps is Dedication. In taking this step, the candidate is not making a commitment to the circle itself, but rather s/he is making a formal pledge to the Goddess and the God of his/her choice to follow the path and learn the ways of the Craft. The purpose of the Rite is to call the attention of Goddess and God to the individual and specifically to her/his desire to enter the Craft.

Before a candidate is Dedicated, we require several questions to be answered in writing. The questions are not ones that have "textbook" answers. They require thought. What the HPs are looking for is evidence that the seeker has given serious thought to what s/he is doing. We want to know how s/he perceives the ethics of Craft, and if s/he understands the potential consequences of the path. (Our questions for Dedication and for the degrees are in Chapter 11.)

A copy of the ritual of Dedication is always given to the Dedicate at the same time as the questions are given. Before the candidate decides to make this promise to the Lady and her Consort, it is important that the candidate read and understand exactly what s/he will be asked to promise.

By the time a candidate asks to Dedicate, s/he has probably attended several of our rituals and/or classes, and we have come to know him/her fairly well. The written answers help give both candidate and HPs the opportunity to clarify the candidate's thinking, and provide a focus for discussion, if the candidate's answers indicate an incompatibility with ethical values or a lack of clear understanding of basic concepts.

This ritual is normally done within a regular Full Moon ritual, and you will have noticed in reading the Moon ritual chapter that some of them indicated that a Dedication had taken place, between the Charge and the Great Rite.

It is not necessary that a Dedication be performed at Full Moon, however. It could be done at a Sabbat, or at another time separate from either Full Moon or Sabbat. All that is required to perform the Dedication is a candle. The lunar phase is not of essential significance, but waxing is considered preferable to waning.

When a male candidate arrives to be Dedicated, he has a few moments of private talk with the High Priestess. A female candidate will have her private talk with the High Priest. This allows for clarification of any last questions that might remain. The Dedicate is given a white candle to anoint and bring into the ritual. Once the candle is lighted, it should be left to burn out completely, symbolizing that once the candidate is Dedicated s/he will live out this lifetime in the Dedicated state.

We have a booklet with the ritual printed in it, so that the candidate can read from it during the ritual. Some people prefer to try to memorize their part, but a new candidate tends to be a little nervous, so it is best to give them a booklet, anyway, to be used if need be. This ritual comes from Circle Atheneum, who received it from their mother circle, Circle of the Soaring Spirit. It is apparently a generally known traditional one. Later, I found it published in a compilation of rituals edited by Herman Slater, called *A Book of Pagan Rituals*.[1]

The Dedication Ritual

The candidate is asked to kneel at the altar (provide a pillow!). The HP or HPS of the opposite sex of the candidate says the parts marked HP/S.

> *HP/S: Do you wish to be Dedicated to the Goddess and the God of the Craft, that you may learn of them, and that you may join the Craft of the Wise when you are ready?*

> *Candidate: I do. Blessed be my eyes that have seen this day ...*

> *HP/S: Blessed be thine eyes.*

> *Candidate: Blessed be my ears that hear Thy voice ...*

> *HP/S: Blessed be thine ears.*

> *Candidate: Blessed be my mouth that it may speak of Thy blessings ...*

> *HP/S: Blessed be thy mouth.*

> *Candidate: Blessed be my feet that have led me in these ways ...*

> *HP/S: Blessed be thy feet.*

> *Candidate [lights the candle]: O Mother of all creatures and all living things, O Father of the woodlands, will you teach this seeker that I may learn of Thee and become wise in the love of the Gods, strong in the aid of humanity, learned in Thy arts and skillful in Thy ways?*

> *HP: Beloved (name), do you pledge yourself to the Goddess, to love Her, and to the Horned God, to honor Him?*

> *Candidate: Gladly do I pledge myself to the Goddess, to love Her, and to the Horned God, to honor Him.*

> *HPS: Beloved, do you pledge yourself to keep silent of what you shall learn, and to respect that which is taught you?*

Candidate: With honor do I pledge to keep silent of what I shall learn and to respect that which is taught me.

HP: Then hear the charge of the Great Mother, called by all names of power among men, before whose altars all the world has approached in reverence:

HPS: I am the eternal Goddess. Yet I demand no sacrifice, rather I give to those who honor Me. Yet I charge you that if you would be Mine and follow in my ways you shall gather yourselves, once at each Full Moon and give worship to Me, your Queen. Each of you must recognize Me and look at Me, lest you forget from Whom you come and to Whom you are called. If you would be Mine you must honor My charge, for those things which I have made law may be dissolved by no one.

(Name), shall you obey this charge?

Candidate: Gladly shall I obey the charge of the Goddess. I pledge myself to the Goddess, to love Her, and to the Horned God, to honor Him, to keep silent of what I shall learn and to respect that which is taught me.

HP: Then you shall be taught to be wise, that in the fullness of time you shall count yourself among those who serve the Gods, among those who belong to the Craft. Let thy life, and the life to come, be in the service of our noble Lady.

Candidate: Blessed be this time that marks my life, that I shall ever after be a child of the Gods, that I shall learn of them and embrace them as my own.

HP/S makes the sign of the pentacle in blessing the candidate and says:

May the blessing of our gracious Lady and of Her hearty consort go ever with thee.

The Dedicate arises and is kissed and congratulated by High Priestess and High Priest and is then passed deocil around the circle for the congratulations of all. The white candle is left to burn all the way down. (We move it to the fireplace, behind the fire screen, because a taper usually burns all night. Use a metal candleholder. Candles burning all the way down can crack a glass holder.)

Spinning Off to Form a New Circle

Our spin-off ceremony for Terra was conducted in a similar way to my own spin-off from Circle Atheneum. (The idea of "cutting the cord" was devised by Lady Beckett.) In both cases, the ritual acknowledged a passage to High Priestess. No High Priest was designated. The ritual for Terra took place during our 1992 Autumn Equinox ritual, right after the Great Rite. My own spin-off was during a Spring Equinox. It is customary among the circles in our area to hold spin-offs during some Sabbat ritual. That particular Sabbat then becomes the official "birthday" of the new circle, and is celebrated as such in the years to come.

Spin-off Ritual for Terra
(Autumn Equinox 1992)

> *HPS: A very special working must yet be done this rite. I call to the Crone! Grandmother, is my daughter prepared?*
>
> *Crone: She has been challenged and has answered the challenge. She has been taught, and yet she knows how much more there is to learn. She has been guided and has learned how important are guardians and teachers along the path. She has looked into her heart and knows her need and fulfillment. She is ready for that which she seeks to do.*
>
> *HPS [gives Terra one end of a green cord]: I place within your hand this green cord. At other times there have been other cords. Each one marking a change in your life—each one an indication of your growth in the Craft.*
>
> *From your first steps in the Craft, we have come closer and closer together. As a child of the Craft you studied and learned, and then reached out into the larger world. We have watched and nurtured you safely within the embrace of this circle, but now the time has come for you to begin your next steps on the path you have chosen.*

Terra and I are each holding one end of the cord. We begin to circle, each on opposite sides of the altar, holding the cord over the center. I continue to speak extemporaneously of personal memories specific to our relationship ... the cord becomes more taunt as the circle being walked gradually grows.

> *As we now move in this spiral dance, you will perhaps at first stay close, but gradually will spiral farther out and away as you become more involved with the new seekers that will come to you ... and that is well ... yet know that even though a continent or an ocean may lie between us, this cord is never truly severed, for always it will link us together in our souls.*

At this point my High Priest cut the taunt cord in the center with the boline, and then I said:

> *I now do name thee Lady Terra!*

> **HP** [*crowns Terra with crescent crown*]: *With all of the joy and promise of the Maiden you have so beautifully been for our circle, I now crown you with this circlet of your new rank as High Priestess, and give you our blessings also to your own circle of potential and dreams. May you dance among the stars and weave magic from their light.*

> **Crone** [*gives Terra Book of Shadows*]: *This gift is a tie of the past to the future. It is the Book of Shadows of the Circle of the Cosmic Muse. Guard it well. It contains the rituals our entire circle has shared, but also a few things that are for you alone, to share only with a High Priest or Crone whom you might one day choose to share your work, or with a new High Priestess who may one day emerge from your circle.*

Then, Lady Terra, the new High Priestess made a somewhat unexpected presentation of her own! These are her words:

> *Great Lady of Earth, Sea, Fire, and Sky, I beseech you to hear my words at this time. Your daughter, Lady Mari, has provided great gifts to me upon my path to you. She has been the cool intellect that informs my conscience, the bright beacon that lights the nights of my wanderings, the*

refreshing waves that cleanse my soul, and the firm rock of wisdom upon which my knowledge stands. But most of all, and most importantly, she has guided me on my path to you, my Lady.

In the tradition of the Old Religion, the High Priestess was honored with a black garter to signify her sagacity and esteem in our eyes. However, the Circle of the Cosmic Muse and Circle Atheneum, the parent circle, have brought forth so many new traditions that you, my great Lady, have inspired. So too, have you inspired a new way of honoring those who have guided my footsteps.

Lady Mari, sweet soul of the great oceans, Mer-mother of us all, I request that I might honor you with this gift. It is a cord, woven with love, spun with the energies of the Maiden's white of purity, the Mother's red of passion, and the Crone's black of wisdom and protection.

Ah, but how can we forget my Lord standing beside you? So too, have the colors of the Lord been woven next to yours, for balance and the blending of polarity into the great Unity of the One which you, my Lady, have taught us. So blending and braiding with yours are the green of the young Lord, the Green Man of growing things, the yellow of the Sun King, the Bright Lord at his peak, and the brown of the Dark Lord, Herne the Hunter, as he chases down the Great Stag.

Upon this cord of Lady and Lord, you will find a token, symbolizing the Goddess Mari, Queen of the Sea and the Stars. Lady Mari, will you accept this gift, as a token of my love for you, and in remembrance of our bond? [my gift is a little silver Goddess dancing in waves poured from a starry urn]

Great Lady, Mother of all realms, just as we cannot forget your mighty consort, the Lord of all things, neither can we forget your servant, Lord Willow. His has been the bright insight that clears my mind, the flame of hope that leads me forward, the waters of passion that inspire my desires, and the amber grain bowing in waves to honor the wind, steadfastly nourishing my soul.

> *So too, I present Lord Willow with a cord, weaving the love of Lord and Lady, and with a token of my love and honor for him. Lord Willow, will you accept this gift as a token of my love for you and in remembrance of our bond? [Willow's gift was a miniature silver wolf]*
>
> *And finally, to honor the spirit of our past, our noble ancestry on this path, I would like to acknowledge the wise guiding hands of our elders, whose presence was always felt and appreciated. Just as the owl gave birth to the mermaid, so the mermaid has given birth to another sea-child. Lady Beckett, will you accept this gift as a token of my love for you and in remembrance of our bond? [Lady Beckett received a little silver sand dollar, with its natural pentagram]*
>
> *And my Lady, if I might make one more offering, I would like to give a gift to my sister Greraven, whose loving nurturance has provided wisdom and strength along my path to you.*
>
> *Greraven, will you accept this gift as a token of my love for you and in remembrance of our bond? [Greraven was given a tiny silver pentagram]*

At the close of a Spin-off Ritual the new High Priestess is acknowledged by the entire group by walking the circle three times to applause. On the second time around she takes the hand of her High Priest (if she has one) and brings him around with her, and on the third time around, any of the members of the new circle who are present join hands with their HPs and follow along.

Spin-off for a High Priest or for Working Partners

Atheneum's first spin-off High Priest was Mark. Since he was leaving Atheneum to become my High Priest, the following ceremony was for him alone, during the Spring Equinox ritual that we shared with Circle Atheneum on the occasion of the first "birthday" of Circle of the Cosmic Muse. Since then, all of Atheneum's spin-offs have been for couples. In those cases, the ceremony for the daughter was given first (in much the same manner as the ritual above for Terra). After the cord was cut and the new High Priestess acknowledged, Lord

Landerthorn called her designated High Priest forward and continued as is given below:

> **HP:** *In the days of old, when the daughter left the family
> or tribe there was given a dowry and lavish gifts. When a
> young warrior left the tribe he was expected to make it on
> his own and received very little. At most he kept his skills
> and his weapons.*
>
> *You, (name), have begun a new journey, and with your
> lady have begun a new circle. And so as in the times of old
> I now gift you with this knife. [Landerthorn's hobby is
> metal work, and he is very skilled. He makes the blue han-
> dled knives that he presents to his new High Priests] It is
> the symbol of the guardian. With your new responsibilities
> you will be a warrior alone no longer. With your own cir-
> cle you now become a guardian—for not only do you pro-
> tect yourself, you will protect your lady and the children
> of the circle.*
>
> *As your lady forms the circle each of the cardinal points
> is formed with a green pentagram. But the line that con-
> nects those points—the walls and protective boundary of
> the circle are of blue light. And so—as her cord is green,
> yours is blue. [HP then adds extemporaneous words spe-
> cific to the relationship]*

A token is presented by the new High Priest to the initiating High
Priest.

At this point, in Atheneum custom, the HPs of the sister circles are
called forward to gift the new HPs with a few personal words of
experience and encouragement, and a item to be used in the new circle's rituals. At Terra's spin-off, the "grandparents," Lady Beckett
and Lord Landerthorn, were also present and came forward to gift
Lady Terra.

Spin-off Tokens and Gifts

Our adjustable-size crowns with crescent Moon at center, that I gave
Lady Terra and expect to give to future daughter High Priestesses,
were purchased from Abyss, a phone/mail order distribution business in Massachusetts.[2]

Since our Book of Shadows is a "disk of shadows" (Macintosh), it was a relatively easy task to print out our rituals, recipes, etc. We bound the pages with black cover stock and stamped a silver pentagram on the front cover.

Presentation from New High Priestess to Initiating High Priestess

It is an old tradition in the Craft, mentioned in a number of books, for a High Priestess, who has had new circles hive off from hers, to wear a black garter, on which is a silver buckle for each new circle. Three buckles and she is designated "Witch Queen." At my spin-off ritual from Circle Atheneum, since I was the first, I presented a black lace garter to Lady Beckett, on which was sewn a small dragon as the "buckle" (dragons are a special symbol for her). The only problem with garters is that they don't show very easily when one is robed. Lady Aanja of The Circle of the Wildewood, Atheneum's second spin-off, improved the idea by creating a long black ribbon tie that could be pinned to the front of Lady Beckett's robe or worn on her cord belt, thus providing a place to display each of the tokens given by the daughters.

Lady Beckett received her third little dragon token Midsummer 1992, from Lady Joy-of-Heart, who had formed Circle of the Fates. This Midsummer, which was Atheneum's fifth birthday Sabbat, was a joint celebration with all three daughter circles and Atheneum's mother circle, as well. Following the spin-off, Lady Olwen-Vivianne and Lord Hephaestus of Circle of the Soaring Spirit came forward to proclaim Lady Beckett "Witch Queen." Since then, Lady Shelayne and Lord Oberon became Atheneum's fourth spin-off at Yule 1992, forming Amber Grove, and two more spin-offs are planned.

As you have read, within the spin-off for Terra, Lady Terra devised a new "tradition" of her own, in presenting my High Priest and I each with her lovely woven ribbons, designed to hold our daughter circle tokens.

Presentation from New High Priest to Initiating High Priest

No time-honored tradition apparently exists for a High Priest that is equivalent to the High Priestess' black garter. In hindsight, after

Atheneum's first two spin-offs, Mark (Lord Willow) and Lord Falkan (of The Circle of the Wildewood) decided that there ought to be a tradition, so Mark carved an oak staff for Lord Landerthorn, and mounted an owl token on top (the owl is Atheneum's emblem). This was presented to Lord Landerthorn at that '92 Midsummer, along with tokens from Lord Falkan and from Lord Brujo of the new Circle of the Fates. These tokens, and now a fourth, from Lord Oberon, have all been mounted on the staff.

Wiccaning

The Wiccaning ritual is for the purpose of naming and blessing a child. It can be incorporated into a Moon ritual, and in that case, the ritual given below would come immediately after the Great Rite. Or a special circle could take place just for the Wiccaning. In that case, the standard format could be followed (casting the circle, consecration, calling Watchtowers, etc.). The ritual as given below would proceed after the invocations.

This following ceremony took place during our September 11, 1992 Full Moon ritual. The ritual honored a newborn baby boy, and I've used the male pronouns and the names used then so that the reading of it will flow more smoothly than if it was peppered with "he or she" notations. The ritual format and wording is nearly identically patterned after that of Circle Atheneum, and Lady Beckett constructed Atheneum's ritual by starting with ideas from the Wiccaning in *Eight Sabbats for Witches* by Stewart and Janet Farrar.[3]

The Wiccaning Ritual
(Pisces Full Moon 1992)

> *HPS: We are gathered in our circle to ask the blessing of the gracious Goddess and the mighty God on Damien Malachi, the son of Dara and Sar, so that he may grow in beauty and strength, in joy and wisdom.*
>
> *There are many paths, and each must find their own: therefore we do not seek to bind Damien to any one path while he is still too young to choose; rather do we ask the God and the Goddess, who know all paths, and to whom*

all paths lead, to bless, protect, and prepare him through the years of childhood: so that when at last he is truly grown, he shall know without doubt or fear which path is his and shall tread it gladly.

Dara, mother of Damien, bring him forward that he may be blessed.

The father helps the mother stand, and both of them bring the child to the High Priestess, who takes the child in her arm and anoints him on the forehead with oil, marking an invoking active spirit pentagram and saying:

I anoint thee, Damien, with oil, and give thee our blessings.

HP, using consecrated water, makes the solar cross of greeting on the child, saying:

I anoint thee, Damien, with water, in the name of the God and the Goddess who within thee dwell.

HPS gives the child back to the mother and then she and the HP lead the parents and child to each of the Watchtowers in turn.

HPS: *Hail, Guardian of the East, we do bring before you Damien, who has been anointed within our Wiccan circle. Hear ye therefore, that he is under the protection of the Lord and the Lady. And we do now seek your gifts for this child.*

East: *Within the child shall be*
Fresh, new beginnings
Communication of the mind and heart and soul
Knowledge of the Goddess and the God
Memories of his parents
Love with each touch of my gentle breeze.
These are my gifts to this child
His to know when he seeks them.
[to parents]
Teach him to seek.

The child is given a small token of Air. In this case, it was a feather.

HP: *Hail, Guardian of the South, we do bring before you Damien, who has been anointed within our Wiccan circle.*

Hear ye therefore, that he is under the protection of the Lord and the Lady. And we do now seek your gifts for this child.

South: *Within the child will be*
Energy of spirit and passion well spent
Fire that comes from embers carefully tended in a loving home
A heart that shares the warmth.
These are my gifts to the child
His to know when he seeks them.
[to the parents]
Teach the child to seek.

The child is given a small token of Fire. In this case, it was a piece rose quartz.

HPS: *Hail, Guardian of the West, we do bring before you Damien, who has been anointed within our Wiccan circle. Hear ye therefore, that he is under the protection of the Lord and the Lady. And we do now seek your gifts for this child.*

West: *Within the child shall be*
Understanding of the quick brook and deep lakes
That will be his emotions.
A willingness to face and know the silences within himself
So that he will understand the path he will follow.
This is my gift to the child
His to find when he seeks them.
[to the parents]
Teach the child to seek.

The child is given a small token of Water. In this case, it was a seashell.

HP: *Hail, Guardian of the North, we do bring before you Damien, who has been anointed within our Wiccan circle. Hear ye therefore, that he is under the protection of the Lord and the Lady. And we do now seek your gifts for this child.*

North: *Within the child shall be*
A stable and firm base on which to build

Security and serenity within
Affinity with all things that grow
And knowledge of the Earth's love for her child.
This is my gift to the child
His to find when he seeks it.
[to parents]
Teach the child to seek.

The child is given a small token of Earth. In this case, it was a tiny vial of salt.

Return to the altar, parents and child standing between HP and HPS.

HP: *Mighty Lord, bestow upon this child the gift of strength.*

HPS: *Gentle Lady, bestow upon this child the gift of beauty.*

HP: *Mighty Lord, bestow upon this child the gift of wisdom.*

HPS: *Gentle Lady, bestow upon this child the gift of love.*

Who stands as Godparents to this child?

The Godparents come forward and face HPs.

HP *[to Godmother]: Do you, Joanna, promise to be a friend to Damien throughout his childhood, to aid and guide him as he shall need, and in concord with his parents, to watch over him and love him as if he were of you own blood, till by the grace of the Lord and Lady, he shall be ready to choose his own path?*

Godmother: *I, Joanna, do so promise.*

HPS *[to Godfather]: Do you, Jim, promise to be a friend to Damien throughout his childhood, to aid and guide him as he shall need, and in concord with his parents, to watch over him and love him as if he were of you own blood, till by the grace of the Lord and Lady, he shall be ready to choose his own path?*

Godfather: *I, Jim, do so promise.*

HPS *[taking child in her arms again]:*
The God and the Goddess have blessed him
The Guardians of the Watchtowers have gifted him
We his friends and family have welcomed him
[now holding child gently up toward the sky]
Therefore, lights of the Cosmos
Shine in peace on Damien Malachi.
As it is willed, so mote it be.

Handfasting

So far, my circle has not been called upon to conduct a handfasting, but on February 21, 1993, my High Priest and I were handfasted. This ritual is the standard one used by Circle Atheneum, and is printed with the permission of Lady Beckett, who, of course, offici-ated when Mark and I were handfasted. Atheneum has, at this point, done a number of handfastings, and Lady Beckett has obtained the necessary license to do a legal wedding if the couple so requests. Handfasting is a public declaration of commitment between a couple who may be joining in a legal marriage, may be already married and desire a Wiccan ceremony, or may be living together (or planning to) without legal marriage. In the latter case, the commitment is often said, within the wording of the ritual, to be "for a year and a day," after which the couple may or may not choose to continue.

The circle is set and all participants are brought in, except for the Bride and Groom. The Watchtowers are called, and then the Red Priest opens a door in the circle for the couple to enter, and gives them the traditional greeting. They are then greeted at the door by the Crone.

> **Crone:** *Know now, before you go further, that since your lives have crossed in this life you have formed ties between each other. As you seek to enter this rite you will become a focus for the power that has been raised herein, and those ties will become strengthened.*
>
> *With full awareness, know that within this circle you are not only declaring your intent to be handfasted before your friends and family, but you speak that intent also before your Goddess and your God.*

> *The promises made today and the ties that are bound here greatly strengthen your union; they will cross the years and lives and future lives of each soul's growth.*

Or alternatively, if this is to be a "year and a day" rather than a life partner commitment:

> *Though the promises made today are for but a year and a day, the ties that are made here are strengthened; they will cross the years and lives of each soul's growth.*
>
> *Do you still seek to enter this rite?*
>
> **Couple:** *Yes, we seek to enter.*

Crone takes the couple to the front of the altar.

> **HPS:** *Grandmother, do they know the full significance of what they seek?*
>
> **Crone:** *Yes, for I have questioned them and told them the meaning of this rite.*
>
> **HP** [to the couple]: *And do you still seek this handfasting?*
>
> **Couple** [each answers]: *Yes.*
>
> **HPS** [to Maiden]: *Take them to the Guardians to seek their blessing on this union.*
>
> **East:** *What seek you of the Guardian of the East?*
>
> **Couple:** *We seek your blessing on this union.*
>
> **East:** *Blessed be this union with the gifts of the East.*
> *Communication of the heart, mind, and body*
> *Fresh beginnings with the rising of each Sun.*
> *The knowledge of the growth found in the sharing of silences.*

East wafts air at the couple with a fan, and then Maiden leads them to the next quarter.

> **South:** *What seek you of the Guardian of the South?*
>
> **Couple:** *We seek your blessing on this union.*
>
> **South:** *Blessed be this union with the gifts of the South.*
> *Warmth of the hearth and home*

The heat of the hearts passion
The light created by both
To lighten the darkest of times.

South directs the scent of burning incense toward the couple, and then Maiden leads them to the next quarter.

West: *What seek you of the Guardian of the West?*

Couple: *We seek your blessing on this union.*

West: *Blessed be this union with the gifts of the West.*
The deep commitments of the lake
The swift excitement of the river
The refreshing cleansing of the rain
The all encompassing passion of the sea.

West sprinkles water on the couple, and then Maiden leads them to the next quarter.

North: *What seek you from the Guardian of the North?*

Couple: *We seek your blessing on this union.*

North: *Blessed be this union with the gifts of the North.*
Firm foundation on which to build
Fertility of the fields to enrich your lives
A stable home to which you may always return.

North offers salt to the couple to taste, and then Maiden leads them to the altar.

HPS: *You have received tools from the Guardians that will help you to build a happy and successful union. Yet that is all they are—tools. Tools that you must wield together in order to create what you seek in this union. I bid you look into each other's eyes.*

HPS [to Groom]: *Will you cause her pain?*

Groom: *I may.*

HPS: *Is that your intent?*

Groom: *No.*

HP [to Bride]: *Will you cause him pain?*

Bride: I may.

HP: Is that your intent?

Bride: No.

HPS: Will you share each other's pain and seek to ease it?

Couple: Yes.

HPS: And so the binding is made.

HP: Join your hands.

A orange cord is draped across their joined hands.

HP [to Bride]: Will you share his laughter?

Bride: Yes.

HPS [to Groom]: Will you share her laughter?

Groom: Yes.

HPS: Will both of you look for the brightness in life and the positive in each other?

Couple: Yes.

HP: And so the binding is made.

A yellow cord is draped across their joined hands.

HP [to Bride]: Will you burden him?

Bride: I may.

HP [to Bride]: Is that your intent?

Bride: No.

HPS [to Groom]: Will you burden her?

Groom: I may.

HPS [to Groom]: Is that your intent?

Groom: No.

HPS: Will you share the burdens of each so that your spirits may grow in this union?

Couple: Yes.

HPS: And so the binding made.

A brown cord is draped across their joined hands.

HP [to Bride]: Will you share his dreams?

Bride: Yes.

HPS [to Groom]: Will you share her dreams?

Groom: Yes.

HPS: Will you dream together to create new realities and hopes?

Couple: Yes.

HP: And so the binding is made.

A blue cord is draped across their joined hands.

HPS [to Groom]: Will you cause her anger?

Groom: I may.

HPS [to Groom]: Is that your intent?

Groom: No.

HP [to Bride]: Will you cause him anger?

Bride: I may.

HP [to Bride]: Is that your intent?

Bride: No.

HP: Will you take the heat of your anger and use it to temper the strength of this union?

Couple: We will.

HPS: And so the binding made.

A red cord is draped across their joined hands.

HP [to Bride]: Will you honor him?

Bride: I will.

HPS [to Groom]: Will you honor her?

Groom: I will.

> **HPS:** *Will you seek never to give cause to break that honor?*
>
> **Couple:** *We shall never do so.*
>
> **HPS:** *And so the binding is made.*

A purple cord is draped across their joined hands.

> **HPS:** *The knots of this binding are not made on this plane. Either of you may drop the cords, for as always, you hold in your own hands the making or breaking of this union.*

Immediately after she says this, she and the HP hold the hands of the couple, with the cords, high in the air, to the applause of all. Then the couple carefully ties all of the cords together with one center knot and places them on the altar, because they will need their hands free for their exchange of gifts.

> **HP:** *What gifts have you as tokens of your love?*

Bride and Groom then exchange rings or other gifts.

Mark and I gifted each other with both rings and new crowns, the latter in acknowledgment of each other as working partners in the Craft. Both crowns and rings were designed and made for us by Blake Hubbard of San Diego. Blake offers beautiful handcrafted jewelry through his business, Wren Faire Designs. Our rings are in an earth/water motif—stylized silver ocean waves in the center, with gold rims in a leaf pattern. Mark's crown has a small silver stag head at center, set with a sapphire, and the band is wrapped with gold leather. My crown, also a silver circlet, but not wrapped, has a round moonstone at center, flanked by outward turned silver crescents—the symbol of the Triple Goddess—waxing, full, and waning Moons. I made the first presentation, and then he followed. The words we used were:

> **Bride:** *I crown thee with this circlet in recognition of thee as my priest and partner. As into thee I call and see my Lord God, my brother, father, son, and lover, I learn to know and see and love him more within us all.*
>
> *I give thee this ring and call you also my husband and companion, for it symbolizes the endless cycle and the neverending nature of my love for you.*

Groom: I *crown thee with this circlet in recognition of thee as my priestess and partner. As into thee I call and see my Lady Goddess, my sister, mother, daughter, and lover, I learn to know and see and love her more within us all.*

I give thee this ring and call you also my wife and companion, for it symbolizes the endless cycle and the neverending nature of my love for you.

Great Rite

Performed by the handfasted couple alone, if they are initiated priest and priestess. If they are not, the officiating HPs hold chalice and athame with the couple for the Great Rite.

Sharing

The couple alone, or with HPs, blesses the cakes and wine. They serve each other first, and then all participants. If the group is large, it is better to call the Guardians of the Watchtowers forward to help serve.

HPS [holding broom]: This *broom shall represent the hearth and home, and the woman who is traditionally in charge of it.*

She places the broom on the ground, about halfway between the altar and the East Watchtower.

HP [holding sword]: This *sword shall represent protection, and the man who is traditionally responsible for protecting his lady and their home.*

He places the sword in a position that crosses the broom. It's best to cross sword and broom in an "x" rather than a full cross—not so far to jump that way! Following an old Pagan custom symbolizing the commitment of Bride and Groom to the establishment of a home, the Bride and Groom now hold hands, clasped around their cords, and walk the circle three times, jumping the broom and sword each time, while everyone else applauds.

Variations

Variations in this ritual, as with all rituals, are motivated by numbers of people, time, place, weather, etc. As an example, Mark and I were somewhat limited as to time and place because we wanted to make sure that my daughter Molly would be able to come home from Florida to work as Maiden. After Molly's vacation time was determined, we found that Lord Landerthorn would be out-of-state. We were, of course, very disappointed about that, but could not change Molly's vacation or plane tickets. Molly worked as "official" circle Maiden, or one could say, the Maid of Honor. In this case, though, there were two Maidens, with my teenage daughter Elizabeth also participating as Bridesmaid. The two of them entered the circle escorted by the Red Priests of Circle of the Cosmic Muse (Jered) and Circle Atheneum (Wolf Spirit).

Lord Falkan of The Circle of the Wildewood agreed to work center with Lady Beckett. As it turned out, having him, with his fine bass voice and guitar as High Priest, provided a perfect foil for Elizabeth, with her lovely soprano, to sing her young Maidenly questions about what was happening. He sang the answers, thus teaching, to everyone's delight—and to the benefit of the few non-Wiccan guests—what our primary symbols meant. The duet, a very pretty and singable piece called "The Handfasting Song" can be found on a tape called *Libation*. Each verse by the woman begins, "I'll sing you a riddle ... " and each verse by the man begins, "I'll sing you the answer ... " The words describe first the Goddess, then the God, how their union began, and continue to the final Maiden's question, "How long will it last ... " to which the final reply is "It cannot last longer than my love for you. The answer's forever, the day it is done. Come to me, my love!"[4]

The theme of the day was taken from the earth/water motif of our rings, including green and blue for altar colors, and for exceptional robes for Mark and I, and dresses for Molly and Elizabeth, all made by Lady Aanja, who is an excellent seamstress and a most generous friend. Mark's dark green robe had a long gold overpiece, and my deep blue one had a matching silver overpiece.

We had "double Watchtowers"—a couple working at each quarter. This is often done when the ritual will involve a large group. At the sharing of cakes and wine, the four couples come forward, each man taking a goblet and each woman a plate of cakes. The HPs bless all the offerings at once, and then the four couples return to their posts and serve the people from there, deocil to the next quarter.

Another variation from standard practice was taken to resolve the logistical problem of space and time. My house is small for a

large group, and a ritual with full circle casting is long and confusing, and potentially troubling, for non-Wiccan guests who have not
been taught about all the tools and symbols. We decided it was best
to build the circle with just the main participants, before everyone
else arrived. The HPs cast the circle, and then formally greeted and
admitted the Guardian couples, Crone, Maidens, and Red Priests.
After a final briefing on the procedures for the handfasting, they dismissed the others and pulled in the circle from each quarter, com-
pacting it at the altar. That way, the entire circle area would not have
to be ribboned off, and guests could move freely through the room
as they arrived.

When the time came for the Handfasting to begin, the HPs
returned to the circle area and rang the bell. The Red Priests called
everyone into the room and placed them. To help settle everyone and
make the proper transition, Elizabeth sang "Look to the Rainbow"
from *Finian's Rainbow*, accompanied by Lord Falkan on his guitar.
Now it was time to reestablish the full circle.

Lady Beckett called forward the Guardians of the East, who
entered the circle, went to the altar, and received the fan. They proceeded to the East candelabra, called the East, and lighted the candles. In this way they expanded the circle out again to encompass the
entire room, as it was originally cast. The same procedure, with the
same general call, took place for each set of Guardians.

Habondia (the Crone), and the Maidens, escorted by the Red
Priests, entered, and the Red Priests returned to stand on either side
of the door. Lady Beckett gave an extemporaneous welcome and Circle Dedication. The final step to recharge the full circle was the duet.
Elizabeth whispered in Lady Beckett's ear, who said to Lord Falkan,
"She has questions, but she is shy," to which he answered, "I think I
have a way to bring out her voice." He picked up his guitar, began
the introduction, and their sung questions and answers quite nicely
set just the right tone and feeling within everyone for the handfasting
to begin. Then the red priests escorted Mark and I to the edge of the
circle, where we were challenged by the Crone, and the remainder of
the ritual proceeded as it was given above.

The point to all this: if one thing won't work, try another. Be
creative. There is never only one way to do anything. The intent is
what matters!

A Wedding Ritual

This ceremony for my wedding to Neil was held on the beach of Coronado, on October 2, 1987, at sunset. Taped music, especially composed by Gerald Markoe for this occasion, was played in the background. It was based on the astrological configurations in our Composite Chart. (A Composite Chart is a chart of a relationship made from the midpoints of each planet and house cusp in the charts of each individual.)

Gerry improvises his music using the notes that correspond, mathematically, to planetary positions. Quite a number of years ago he collaborated with Neil to program his system for Astro's computers, so that he could get a print-out of those correspondences, which he reads and plays almost as if it were sheet music—sheet music for Gerry, that is. I doubt if most other musicians could read it! Gerry, who has been doing "Astromusic" for years, has more recently cut albums of his compositions, inspired by the stars of the Pleiades, that are doing very well on the New Age music charts. All four—so far— of his albums make wonderful background music for ritual, and you will find their titles in my Annotated Bibliography.

At the time of the wedding, I was not yet formally involved in Wiccan ritual. This ceremony was devised in collaboration with Maritha Pottenger, an ordained minister of the Church of Religious Science, who is much better known as an astrologer, author, and the ACS Editorial Director. She has officiated at quite a number of uniquely written weddings, and was very open to my wish to call on the blessings of the Goddess. Our main point, however, was to base the wording of the wedding ceremony on astrological symbolism.

Here, the directions were based on the Composite Chart of the Bride and Groom. Neil's and my Composite Ascendant is in Aquarius, hence East as Air. Taurus, an Earth sign is the 4th house cusp, therefore North—and so far, the directions are the same as Wicca! The other two, however, follow astrological polarities, rather than magickal ones. South is Water, the Composite Midheaven in Scorpio; and West is Fire, the Composite Descendant in Leo. Geographically, this worked great, for on this particular stretch of the beach, the ocean is south, and since the ceremony was at sunset, lovely fire colors filled the western sky!

Although this ritual is not strictly Wiccan, I have included it because it shows good use of the astrological symbolism that could spark the creativity of some readers who wish to write similar rituals.

One thing is not recommended: at the time we did this ceremony, it was not yet generally known that balloons can be dangerous for marine life. If planning such an event again, I would not release balloons. Instead, perhaps element colored poles with ribbons and flower garlands could mark the directions, and the bridal couple could be showered by guests with appropriately colored flower petals at the climatic moment.

> *Maritha: Let us gather within a circle of unity to celebrate the marriage of Maria and Neil, and call upon the elements of the ancient world to symbolize the blessings that we would wish for their union.*

Guests gathered in a circle, with the couple and minister in the center, the couple facing the ocean, and the minister facing them.

Six balloons of appropriate colors marked each compass point. Maritha began by taking the white ones (readers: yellow was not available) to the East, and giving them to six people standing there as she spoke:

> *Maritha: We mark the East, the direction of the rising Aquarius Sun in the Composite Chart of Maria and Neil. Here, tonight, the Moon will also rise. And so we call first upon the Air. May Maria and Neil be blessed with intellectual understanding, objectivity, detachment, and the willingness to communicate freely with one another.*

Green balloons were passed out to people in the North.

> *To the North we call upon the Earth. May the bond that we celebrate today be blessed with endurance, fidelity, stability of purpose, and the dedication to grow within a lasting relationship.*

Red balloons were passed out to people in the West.

> *To the West we face the fire of the sunset, and call upon the spirit of Fire in the hope that they will always be blessed with passion and with intensity of commitment.*

Blue balloons are passed to people in the South.

> *To the South are the waters of the ocean. May Neil and Maria be blessed with the empathy to truly share on a*

deep level, with non-verbal understanding and with psychic openness to one another.

Our circle is almost complete. We need only to call upon the Source of all Unity.

Because She is of special significance to the union we celebrate today, we call upon the One God in the aspect of Mari, Goddess of the Sea and Mother of our age. For a moment of meditation: the words of She whose body encircles the universe:

"I who am the beauty of the green earth and the white moon among the stars and the mysteries of the waters, I call upon your soul to arise and come unto Me. For I am the soul of nature that gives life to the Universe. From Me all things proceed, and unto Me they must return. Let My worship be in the heart that rejoices, for behold—all acts of love and pleasure are My rituals. Let there be beauty and strength, power and compassion, honor and humility, mirth and reverence within you. And you who seek to know Me, know that your seeking and yearning will avail you not, unless you know the Mystery: for if that which you seek you find not within yourself, you will never find it without. For behold, I have been with you from the beginning, and I am with you always."

As all of the elements remain true to their own natures yet create together a world of great beauty, so do these two people commit to remain true to their own natures, yet create together a relationship of great beauty. Individuality reigns within Oneness.

With a ground of solid foundation, the breath of knowledge, the flame of inspiration, and an ocean of understanding, do you, Maria, now pledge yourself to Neil?

Maria: *Yes, I do! I love you, Neil. I pledge myself to be your wife, your companion, your colleague, your lover, and your friend. I will share with you and care for you through joys and sorrows, through all the varying experiences toward fulfillment of our purpose.*

Maritha: With a ground of solid foundation, the breath of knowledge, the flame of inspiration and an ocean of understanding, do you, Neil, now pledge yourself to Maria?

Neil: Yes, I do! I love you, Maria. I pledge myself to be your husband, companion, friend, student when appropriate, mentor when appropriate, co-worker, and lover. I will be with you through the joys, sorrows, and fulfillment of our physical, mental, emotional, and spiritual journeys together.

Maritha: This ring is a circle, formed with the waves of the eternal sea. For he who gives it and she who wears it, let it symbolize an eternal bond of love.

Let all of us now join Maria and Neil in extending the blessings symbolized by the elements to all of their family and especially to Elizabeth, who will share a home with them. May the three of you share a home environment that will enrich your lives.

And now, as you, Neil, and you, Maria, have pledged yourselves to each other as partners in life, by the authority vested in me, I pronounce that you are husband and wife.

Music of the moment—especially composed by Gerald Markoe, based on the astrological configurations at 6:18 PM.

We thank the spirits of North, East, South, and West, and of Earth, Air, Fire, and Water, and especially our Divine Mother, for their blessings and for their presence in our circle.

Balloons were released into the air.

The circle is now open, but unbroken. Peace go with you.

Maria's three daughters, each carrying a basket, passed flowers to all present.

Memorial Ritual

This ritual was held on the beach of Coronado, May 26, 1990, at sunset, as a funeral service for Neil, who died on May 15. (Neil was cremated, and the delay allowed family and friends from other states to gather in San Diego.) Rob Hand, a widely known astrologer, and our friend and business associate, flew here from his home in Massachusetts to help me conduct the ritual. (Rob is not Wiccan, but he has studied ritual magick in Kabbalistic tradition, and was comfortable with my proposal to do this funeral service as an astrological circle ritual.)

Also assisting were Maritha Pottenger, Dr. Zipporah Dobyns (Maritha's mother, and an internationally known astrologer who had been an important catalyst for Neil when he first became interested in the possibilities of computerized astrological calculations), Lady Beckett, and Atheneum's Crone, Habondia. At this time I had completed my Third Degree with Circle Atheneum, but had not yet officially begun my own circle.

The four directions were marked with candles atop poles in the sand, decorated with ribbons in the element colors. A white candle pole stood in the center (the only one lighted at the beginning) and was flanked by one candle pole of silver and one of gold. A small table held the oak crematory urn, a censer, a bell, and containers of water and salt. No other ritual tools were used.

This was a ceremony attended by mostly people who were not Wiccan, and who might not have understood, or been comfortable with, tools such as an athame, sword, wand, etc. Tools are not necessary. For this ceremony, attended by either people who are astrologers, or if not, were well aware of Neil's dedication to astrology, the format of using astrological symbolism was the common denominator which was understood by all.

I am told that this ceremony had a healing effect, and that was its intent. In deciding, after considerable thought, that it is appropriate to print it here, I draw upon the knowledge that Neil, who encouraged my work with ritual and shared so much of himself, would say, "Do it!"

Rob [*as he directed people to gather in a circle as marked by the candles*]: *We are of varied traditions and faiths, yet we are united by our connection to Neil Michelsen and to* *his love for astrology, a craft that owes much of its contemporary development to his work. It is fitting to remember him with the rich symbolism of that craft. We will begin by defining our circle with the symbols of the four ancient elements. Let the ceremony begin.*

Maria gives Beckett the incense and Habondia the salt water. While they cast the circle, Rob asks the people to join hands and leads a brief centering meditation:

Above us is the zenith. This is a point that humanity has traditionally associated with God. Visualize coming down from the zenith overhead, a golden ray of light. Let it come down within you, through your head, and illuminate your heart. Beneath you is the Earth, our ultimate Mother. From the center of the Earth, visualize a silver ray of light, coming up into you through your feet and illuminating your heart. Visualize this as mixing with the golden ray and producing a pure, white light. Now visualize that light moving through your hands to the person clockwise next to you and on around the circle. Visualize it moving around and around and around, and thus our circle is formed.

Circle Consecration

Maria: We have gathered here to honor the memory of a very special man who has passed out of our physical world into the world beyond. Let this circle be formed in perfect love and perfect trust in the continuous cycle of life and death and life again. Be it a sacred place, out of time and space, a boundary between the visible and invisible worlds, where we can know and feel the presence of Neil—as father, son, husband, brother, colleague, mentor, leader, and friend—and know and feel that in a profound way he has not gone from us at all, but lives among us still.

Rob: In the symbolism of the ancients, let us now call upon the spirits of the elements for their message.

Rob sounds the bell three times just before Maria calls each direction.

Maria: To the East I call the Air!

Maritha [lights candle and answers]: I am the Gemini winds of change, the fresh Aquarian breeze of new ideas, Libra's sense of balance and the Power of Mind. Neil lives in me and in you as you continue to use and expand the gifts of his intellect, communicate to others what you have learned from him, and remain open to innovation and growth through change. And so he is with you always.

Maria: To the South I call the Fire!

Lady Beckett [lights candle and answers]: I am the surging energy of Aries, the bright radiance of Leo, the vibrant enthusiasm and idealism of Sagittarius, the Power of Spirit. Neil lives in me and in you whenever you follow his example by charging forth to take charge and pioneer a new idea in which you believe, and when you glow with vitality in the sheer joy of life. And so he is with you always.

Maria: To the West I call the Water!

Habondia [lights candle and answers]: I am the nurturing womb of Cancer, the deep mysterious pools of Scorpio, the ocean of compassion that is Pisces, the emotional Power of Soul. Neil lives in me and in you as you nurture the development of others, fearlessly probe for self-awareness, and connect with others in compassion and in love. And so he is with you always.

Maria: To the North I call the Earth!

Zip [lights candle and answers]: I am the solid ground of Taurean stability, the bountiful natural order that is Virgo, and the Capricorn mountains life calls you to climb. Neil lives in me and in you when, like him, with quiet, stubborn persistence, you stick with a task until it's right, ground your idealism in practical structure, and always strive to "climb the highest mountain." And so he is with you always.

Power Chant

> *As above, so below*
> *As within, so without*
> *As the Universe, so the Soul ...*

Invocations

> *Maria: I now do call the presence of the Father of light and life and love, bright Lord of Day and Christ within. Flow now through this your son and through him shine forth to touch your light within us all.*

Rob lights gold candle and answers:

> *Rob: I am spiritual energy, the active aspect of the Eternal One that permeates the Universe and dwells within you all, in this world and in the world beyond.*
>
> *From ancient scripture you were told that "For every time there is a season, a time for every purpose under heaven. A time to live, a time to die; a time to plant, a time to reap ... a time to weep and a time to laugh; a time to mourn and a time to dance; a time to gather and a time to cast away ... a time of silence and a time to speak ... "*
>
> *The music you hear is Gerry Markoe's "Music from the Pleiades." These stars of Taurus are known as the weeping sisters, and this is a time to weep for our loss, but do not weep for Neil, for his spirit goes on to a new adventure, free of the physical pain that bound him in recent months. Remember how much he loved to travel? Thinking of that can ease the pain of missing him.*
>
> *You come here because a death has touched your heart, but what is death? Only a change in form—*
>
> *I now do call the presence of the Mother of light and life and love, gracious Lady of the Night who receives my light and clarifies it into form, Goddess within. Flow now through this your daughter and shine forth to touch your light within us all.*

Maria lights silver candle and answers:

Maria: I am the form of spirit, responsive aspect of the Eternal One, whose body is the Universe. I speak first to you in the same words as were spoken at the marriage of Neil and Maria, for they are as appropriate now as they were then ...

"I am the beauty of the green earth, the white Moon among the stars, and the mystery of the waters, and I call upon your souls to rise up and come to me. For I am the soul of nature which gives life to the Universe. From me all things proceed and unto me they must return. Yet let my worship be in the heart that rejoices, for behold, all acts of love and pleasure are my rituals. Let there be beauty and strength, power and compassion, honor, humility, mirth, and reverence among you. And for you who seek to know me, know that all of your seeking and all of your yearning are of no avail unless you know the mystery. If that which you seek you find not within yourself, you will never find it without. For behold, I am with you always, and I am that which you will find at the end of desire."

[pick up urn] Here is all that remains of the physical form of the man that we have loved so well.

Rob: We have seen the many ways that the works of his form and spirit remain among us and always will, though this, too, will change and evolve through our own manifestations, for this is the nature of life.

Both take urn to the East.

Maria: I now commend this body to the Air.

Maritha directs incense toward urn with feather, says:

Maritha: May the currents of thought carry forth the products of his intellect throughout the world to the continued stimulation of the growth of our astrological craft.

Maria: So mote it be! [all repeat]

Move to South quarter.

Rob: This body has been given to physical fire. I now commend it to the Fires of spirit.

Beckett makes the solar cross over the urn with a lighted fire wand and says:

> **Lady Beckett:** *May the flames carry forth his vitality and enthusiasm as a beacon of inspiration for us all.*
>
> **Rob:** *So mote it be! [all repeat]*

Move to the West.

> **Maria:** *I now commend this body to the Womb of the Mother, cauldron of rebirth.*

Habondia sprinkles urn with salt water, saying:

> **Habondia:** *In oceans of feeling may we remember his love and compassion, and in so doing, love one another more.*
>
> **Maria:** *So mote it be! [all repeat]*

Move to the North.

> **Rob:** *And finally, I commend this body to the earth, into the keeping of his own beloved mother, until he is returned to the body of Mother Earth in the city of his birth.*

Neil's mother, seated in the North near Zip, is given the urn after Zip sprinkles it with sand and speaks:

> **Zip:** *With the solid foundation he has given us, may we continue to build, in understanding of the importance of the practical application of our ideals.*
>
> **Rob:** *So mote it be! [all repeat]*

Rob and Maria return to center.

> **Rob:** *Some of you have expressed a wish to make a personal statement. We will pass clockwise around the circle and if you wish to speak, step slightly forward. Please be brief so that we can finish and be off the beach before night falls. You are welcome to gather at Maria's home afterwards.*
>
> **Maria:** *Symbolically it is said that the departing soul goes west to the waters into the womb of rebirth. When your statements are finished I will open the circle, and as a final gesture you might send a single flower into the waves with your wishes to Neil for a wonderful new journey.*

Personal statements from many present who wished to speak.

> *Maria: All join hands. I now thank the spirits of the elements, and the Lord and Lady of the Universe for their presence within. I declare that this circle is open but never broken. Go forth in love and peace. Blessed Be.*

Everyone walked to the ocean and threw in a flower.

Memorial to be Held within a Full Moon Ritual

This is a short memorial ritual, devised by Lady Beckett and Lord Landerthorn of Circle Atheneum, for the benefit of any circle member who has lost a loved one, when the actual funeral was held elsewhere or in the rites of a different faith. It takes place during the first appropriate Full Moon, and comes between the Charge and the Great Rite.

HP steps back to the West quarter, and the HPS takes the person who has asked for the service to the East. Holding the person's hand, she turns to the West and calls:

> *HPS: I call to you who are the Dark Lord of death, I who am all life, I call to you, my other half.*
>
> *HP: I hear. What do you seek of me?*
>
> *HPS: One we have loved and cherished has passed from my halls to yours. Speak now of your gifts to the one who has come to you. Speak now of your gifts to those who are left behind.*
>
> *HP: I am the Lord of death. I do not come hunting for those who fill my halls, because all come to me in the end. I am not the specter of bad dreams, but the guardian of a realm of peace, contemplation, and memories. I guard those who come to me as a father watches over his children. Within my halls old friends are reunited, old hurts healed, pain washed away, and bright memories polished. And because you are my knowing children, my gift to you, the living, is this knowledge.*
>
> *HP [to the bereaved]: And my gift to you is, once again, the Great Rite and the affirmation of life therein.*

The HP returns to the altar, and HP, HPS, and the bereaved person join their hands together, over athame and chalice, to perform the Great Rite.

A Ritual for Healing

Fairly often a "healing circle" will be held during a Moon ritual, if requested by any of the members. Such rituals will usually involve sitting in the circle, holding hands, while the HPS or other designated person leads a guided meditation designed to assist the visualization of healing light energy building around the circle, filling it, and rising into a cone of power that is directed to the person who has asked for the healing either on his/her own behalf, or for someone outside the circle who may be unknown to the others. Again, I remind you that it is only appropriate to direct specific healing to one who has asked to receive it. If the person outside the circle is not actively cooperating with the healing, it is only appropriate to send healing light into the area around him/her, to take in or not as the soul chooses.

Sometimes a group may be asked for a special ritual for the purpose of healing. If the person who wishes to be healed can be present, the best technique may well be a "laying on of hands" with the person sitting or lying down in the center of the circle.

The technique below can be used for a person who is at home, actively participating in thought, but too ill to come into the circle.

I led a ritual worded very much like this one at Atheneum in the summer of '89, at Neil's request. The ritual incorporated the color correspondences that he was also using at home with projected light through color transparencies. Neil was involved with wholistic health techniques for many years and had often lectured on color healing at conferences. In the early stages of his cancer he was very focused on healing, using wholistic and conventional medicine. By the end of the summer the cancer had gone into a remission that held for six months. By the end of January 1990, however, it was evident that the disease was advancing again. From that time on, his primary concern seemed to be on finishing things, and in fact he finished his last book, *Tables of Planetary Phenomena*, on the evening of his birthday (May 11), just a few days before he died. Sometimes the soul has another agenda than the conscious mind, with which the conscious mind either does not agree, or simply does not recognize.

Consecration

HPS: There is one tonight who has asked our assistance for healing, and I do dedicate this rite to that purpose. I do conjure that this shall be a circle of power and love, a sacred sphere of healing light that shall contain, preserve, and expand the energy that we shall raise within it, reaching out to he who is with us tonight in spirit, with thoughts focused to receive the healing light that we shall direct to him. In all the names of the Threefold Goddess and her Mighty Consort, I do bless and consecrate this circle. As it is willed, so mote it be.

Watchtowers

East: To the Watchtowers of the East I call forth the Air, healing powers of mind. Increase the focus and projection of thought. Blow forth, winds of change! Be here this night!

South: To the Watchtowers of the South I call forth the Fire, healing power of spirit. With passion I greet thee ... your inspiration, your energy, your vitality. Charge forth! Be here this night!

West: To the Watchtowers of the West I call forth the Waters, healing power of soul. Wash over this circle in indigo purity, reveal thy mysteries, charge us with thy deepest knowing. Flow Waters! Be here this night!

North: To the Watchtowers of the North I call forth the Earth, healing power of body. Charge this circle with thy strength, that we may channel thy regenerative energy. Come forth! Be here this night!

Invocations

Here the High Priest invokes the God into himself, and the High Priestess, the Goddess into herself. This is usual preference at Circle Atheneum.

HP: Hearty and powerful Lord of the Sun, I ask your vibrant presence now. I exalt in your strength, now may I share in your energy. Charge this circle with light and vitality and glowing health that we may project to he who asks thy healing light.

HPS: Threefold Goddess, Mother of the Earth, Lady of the Moon, I feel your light shine down on me ... you who create, preserve, destroy—and yet create again. Connect that light with your spark that lives always within me. Expand the light that I may feel your healing presence within me ... that I may speak your words of inspiration.

Charge of the Goddess

Open with the Charge of the Star Goddess, as has been given in previous rituals, then:

You call me tonight for a special purpose. One you love is ill and asks for a rite of healing. The only constant in my Universe is change. With the power of mind and soul and spirit the body can heal itself. You know that. Hold an image of wellness, visualize glowing health and vitality, and so it will be. Join your energy now with he who waits to receive it, and with my love, my blessings, and my healing light, we will help him to heal himself. I light his candle with my fire and that of the Sun.

An image of the person to be healed is passed around with a description of where he is, along with various colored magic markers. We used a blown-up computer scan of Neil's picture, but a simple line drawing of a body would do. Explain that each may mark it with a symbol of health and protection. For the ritual for Neil, I also explained how the working would proceed in regard to the colors, which I projected during the visualization by shining a flashlight through some of Neil's color slides.

HPS: Thou art a creature of art and paper. By art made and by art be changed. Yet thou art also (Name), a creature of body, mind, soul, and spirit. Be ye also changed and charged with health and vitality.

For Neil's ritual, while the paper was passed around, all sat silently, breathing deeply three times as they visualized Neil surrounded by lemon-green light, then three more times visualizing indigo, three more times visualizing orange, and finally three times visualizing white light. The paper was passed a final time so all could see what was added. If color projections are not meaningful for you, alternatively effective ways of assisting the visualization might be through musical sounds or steady drum beats. We used the color projections because that was what was meaningful to the recipient, and that, I feel, is what is most important. Neil's color correspondences to the body and its functions are not known well enough to me that I should attempt to explain them here.[5]

> *HPS: I do now charge this image with the earth and water of the Mother's womb for the renewal of (Name)'s health, and I send it forth on the winds of change and the fire of spirit, and on the energy we have raised tonight. Receive it, (Name), and be healed!*

Here the image is charged by sprinkling with the consecrated salt water, and then burned in the cauldron. The group should remain in silent visualization, directing the energy, until the fire burns out.

> *And as it is willed, so mote it be.*

The ritual is then ended in the usual way, by thanking the Goddess, the God, and the Guardians, and opening the circle.

Ritual for Cleansing and Charging a Place

A new home, apartment, or place of business should be cleansed and charged. This could also be done to a location that you've already been in for a time, if you feel a need to cleanse it of unwanted energies and charge it with a new or renewed intent.

On a table, set out a white candle, a censer on which is burned incense made from cleansing and protection herbs, a container of water and one of salt, an athame, a wand, and a broom. Meditate for a moment and center, then cleanse and charge the elements and mix the salt and water in the same manner as is done when beginning to cast a circle. The work, as described here, is done with a team of four people, although, of course, it could be adapted for fewer, or could even be done by one.

Consecration

HPS [or other leader]: We are gathered here for special work. [continue with statement of intent specific to whether this is a place of domicile or business] We will begin by sweeping and cleansing this place thoroughly. If any unsupportive energies dwell within this place from those who have been here before us, let them be banished. I charge that any and all spirits of dissension, pettiness, uncooperativeness, pessimism—any thoughts or energies that currently interfere with a positive environment—be gone. I charge that any ill will from without be banished also, prevented from any present or future entrance or interference. [to participants] Begin at the center east wall. Move deocil around the entire building. Keep focused on our intent. When you have finished, meet back here.

For the cleansing, the first person sweeps with the broom, the second sprinkles salt water, the third directs incense, and the fourth draws banishing pentagrams with an athame at every window and door, and at other significant places, as well, if desired.

We now must charge and fill this place with all of the energies that we wish to prevail within and project without. Go forth to charge and seal the physical boundaries of the smaller circle that is this building, but project the light, also, into a larger circle that extends beyond. Be focused on our intents as you work. You who will live (work) within this place, state mentally or aloud your intents as you work. Let an aura of peace, harmony, and cooperation settle over this place and dwell within all who enter here. And let that aura be projected outward to all of our contacts throughout the community.

For the charging, the first person charges with the wand, drawing a solar cross—"With will, intent, and purpose, I do charge this place." The second sprinkles salt water, the third directs incense, and the fourth seals the intent by drawing a solar cross with a white candle at each window, door, and other significant area, saying,

In perfect love, and perfect trust, in the name of the Lady and her Consort, I do seal and protect this place.

HPS: I now do thank the mighty powers of Air, Fire, Water, and Earth, for their presence within our lives and within this rite. I do most gratefully acknowledge the power of the unseen One, the force of Life whom we call Goddess and God, separate yet never separated, for they are One. The One unites us all in bonds of Perfect Love and Perfect Trust. Though this physical symbol of light [the white candle] be now extinguished, the true light is ever present. Let the sacred sphere of light that we have created within this place be now open, but remain ever-present, serenely felt by all within. Merry meet, merry part and merry meet again, Blessed Be!

Solitary Ritual

Circle members are encouraged to do rituals on their own. This might be for a particular intent, or just as a centering meditation. Some people like to have a small, permanent altar in the bedroom. Mine is inside a small secretary, one of those with a slanted door that opens down to form a little desk. Inside I keep candles, a small incense burner and stick incense, a little shell containing salt, another small shell for water, a pentagram, and a vial of oil.

Another tool I have used for solitary ritual is a five-holder candelabra. I have a white candle in the center, and yellow, red, blue, and green candles in the other four holders. I can place it in front of me, and call the Guardians around me, lighting each appropriate candle as I do.

I think the best solitary ritual form is spontaneous. You could use an accustomed format, similar to that used in your group practice, but make up your own words as you go. To focus intent, you could incorporate magickal tools, such as a candle, poppet, or cord as described in Chapter 5.

Or—you don't need tools at all! You can improvise, wherever you are, with whatever is available. You could perform a beautiful ritual meditation outdoors by drawing a pentagram in the sand at the beach or by sprinkling salt or leaves on the ground, and then stand or sit in the center of it.

Tools are nice, but they are only accessories for focus and intent. Your primary tool is always your mind—your imagination.

I have shared with my circle a little song I made up to call the quarters when working solitary, and they have told me I should write it down. I adapted it from one I heard during a lecture on the Kabbalah. The original words called the four archangels and the Shekinah. So, for those who might like some formal words to use, here they are. The words, with music, appear in Chapter 11.

Here within this sacred space
My Guardians gather near
Fire's bright flames protect my right
At left, Earth's strength is here
Before me Air my vision clears
Behind the tides do swell
And all around, throughout this space
The Lord and Lady dwell.

Centering Meditations

I have mentioned, in various rituals, the process of centering before entering the circle. One meditation is printed within the Memorial Ritual for Neil, earlier in this chapter. Following are a few other suggested wordings.

Gather together, my brothers and sisters. Stand comfortably but straight and take three deep breaths. Picture a beautiful white light forming above your head, the peace and light of spirit. Allow the white light to pour down into your head, through the crown chakra, where it fills to overflowing, and courses on down to your third eye. And now feel the light pour into your throat chakra, fill and then overflow on downward to surround and fill your heart. The warmth and light flow on into your solar plexus, and downward into the root chakra. You are filled to overflowing with the white light. Let it flow downward, through your feet, into the Earth below. Now it reaches down to meet and gather the energy of the Mother. Feel that energy now move upward, through your feet, coursing through each chakra until it passes through the crown and cascades out and around you. Feel the energy around

*and through you, a pillar of peace and light, as you
ground and center, prepared now to enter our circle.*

*Gather 'round, now, in a relaxed position, close your eyes,
and take three deep breaths. Let your thoughts reach
upward and gather the silver and golden lights of the Cosmos. Draw them in a stream of light, down, down, down
until they flow into your body, filling it from head to foot.
Feel the warmth, the glow within. Now send your
thoughts downward, deep into the Earth, and gather the
strong, green energy of the Mother and her Horned Consort. Bring that energy up, up, up until it flows into your
body, filling it, blending with the silver and gold of the
Mother and Father of the Universe. Feel it blend and
become the pure, luminous light of the One. Feel it glow
and radiate, both within and without, reaching out to
touch and enfold those around you, as well. Now in the
center of your being, you are a pillar of light, from Cosmos to Earth and from Earth to Cosmos, all with the One,
at peace and ready to enter the circle.*

*Relax now and gather near; close your eyes and breathe
deeply. Inhale and breathe her breath of life. Visualize it
as pure, white, and cleansing. Take it into your body,
hold, and then slowly exhale, letting out of your body all
of the mental tensions of your day, all those thoughts of
difficulty, all problems which have evaded solution.
Replace them with another deep, long breath of pure,
luminous, golden light and clarity. Exhale again, letting go
of any heat of anger that may dwell within you, and draw
in the bright and fiery light of spirit and faith, and the
warmth of love all around you. And again exhale, letting
go of all negative emotions of the day, all doubts, all fears,
all worries. With another deep breath, now inhale the
cool, blue, fluid lightwaves of the Mother's love, nurturing
and soothing. And once more exhale, banishing all tired-
ness and discomfort, all the shifting sands of your concerns. Let them go. Let them go. Now deeply, deeply, take
in the green, healing light of Earth energy, opening yourself to new growth. Within you now, the lights of Air, Fire,
Water, and Earth, all lights of the spectrum, now blend*

together into the luminous, white light of the One. Feel that light fill you, as in the center of your being, you are at peace and secure, and let it now overflow, cascading all around you, back into the Earth, and reaching out with love to your brothers and sisters, as we prepare to share in our sacred circle.

Endnotes

1. Slater, Herman, Ed. *A Book of Pagan Rituals*. York Beach, ME: Samuel Weiser, Inc., 1978.

2. Abyss, RR 1, Box 213, Chester Road, Chester, MA, phone (413) 623-2155. Ask for information on crowns.

3. Farrar, Stewart and Janet. *Eight Sabbats for Witches*. Custer, WA: Phoenix Publishing, Inc., 1981.

4. James, Tamara and Jennifer Holding, *Libation*, 1988.

5. For those who are interested in pursuing more information, one of his primary references was the Dinshah Health Society, 1399 North Orchard Road, Vineland, NJ 08360.

Concerns, Hints, and Helps

Finding a Circle

A frequent complaint that I've heard from people here in San Diego and from other areas around the country (once they have found out that I am involved with Wicca) is about the difficulty they've had in finding Wiccan contacts. Often it is truly not easy. As has been said before, Wiccans are not out looking for converts, and in many cases, a reluctance to expose themselves to possible prejudice dictates a very "low profile" and considerable caution in revealing themselves to strangers.

Often you can locate Pagan groups through your local metaphysical book shop(s). Look to see if the shop carries a wide selection of books on Wicca, Magick, and Goddess revival. If it does, that means it has customers who are interested in those topics, and that among those customers are surely some who are doing ritual either as solitaries or with groups. Ask the proprietor. There's no guarantee, of course, that s/he will know, or will tell you if s/he does, but it's a start. The proprietor may have been quietly told by a Wiccan leader or two that it is okay to give out their phone number if the seeker seems seriously interested. Also, find out if the shop offers classes—many of them do. See if the class schedule has any topics that suggest sacred ritual work or "relating to the Goddess within," etc. The teacher is probably Pagan, or if not, may know of contacts you could make.

Most cities I've lived in have one or two weekly newspapers that cater to New Age readers and are often passed out free at book shops and health food stores. In this type of paper you may find listings of local events. Scan those to see if anyone is offering a Full Moon gathering or a class on a Wiccan-related subject. If you go, and ask questions of the people you meet there, you may find a contact.

When you seek contacts, do not expect to be met with immediate "open arms." Expect to answer a few questions about yourself, when you ask questions of others. Since Wiccan circles are small, close groups that meet in private homes, an invitation to come to a ritual is usually not given too freely. As has been said before, misunderstandings about Wicca exist, and many practitioners feel it necessary to remain anonymous to the general public. They will want to know you a little better first, so you should understand why, in such circumstances, they would want to "check you out" before letting you in on the place of circle meetings and the identities of those who meet there.

Also notice in the papers if there are any Renaissance Faires going on in your local area. Most Craft people are attracted to "Ren Faires." You can bet that many of the costumed attendees are in the Craft, and a good share of the vendors. Look what the vendors are selling. If their wares include items that could be used as ritual tools; or pentagrams, Wiccan books, etc.; then try to strike up a friendly conversation and ask questions.

In the Bibliography are addresses for a few of the Wiccan publications that I know of. Sending for any of these may possibly lead you to a contact in your area.

When you do make a contact, you should exercise the same kind of caution that they do! Arrange to meet the High Priestess and/or High Priest. If you feel comfortable with them, you might ask if you could attend a ritual. If they are comfortable with you, they may invite you—or they may wish to get to know you better first, perhaps suggesting that you come to a class, instead. Go, with openness and friendliness, but with your "antenna" alert. Choosing a circle is choosing a very close group of friends—a family. You want to feel comfortable with them, with their values, with what they do. Every group is different; all are autonomous. Ask questions. Don't assume that just because you've read this book, or a hundred other books on Wicca, you know what this particular group is about.

Yet, in spite of the above caveat, I do recommend that you attempt to find a compatible existing group, rather than to just start one of your own without training. There are things you just can't learn from books, no matter how strong a leader-type you may be. When you start out on something new, it's best to be a student before you become the teacher. I came to Wiccan training with a background of many years of involvement in various metaphysical activities, and a lot of experience as a speaker. I was still not ready to handle the energies of leading ritual. The training, the experience of working within a group, one step at a time, the initiations, and perhaps most of all the example set by Lady Beckett and Lord Landerthorn, changed me enormously—from the inside out.

It is possible, though, that you will not be able to find a circle in your area with which you would like to train. In that case, discuss your interest with a few like-minded friends, and perhaps you can start a circle with them. This is the way a good number of feminist Wiccan groups have begun, and some beautiful ritual work and a lot of mutual support has come out of them.

Starting a Circle

No matter what your background, before you have others to work with, you can work alone—solitary. Use meditation techniques and study ideas offered in this book and in others. As you practice ritual, you will become increasingly comfortable with the thoughts, feelings, energies, and motions involved.

If you have formally trained with a circle and wish to "spin off" and start your own among your friends and acquaintances, outside the circle in which you have trained, you can probably already identify some people who might be interested. If you open yourself to conversation, they will seek you out. When you think you have a little group that will work comfortably together, invite them for an organizational meeting. Or, you might first offer to conduct a ritual for them, so they can see what it is like to participate.

If you have not trained and have no access to a training circle, but still want to be part of one, initiate some informal meetings with a like-minded friend or a few friends, for conversation and group study. You might read and discuss some Wiccan books and talk over how, what, and where you would like to work together. Plan a ritual together, and do it!

If you are taking a leadership role in organizing your group, be aware that you are taking on a large responsibility. This issue was already addressed in the discussion of hierarchy in Chapter 6, but because I consider the topic to be of great importance, I will add a few thoughts here.

Whether you like it or not, invite it or not, there will be tend to be some people in any circle who will put the HPs on a pedestal. There's no doubt it can be a "heady" experience, but if you let it "go to your head," sooner or later you're likely to find out that the pedestal isn't so solid. I've heard of more than one circle in trouble because the HPs turned out to be human after all, and didn't catch on to that fact as soon as the others did.

You must guide your seekers, give them all the love and support that you can—but, at the same time, you must not encourage them to become in any way dependent on you. You must, indeed, actively encourage them to read, compare, discuss, disagree, question, and draw their own conclusions—in short, you must encourage independence and responsibility for self.

Never forget that teaching is a growth experience for the teacher as much as it is for the students. And that no matter what you say, the most profound influence you will have is through what you are. There is a quote I remember being given in a seminar I attended: "Example is not the best way to influence people—it is the *only* way."[1]

Having a circle takes a lot of time and thought—more than probably anyone truly realizes until they are a few months into it. It is best not to attempt to organize and lead one alone. A would-be High Priestess needs a reliable person whom she can count on for help, advice, and general moral support. This could be her High Priest or her Crone or her Maiden, but I would recommend not actually starting a circle until at least one such person is willingly available.

Circle Names

Various times throughout this book I've referred to others by names that I'm sure you realize are not the ones they were given at birth. It is a common practice in Craft to choose a "magickal name," or spiritual name, by which one is thereafter to be called during ritual. (Sometimes we slip up, but you are supposed to use only circle names during ritual.)

The idea of choosing a new name as part of a spiritual tradition is far from unique to Wicca. For example, in Judaic practice, the taking of an additional name in the temple (usually for a special purpose, such as a new start in the case of grave illness) is based on Midrash interpretations of the Genesis story where the patriarch Abram's name was changed by God to Abraham. Later in Genesis, the patriarch Jacob became Israel.[2] In the Catholic church, one takes a new name at Confirmation.

The practice of taking a new name in Wicca is often related to the "burning times" when life preservation could rest on not having anyone know one's true identity, but I think the "new name" practice is much older than that, and runs through many traditions and cultures.

Wiccans often take a new name at Dedication, and although my tradition does not require that choice at that time, most of our Dedicates have done so. We do expect that a First Degree Initiate will choose a circle name. The reasons for choices of new names vary widely, for the name should have a personal significance for that person. The name may evoke an example toward which the person aspires, or a trait by which the person is already known, or at least sees within self. It may be a Goddess or God name, or refer to something from nature (plants, animals, birds, etc.), or perhaps the choice could be an emotion or a state of mind.

My name, Mari (pronounced with a short "a": MAR-ee), was chosen in part because I really didn't want to change my name! My given name, Maria, means "the seas." I have Sun and Mercury in Scorpio, Moon in Cancer, and Neptune closely conjunct my Midheaven, with Pisces as my 4th house of home, ancestry, and foundation—a very "watery" chart! I remember my late teacher and mentor in Uranian Astrology, Charles Emerson, discoursing one day on the topic that people nearly always have their chart in their name, whether anybody intended it or not. He went on to illustrate his point with everyone present, and my name, he pointed out, was derived from the root *mar* for the sea, which was perfect for my chart, and also could be related to Mars, which would be the ancient ruler of my Sun sign. Others' names he associated with planetary mythology, rulers of the Ascendant—one thing or another—but always with a pointed correspondence.

Maria is also the equivalent of Mary in several languages, including that of my mother's origin, Denmark. (It is a family name—that of my great-grandmother and one of my aunts, as well.) I felt strongly, as said earlier in this book, as well as in *Twelve Wings* and in numerous talks I've given, that Mary is the mother of the Age of Pisces, and should be acknowledged as Goddess, just as much as Jesus is equated with God. So somehow, that name connotation also seemed appropriate, in setting my feet on the Path of service to the Goddess.

Additionally, I had spent much of my life actually suppressing my watery intuition (even in spite of a few incidents when it had come through quite strikingly), in favor of doing all the left-brain things that enabled me to achieve success in a culture that strongly favored that approach. Only in the best of my pre-astrology paintings, which are abstracted human figures emerging from and fused with natural forms, had the right-brain fully emerged, even though my logical side didn't understand them even after I'd painted them. How very Pagan they are—even though I had no knowledge or intent at the time of where I was going!

In any case, now I really wanted to allow that mysterious part of myself to open up and blossom. Somehow it just seemed that maybe I was "meant" to be "Maria-of-the-sea" for reasons beyond any that were ever intended by my mother. (Her name, coincidentally, is Anna, the traditional name for the mother of Mary, though I am quite sure that nothing was intended by the choosing of either name other than family tradition and individual preference.)

With the necessity of choosing a circle name, I decided upon Mari, whom Barbara Walker in her *Women's Encyclopedia of Myths and Secrets* identified as the pre-Christian Goddess of the Sea, sometimes seen as a mermaid. I have carried out that theme in a number of ways, beyond my sea motif for my altar tools (as described in Chapter 6). Messages sent to members of my circle have a mermaid stamped on the envelope, and I frequently wear mermaid jewelry.

My outdoor altar often has a mermaid statuette as the Goddess image, there's a mermaid relief sculpture on the outside wall of my house, and a mermaid fountain at the West Watchtower. The western wall of my interior room used for ritual has a large, beautiful painting of a mermaid by my daughter Molly.

Enough of my own reasons—possibly a bit more complex than some—but you should certainly get the idea of the personal significance of choosing a circle name. Prior to her Dedication, Molly spent hours and hours deliberating over the choice of her name, pouring through books, asking me for suggestions. In the end, she chose a name from within herself, suggested by nobody else. Meadow, she said, evoked an image of Nature, of peace, beauty, happiness, and freedom. And, so mote it be!

Mark (m'Lord Willow!) chose Willow because the bark is used in many healing preparations, and he is very interested in (and effective at!) healing. Additionally, he admired the flexibility of the willow branch, able to bend and yet remain very strong. (Mark, with Sun and other planets in Virgo, has earth strong in his chart, though this was not his reason for choosing an earthy Nature name—astrology was a very minor interest before he met me!)

I have not asked the specific reasons why others have chosen their names, but I do know that each person gives the choice serious thought. Names may express a particular stage of growth or state of mind at the time they are chosen, and later, with change, a new name is chosen to express the new consciousness that results. Or as Eldar told me, one name may be a "public" Wiccan name, for use in any circle or on computer bulletin boards, while another name may be chosen for more private use within a particular circle. It is not uncommon for a High Priestess spinning off to start her own circle (and/or her High Priest), to take a new name(s) at that time. Some of my close friends did so: Freya became Lady Aanja and Greraven became Lady Shelayne (while her HP Eldar became Lord Oberon). I kept my originally chosen name (becoming Lady Mari), as did Lady Joy-of-Heart, Lord Willow, Lord Falkan, and Lord Brujo. (A High Priestess is addressed with the title of "Lady" before her name, and her High Priest is addressed as "Lord.")

Preparation for Degrees

In Circle of the Cosmic Muse, as in Circle Atheneum and all of its daughter circles, part of the preparation for Dedication and for each of the three degrees is the completion of paperwork—written answers to a series of questions. The "paperwork" is not an arbitrary requirement, to be done merely for the sake of having to do something. It provides a framework for thought and discussion that helps both candidate and HPs determine whether or not it is the right time to move to the next step. It is not the only criterion. The HPs will have been observing the candidate's progress in performing the various parts of ritual, in handling the energies, in relating to the others, and in general personal growth. Yet these candidates are adults, not schoolchildren. By the time most of them actually complete their paperwork for a particular degree, they know, themselves, that they are ready. Thus these questions are more of a self-test than they are a device to prove anything to the HPs.

Questions to be Answered Before Dedication

Dedication questions do not have "textbook" answers. They are designed to provoke the candidate to carefully think through what s/he is doing and why. The candidate is given the dedication ritual to read at the same time as these questions are given. A Dedicate is making a promise to the Goddess and the God, not to the HPs or the circle. No commitment to the specific circle is required.

1. What does Wicca mean to you? And the term "Witch"?

2. Why do you wish to worship the Goddess?

3. What are you looking for in this religion?

4. Explain the threefold law and how it applies to you, or will apply to you, in your day-to-day life.

5. What does Dedication mean to you, and why are you doing it at this time?

6. Who or what are the Goddess and the Horned God?

7. What are your responsibilities as a Dedicate?

Questions to be Answered before First Degree

Again, these questions do not seek textbook answers, although looking up some of the words below in the dictionary has lead to a number of very deep and well-thought-out opinions from some of our initiates. (See "Ariel's Definitions" in Chapter 12.) Here we are still much more interested in the candidate's general self-awareness and careful thought about the step s/he is taking and why, than we are concerned about testing specific knowledge of our tradition. On completing this degree, the initiate is actually joining the circle into which s/he is initiated, committing to assist in the work of the circle and to continue learning its traditions, as well as seeking to grow in his or her own special interests. (Wiccans tend to develop specialties or primary interests; for example, one might study astrology, another might research herbs and become adept at using them, while another develops skill in the Tarot, etc.) The HPs are committing themselves to the initiate, to guide and assist him/her on the path. The HPs do not coerce progress, or pressure initiates on a timetable of achievement. They provide opportunities through classes and networking contacts, and they make themselves available to help when requested.

An exception to the above is when the HPs of a circle are occasionally asked to initiate a solitary practitioner. Some solitaries prefer not to be regular members of a group, but still want to experience initiation. In this case, the initiation rite may be altered slightly, and no extended obligation exists between the HPs and initiate.

Define in your own words and describe the purpose of each of the following:

1. religion
2. philosophy
3. clergy
4. worship
5. dedication
6. meditation
7. church
8. symbols
9. ritual
10. initiation
11. occult
12. prayer

13. Define the terms immanence and transcendence. Use a dictionary if you wish, but also explain how they relate to the Craft world view.

14. Do you consider Wicca, or the Craft, to be a religion or a philosophy or both? Why?

15. What do you think astrology is?

16. Who and what is the Goddess, and why is She so important in our times? (The answer expected here should be in greater depth than the description of the Goddess you gave for Dedication.)

17. What do you consider to be your responsibility as a First Degree Initiate?

18. What do you consider to be the responsibilities of a High Priestess/High Priest of a circle?

Questions to be Answered Before Second Degree

At this point we want to determine what the candidate has actually learned about our tradition, and if s/he is truly ready and able to handle the various aspects of our practice. The actual initiation begins with the candidate doing a complete ritual of his or her own writing, entirely unassisted, in the presence of the HPs and any other guests or circle members who have already completed Second Degree. A Second Degree initiate is considered to be completely ready to be responsible for self and to conduct ritual as a priest/ess, but is not yet acknowledged as being ready to lead his or her own circle. The Second Degree initiate will be scheduled to "work center" (meaning conduct the ritual as High Priest/ess) for one of our Full Moon rituals soon after his or her initiation. (I may have to make these questions a bit tougher now that our candidates will have this single textbook in which to look up nearly all the answers!)

1. Why do you wish to attempt the Second Degree?

2. What is the full purpose of ritual?

3. Define the terms invocation and evocation. Explain how each of them is used in the Craft.

4. Why is a circle cast before beginning a ritual? Briefly describe the specific procedure used in the Circle of the Cosmic Muse, with the order and intent of each action performed.

5. Briefly describe the purpose of each of these parts of ritual:

    Dedication

    Consecration

    Watchtowers

    Invocations

    Charge

    Great Rite

    Sharing

    Farewells

6. List the four elements with ten correspondences of each, including the signs of the zodiac and the Watchtowers.

7. What tools are used on the altar, and what is the elemental correspondence of each?

8. What symbols are used for cleansing and charging, and how?

9. Why are spaces, items, and intents cleansed and charged?

10. Why do we call the presence of Goddess and God to circle? In what order are they called and thanked, and why?

11. How many people do you need to set circle and worship the Goddess and the God?

12. What is an Esbat? Within this circle we have used astrological sign polarities to individualize the Esbats. List each sign with its complementary opposite and one or two keywords of each that show the contrasts between them.

13. List the eight Sabbats, the aspects of Goddess and God in each one, and how each one corresponds to the astrological and seasonal cycles.

14. Why are symbols of the past used in today's circle?

15. What are some modern symbols that could be used in the Craft, and how would you use them?

16. What is the purpose of music, poetry, and drama in ritual?

17. Write and present one Esbat ritual.

Questions to be Answered before Third Degree

Here we are looking for both demonstration of knowledge and depth of personal thought. A Third Degree Initiate is acknowledged as ready to spin off and start his/her own group if desired, so we want the candidate to think through potential plans for that. If s/he decides to stay within the home circle, s/he will be considered an elder whose input and advice is sought and valued in the scheduling and leading of circle activities. S/he will be expected to teach an occasional class, and will be scheduled to lead the Sabbat ritual s/he has written for the circle.

1. Choose a Goddess. Describe Her attributes for each of the three aspects, and explain how you relate to Her.

2. Choose a God. Describe His attributes to the waxing/bright and waning/dark aspects, and explain how you relate to Him.

3. Describe the Great Rite, list its purposes, and three ways that it can be performed.

4. List a schedule of classes for Wiccan training. Specifically, list at least twelve topics you feel should be presented ranging from an introduction to new seekers, through Dedication to Second Degree. List six others that you feel would be helpful/interesting to present, although not as essential as the twelve. Include at least a one-sentence description for each class.

5. Choose one of the topics listed below and prepare a paper that develops the material for class presentation. The paper would be at least the equivalent of five typewritten, double-spaced pages. (You may submit your own topic for approval, if you prefer. However, even though this is an astrology-intensive circle, the degree program is primarily Wiccan, so your topic must apply directly to Craft.)

    Ethics and the Craft

    Tools of the Craft

    Watchtowers

    The Threefold Goddess

    The Bright and Dark God

The Wheel of the Year

The Path of Wicca Today and in the Future

6. Write, plan, and present a Sabbat ritual.

Ritual Robes

Our circle and other circles we are acquainted with all work robed. Strict Gardnerian tradition calls for working "skyclad" (nude), and some readers familiar with that tradition may have wondered why I haven't mentioned it yet.

One of the rationales for working skyclad is that it expresses "freedom" and it "equalizes everyone." And supposedly, in the "burning times," Witches met in the forest skyclad to help avoid identifying clothing. If the latter was ever valid (which I question), this is *now*, and the rationale is valid no longer.

Working alone or with a close working partner aside, I know I am far from the only one who feels quite sufficiently free (and probably even a greater sense of freedom—not to mention comfort) working within the group while wearing a loose and flowing robe. The very act of putting on a robe that is made and reserved only for ritual begins a transition from the mundane that contributes to the mood and focus. As for equalizing—sorry, I do not agree that skyclad is equalizing. To the contrary, in fact. Every priestess and priest, no matter what their physical attributes, looks and feels attractive, special, and even grand, in a robe. The ladies look glamorous; the lords look as regal as they would in a tuxedo.

A fine robe that anyone will feel great in can be made very easily and inexpensively. We occasionally schedule a Saturday robe workshop to make new robes for new members, and often additional robes in a new color for older members. Those who have portable sewing machines bring them, and everyone gets involved helping others cut and pin and sew. Sometimes, prior to the actual sewing day, we've gone in groups to a fabric store so that those who have no previous experience with this sort of thing can have the benefit of shopping help. Following are some specific instructions for making simple, but very satisfactory, ritual robes.

Choosing the Fabric

Tradition says it should be "natural," as in all cotton or some other natural fabric. 100% cotton is nice—until you wash it, and have to spend almost as much time ironing it as you did making it. In this age of computerized "Books of Shadows" I fail to see why it hurts to have just a little mix of synthetic with the cotton, just enough to make the robe come out of the dryer ready-to-wear! It is usually possible to get 60-inch wide sheeting, or T-shirt/sweatshirt knits, in a wide variety of colors. Another good choice is desert cloth, which is supposed to look wrinkled—most convenient! You need three yards of 60-inch wide material for most people. Add another yard if the fabric is 45 inches wide, and you want sleeves. With a little comparison shopping, you should be able to get adequate fabric for about $10 to $15. Trim would add more, but having a nice robe will certainly be within the means of nearly everyone.

To be specific, figure exactly how much material you need by how tall you are from neck to floor. Double that, and add another foot for facing and hem. If the fabric is 60 inches wide, double your height plus a foot will be plenty. If the fabric is 45 inches wide, and you do not require long sleeves, the same formula will do. If you want sleeves, get an additional yard. Buy a spool of thread to match. Some like to edge the neckline and sleeves with one of the many types of gold, silver, or other colored braid trims that are available.

Some circles have specific color requirements for robes. We discourage black, unless one is either a Third Degree initiate or is of "Crone age." Our people choose whatever color pleases them. We ask that they choose solid colors rather than prints, unless the print is very subdued, because bold prints can be distracting in circle. Sometimes a border design or symbol can be painted on or appliquéed with trim. The circle Maiden usually wears white, the Crone black, the Red Priest red, the HPS red, the HP either gold or red—although we all have other colors and wear them at times.

Cutting Out and Sewing a Robe

Diagram #1 shows folds and cuts for basic robes with 60-inch wide fabric. Fold the material in half lengthwise, so that it is slightly longer than you are from neck to floor (about two inches longer is enough), with the fold at the shoulders. Now fold it in half across the width. The fold is now a line that would go down the center of your

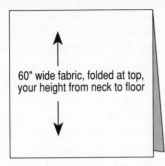

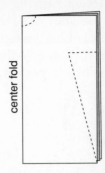

Fold the fabric again at the center. You will be cutting through 4 thicknesses of fabric. Use good, sharp scissors! Cut neck opening through top and center folds. Cut sleeves, if desired. (See robe #3)

60" wide fabric, folded at top, your height from neck to floor

center fold

Some fabrics look the same on both sides. Others are definitely more attractive on one side, and that's what you'll want outside, where it shows! For the purpose of all of these robe-making diagrams, "outside" is white and "inside" is gray.

Diagram #1: How to Cut the Fabric

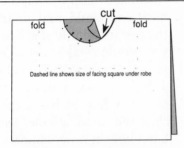

Dashed line shows size of facing square under robe

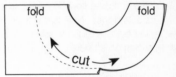

Trim outer edge of facing into a curve.

Cut a hole in a square of fabric that matches your neckline. You could trace it with chalk, or pin robe to fabric square, to make sure both neck holes are the same. Be sure the square is a least 2" bigger than the neckhole on all sides.

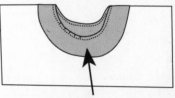

Pin neckline facing to outside of robe, with the right side (outside) of the facing down. Stitch about 1/2" from the neck edge, and then trim the edge to about 1/4" from the stitching. Making a few little scissor snips along curves will help you to press the facing to the inside smoothly. Snip almost to stitch line, not through it!

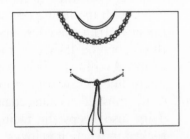

LAST: Press the facing to the inside of robe. The basic robe is finished! Trim as you wish. To make a place for a cord belt to tie through just the front of the robe, as on Robe #2, make two machine buttonholes. Run the cords through one, around your waist and out through the other.

Diagram #2: How to Finish the Neckline

body. Cut a small curve across the folded corners, as shown. Then unfold the material, put your head through the hole, and see if you like the neckline. If it's not big enough, fold it up again and cut out a little more—cautiously. (You can always cut the hole bigger, but if you get it too big, you have a problem! Not an insurmountable one, mind you. There are trims, etc., but ...)

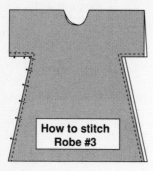

Stitch under the arms and down the sides as is shown by the dotted lines. Note that you stitch with the "inside" out! It's easier to stitch if you pin first, as shown on left side.

How to stitch Robes #1 and #2

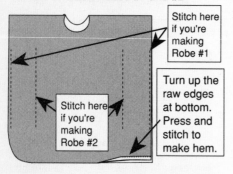

Stitch here if you're making Robe #1

Turn up the raw edges at bottom. Press and stitch to make hem.

Stitch here if you're making Robe #2

The lower left corner of this robe shows the option of cutting off the corners into a curve. This is a good idea with this type of robe. It is graceful, and it prevents the sides of the robe from dragging on the floor when your arms are down at your sides.

Also note that the stitch line does not go all the way to the bottom, thus leaving side slits from about knee down. The neckline has been cut lower in the front than in the back. These are among the ways you can easily vary the basic design.

Diagram #3: How to Stitch Robes

Once you have the neckline a size that pleases you, you need only to finish it. (See Diagram #2. Note: If you want a hood on the robe, it must be added before the neckline is finished. See hood in Diagram #6.) You could fold under the edge twice and sew it, or you could make a facing (See Diagram #2). To make a facing, take a square of fabric a few inches larger than the neckline hole, and cut a hole in it the same size as your neckline. (You could trace with chalk.) Round off the corners on the edges of the square, and sew the two pieces (facing and garment) together at the neckline edge, with the facing on the outside. Trim the edge, and then iron the facing to the inside. As a final touch, you might like to sew some trim to the finished neckline edge. Trim also keeps the facing tucked in where it belongs.

Alternatives other than facing for finishing raw edges are possible. For example, you could press under the edges of the neckline as if you were making a narrow hem, and stitch. Or you can purchase decorative bindings that cap the edges. For soft, thin, or flimsy fabrics, however, you will probably need the facing to give the neckline enough substance to hold its shape.

All you have left to do now is sew up the sides and hem. (See Diagram #3.) Turn the robe inside out and sew a seam on each side as shown. You might like to trim the bottom edge corners into a curve, leave a side slit to the knee, or you could sew all the way down. Iron the seam open and then turn the robe right side out again. Try it on, and have someone else pin the hem up, just a half-inch or so from the floor, so you won't trip over it. Iron the hem up along the pin lines, turning under the raw edge and then sewing it. You may not need to finish the sleeve opening if you used the entire width of the fabric, because the selvage edge is finished enough. If this is not the case, you will need to turn in the raw edges of the sleeve opening, too—iron first, then sew.

These basic robes (Robe #1 is shown at right) can be made in a very short time, with a sewing machine and someone to help pin the hem. We've turned out a half-dozen or more in an afternoon. It works for either women or men. It would not take more than an evening of stitching, even if you had to sew it by hand. A woman from one tradition told me that her High Priestess required everyone to sew the initiation robe entirely by hand, focusing intent into every stitch. This is fine, but I'm afraid I am a confirmed "techno-Pagan." I prefer a sewing machine. (I can focus intent during that process, too!)

Robe #1

A pretty alternate for the women is to sew the side seam about a foot in on both sides. This creates a pretty ripple effect down the side (Robe #2, Diagram #3).

Some men prefer to have actual sleeves. If so, the variation for cutting is as shown in Diagram #1 and the result is illustrated as Robe #3. The man can lie down on the fabric while someone traces around him in chalk. Always err on the side of cutting too big. You can always sew the garment smaller, but if you cut too deep under the arms, it can be a real challenge trying to fix it. Insetting extra fabric under the sleeve is no fun!

Some like to add a hood (Robe #6, Diagram #6). For that you need additional fabric. If you bought an extra half yard of fabric, you will be able to do it. You need a rectangle about a half yard by one yard. Cut it as shown. Run a double line of loose machine stitching along the curved edge, and pull the threads into a gather. Or, use a neat trick discovered by Lady Aanja, if your machine does zig-zag

Robe #2   Robe #3

Robe #4

Robe #5

Robe #6

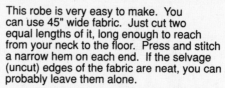

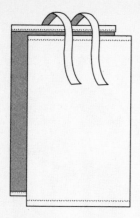

This robe is very easy to make. You can use 45" wide fabric. Just cut two equal lengths of it, long enough to reach from your neck to the floor. Press and stitch a narrow hem on each end. If the selvage (uncut) edges of the fabric are neat, you can probably leave them alone.

Purchase enough grosgrain ribbon or decorative trim to make shoulder straps, with extra for trim, if you wish. Hold one length of fabric in front of you, decide how high up on your chest you want it to be, and then pin a ribbon strap on each side.

Drape the ribbons over your shoulder and mark with a pin about where the back of the fabric should be. Be sure the ribbons are equally distant from the sides of the fabric. Pin the ribbons to the back piece and try it on again until you're satisfied, and then stitch the ribbon to the fabric.

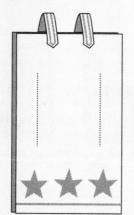

Try it on again. This time decide about how high under your arms you want the sides closed, and mark it with a pin, keeping the measurement the same on both sides. You'll be able to place the stitch line about 8" or so in from the edges, depending on how big you are. Pin the fabric together, outsides out. Run a line of stitching on each side, as shown by the dashed lines. You can leave the sides open from floor to knee, or higher. When you try the robe on now, you'll see that the sides fall in a pretty ripple effect.

Simple non-distracting designs can be made with fabric paint. Shown above are stenciled stars, which could be subtle but nice in silver gilt paint on a white robe, for example. Freezer paint makes a good stencil. Cut out the design and then lightly iron the paper on the fabric. It will stick enough to prevent the paint from getting where it shouldn't be, and will easily peel off when the paint is dry. Dab the paint into the stencil opening with a little piece of sponge.

Diagram #4: How to Make Robe #4

stitching. Zig-zag over a length of embroidery thread which is laid along the edge you want gathered. You can then pull the embroidery thread to create the gathers. (The standard double stitch of machine thread tends toward frustrating breaks, which is why standard sewing instructions tell you to use a double row of stitching rather than just one. Lady Aanja's method works faster, and virtually eliminates breakage.) Iron under the raw edge of the straight side and sew to finish it. Pin the gathered edge into the unfinished neckline of the robe as shown. When you add the facing, the raw edge of the hood will be inside.

Other variations in style are shown in Robes #4 and #5. These two ideas can use 45-inch wide fabric, which is easier to find in a wider variety of fibers and colors than 60-inch fabric. The instructions for making Robe #4 are given in Diagram #4.

Simple, non-distracting designs can be added with fabric paint. The stars on Diagram #4 could be stenciled on with fabric paint, which is easy to find at any craft shop and most fabric stores. I made a pretty Maiden's robe by stenciling a border of silver glitter-paint stars along the hem of the fabric, which was a very subtle white-on-white print of tiny stars. Freezer paper makes a good stencil. Cut out the design and then lightly iron the paper on the fabric. It will stick enough to prevent the paint from getting where it shouldn't be, and will easily peel off after the paint is dry. You can dab the paint into the stencil opening with a little piece of sponge.

Robe #5 shows a sleeveless overpiece, for which 45-inch wide fabric would be more than adequate for most people. For this you would fold the fabric as in Diagram #1 and cut the neck opening. Then, while still folded, carefully slit the center front *only* from the neck opening to the bottom edge. You would have to finish the entire neckline and front opening edges by either facing them, by pressing under and stitching, or by binding the edges with commercial decorative binding. The stitching is shown below on Diagram #5.

The under-robe shown in Robe #5 is exactly the same as Robe #3. It's best to use 60-inch wide fabric for the under-robe. If you

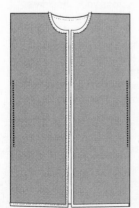

The under-robe is made exactly the same way as Robe #3. The sleeveless, long vest that is worn over it can be made from 45" wide fabric. Fold over a piece long enough to reach, folded, from your neck to your ankles. Fold it again vertically, as in the diagrams for cutting Robe #3, and cut a neck hole. Then slit ONE side of the fabric ONLY, from the neck all the way down the center.

Fold the robe with the inside out, as shown. Starting at least 12" (or more) down from the top, stitch about 1/2" from the outer edges to about 12" to 15" from the bottom. Narrow hem or bind all of the raw edges of neckline, front opening and bottom. Press, and turn right side out. It's done—unless you'd like to add some decorative trim.

Diagram #5: How to Make the Overpiece for Robe #5

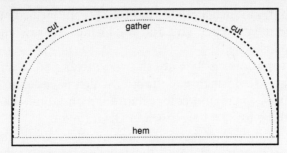

Cut a piece of fabric about one yard long and two feet wide. Trim off the corners on one side into a curve, as shown by the dashed line. Finish the straight edge with a narrow hem or with binding. Run a gathering stitch along the curved edge and pull up the gathers evenly.

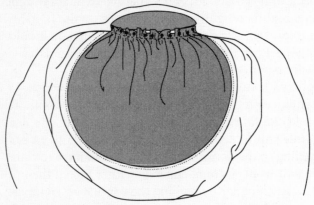

BEFORE you face or otherwise finish the raw neckline edge, pin the gathered hood to the sides and back of the neckline. The front edge of the hood should come to at least an inch or two in front of where the neckline would lie across your shoulders. Stitch the hood in place.

NOW, pin and stitch the facing to the neckline, catching the hood edge in between robe and facing. Trim all the edges, then press the facing to the inside of the robe. OR, trim the edges of hood and neckline close to the stitch line and then bind the edges with decorative binding. (See instructions for How to Finish the Neckline.)

Diagram #6: How to Make a Hood

must use 45-inch wide material to make a robe with long sleeves, it would probably be best to use a commercial pattern. Most pattern books have at least one for a man's kaftan or robe. Of course, if you are experienced at sewing and using patterns (or perhaps have a different skill to barter with a friend who sews), "the sky's the limit." You can find many dress patterns that you could easily adapt for robes. What has been provided here are only the very simplest options that I know, from actually watching it happen. These projects can be done by those who have never even thought of sewing before!

Head Wreaths

It's fun to make head wreaths—especially for Beltane, when at times we've gathered early, before ritual, to make them with live flowers. For lasting and repeated wear, however, beautiful dried flowers or silk flowers are available in craft shops—or you can collect flowers yourself and hang them upside down to dry. This is not just a craft for the women in your group. Men, too, enjoy wearing crowns of natural materials—perhaps the oak or holly leaves of the Oak King or Holly King, or wreaths of grains, or colored autumn leaves—just a bit more rustic and less frilly than the ladies would prefer. Collect an assortment of leaves and flowers, berries and branches, and watch the fabric store sales for spools of ribbon. A few pieces of flower wire can be purchased at a craft or floral supply store quite inexpensively, as can a roll of floral tape. A hot glue gun is a big help, too.

Just make a wire band that fits your head, and then start tying, gluing, or weaving the leaves and flowers around it. For the women, a cascade of ribbons down the back is very pretty. Some of my friends have a wide assortment of wreaths hanging on their walls, to wear when they choose, and provide wall decoration in between. They have wreaths in colors and materials for various seasons, and to represent various aspects of Goddess or God.

As mentioned in Chapter 9 (Virgo Full Moon), I have a beautiful wreath of white silk flowers, silver leaves, and pearls that is worn by my Circle Maiden. It was made by my eldest daughter Shannon, when she and my little granddaughter came to visit shortly before the circle where our first Maiden was to be crowned.

Since that time Ariel, who succeeded Terra as Maiden after Terra's spin-off, made special crowns for the times when three priestesses would take the roles of Maiden, Mother, and Crone in the same ritual. Her idea, which turned out very successfully, was to cut around plastic liter soda bottles in a gracefully curved crown shape.

She covered one of them each with white, red, and black fabric, and then decorated them with a pretty sequin design, with the triple Moons at center.

Masks

As in two of the Sabbat rituals included in this book, sometimes it is effective to use masks. For the Midsummer ritual, we used an assortment of pretty feathered ones that I got in the French Quarter when United Astrology Congress was held in New Orleans a few years ago, but for the public Samhain, we made our own. For the four elements, we purchased inexpensive white plastic face masks at a craft shop. (These are fairly easy to find, if you're in a city where a large arts and crafts store is available.) We cut curves up from the bottom, so the wearers' mouths would be free, and cut the eyes out a little larger. Then we sprayed glue on the front and shook on plenty of glitter in the appropriate color for each element. Each person wore fabric in the color of the element draped over his or her head, and held in front where it concealed the flashlight that was being held pointed upwards to illuminate the face. As said in the ritual description, the flashlights were covered with colored cellophane so they would glow in the corresponding color. The light picked up color and glitter highlights. It looked very striking.

At the public Samhain last year (led by Lady Aanja and Lord Falkan—it rotates every year), the Guardians of the four quarters were resplendent in white hooded robes in which miniature Yule tree lights lined the edge of the hoods (one hood each in yellow, red, blue, or green, of course), which were lit by small hidden batteries. (It's always fun, here among the San Diego circles, to see who will come up with what next!)

In any case, my publisher, Carl Llewellyn Weschcke, has suggested that I should add some instructions on mask-making to this how-to section, so I will reach back into my art teaching background for an idea or two, especially for those readers who may not be anywhere near a large craft shop, or who might have limited money to spend for supplies.

My best suggestion for art from scrap material, with very little cost, is papier-mâché. All you need for that is a bunch of old newspapers and a little wheat paste (wallpaper paste), which you can find at any hardware store or place that sells home decorating supplies, and some kind of paint. (Lacking even wheat paste, you could use a flour and water mixture.) You need something to form the mask over—to hold it in a shape until it dries. A blown-up balloon about the size of a person's head works well, but for a very well-formed and comfortable mask, the face of a willing and patient friend works even better. (I've had grade school students in the distant past who loved to do this for each other!)

To mix the paste, put cold or tepid water in a pan and add paste a little at a time, stirring constantly, until you have a smooth glop that is not too thick, and not too thin. (How do I explain that? Not quite as thick as cooked oatmeal cereal, but not watery, either—maybe more like a rich cream soup. If you are using commercial wheat paste—which is what I recommend—there will be mixing instructions on the bag.)

Prepare some paper by tearing it into usable pieces. For starters, the pieces would probably be, say, a little more than an inch wide and a little less than a foot long. Actually, I tear the paper up pretty randomly and irregularly. My "measurements" are just to give you some idea, if you are one of the rare people who managed to get through grade school without having to do a papier-mâché project!

If you are using a friend's face on which to model your mask, I suggest that you also get a package of cheesecloth (a grocery store or hardware store should have it) and cut a piece to lay over the face before you start applying the paste-soaked paper. It won't protect your friend's face much from feeling a bit sticky and then stiff, but it will make removing the mask a little nicer. Also protect the hair from getting pasty by pulling it back, and covering it with a scarf.

Protect the table you're working on with a layer of newspaper, and wear old, washable clothes. The dried wheat paste will come off most things, but it's no fun. It will also wash off your hands in warm, soapy water—promise!—even though when it starts to dry, you may wonder if you'll have to peel it off.

Take each strip of paper, one at a time, and dip it in the paste. Smooth off the excess with your fingers, and then lay it across your model (balloon or face). Keep adding another and then another, overlapping a little each time until you have one layer over the entire area you want to cover. If the live model is willing to keep eyes closed you could go over the eyes, and cut out shapes later, but I would prefer to work carefully around the eyes, creating opening shapes as I go, that could be refined later when the basic mask is dry. Also for a live model, you will want to leave a small breathing opening under the nose. Build up one layer of pasted paper over another, carefully smoothing each strip into the others. About five or six layers should do it.

I sometimes have used white facial tissue for the final layer, to smooth the surface and provide a white, non-printed surface for painting. Now you must let the mask dry enough to hold its shape before removing it from the face or balloon. Your live model could meditate, nap, or read (if you've left the eyes open). The mask will have to stay on at least until it is dry enough to hold its shape—completely dry is not necessary. Lift the damp but firm mask carefully off and let it dry, perhaps supported in its shape by wadding up a loose ball of dry newspaper to put under it. (For a mask built on a balloon, leave it alone until it is completely dry.)

A softer type of paper, such as facial tissue or napkin, also works more easily than newspaper if you'd like to build up minor ridges to give the face expression, such as eyebrows, character lines around the mouth, etc. I don't recommend that you do very much of this detailing while the mask is on someone's face. It will make the mask too wet and they'll have to leave it on too long to be comfortable. Instead, let the basic face shape dry enough to remove the mask, let it dry completely, and then work your detailing over the dry base. Blend and smooth one thin layer over the whole mask as a final step, so you'll make sure all the details stay where they belong, and you'll have a good crack-free painting surface. (You can, of course, purchase papier-mâché mixtures designed for such modeling purposes at an art store, but a good job can be done with the low cost common household materials I've described here.)

While the basic mask is drying, you could prepare some other papers for shapes to add to it later. Let's say you want a Sun mask that has long, pointy shapes sticking out all around. Lay about six sheets of newspaper together and cut, through all the layers, the shapes you want. That way, of course, you have six of each shape. Soak all six in the paste, smoothing off the excess, and stick them together. Lay each shape out to dry, perhaps on a cookie sheet or waxed paper. Check on them from time to time, because they should dry fairly fast. When they are dry enough to begin holding their shape, you could add dimension by rolling them into a slightly curved or twisted position. You may or may not need to prop them in the curve with a balloon or wad of dry paper, but they will hold the shape when they are completely dry.

When the basic mask is dry, remove it from the face or balloon. Now you can refine the edges, and add things. Trim the edges into a slightly different shape, if you like, with a scissors, and also refine the eye openings. Working with little pieces of pasted paper, you can go over all the raw edges to make them smoother. Adding things is just a matter of using more pasted paper to join one piece to another. You don't want to get the whole thing all wet again, so you're working more carefully now, with smaller pieces, all around each joint. There are lots of lightweight things you could possibly add besides the pointy Sun ray shapes. You might papier-mâché the stem ends of feathers, lightweight sticks or branches (that look like antlers, perhaps!), the stems of artificial flowers or leaves—whatever fits the myth your mask is supposed to portray.

When all is dry, you need only to decorate the mask. An obvious choice is paint. School-type tempera paints will do fine. You can shellac as a final coat, if you want gloss. Shellac will also help preserve the mask for long-term, repeated use. You can add glitz with glitter, trim with beads—the possibilities are unlimited. (For that Midsummer ritual, we had New Orleans masks that were appropriate for everything but the Sun, so Eldar made that mask from a plastic base mask purchased at a crafts store. He built out the rays with long pipe-cleaners and finished it with lots of gold paint and gold glitter.)

Illustrated on the next page is a possible design for a Sun God mask made from papier-mâché, according to the general instructions I've given you. This is a very stylized design because I think that is actually easier to do, and come out with a good result, that to try to do more realistic facial features. I'd suggest painting this one with different shades of orange, gold, and yellow, with metallic gold for trim and highlights. Give the whole thing a final coat of high-gloss shellac.

Crafts stores have lots of choices to make feathered masks, in beautifully colored small, downy ones and in large plumes, but if you're not near a craft store but you are near a farm with chickens, you should be able to collect plenty of feathers. The most spectacular mask I ever saw was an elaborate black feathered concoction on a native dancer at the Polynesian Cultural Center in Hawaii. I was so impressed that I asked where they got the beautiful feathers. The dancer pointed to the black chickens that were running around the

Sun God Mask

grounds. Most of the mask was made from layer upon layer of the downy little feathers that all the chickens dropped. The graceful longer feathers on the edges of the mask were just like those in the roosters' tails. I was surprised that something so exotic was made from chicken feathers, but it was.

To layer with feathers, you'd want to start with the outer edge of the mask and work toward the center, overlapping each row of feathers over the one before. I'd suggest using a commercial white glue that dries translucent.

A possible variation on the newspaper papier-mâché, if you'd like to have a translucent effect that you don't have to paint, is tissue paper and liquid laundry starch. I've never made a mask with tissue paper, but I know it would work, because I've made animal-shaped lanterns for my kid's rooms this way. (I'd hang an electric light bulb in the center, like a swag lamp.) Take a big inflated balloon (or balloons, for different parts), colored tissue paper, the starch, and a paintbrush. Tear off strips of tissue and paint them onto the balloon with the starch, soaking each strip and overlapping as you go. Use the starch full strength—don't dilute it. You will need to build up quite a few layers to make it hold. You can get interesting effects by using several colors, because one will show through the other. When it's dry, pop the balloon, trim where desired, and attach parts, if that's applicable, by stripping them together with a little more tissue and starch. Curved shapes can be cut out of one large hardened balloon shape. This technique makes a lightweight shell through which light will show.

Incidentally, if you like to decorate windows with paint on occasion, tissue paper and liquid starch make a much more effective decoration. This kind of decoration is more translucent and, in my opinion, a bit easier to clean up. I've decorated glass room dividers with this technique and left them up for many months, and my students used to decorate the school windows for holidays. The effect of light shining through the randomly overlapped tissue colors is really pretty, somewhat like stained glass.

With a large balloon to start with, you could even make a papier-mâché mask that would cover the entire head. If you have made a face-only mask, you will, of course, need something to attach it to the head. Thin elastic is easily available at any fabric store, and you can attach it to the edges of the mask by stapling or sewing.

Of course, to avoid the papier-mâché mess, you could get a basic mask of the type that is sold for kids at Halloween, and build on it with your own creative ideas, adding any of the trims mentioned before. I think, though, that some form of papier-mâché gives you the maximum in lightweight flexibility for all sorts of fantastic creations.

Ritual Wands

Besides our robe workshops, we've also held wand workshops, where we share tools and expertise to convert wooden branches into beautiful wands. Mostly we've used driftwood or fallen branches that have nicely dried out.

Lady Mari with her Wand

If you must take a branch from a living tree, you should do so respectfully. Ask the spirit of the tree for its gift, tie off the place to be cut with a red cord, score it with the boline, and pass the boline through the complete cut after the sawing is done. Afterward, thank the tree and give it a gift of water. The branch will need to be thoroughly dry before it can be made into a wand.

The wood is first cut to an appropriate length. The traditional length is from the elbow to fingers, though as with most other things, this rule is not absolute. Some people like them longer, and some petite. After a thorough sanding (and yes, we do use power tools!), we generally oil the wood to bring out the grain. A favorite embellishment is to mount a crystal point in the top end. We do this by boring a hole in the end with a power drill, inserting the crystal, and securing it with epoxy. From there we decorate according to the natural lines of the wood, perhaps mounting smaller stones or crystals in the hollows. Symbols or runes can be added with wood burning tools. My wand has a little silver mermaid and a silver crescent Moon mounted near the top. A cascade of very small crystals surround the base of the top-mounted laser crystal point.

Resourcefulness When Fire is Prohibited

Sometimes you just can't do what you'd like to do. For example, you're having a ritual in a public place, like a park or a hotel meeting room, and you are told okay, but no fire—not even one candle. Use a battery-powered flashlight with colored cellophane over the top—or a white paper bag "lantern" diffuses the light nicely. Around Christmastime it is easy to find battery-powered candle sticks, the flame for which is a Christmas tree bulb. We have used those to call Watchtowers on one public ritual occasion, using a colored bulb of the appropriate color for each element. For the annual public Samhain, Eldar constructed striking Watchtower lights by mounting appropriately colored miniature tree lights in the shape of pentagrams. They were powered by batteries, and had an easy switch-on mechanism. Near Halloween it is usually fairly easy to find (in children's toy departments) "wands" of different colors that glow in the dark. Put modern technology to use! It may not be quite as romantic as candlelight, but it works.

Herbs and Oils

You can buy lots of pre-packaged incenses, healing mixtures, and oils for various purposes at most any metaphysical book shop, but most Wiccans sooner or later get to the point of preferring to concoct mixtures themselves, so they know everything that's in it and what the correspondences are. I am not going to go into lists of correspondences here—there are excellent books available that go into much more detail than I could provide in a small portion of this book. If you want to make your own preparations, you will need to acquire books that specialize in the subject. Look in the bibliography for my recommendations.

Although I am beginning to experiment with some recipes of my own, my primary ones were handed down by Habondia, Crone of Circle Atheneum, under a strict pledge of secrecy, so they, like our initiation rituals, are withheld from this public Book of Shadows. I will, however, give you a few recipes that are the result of a full day that I spent with several of my friends who are High Priests or High Priestesses. We pooled our collections of herbs and oils, tried out various combinations, and tested them to see how they behaved as incense. This prior experimentation is an idea I'd highly recommend. You don't want to find out after your ritual begins that your concoction burns with such heavy smoke that it threatens to drive people out of the room, or that it starts out smelling heavenly, and after awhile, smells quite the opposite. Habondia still laughs about her first experimentation with a Yule incense containing cinnamon that was wonderful—until it began to smell like very badly burned cookies!

First, here are a few bits of general information on working with herbs and oils.

Harvest fresh herbs with your boline, meditating on proper respect for the plant and thanking it as you do so. The herbs will need to be dried, which you can do by tying them upside down in bunches. Pinched for time and in need of a particular herb *now*, however, I have been known to again use modern technology and quick-dry them in my microwave! (I have an old newspaper cartoon on that—a typical Halloween hag-type witch is consulting a book, before her microwave. The caption: "... add one bat wing and a dash of cobwebs, microwave on high 3-4 minutes, rotate ½ turn once during heating. Remove from oven, leave covered for 2 minutes. Hexes six.")

It's okay to store individual dry herbs in a plastic bag, but once you have mixed them into an incense, tea, or whatever, you should store the mixture in a glass jar—opaque glass is best if it's to be kept out in the open. If the jar is clear glass, store it in a closed cabinet.

When you mix herbs for a magickal purpose, the intent for which the mixture is to be used should be clearly in mind. Cleanse and charge your tools, and meditate on the intent all the time you are working. Balance your selections for aroma and texture, but also for male/female and elemental correspondences.

One of Habondia's hints that she does want me to pass on is the warning that essential oils are strong and highly flammable. It is important that you work with them in a ventilated area, for inhaling too strong a dose of some of them could make you feel ill. It is even more important that you not work with them near a source of fire. She says no book she's seen so far tells about this danger, but she has tested them, and was shocked at first, at how quickly these oils go up in flames. A few drops of oil in an herbal incense mixture is an asset in improving the aroma, but you definitely do not want to chance accidentally spilling the bottle of oil near the burning charcoal! Do your mixing away from the fire.

Some essential oils, in their pure form, burn the skin. You can check this possibility by testing a drop on the inside of your arm, but even this is not a sure test. An oil may seem fine when you are serenely working alone, but it seems that somehow within the energy of being in circle, the pores of the skin are more open and sensitive, and what did not burn before, may. I have personally experienced this, and so have several friends. Some people are more sensitive than others, or more sensitive at some times than others. For this reason, you should avoid using anointing oil mixtures at full strength. Cut them with a base oil, such as canola, saffron, almond, or jojoba. They will smell just as nice and will not burn the skin. If it should happen, during a ritual, that someone is experiencing an uncomfortable burning sensation on their forehead, where they've been anointed with oil, offer the water from the altar. Rubbing a little water over the area will usually diminish the effect.

Now, for a few of the recipes that passed the "scent approval" tests of our experimental day. Most of these were based on suggestions from Scott Cunningham's books (see Bibliography), although we changed some of the ingredients. After our session, Lady Joy-of-Heart compiled the correspondences given after each ingredient, mostly, she says, from Cunningham's books.

Air Incense

4 parts benzoin	(Air-Masculine-Sun)
2 parts gum arabic	(Air-Masculine-Sun)
1 part lavender	(Air-Masculine-Mercury)
1 pinch wormwood*	(Fire-Masculine-Mars)
1 pinch mint or sage+	(Fire-Masculine-Mars)
*Can substitute mugwort	(Earth-Feminine-Venus)

+With sage it is pungent; with mint it is fresh and clean smelling. We liked it better with some mint oil added.

Fire Incense

This is a very nice blend.

3 parts frankincense	(Fire-Masculine-Sun)
2 parts Dragon's Blood	(Fire-Masculine-Mars)
1 part red sandalwood	(Air-Masculine-Mercury)
1 pinch saffron*	(Fire-Masculine-Sun)
Few drops musk oil	(Earth-Feminine-Venus)

*Orange oil as an alternative is good, perhaps preferable.

Water Incense

We found this one to be great, just as given.

2 parts benzoin	(Air-Masculine-Sun)
1 part myrrh	(Water-Feminine-Moon)
1 part sandalwood	(Air-Masculine-Mercury)
Few drops lotus oil	(Water-Feminine-Moon)
Few drops ambergris oil	(Earth-Feminine-Venus)

Earth Incense

We liked this one quite a bit; we found we didn't really need the salt, in regard to burning behavior or smell.

2 parts pine needles	(Earth-Feminine-Saturn)
1 part patchouli	(Earth-Feminine-Saturn)
1 pinch fine powdered salt	(Earth)
Few drops cypress oil	(Earth-Feminine-Saturn)

Esbat Incense 1

This one is romantic and sexy, but it is heavy-burning—best for out-doors.

4 parts frankincense	(Fire-Masculine-Sun)
3 parts myrrh	(Water-Feminine-Moon)
2 parts benzoin	(Air-Masculine-Sun)
1 part sandalwood	(Air-Masculine-Mercury)
Few drops gardenia oil	(Water-Feminine-Moon)
1/2 part orris	(Earth-Feminine-Venus)
1/2 part thyme	(Water-Feminine-Venus)
1/2 part rose petals	(Air-Feminine-Venus)
Few drops rose oil	

Esbat Incense 2

We found this one to be musky—not sweet. It reminded us of autumn; does not burn as heavily as the one given above.

Equal parts:

Patchouli	(Earth-Feminine-Saturn)
Calamus	(Water-Feminine-Moon)
Mugwort	(Earth-Feminine-Venus)
Cinnamon	(Air-Masculine-Mercury)
Sandalwood	(Air-Feminine-Venus)
Few drops ambergris	(Earth-Feminine-Venus)
Few drops camphor	(Water-Feminine-Moon)

Esbat Incense 3

Use this one in a small room. It is soft and nice; not smoky.

3 parts lavender petals	(Air-Masculine-Mercury)
2 parts frankincense	(Fire-Masculine-Sun)
1 part rose petals	(Air-Feminine-Venus)
1/2 part orris	(Earth-Feminine-Venus)
Few drops sandalwood oil	(Air-Masculine-Mercury)
Few drops gardenia oil	(Water-Feminine-Moon)

Circle Incense

This is another one that is very soft and subtle—good for indoors.

4 parts frankincense	(Fire-Masculine-Sun)
2 parts myrrh	(Water-Feminine-Moon)
2 parts benzoin	(Air-Masculine-Sun)
1 part sandalwood	(Air-Masculine-Mercury)
1/2 part cinnamon	(Air-Masculine-Mercury)
1/2 part rose petals	(Air-Feminine-Venus)
1/4 part vervain	(Earth-Feminine-Venus)
1/4 part rosemary	(Fire-Masculine-Sun)
1/4 part bay	(Fire-Masculine-Sun)

Here are a few oils that we concocted ourselves, by experimentation, and especially liked. Remember, use 1/2 of a base oil (almond, jojoba, canola, etc.) and 1/2 of all essential oils combined.

Imbolc Oil

Use almond for the base oil on this one.

10 parts clove	(Fire-Masculine-Sun)
5 parts wisteria	(Air-Feminine-Venus)
5 parts lotus	(Water-Feminine-Moon)
5 parts musk	(Earth-Feminine-Venus)
20 parts Dragon's Blood	(Fire-Masculine-Mars)

Cleansing/Protection Oil

Equal parts:

sandalwood	(Air-Masculine-Mercury)
rosemary	(Fire-Masculine-Sun)
rose geranium	(Fire-Masculine-Mars)

Waxing of the Year Circle Oil

18 parts carnation	(Fire-Masculine-Sun)
3 parts ambergris	(Earth-Feminine-Venus)
4 parts musk	(Earth-Feminine-Venus)
5 parts sandalwood	(Air-Masculine-Mercury)
5 parts lavender	(Air-Masculine-Mercury)

Music

Following are the songs and chants mentioned within the rituals in this book, and a few extras that weren't. We usually sing or chant while people are being brought into circle, when the kiss is passed, and during the time that the HPs are passing around the chalice and cakes. Sometimes we use chants to help raise energy during the working.

The first group of songs and chants comes from the "oral tradition" of the Craft. Everyone seems to know them—I've learned them by hearing them sung in various circles. I do not know who originally wrote them—if I did, I would most certainly give proper credit. If anybody knows for sure, I'd like to hear from you, so that I can credit the source in the future.

I have provided a melody line as I've heard it, in a range that is comfortable for me to sing. My voice is an ordinary limited range medium-low, and I find that I usually instinctively start in a key that is comfortable for most people, male or female, so hopefully, these will work for you.

The second group is made up of songs that I have written, and words that I have written to fit popular tunes. For the latter, I can't provide the melody line, because the music is copyrighted, but I have, when possible, given you the information you need to buy the sheet music.

For the Yule songs only the words are given, because the melodies are familiar and can be easily found in numerous Christmas song books.

All the short songs and chants are sung repeatedly, over and over, during "waiting times"—while everyone is being individually greeted and brought into the circle, while the kiss is being passed, while the chalice and cakes are being passed. This keeps the energy "up" and keeps everyone involved. Many of the short songs can be very effective as rounds, too.

Traditional Songs/Chants

The River is Flowing

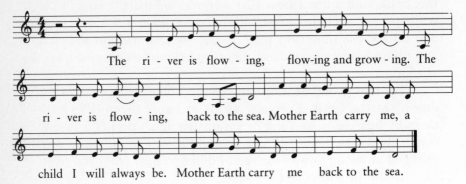

The ri - ver is flow - ing, flow-ing and grow - ing. The
ri - ver is flow - ing, back to the sea. Mother Earth carry me, a
child I will always be. Mother Earth carry me back to the sea.

We All Come From the Goddess

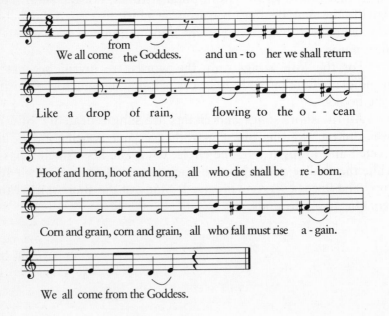

We all come from the Goddess. and un - to her we shall return

Like a drop of rain, flowing to the o - - cean

Hoof and horn, hoof and horn, all who die shall be re - born.

Corn and grain, corn and grain, all who fall must rise a - gain.

We all come from the Goddess.

Tall Trees

Recorded on *First Chants,* by Prana, The Creative Source, P.O. Box 11024, Costa Mesa, CA 92627.

This one was introduced at Atheneum by Sidhe-the-Ri, who often leads the singing with her strong, clear soprano. We pantomime in spontaneous, flowing arm movements as we sing:

Tall trees: Arms up high.

Warm fire: Arms out front as if warming them over a flame.

Cool breeze: Arms out at the sides, like wings in motion.

Deep waters: Reach down, as if dipping hands in water.

I feel it in my body: Give yourself a swaying hug, with arms crossed from shoulder to shoulder.

And feed it to the source: Arms out and forward, hands uplifted, as if giving to all around.

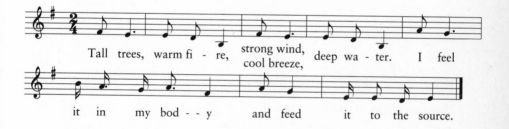

Mother, I Feel You

The first time I heard the following chant was when I attended a Margot Adler lecture at a large Unitarian church in San Diego. At the close of her presentation, Margot led a spiral dance with all of the large crowd of people who attended. The chain danced out of the church and into the courtyard, where the Full Moon shone overhead. It was wonderful! I don't remember most of the series of chants that were used, but this one particularly stuck in my mind because it was so effective (or maybe just because it appealed to the Scorpio in me). Several people were drumming in the background, which added lots of energy.

Mother, I feel you under my feet, Mother, I hear your heart beat.

Mother, I see you as the eagle flies, Mother take me high - er.

Turn, Turn, Wheel of the Year

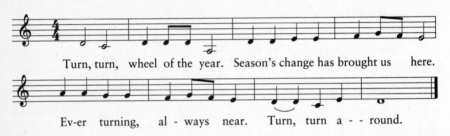

Turn, turn, wheel of the year. Season's change has brought us here.

Ev-er turning, al - ways near. Turn, turn a - - round.

Turn, Turn, Wheel of the Year (for Spring)

This variation was written by me for our Imbolc, because it seemed more "upbeat" for Spring.

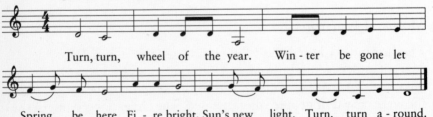

Turn, turn, wheel of the year. Win - ter be gone let

Spring be here. Fi - re bright, Sun's new light. Turn, turn a - round.

Lady Weave Your Circle

Here's another that we use, with the same basic tune as *Turn, Turn*. This one I have seen published in a Llewellyn book by Pattalee Glass-Keontop, entitled *Year of Moons, Season of Trees*. The songwriter is given as Llewyn.

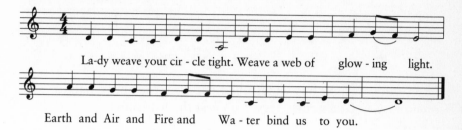

La-dy weave your cir - cle tight. Weave a web of glow - ing light.

Earth and Air and Fire and Wa - ter bind us to you.

Horned One

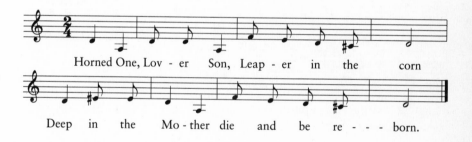

Horned One, Lov - er Son, Leap - er in the corn

Deep in the Mo - ther die and be re - - - born.

Elements

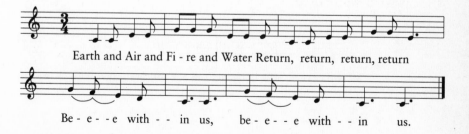

Earth and Air and Fi - re and Water Return, return, return, return

Be - e - - e with - - in us, be - e - - e with - - in us.

Goddess Chant

The Goddess chant has widespread use with the above names, but versions with God names vary. I suggest the list below.

God Chant

All Will Change

I've seen this one in *Spiral Dance* by Starhawk, with no tune given. Here is what we've used.

Long Winged Feathers

I circle around, I circle around, the bound'ries of the Earth

I circle around, I circle around, the bound'ries of the Earth

Wearing my long winged feathers now I fly

Wearing my long winged feathers now I fly.

Lord of the Dance

The words we use were provided by Theseus, who obtained them from Joe Bethancourt, a Bard, who performed "Lord of the Dance" on a tape called *Celtic Circle Dances*. I contacted Joe (P.O. Box 35190, Phoenix, AZ 85069) and he generously sent me a computer disk full of songs he's compiling for a "Green Book of Song." According to Joe's notes, the words were written by Aidan Kelly, C. Taliesin Edwards, and Ann Cass. Then he adds "Aidan Kelly and C. Taliesin Edwards may be the same person." Also, "Gwydion recorded the song, with variant lyrics on his *Songs of the Old Religion* tape (not the entire song, though)."

The tune on *Celtic Circle Dances* has a strong beat, very singable. Joe says "the tune (when it isn't 'Simple Gifts') is credited to Jenny Peckham-Vanzant, and may be an old shape-note hymn." A similar, somewhat more melodic tune can be found in a number of Christian song books. One that I have is *The Genesis Songbook*, published by Agápe, Main Place, Carol Stream, Illinois 60187. The lyrics (Christian version) are given as "traditional," and now that I read Joe's notes, I can "hear" somewhere in the back of my mind

"It's a gift to be simple, it's a gift to be free ... " so I guess the Christian version must be to the tune of "Simple Gifts"—I'd never thought of that before!

Here are the verses used by Joe on *Celtic Circle Dances*:

She danced on the waters and the wind was her horn
The Lady laughed and everything was born
And when She lit the sun and its light gave Him birth
The Lord of the Dance first appeared on the Earth.

Chorus:
Dance, dance, wherever you may be
For I am the Lord of the Dance, you see!
I live in you, and you live in Me
And I lead you all in the dance, said He.

I dance in the Circle when the flames leap up high
I dance in the Fire and I never, ever die
I dance in the waves on a bright summer sea
For I am the Lord of the wave's mystery.

I sleep in the kernel and I dance in the rain
I dance in the wind and through the waving grain
And when you cut me down, I care nothing for the pain
In the Spring I'm the Lord of the Dance once again!

I dance at the Sabbat when you chant out the spell
I dance and sing that everyone be well
And when the dancing's over, do not think that I am gone
To live is to dance! So I dance on and on!

The Horn of the Lady cast its sound 'cross the Plain
The birds took the notes, and gave them back again
Till the sound of Her music was a Song in the sky
And to that Song there is only one reply:

The Moon in her phases and the tides of the sea
The movement of the Earth, and the Seasons that will be
Are the rhythm for the dancing, and a promise through the years
That the Dance goes on through all our joy and tears.

They danced in the darkness and they danced in the night
They danced on the Earth, and everything was light.
They danced out the Darkness and they danced in the Dawn
And the Day of that Dancing is still going on!

I gaze on the Heavens and I gaze on the Earth
And I feel the pain of dying, and rebirth
And I lift my head in gladness, and in praise
Of the Dance of the Lord, and His Lady gay.

"My" Songs

Her Breasts are the Mountains

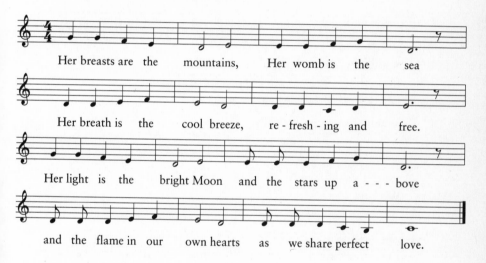

Her breasts are the mountains, Her womb is the sea

Her breath is the cool breeze, re-fresh-ing and free.

Her light is the bright Moon and the stars up a - - - bove

and the flame in our own hearts as we share perfect love.

May You Not Hunger

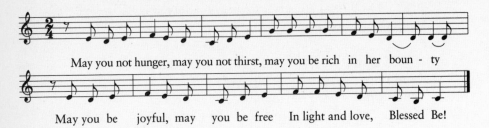

May you not hunger, may you not thirst, may you be rich in her boun - ty

May you be joyful, may you be free In light and love, Blessed Be!

Chant for the Sagittarius Full Moon

Live with - in us now, Di - - a - - - na   Live with -

in us now, A - - po - - - llo.

Weave, Weave

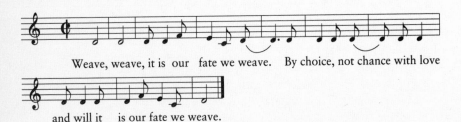

Weave, weave, it is our fate we weave. By choice, not chance with love

and will it is our fate we weave.

The Goddess and the Rose

For music use "The Rose" by Amanda McBroom. Sheet music easily available at most music stores.

Some say you'll find her in the bright Moon
That shines to light this night
And some say she is the cool breeze
That lifts the birds in flight
Some say she is the ocean, the tides that ebb and flow
And they say she is the green Earth
And the beauty of a rose.

She is called the soul of nature
The source of all who live
All return to her at dying and new life is hers to give
Yet we honor her in pleasure, in all acts of joy and love
When we gather in our circle
As the full Moon shines above.

Let there be among us beauty
Honor, strength, humility
Reverence, power, and compassion,
Mirth and joy and spirit free.
Now, where is she, where can we find her
We who truly seek to know
Stop all searching through the wide world
And look deep within each soul.

Yes, nowhere will we find her
If this we cannot see
Behold, she is the truth within us
That unveils the mystery
And she has been with us always
For she is our love that grows
She is the seed that gives our spirits
The beauty of a rose.

John Barleycorn

This is an old traditional folk song for which Terry Lamb and I collaborated on rewriting words, because she wanted to use it in the Lughnasad ritual that was part of her Third Degree requirement. We sang and enacted it as a mini-pageant, with Terra as Mother, Irisa as Maiden, me as Crone, Lord Willow as John Barleycorn, and Lavender, Hare, and Otter as the townspeople. It was lots of fun and quite successful! The tune, as Terry taught it to us, is rather tricky, but I'll try to come close!

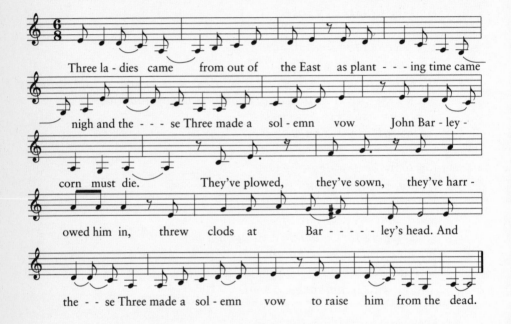

They lay with him for a very long time
Till the rains from the sky did fall
And little Sir John sprung up his head
And brought great joy to all
They've let him grow till Midsummer's Day
Till he stood both straight and tall
And little Sir John's grown a long, long beard
And become the Lord of All

Then came the Crone with a scythe so sharp
To cut him off at the knee
She's rolled him and tied him by the waist
Serving him to humanity
The townspeople came with sharp pitchforks
And gripped him to the heart
And the loader has served him worse than that
For he's bound him to the cart

They've wheeled him around and around the field
Till they came unto a barn
And there they cut him head from stalk
Oh, poor John Barleycorn!
The townspeople came with crabtree sticks
To cut him skin from bone
And the miller has served him worse than that
For he's ground him between two stones

Yet little Sir John and the Ladies Three
As we've learned from cycles past
Yes, little Sir John and the Ladies Three
Prove that death will never last
For the Lord will die and rise again
Child of our Mother Earth
For the Wheel of the Year goes round and round
From death to Spring's new birth.

Magic of the Night

For music use "The Music of the Night" from *Phantom of the Opera* by Andrew Lloyd Webber. For my ritual I sang to a tape by DreaMaker Productions, Inc., one of the "Sing Along Tapes Hot-25" series, which I purchased at a music store. Such tapes are widely available.

Night time comes and heightens each sensation
In the dark, I wake imagination
Silently your senses abandon their defenses
Helpless to resist my soft moonlight
For I bring you the magick of the night.

Softly, slowly ... night unfurls her splendor
Can you sense it? Tremulous and tender.
Feeling is believing, sight alone can be deceiving
Trust this spell I weave by candlelight
Join me in the magick of the night.
Come closer and gaze into my candlelight
In the flame see the dreams you wish to be
In the darkness it's easy to create
A dream that can become reality.
Softly, let my silver Moon caress you
Feel it, sense it, let it now possess you.
Open up your mind, let your fantasies unwind
As you dream into my flame of candlelight
Glowing in the mystery of the night.
Come with me, I'll take you to another world
Leave all thoughts of the life you've lived before
Let your soul take you where you long to be
There you'll know that you belong to me.
Floating, dreaming, sweet intoxication
Touch me, trust me, savor each sensation.
Now our spell is cast, let all doubts and fears be past
Know the power of your dreams by candlelight
The power of the Full Moon on this night!

(musical interlude)

Only you can truly be my light ...
Help me make the magick of the night.

Spirits of the Elements

These are sung Watchtowers, with a refrain to be sung by the others
in the circle. I've only actually tried it once, some time ago, with a
small women's group. It would require at least four people who are
willing to sing solo, with a facilitator who could lead the group
singing of the refrain. The tune is from "Here I Am, Lord" by Dan
Schutte, S.J., from *Glory and Praise*, Vol. 3, Northern Liturgy
Resources, Phoenix, AZ. (Words or phrases in parentheses are alternatives for a male voice.)

Eastern Priest/ess:
I, the Queen (Lord) of Wind and Air
My breath of life with all I share
Wisdom is my gift to you
Who seek to know.
My truth be seen with clarity
In cosmic cycles, land and sea
All continue, all renew
All live in me!

Refrain (sung by all, and repeated after each Watchtower):
Live within us, we will serve you
We feel your love within our souls
Let it grow now, ever stronger
As we live in peace and joy and love.

Southern Priest/ess:
I, the Goddess of the flame (I, the bright Lord of the flame)
Come to all who call my name
Live within each heart and soul
With spirit glow.
Let my spark within you be
A shining flame for all to see
Energy, the joy of life
The flame of love!

Western Priest/ess:
I, the Goddess of the sea (I, the Lord of lakes and sea)
Speak to you of mystery
Intuition, psychic vision
Flow now through me.
Open up your soul to me
Mystic waves will help you see
Strength within, and power of love
Serenity!

Northern Priest/ess:
I, the Mother of the Earth (I the Lord of all the Earth)
To all living things give birth (Live within you from your birth)

All who come from me return (I grow with you and die for you)
Then are reborn (And am reborn!)
Worship me in seeds you sow
Seeds of love that bloom and grow
Spread my love thoughout the Earth
I love you so!

Call to the Guardians for Solitary Ritual

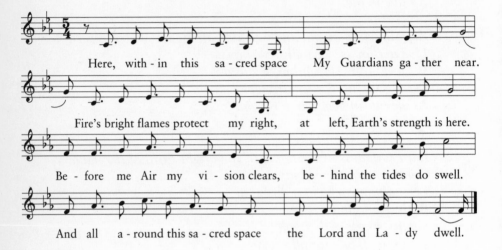

Here, with-in this sa-cred space My Guardians ga-ther near.

Fire's bright flames protect my right, at left, Earth's strength is here.

Be-fore me Air my vi-sion clears, be-hind the tides do swell.

And all a-round this sa-cred space the Lord and La-dy dwell.

Chants Sung on One Note Only (Spoken)

These chants are spoken, rather than sung. The words or syllables in bold type are the ones to be accented.

Fire Chant

*Fire, fire, **burn** higher*
*Fire, fire, **burn** higher*
*She **shines** in me, She **burns** in me*
*To raise our circle **energy.***

Power Chant

> *Let it **flow**, let it **flow***
> *Build the **power**, raise it **higher***
> *See the **light**, make it **bright***
> *Magick be our **will** tonight!*
> *[alternate last line: Let (name) be **healed** tonight!]*

Yule Songs

Pagan versions of Yule songs are around on various tapes. We've obtained a bunch from reading computer bulletin boards, which unfortunately hardly ever include credits for their sources. That is how we got the words to "Silent Night, Solstice Night." We rearranged the order of the verses, because they worked better in our particular Yule ritual that way. Later, in the *Green Egg* Yule 1991 issue, we saw nearly identical words to those we had downloaded, attributed to the "Greenwood Singers." Later, among the song lyrics sent to me by Joe Bethencourt, I found the same words again. Joe lists Ellen Reed as the author of the words.

Silent Night, Solstice Night

> *Silent Night, Solstice Night*
> *Quiet rest, dim the light.*
> *Turning ever the rolling wheel*
> *Brings the winter to comfort and heal.*
> *Rest your spirit in peace.*
> *Rest your spirit in peace.*
>
> *Silent Night, Solstice Night*
> *All is calm, all is right.*
> *Nature slumbers in forest and glen*
> *Filling streams as She wakens again*
> *Sleeping spirits grow strong.*
> *Sleeping spirits grow strong.*
>
> *Silent Night, Solstice Night*
> *Silver Moon, shining bright.*
> *Snowfall blankets the slumbering Earth*

Yule fires welcome the Sun's rebirth
Hark the light is reborn!
Hark the light is reborn!

Here are a few extras that I wrote words for. The first two are only slightly revised from the traditional Christmas versions, the rest are total rewrites.

We Three Kings

This one is only a slight rewrite from the traditional words by John H. Hopkins, 1857. The first and last verses and chorus are unchanged.

We three kings of Orient are
Bearing gifts we traverse afar
Field and fountain, moor and mountain
Following yonder star.

Chorus:
O star of wonder, star of night
Star with royal beauty bright
Westward leading, still proceeding
Guide us to the perfect light

Born a king at sunrise so bright
Gold I bring to honor the light
King forever, ceasing never
Light is reborn this night

Frankincense to offer have I
Scent of praise for birth that is nigh
Joy and praising, all now raising
Worship the God most high.

Myrrh is mine, the incense of night
Gone is he away from our sight
Yet in sorrow, know tomorrow
Surely will bring new light

Glorious now behold him arise
King and God and sacrifice
Alleluia, alleluia
Earth to the heav'ns replies.

Joy to the World

This carol was written by George F. Handel in 1742. The first verse is appropriate enough for our Yule as is, the other two verses I altered slightly to make them fit our celebration.

Joy to the world! The Lord has come
Let Earth receive her king
Let every heart prepare him room
And heav'n and nature sing
And heav'n and nature sing
And heav'n and heav'n and nature sing.

Joy to the world! The Sun returns
Our Lady gives him birth
His living light will warm our hearts
And wake the sleeping Earth
And wake the sleeping Earth
And wake, and wake the sleeping Earth

Light we the fires to greet our Lord
Our light, our life, our Lord
Let every voice sing holy praise
As heav'n and nature sing
As heav'n and nature sing
As heav'n, as heav'n and nature sing.

Ave Maria

Sung to the very well-known melody by Franz Schubert.

Maiden of beauty, hear us as we call to thee
Come forth and take thy place as Mother
Reborn the child of light must be
Queen of night, O lady of wisdom we call
Weave thy magick tonight

Here we stand and humbly wait to serve thee
Come within and fill our souls with love
As thy sphere of stars is slowly turning
Bring us new light, the light of your glorious Son
Ave Maria

Bring a Torch

Tune: Bring a Torch, Jeanette Isabella

Bring a torch, O brothers and sisters
Bring a torch, light Yule fires bright
We gather this night to wait for the dawning
Come quickly; I see the first rays of light
Ah! Ah! How radiant the Mother
Ah! Ah! How brightly shines the Sun

Sing in praise of our gracious Lady
Sing in praise of her glorious Son.
The wheel has turned
Tis time for the new year
Dance gaily; we shall welcome the Sun
Ah! Ah! How radiant the Mother
Ah! Ah! How brightly shines the Sun

Lady Moon Shines Softly

Tune: O Little Town of Bethlehem

Lady Moon shines softly down
To light the Earth below
As we, her children, gather here
Around the Yule fire's glow
We wait for morning's dawning
First light of holy birth
Our Lady turns the wheel of life
Her Son returns to Earth
With joy we'll greet his dawning
A new year has begun
With increased light is bright new hope
Reborn in everyone.

Good Pagan Folk, Rejoice

Tune: Good Christian Men, Rejoice

Good Pagan folk, rejoice
With heart and soul and voice
Give ye heed to what we say
News! News!
Our Lord the Sun is born today
Greet him as the dawn's first light
Bids farewell to dark of night
The Sun returns today
The Sun returns today.

Good Pagan folk, rejoice
With heart and soul and voice
Gather round the Yuletide tree
Peace! Peace!
Hope he brings for you and me
Winter's cold is nearly gone
We wait for spring with joyous song
Our Lord returns to Earth
Our Lord returns to Earth

Good Pagan folk, rejoice
With heart and soul and voice
Praise our Lady, praise her Son
Joy! Joy!
New life they bring to everyone
Dance and sing and merry meet
As the Lord of Light we greet
The Sun returns today
The Sun returns today.

O Yuletide Tree

Tune: O Christmas Tree

O Yuletide tree, O Yuletide tree
How lovely are thy branches
O Yuletide tree, O Yuletide tree

How lovely are thy branches
The thought of you as Yule draws near
Brings joyful tidings of great cheer
O Yuletide tree, O Yuletide tree
To us you are so lovely.

O Yuletide tree, O Yuletide tree
Evergreen and fragrant
O Yuletide tree, O Yuletide tree
Evergreen and fragrant
We bring you in our home to be
A sign of life's eternity.
O Yuletide tree, O Yuletide tree
Forever green and lovely.

O Yuletide tree, O Yuletide tree
We thank you for your blessings
O Yuletide tree, O Yuletide tree
We thank you for your blessings
With golden stars and twinkling light
You cheer us on this holy night
O Yuletide tree, O Yuletide tree
Thou art most fair and lovely.

O Holy Night

O Holy Night
The stars are brightly shining
It is the night of the Sun's rebirth
Long lay the land, in cold of winter pining
Till he appears to shine warmth on the Earth
A thrill of hope, the weary world rejoices
As yonder breaks the new and glorious dawn
Sing now with joy
O sing in celebration
O night divine
O night of holy birth
O night, divine
O night, O night divine

Moon up above
We gather in your soft light
And wait for him, Son of light to appear
Orb of our Mother
Who holds us in her keeping
Send us your child
To bring warmth to our souls.
The winter is cold, the nights are long in darkness
We long for the spring, the hope that now begins
Sing now with joy
O sing in celebration
O night divine
O night of holy birth
O night, divine
O night, O night divine

Endnotes

1. Career Track Seminars, "High Impact Communications Skills," given in San Diego in 1992. This seminar group gives very useful and helpful presentations in cities all over the country, and most of their material is available on tape. For info: Career Track, 3085 Center Green Drive, Boulder, Colorado 80301.

2. From Chapter 9 of *Twelve Wings of the Eagle,* based on material from Rabbi Joel Dobyn's *To Rule Both Day and Night.*

Concluding Reflections

On Children in the Craft

The topic of the presence and participation of children in Craft activities provoked one of the liveliest class discussions held at Circle Atheneum during this past year. Those present included married parents, separated/divorced parents, step-parents, grandparents, and may-be-parents-someday. All expressed a myriad of serious concerns, not many of which were resolved. It is definitely apparent that this topic requires special consideration. The concerns that were expressed can be summarized under four main categories.

1. The Relationship of the Child to the Craft Parent(s)

Many Wiccans still find it necessary to keep a very low profile about their religion. Small children who are present at rituals and other circle activities will talk—just as small children everywhere talk about things their parents do. Ask any kindergarten teacher what an earful she often gets! It was a child about kindergarten age drawing pentagrams on the sidewalk with chalk that added to the "evidence" provoking the tire-slashing incident related earlier, on page 43.

A suggestion that it would be helpful to lose the "hot button" language provoked controversy. Some Wiccans really like the word witch (non-conformist as we all are, to some degree), and they bristle at the very thought that we should suppress the word to please anybody.

Yet the majority present at the class saw the point. There is practically nothing any child could say in describing one of our Sabbat rituals that would send up any red flags in a teacher's or friend's parent's mind. A small child's description would probably just sound like a big party/picnic at which a circle game was played, with singing and dancing. But if the child said, "Mommy and Daddy are Witches, or we went to a coven meeting … " that could definitely raise eyebrows, and provoke concern and possible adverse action. What is more important—protecting our free use of a few controversial "hot-button" words, or being able to have our children freely participate in our spiritual activities without fear about what they might say to outsiders? As I said earlier, when discussing the "w" word in Chapter 4, I think it would be wise for us to get in the habit of referring to ourselves as Wiccans rather than Witches, and to calling our groups circles instead of covens.

Then, as children get older, parental perception of a necessity for a low profile brings up the issue of secrecy. Older children can be told that, even though we know that what we are doing is loving and good and fun, other people may not understand, so we should not talk about it to them. Is this, however, a constructive thing to convey to our children? Might it not be pretty confusing? If it is good, why must we hide it? Is there really something here to be ashamed of? Are we, the parents, being unnecessarily paralyzed by fear—and thus conveying that negative emotion to our children? This brings us to a closely related second point …

2. The Child's Relationship to the Community

Most application/enrollment forms have, in recent years, dropped the question of religious affiliation. But it still comes up. A mainstream religious affiliation is an identity factor that links a child with others in his/her peer group. What happens to a child who publicly identifies himself or herself with Witches—or even as a Wiccan or Pagan? What happens to a child who is told to hide that identity? Like it or not, the first alternative may involve a safety issue. Children have been ridiculed and taunted by peers—kids can be very cruel.

Worse, some child protection agencies here in southern California (and in a number of other areas, too, I've heard) are permeated with counselors who are quite paranoid about Satanic ritual abuse. The fact that nothing has been substantiated does not stop them from looking for anything remotely suspect, and being quite sure that not finding it only means a very cleverly concealed conspiracy. One case, covered in the San Diego papers recently, involved some children who were taken away from their parents and kept away from them for many months, solely on the "evidence" that a woman in a psychiatric hospital had related "memories" of ritual abuse in her childhood to her psychiatrist. Authorities began following the sister of the insane woman, to see if anything suspect was happening in that family. The woman, driving with her children one night, became frightened by her growing awareness that men in unmarked cars were following her. Thinking they intended robbery, she panicked and fled. This, too, became "evidence" that led soon after to the children being taken into protective custody. (Fleeing equates with guilt, they reasoned.)

I know that to many readers, this whole tale sounds impossibly insane, but it happened, and it is not the only local incident in which children have been wrongly taken from their parents. It seems as though in cases of suspected child abuse, the parents are truly guilty unless they can prove innocence. Meanwhile, the children are kept apart from them, and are literally brainwashed by social workers until, desperate for relief, they will finally say something that the social worker wants to hear, which will then be introduced as "evidence." And meanwhile, the parents are running up a fortune in legal bills trying to prove their innocence.

The various San Diego incidents, of course, finally caused a great deal of public outrage and calls for reform from the City Council. Recent letters on the editorial page have indicated that some of the overzealous counselors are still on the job, and still refusing to acknowledge any wrongdoing, but I've heard on good authority that they are no longer sent to evaluate suspected emotional abuse cases.

So far as anyone knows, there is no connection of the family involved in the above story with anything to do with actual ritual of any type, either Satanic, or of any type of alternative religion. The apparent "ritual" story exists only in the fantasies of the institutionalized sister, which "came out" under psychotherapy. Meanwhile, controversial stories and even court cases continue to surface, involving alleged memories of ritual abuse that are "remembered" by children only after extensive questioning by therapists, and are "remembered" by adults after they have been involved in psychotherapy programs which attempt to solve the problems of today by probing for childhood abuse of some kind to blame it on. Despite the fact that none of these ritual abuse cases have been substantiated by hard evidence, quite a number of people (including therapists who have written books on the subject, thus developing a vested interest in it) apparently believe that a widespread Satanic conspiracy exists, perpetuated by a vast and clever cover-up.

How much truth is to be found behind this "ritual abuse therapy," I do not know. A few isolated cases, perhaps, but that it could be as widespread as many seem to believe, I find implausible. A recent article in *Ms.* magazine related a personal account of ritual abuse, obviously fervently believed by the author and taken seriously by *Ms.* Then, a few weeks later I saw an editorial in the *San Diego Union-Tribune* in which the author said that she considered herself a feminist, but found it necessary to take a stand against widespread feminist acceptance of the memories of incest and ritual abuse that were being discovered after psychotherapy. She said it had become a feminist heresy to even question such memories. I consider myself a feminist, too, but I agreed with the writer in her points about the importance of questioning. "Politically correct" thinking can be dangerous when it seeks to suppress freedom of thought and speech.[1] Unfortunately, it is not uncommon for people—even some professionals or officials—to see only what seems to fit their preconceived assumptions, and refuse to see all contradictory evidence.

The implications of all this could be very serious for a Pagan family with young children, and fundamentalist neighbors who might consider it their Christian duty to make erroneous assumptions about ritual activities and report them to child protection agencies. It bears sober thinking among us all—and that most certainly includes feminist Witches. (That same *Ms.* issue also had an article about the Witchcraft revival!)

So there are valid reasons to teach a child to be discreet, and to be careful what a child sees or hears, when he or she is too young to be discreet, or to clearly understand just what is going on. On the other hand, what happens to us if we give in to fear of potential prejudice, and hide our spiritual life from our children? What does that do to our self-esteem—and what does it feed into the self-esteem of our children? Is this not, at best, confusing to them?

It is easy for those who do not have children—or public vulnerability in regard to jobs or housing—to say we must not give energy to such fear. And easier for me to say, too, when my only child still at home is 15, and is therefore at or near an age when her own choices and perceptions would be given credence, should it come to that, before most judges. Not so easy, though, for some of my friends who have small children. Their concerns are very real.

It is potentially destructive to self-esteem to convey secrecy about our religion and fear of persecution to our children. On that, everyone at the class agreed. What to do about it? That is another issue. Some feel that they have no choice but secrecy for the time being. This adds to my own resolve that is important for those of us who feel that we do have a choice to become much more open about our involvement with Wicca, so that by our example we may gradually raise public perception, and dispel the fear that keeps so many still "in the broom closet." Only then can all of our children fully share in our religious life—and perhaps also identify with other Pagan children in their peer groups.

3. The Child's Relationship to non-Craft Family Members

Another issue that provoked much conversation was the experience of dealing with family members who range from barely tolerant to openly hostile in regard to Wiccan activities, particularly those involving children. Various personal stories were related of grandparents, aunts, and uncles who looked for every opportunity to preach to the Craft parent's child about various Christian doctrines, even to the point of scaring the child with worries that the parent would go to hell if s/he did not turn away from Wicca and return to Jesus.

Then there were the concerns of non-custodial fathers who had the very real threat that the mother, if she found out about the father's Wiccan identity, would use it as a club to prevent the children visiting.

Or of non-custodial parents who could use the custodial parent's affiliation with Craft as leverage to gain custody. Those who say this could not happen in this country where freedom of religion is supposedly protected and church and state are separate, should consider that "blue laws" still exist on the books in many states that are clearly based on the religious beliefs of those who passed them.

The function of the state to maintain order and provide for the general welfare often gets muddied with assumptions about reality that are rooted in religious faith. Sometimes the fact that such assumptions grow out of unprovable matters of faith are quite unconscious to the authority who sincerely feels that s/he is basing a decision on logic and evidence. Free choice may then be protected only if the choice agrees with an authority's assumptions.

Much of the emotionalism over such issues as right-to-life for the terminally ill or the unborn could dissipate if people could be clear about the religious basis for their assumptions. A lot of the hysteria is rooted in beliefs of a linear world view—one body for one soul for one life only. When does potential life actually become full-fledged human life? At conception? At viability? At birth? When does effective life end? When breath stops (without artificial support)? When functional brain activity ceases? When does the soul enter a body? At conception? Sometime during pregnancy? At birth? Is there a soul at all? Are body and soul one for all eternity? Or does a soul take on a body like a garment for one physical life, discard it at death, and later take on another body, and another? Science cannot prove these things; it can only prove viability—capability of survival without extraordinary artifical support. All other assumptions are based on faith—and people vary widely in their beliefs on these matters.

A government that is supposed to protect the right of people to practice different faiths, and is not supposed to establish any one faith as the law of the land, clearly should stay out of these right-to-life issues. Religion should teach, not legislate, or coerce legislation. Legislators should be ever-mindful of the fact that they represent people of varied beliefs. On matters that are so clearly based on assumptions rooted in faith, which do not threaten public order, citizens should have the right to choose for themselves, according to their own particular beliefs.

Forgive the not entirely related digression. Back to the topic at hand:

I have had a personal issue over my work in the Craft with my 15-year-old daughter's father, who very much wants her to be confirmed as a Catholic, just like all of his older children were. "Family tradition," he says. "She needs an identity; she needs clear-cut moral rules." He lives across the country, and although he takes her to Mass during the summer, he can't force the issue of confirmation because she lives with me during the school year, and that is when she would have to take the catechism classes. I have refused to force her to go. I do not discourage her from going to catechism if she wishes. A church is close to us—within walking distance—and I have even said I will drive her there if she requests. But I will not go to Mass with her, nor will I coerce her to go. It is her choice.

Neither have I coerced her to participate in my rituals. Often she chooses to do so—after all, it's fun. And therein is the rub, for her father. After all, when the now-adult kids were young teens, I taught their confirmation catechism classes. I didn't force them to come to those classes, either. The church, in fact, instructed the catechists to stress the importance to the kids of making their own choices, free of parental insistence. But the truth is, kids learn a lot more by example than they ever do from what you tell them. I made those catechism classes as interesting and enjoyable as I could, and they responded. Now I am a Wiccan High Priestess, making my rituals as interesting and enjoyable as I can. So, I cannot deny that my ex-husband has a valid point in regard to my potential influence on our daughter. I can only point out a fact that he, too, well knows. She is being taught to be responsible for her own decisions and to think for herself—and she does. This is a child who decided at the age of ten to become a vegetarian, and has never once deviated from that choice in the four years since. Neither I, her father, nor her stepfather were vegetarians, nor was anyone in her peer group. It was entirely her own idea, based on her adoption of the cause of animal rights. Yes, Liz will choose her own path, for her own well-thought-through reasons, and when she does, I will respect her choice.

And that leads to the final summary point from that Atheneum discussion:

4. The Child's Relationship to a Religious/Ethical/Spiritual System

There is strong feeling among Wiccans that each must be free to choose his/her own path, which includes the non-coercion of children.

(Note the wording of the Wiccaning ceremony in Chapter 10, in which the parents are directed to "teach the child to seek" and when s/he chooses a spiritual path, to respect it.) Some translate this into a reluctance to directly teach Wicca to their children, preferring to teach only the ethic of personal responsibility and harming none. This is partially driven by the accompanying wish to protect the child from the possible adverse reactions of others to an open Wiccan identity.

Most of those present, however, recognize the difficulty of teaching ethics as a purely intellectual matter, without a spiritual basis; and they acknowledge that a child brought up with no spiritual identity has little foundation on which to build his or her own thoughts. Too much of our society is heavily secular and we can see that the resulting spiritual void drives many either to negative forms of escapism or, for the very spiritually hungry, to vulnerability to controlling sects or cults.

The majority of people now involved in Wicca, or other alternative new age religions, were raised in mainstream religions. Someplace along the way the particular forms of those religions ceased to be meaningful to us—yet the quest for spiritual experience remained. Still yearning for a spiritual center, for a path to seek the unseen and unknowable, for a interconnectedness with others who shared our ethical ideals, we sought a different form—one which, at this particular step on our Path, was relevant to us. The point is, that a person who is taught a religion—most any religion—is in a better position to evaluate and compare, than one who is brought up with only a secular framework.

We no longer practice the religions in which we were raised. We have found a new form that is very meaningful to us. Do we not then have an obligation to translate that form into a meaningful experience that includes our children? I feel strongly that we do. But there are considerable challenges.

A major challenge is the necessity to get past the fear of open identification with our religion. Being aware of our numbers would help. Again I say that if we can focus on our similarities rather than our differences, we can benefit from networking with each other, and forming large groups that can share, without harming the autonomy of individual circles. So long as we remain only in contact with our one small circle, it is difficult to include children. The reality is that most circles include only some parents, and the children of those parents may be of very different ages—and, just as in church or temple, most adults are less than thrilled with the distraction of small children in a religious service they are too young to understand.

An obvious advantage of networking is that parents can get together to organize activities for children of similar ages. A joint Sabbat celebration could include a special ritual designed for child-size concepts (and I expect this will soon happen within the Atheneum circles). Parents working together could help each other devise ways of discussing "The Wiccan Way" in terms that are understandable to even a small child, and in terms that the child can repeat to others.

One little story was related about a family that is openly Wiccan. The seven-year-old asked if he could wear a pentagram pendant, and the parents told him that when he could clearly explain what it meant, he could wear it. One day in a fast food restaurant, someone accused the child of wearing a Satanic symbol. The child answered, "No, it's not," and proceeded to calmly and accurately explain all about it, totally disarming the accuser. A good lesson for all of us, I think!

Wiccan groups in some areas have apparently done an effective job of addressing Wicca for children. I have never met anyone from the Oregon-based Church of All Worlds, but I subscribe to their adult magazine, *Green Egg,* and to their special magazine for children/youth called *HAM* (How About Magic). (*Green Eggs and Ham* is a popular Dr. Seuss children's book that I must have read a thousand times for each of my three children, to the point that I still have large parts of it memorized. Sometime it would be fun to know what is behind the choice of those titles for the magazines—perhaps only whimsy.) I enjoy both magazines a great deal, and recommend them highly. And Liz looks forward to reading *HAM.* A good share of its articles are written by young people, and it is beautifully illustrated, too.[2]

On Social Change

Some of my astrologer friends say to each other from time to time, that the best way to get astrology accepted by the mainstream would be to convince the business community in general that it can work for them. A focus on forecasting techniques most likely will not be the key, though, because for a business person to admit using astrology successfully would be to perhaps give up a competitive edge. As for its use toward improvements in self-awareness, job satisfaction, successful teamwork—that is another story. But as more of us are discovering, we do better when we tone down the "astrospeak" (my word for speaking in astrological jargon, with the mistaken assumption that those who have not studied astrology will understand what is being said). The concepts behind the astrology sell better than the outer trappings (the jargon and even the very identification of astrology) which are still burdened with fringe element connotations.

I've been fascinated the past two years with the acceleration of concepts in business and management training that were not many years ago the province only of new-agers and feminists, with which the mainstream was, at best, uncomfortable. The new management style is non-autocratic, team oriented, consensus building, and caring toward the individual worker. It is thoroughly geared toward the empowering of the individual, rather than gaining or exercising power over others. It emphasizes relating, flexibility, and communication skills, rather than competitiveness and rigid procedures. Led at first by smaller businesses (many of them female entrepreneurial ones), the new ideas are now being adopted even by some of the largest corporations. They don't associate them with the so-called new age movement, though sometimes I have heard them identified with "feminine" style. There are new names, seminars leaders, authors that I can never remember associating with any of the alternative philosophy, metaphysical, or new age activities with which I've been associated in the past. Yet the ideas are right from the core of the paradigm shift that we've been hearing about and talking about for many years. Now they've been repackaged, renamed, and are being taught to business people all over the country. Why? Because business, unlike more unwieldy bureaucracies like government, is driven by the bottom line. The companies that are buying the new ways of thinking are doing so because it works—because it creates more satisfied workers who are consequently more productive, thus improving that bottom line. I am not just speaking theory here. I am a businesswoman who is seeing the results as I, my management team, and my entire staff continue to improve our ability to work within the new style.

I still think we're a long way from a shift in mass consciousness, even in Western society alone, and in some other parts of the world, it will be much longer yet. The pace of change is accelerating, though. I still see it more as a reflection of Pisces Rising, rather than the Age of Aquarius—but it really doesn't matter what we call it. It's happening, it's exciting, and I'm glad to be a part of it.

On Religions—Present and Future

Why is Paganism, including Wicca, expanding so rapidly today, while this country's dominant religion, Christianity, seems either to be losing its hold in an increasingly secular society, or backlashing into minority groups of intolerant fundamentalists who seek to impose their beliefs into law? I am remembering the paperwork that Ariel turned in to me, in preparation for her First Degree. I constantly learn from those in my circle whom I suppose I could call my students, but prefer to call my sisters and brothers. Ariel wrote far more lengthy answers than we expected, and they were thought-provoking and insightful. With her permission, I'll share a just a few of the things she wrote, for they provide one person's heartfelt answer to the "why" with which I began this paragraph.

For your added understanding, Ariel's college degree was in languages and etymology, so she used those skills to define the words given at the beginning of the First Degree questions. She is in her 60s, a Crone of wisdom, but with all the joy, freshness, and wonder of spirit of a Maiden.[3]

Ariel's Definitions

Religion

Webster [begins its entry with the] old French and Latin *religio,* defined as "taboo" and "restraint."[4] This confirms that which I have always suspected. The purpose of religion is to control—masses, smaller groups and me ... to bring about "order," to prevent the mayhem inherent in our disobedience to the principles underlying the Ten Commandments, which are found in almost every religion in some form ... Notice, they are not the ten "it would be nice if you woulds" or ten "I feel you shoulds" or ten "it would only be intelligent if you dids." We are commanded by God! Good Lord! Whew! ... A leader or leader group who possesses power uses this idea for the purpose of control. Throughout the time of my life, I have learned not to trust that the enforcers are benevolently controlling me for my own good, or the well being of others.

Jesus saw it differently. He taught that if you loved your source and your fellow persons, as completely as you love yourself, you won't need to be commanded to obey those ten laws ... we would not be under the principle of law, but under the power of love.

Buddha taught the identical truth ... compassion was his theme, in spite of the "Ten Grave Precepts" of his time. Krishna the same, Mohammed the same, and so on.

[In the second part of the definition, Webster continues] "the awareness and conviction of the one power, arousing reverence, love, gratitude and the desire to serve." Then ... the key words, "devotion, fidelity and consciousness." There is hope for Webster after all ... and there is hope for me ...

The first half of [Webster's] definitions are in clear and direct contradiction with the second half, as they are two opposing methods used to bring about the same result.

Wicca is a religion in the sense of the second half. Because Wicca, in its nature, is not restricting, but expanding. It does not strive to control, but to set free. Its goal is not to encapsulate us inside its repetitive, collective observances and stagnate us inside its enclosed structures. No, its goal is to release me to the development of my highest potential through rituals that cause me to be deeply aware of Nature, its cycles, my nature, and my interconnection with "all that is"—and therefore know that the same power that is in all, is also in me!

Philosophy

Derived from the Greek, it is a search for knowledge, truth, and ultimately, wisdom ... our concept of what we call reality ...

[After giving examples of the diverse ways of perceiving reality, Ariel continued ...] Energy is vast and beyond our total cognition. Because energy is limitless, and because there are an infinite variety of truths, magick is real! Magick is no metaphor! [... and concluded that philosophy would hopefully] lead us back to the Goddess. After all, look what it really means:

Philo   Sophia
Love of   the Goddess

[Sophia is the Christian Gnostic name for the Goddess, said to be Wisdom.]

Clergy

This word is derived from French and late Latin *clergie,* meaning priest. Webster defines [this along the lines of one who is] ordained ... and therefore given sanction to be a bridge between their religious congregation and their deity. In contrast, the Wiccan concept of the One Power, Goddess and God, is that it is not apart or separate from anyone or anything, but within and throughout all. Therefore it would be ... just plain silly to place an intermediary between the self and the self. We initiates are lovingly and assiduously taught ... understanding becomes a portion of wisdom, and we are educated and trained so that we can give back in the same lavish manner in which we have received, we become clergy. In Wicca, we are all priestesses or priests. We are clergy!

Worship

Taken apart, this Anglo-Saxon word, *weorthscipe, weorth* ... worth and scipe, means to give honor and respect to ... [This] illustrates clearly the positive meaning of this beautiful word: to honor or respect worth ... It shows intelligence ... as one has to be cognizant of worth, and then respond by cherishing it.

When reality is pictured as creatures separated from the divine, then longing for the divine, and waiting to someday join the divine ... and any communication is attempted with the divine, this is believed by the creature to be worship. But truly, this is homage or adoration. Homage was a ceremony in which a man acknowledged himself as vassal to a lord ... obeisance, self-abasement. Adoration is homage paid to one in high esteem. It is devotion to a superior. It means to idolize.

In Wicca we see the oneness in all that is; no separation in reality of the material from the divine. We marvel at existence, we feel a deep awe and reverence for it. We have a joyful awareness of the worth of everything, and we respond by holding it dear and nourishing it. "Let my worship be in the heart that rejoices," is the charge of the Goddess. We worship!

Church

Since before my first birthday I had been in church. My amazed little person (held usually on my father's lap, as my mother played the piano and sang) heard, saw, and felt ... hell, fire, and damnation, fear-inducing ... stories. For years I worried ... It was all so ugly. I felt ugly. It was contrived to wrench your passions and drive you to the altar to beg forgiveness from the pure and beautiful Jesus, as you were ugly and filled with sin, and born in sin ... This is how I was conditioned ... If this stuff impressed adults so intensely, imagine what it did to a little kid ...

Oh, Wicca, the purifier! The soul, body, and mind healer!

There are several root words for church—Greek *kyros, kirkinos, kyriakon.* French *circus kyros* means power, *kirkinos* means circle; *kyriakon* (old Greek) was a place where people gathered. It was circular, and believed to contain a being, their source of great power from which they could draw. Circus means circle. *Circe* is an Anglo-Saxon word, meaning circle of power or holy ring. The Russian word is *tzerke*. So the historical meaning is a circle in which people gather to find the source of their being and partake of the power within.

Imagine a church outdoors in beauty, in nature, and there a group that loves me, that likes and respects me. Imagine me a daughter of the Goddess ... divine! How wonderful that my body is sacred and that sex is holy, that I have the power to bring forth life and nourish it, that the earth is sacred ... nobody to make me ashamed.

So my circle is my church, and my round, precious, beautiful earth and my people. I am growing and relearning in my church. I am cleansing myself of fear and shame. I am claiming my birthright and taking back my power. I am a child of the Goddess.

And that, at least in part, is why!

On Evolution

Among neo-Pagans there are countless Ariels, who have left mainstream religious backgrounds that bred fear, shame, and helplessness, and perpetuate stereotypes that no longer resonate with their evolving spiritual consciousnesses. In *Twelve Wings* I compared the shifting religious paradigm to a pendulum swing, from an age of a feminine sign (Taurus, when Goddess worship predominated) to a masculine sign (Aries, when God and the patriarchy gradually took over), to a feminine sign (Pisces) in which the Goddess is emerging once again. Feminist spirituality literature, and much of general Pagan thought, too, seems often to dwell heavily on a return of the "old religion"—the idea that we are returning to an older form, recreating a time when the Goddess was the primary deity, society was matrifocal and women were powerful, and that we could save the Earth by returning to the old ways.

Often I've read expressions of pessimism and despair, whose authors compare present day acts of violence to past atrocities, current social problems to times from the past, and lament that society is not only sick but getting worse ... "We are no better than barbarians" some have said. It is also a popular "mainstream" idea to look toward past eras, idealize their perceived values, and propose that the ills of society can be cured if only we could return to these times. Currently, the favorite idea of many editorial writers and politicians seems to be "if only we could return to the two-parent family, with Mom at home with the kids," and along with that comes usually "a return to Christian values." In this sense, the ideas of would-be social reformers, be they Pagan or Christian or neither, seem to fit my pendulum model: when a paradigm of mass thinking swings far enough to one extreme, it begins to swing in the other direction. This fits with a cyclical, rather than a linear model—the wheel keeps turning, and "what goes around, comes around." While I still see some validity in that model for illustrating change, it (like everything else) is still only part of an elusive Whole.

The Great Ages are only a turn of the wheel in the spiral dance of a continuous evolution. Consider the spiral. Is it not just a curved linear progression? Or is it something else? Which way are we going? In toward a center One, or out toward the All? And does it matter, for is it not the same either way? The All, spiraling in, becomes the One. The One, spiraling out, becomes the All.

Just as no two persons are exactly the same, neither are any two moments in time. We can look to the past for ideas about what seemed to work or what didn't—yet when we apply these ideas to the present day, they cannot work in the same way because so many other things that supported those ideas have changed. Can we go "back to the earth?" Perhaps a few isolated communes could, but as a model for the masses? With our world population and interdependent economy? Hardly. Can anyone who really looks at what *is*, in terms of the population, economy, and changing male and female roles truly think that preaching, tax incentives, or *anything* can restore the two-parent family model? No, *new* models must be built, based on where we are *now*, not where we were, or even where we might be, "if only." We can fantasize about, or even concretely plan for, the future, but when we get there, factors unknown to us now will have changed it, and our plans may not fit the new circumstances in which we find ourselves. We can only live in the Now, and our thoughts of either past or future are solely an experience of the Now.

Scary? Only if one chooses. Is there nothing we can count on? Yes, one thing—whatever *is*, will change! Fear can paralyze. That which adapts to change will survive and grow—evolution.

Considering the billions of people now on this planet, I wonder how they would really compare by percentages with any earlier period of history, in terms of living conditions, literacy, and physical, mental, and spiritual health? Some will disagree with me, I know, but I think, as a whole, we are evolving. I'd rather live now than at any time in the past, and while many of those past eras were fascinating, none are quite so interesting as it could be as we go into the new millennium.

Now, where are we, who are Wiccans, and where are we going? We are (judging from the large numbers of books and periodicals now available), in fairly numerous company—although no one knows how many Wiccans there really are. I remember reading a newspaper article in the *San Diego Union* about three years ago, that featured a woman who had just written a scholarly book about Wicca. She had managed to be allowed to participate in a coven in England, and had talked to a number of Witches in the United States, and was estimating that there may be perhaps as many as 1,000 practitioners of Wicca in England and maybe even as many as 5,000 in the United States. My friends and I laughed, remarking that there could be nearly that many in San Diego county. But—we don't really know. How many are we? There must be many more than various writers' estimates I've read (from around 50,000 to about 100,000 tops), otherwise how are all those publications being supported? Estimates vary widely according to what the estimater is counting, whether only initiates are counted, or how many have taken courses, etc. The obvious truth is, nobody really knows.

Who are we? Another feature article in the *Union* once covered feminist spirituality and the revival of Wicca among women who are searching for a female image of deity. The article said that there were a number of women's groups around the area, and gradually just a "few" men seemed to be becoming interested, too. No mention whatever was made of mixed male and female circles, as if feminist Wicca was all there is, even though I am quite sure that the resources for information that were listed (area bookshops) know very well the members of quite a number of mixed circles.

Where are we going? I hope it is toward increased networking with each other.

On Networking

At the end of March 1993, just as I was preparing the final draft of this manuscript to send to Llewellyn for editing, a new network was born in San Diego. I am excited by it, for it begins a process in this area (already begun in a few other areas) that I hope will contribute to the more compassionate, balanced, and responsible world view that is just now beginning to emerge beyond the new-agers into a wider consciousness. I hope it will open up this nurturing, empowering form of religion into wider acceptance by the many who hunger for a nurturing and empowering form of spirituality, but cannot find it.

A few months ago, Lady Beckett proposed the thought to several of her contacts among area HPs, that we might all mutually benefit from a leadership seminar, for the complexities of interrelationships in such small family-like groups had been known at various times to result in rather unpleasant and hurtful breakdowns. A date was set, and the expected group grew to a size beyond the average living room, so I volunteered the conference room at Astro (my business). On Sunday, March 28, 1993, twenty-two HPs, representing ten circles and two study groups, met for a seminar conducted by Teri Vodden, a licensed psychotherapist specializing in family therapy. Since Wiccan circles are very much families of choice, if not of origin, Teri's unique perspective and motivation of our discussion provided many useful insights. A number of sensitive issues were discussed quite openly, with growing interaction, until nearly everyone was actively participating.

The discussion turned toward the need to have more of this type of communication among us, and rather spontaneously (although admittedly Beckett and some of the rest of us were hoping the meeting would go that way), a consensus decision was made to form a network, and even a name was chosen: WIN for Wiccan Independent Network. Beckett was elected primary facilitator of activities. I volunteered to see that a networking newsletter was produced, with the cheerful acquiescence of my Managing Editor Daryl Fuller (previously identified in this book as Lord Falkan), who would be the designer/editor.

In a report written for the first newsletter, I summarized the main points made at that meeting which were behind the decision to form WIN. An excerpt follows:[5]

> *We understand that inaccurate assumptions about us [Wicca] are not fair and that we are entitled to the protections as set out in the Constitution, but we must remember that it is not the government that keeps us "in the closet," it is our own fear of community prejudice. We have "freedom of religion," but cultural opinion, even though mistaken, creates pressures. It was pointed out that this will never change. Those of us who can safely do so, without threat to jobs, housing, etc., sometimes choose to become more public—and we can draw upon our numbers. Unfortunately, we cannot become an accepted minority religion if we do not even know who and where we are!*

> *Another issue that keeps us anonymous, is that of control. We all tend to be non-conformists, who fiercely value the autonomy of our individual circles. The fear is that if we form larger organizations, a "right way" to worship could emerge and threaten our autonomy.*

> *WIN is not an institution. It is a network. The concept is very different. We propose to communicate with and support each other, while respecting our individual traditions. The leaders of other groups in the area are encouraged to participate in the exchange of information in the hope that we one day truly become a "community." In the words of*

Lady Beckett's The Wiccan Way: "Recognizing that there is more than one path to spiritual enlightenment ... and there is more than one type of step set to the spiral dance."

During our meeting, we heard later that afternoon, Scott Cunningham passed into the Summerland. Because of our meeting, people who normally would not have called each other did call each other, and planned together how we could pay tribute to this man whose work has been of such value to all of us. On Saturday, April 3, over 70 Wiccans gathered in Presidio Park for a candle lighting ritual, in which messages from others too distant to attend, sent over computer bulletin boards, were also released into spirit via a burning cauldron. Many spoke of Scott's influence on their thoughts and practice, others who were fortunate enough to have known him personally related touching or humorous anecdotes, and said that just the fact we were all together would mean much to Scott. And then we danced, and the Moon rose above the trees, and it was beautiful.

Since then, we've received several requests for more copies of the newsletter, and more meetings of area HPs have been scheduled, to discuss issues that they can then take back and share with their circles. The May meeting was a discussion with a representative from the police department, so we will all be better informed about the best ways to interact with officers in case of any future problems in regard to our ritual activities. (This is an outgrowth of a beginning that Mark and I had already established, through presentations we have made to police academy classes. Mark has a law enforcement background, so he made contact with the officer in charge of teaching the section on ritual crime, who agreed that officers who may be called on a complaint about ritual activity should be able to clearly ask the right questions and make correct observations to know if there is a valid concern, or only an innocent Wiccan circle that should not be disturbed.)

A later meeting has been arranged which will feature a speaker, sympathetic to us, who works within the local child protection services (mentioned earlier in the discussion of children and the Craft), so that we will be better informed on its operation. These seminars, designed to deal with issues of common interest to all of us, could not be possible without networking!

There are established networks in other areas, some at least peripherally known to most of us, such as Covenent of the Goddess

(COG), yet it took that WIN network seminar for us to discover a COG representative within our own community. So there are some who network with others nationally, but many within individual cities who know few outside their own small circles. I doubt if other cities are much different in that from San Diego—in fact, until I moved here in 1987, I knew of no circles anywhere I'd lived before, even though I was professionally involved with new age activities, and even owned a metaphysical bookshop in the mid-to-late 70s. It is in our own areas that we must begin, if we are to ever win the acceptance that will allow all of us to practice our religion openly.

In the first chapter of this book I mentioned the small town where I grew up, with 750 people and four Protestant churches, with the Catholics going to church in the next town. They all had their separate activities, mostly with quite small congregations. I hear that most of them have dwindled even more with the years—small groups of aging people, while the majority of their youth stay away. Think what they could do if they all worked together, but I doubt if they ever will. Small differences in doctrine, significant only to them ... perhaps, also, leaders who fear loss of control or a comfortable status quo, if they allow diversity?

At the beginning of my chapter on ethics, I touched on the importance of Wiccans and other Neo-Pagan groups to not make the same mistake of bickering with each other over such small differences. We have a common world view and a reverence for the Earth and the Goddess and God within that is infinitely more significant than the details of how we do ritual. So much benefit can be gained if we are open to learning from each other and sharing our resources.

I feel optimistic about WIN. By the time this book comes out, some readers may have already been in contact with it, for plans are already being made to establish contact with other networking groups in other areas. It is time for things like this to accelerate. We are just one part of a ground swell to which astrologers correlate the 1993 triple conjunction of Uranus and Neptune in Capricorn. Neptune's highest meaning is spirituality, Uranus symbolizes sudden change and innovation, and Capricorn is a sign of structure, tradition, authority, and government. Unyielding, authoritarian belief systems and structures of all types are under great stress. The agitation, and sometimes near-hysteria or violence, in some factions of the so-called "Christian right" are perhaps the most obvious symptoms of that stress. Such structures will have to change, or continue to lose ground. Innovative, open, adaptable belief systems that offer compassionate understanding and appreciation of diversity have never had a better opportunity to expand.

This year, also, is a slow-moving square (challenge) of Pluto, the planetary archetype of transformation to Saturn, ruler of Capricorn, who represents, for one thing, crystallized structures, which will crumble if they only resist change. If, however, they place the accent on personal responsibility, the transformation will be a rebirth. Tagging all these "heavy" aspects, near the end of 1994, Jupiter, planetary ruler of expansion, philosophy, and religion, will conjunct Pluto—a ray of optimism for our near future.

I look back now over this book I have written, gradually over a period of more than two years, as each ritual and activity in it has been experienced within my circle, and I see that it is not what I started out to create in the beginning. I sought to offer a compilation of our rituals—hopefully, as another potential spark for the creativity of others, such as I have received from the ritual books of other authors. I see now that what I have actually written is a story of evolution—first of my own spiritual seeking and growth, then of the development of my mother circle as it has spread into five-and-growing affiliated groups, and now of a larger networking outreach in our community.

For me, and for all of us, the time is *Now*. Time to take that first small step—and then another, one by one, wherever we are and whatever our nuances of practice and belief—to reach out to each other, to communicate, to value our likenesses, to appreciate and accept our differences, to share our resources. Together may we serve the Lady and Lord, as One, in Perfect Love and Perfect Trust. So mote it be!

Endnotes

1. Rose, Elizabeth (psuedonym). "Surviving the Unbelievable: A First-Person Account of Cult Ritual Abuse." *Ms.* Vol. III, No. 4, 1993.

   Salter, Stephanie. "Asking questions should not be attacked as feminist treason," Opinion page, *The San Diego Union-Tribune,* April 15, 1993.

2. *Green Egg,* quarterly journal of the Church of All Worlds, and *HAM,* or *How About Magic?* P.O. Box 1542, Ukiah, CA 95482.

3. "Ariel's Definitions" by Anne Marie Shiosaki, 1992, printed with her permission.

4. The "Webster" referred to by Ariel is *New Collegiate Dictionary,* Springfield, MA: G & C Merriam Co., 1953.

5. *Wiccan Independent Network News,* Vol. 1, Issue 1, April 1993.

Addendum

Since this book was first published, the "broom closet" has opened even more than I anticipated. Here's an early '96 update:

"WIN" disbanded, after nearly two years, several very interesting newsletters, and a number of contacts from other states that came through readers of this book. Some original participants dropped out in discomfort with the public outreach and organizational goals of others. Gains were made in public acceptance, with notices of our activities listed in the religious calendar of San Diego's *Union-Tribune.* But too few were trying to do the work, and as some of us learned how Covenant of the Goddess (CoG) was already successfully working, nationally, in all of the areas we'd been hoping to direct WIN, and more. Circle of the Cosmic Muse and two other covens of the WIN founders group have joined CoG, and more will follow. To learn more about CoG, try its Web page on the internet: www.cog.org/cog/ or write to Covenant of the Goddess, PO Box 1226, Berkeley, CA 94704.

Because of this book, I have given presentations in several states, circled with other groups, have been enriched by the experience, and am even more convinced that our common ground far outweighs any differences in tradition or form. Locally, I'm finding interest and openness from many who'd never have "come out" two years ago.

Pluto, now in Sagittarius, brings a transformative theme to philosophy and religion. It's a time of upheaval for matters of faith, when some are trying desperately to hang on to a world view that is passing away, and many others are groping for a new spirituality. Pluto tells us it is time to claim our own power—the inner power to seek, find and live our own truth. So again, reach out to one another. Appreciate and accept both our likenesses and our differences. Share your resources, and may we serve the Lady and Lord as One, in Perfect Love and Perfect Trust. Blessed be!

Annotated Bibliography and Resource Guide

Books Specifically Cited

Adler, Margot. *Drawing Down the Moon*. Boston: Beacon Press, 1979.

> This contains most comprehensive information that I know about, in one volume, on Craft traditions, past and present. No matter what tradition you practice, you should be aware of your roots and of how others practice. Don't miss this one.

Baigent, Michael, Richard Leigh and Henry Lincoln. *Holy Blood, Holy Grail*. New York: Dell Publishing Co., 1982.

> Extensive historical research, with particular emphasis on the Knights Templar, provided evidence that led the authors to propose that Jesus married Mary Magdalene, children were born of the union, and that descendants still live.

Budapest, Zuszsanna E. *The Grandmother of Time*. San Francisco: Harper & Row, 1989.

> Good resource for ritual ideas, feminist spirituality, women's holidays. Has stories, anecdotes, poems, too.

Burns, Echo Bodine. *Hands That Heal*. San Diego: ACS Publications, Inc., 1985.

> A good book on healing by laying on of hands, written by a professional healer who believes that anyone can be a channel for healing. Answers many commonly asked questions about spiritual healing. Client examples.

Dechend, Hertha and Giorgio de Santillana. *Hamlet's Mill: An Essay on Myth and the Frame of Time*. Boston: Godine, 1981.

> Scholarly work that cites precessional ages based upon movement of the vernal point against the constellations—the ancients' observation of the helical rising constellation on the first day of spring. This puts the Age of Aquarius still far in the future.

Dobin, Rabbi Joel. *To Rule Both Day and Night*. New York: Inner Traditions International, 1977.

> A most interesting book written by a Rabbi that deals with astrological roots in Judaic tradition and scriptures.

Farrar, Stewart and Janet. *Eight Sabbats for Witches*. Custer, WA: Phoenix Publishing, Inc., 1981.

> Rituals for the eight Sabbats, plus rites for birth, marriage, death. Formal Gardnerian/Alexandrian tradition Witchcraft.

French, Marilyn. *Beyond Power*. New York: Summit Books, 1985.

> Comprehensive, scholarly, and heavily referenced study of the patriarchal system, its social and political assumptions, and the roots and growth of the women's movement.

Gawain, Shakti. *Living in the Light*. San Rafael, CA: New World Library, 1986.

> A popular favorite of new age self-help philosophy that is very complementary to my own (and Astro Communications Services') educational mission in regard to the use of astrology.

George, Demetra with Douglas Bloch. *Asteroid Goddesses*. ACS Publications, 1986.

> Thorough treatment of the mythology behind the names of the four primary asteroids and their use in astrology, with look-up tables for zodiacal positions of the four plus a number of minor asteroids. The text is strongly oriented toward the Goddess and the emerging feminine.

Glass-Koentop, Pattalee. *Year of Moons, Season of Trees: Mysteries and Rites of Celtic Tree Magic.* St. Paul, MN: Llewellyn Publications, 1991.

A very interesting full year of Moon rituals based on the Ogham Tree Calendar, with background on tree worship through the ages.

Greene, Liz. *Relating: An Astrological Guide to Living with Others on a Small Planet.* New York: Samuel Weiser, Inc., 1978.

Correlates the four elements as they are used in astrology with Jungian archetypes. Very insightful and useful for self-awareness and understanding how you interact with others.

Guiley, Rosemary Ellen. *The Encyclopedia of Witches and Witchcraft.* New York: Facts on File, Inc., 1989.

This is a big, thick encyclopedia—just like the title says—in which you can look up alphabetically just about any topic or any prominent person in the history of the Craft. It's a good resource to have.

Guralnik, David B., Ed. *Webster's New World Dictionary of the American Language.* New York: Fawcett, 1979.

Hand, Robert. "The Age and Constellation of Pisces," *Essays on Astrology.* Rockport, MA: ParaResearch, 1982.

This article is primarily cited as another source for the timing of this age, but the other articles in the book are well worth your while, too. Rob is widely respected throughout the astrological community as one of our deepest thinkers and our most articulate philosophers.

Haich, Elisabeth. *Initiation.* Garberville, CA: Seed Center, 1965.

Fictionalized autobiography of a past-life memory makes for thoroughly enjoyable reading, plus a wealth of metaphysical philosophy.

Hines, Lillian M., Edward J Welch, and Doris M. Bacon. *Our Latin Heritage.* New York: Harcourt, Brace, Jovanovich, 1966.

Textbook used at my daughter's high school.

Huxley, Aldous. *Brave New World.* New York: Harare & Bros., 1932.

This novel is a sci-fi classic of a future that we should all hope will *not* be part of the Age of Aquarius! If you are one of the few who escaped reading it in school, you should read it now so you will know what people are talking about when they refer to it, which in my experience, happens fairly often. It's a "good read." Paperback versions are easily available.

Jade. *To Know: A Guide to Women's Magic and Spirituality.* Oak Park, IL: Delphi Press, Inc., 1991.

This is an easy-to-read book that contains a potpourri of good general information on women's spirituality that could be helpful to practitioners of any Wiccan tradition. I list it here because I think that what sets it apart from other books and makes it particularly worthwhile is that it has succinct descriptions of the various neo-Pagan religious movements of today, and an extensive list of resources.

Michelsen, Neil F., Ed. "The Lunar Cycle: An 8-Fold Cycle of Transformation" by Maria Kay Simms, in *Tables of Planetary Phenomena.* San Diego: ACS Publications, 1990.

This is the article in which I first correlated, for publication, the eight Lunar phases with the Wheel of the Year. It precedes Neil's "look-up" tables of the sign positions of the eight phases of the Moon from 1900 through 2020.

Mish, Frederick C., Ed. *Webster's Ninth New Collegiate Dictionary.* Springfield, MA: Merriam-Webster, Inc., 1991.

The New American Bible, Catholic Edition. New York: Thomas Nelson Publishers, 1971.

The New English Bible. Cambridge University Press, 1970.

Actually, just about any translation of the Bible would do, in referencing my comments in Chapter 1. I cite the two listed above primarily because they are my favorites—both written in clear language closely translated by teams of scholars from the oldest possible sources. Additionally, *The New American* has many informative footnotes, and *The New English* contains the entire Apocrypha, including the prophecies of Esdras, on which the final chapter and the title of *Twelve Wings of the Eagle* were based.

Pottenger, Maritha. *Encounter Astrology.* Los Angeles: TIA Publications, 1978.

This is a book on experiential astrology written before experiential astrology was publicly identified! It has lots of games and exercises designed to help you and your group experience the sign and elemental archetypes. You can get some ideas from this that could be used in ritual—I have!

Robinson, James M., Ed. *The Nag Hammadi Library.* San Francisco: Harper & Row, 1977.

Scholarly work on the archeological finds of ancient Gnostic writings from the time of Christ which were unearthed at Nag Hammadi, Egypt.

Regardie, Israel. *The Golden Dawn.* St. Paul, MN: Llewellyn Publications, 1971, 1986.

This is not easy reading, but it is a valuable source for understanding the source of many Wiccan practices. Golden Dawn ritual magick practices were of undoubted influence on Gardner, which in turn, has influenced all of contemporary Wiccan practice to some degree.

Rudhyar, Dane. *The Lunation Cycle.* Boulder: Shambala, 1971.

This book, by the late great astrological philosopher, defines the eight phases of the Moon. His work is the basis for my correlation of the lunar phases with the seasonal cycle, which subsequently led to my structuring of the eight Sabbat rituals in this book.

Schermer, Barbara. *Astrology Alive!* Wellingborough, England: The Aquarian Press, 1989.

A "how-to" on astro-drama, experiential astrology, and the use of astrology for healing. A good potential source for ritual ideas as well.

Simms, Maria Kay. *Dial Detective.* San Diego: ACS Publications, 1989.

How-to for Uranian Astrology and Cosmobiology.

Simms, Maria Kay. *Twelve Wings of the Eagle.* San Diego, ACS Publications, 1988.

Correlates the precessional ages of the zodiac and basic astrological symbolism with religious history, mythical and Biblical, in an easy-reading format combining narrative, dialogue, and paraphrased Bible stories. I was teaching confirmation catechism in a Catholic parish when I began writing it in 1982, yet my world view expressed in it was already neo-Pagan. I just didn't have that word for it at the time. Based on astrology, I project a mass cultural emphasis on matrifocal issues before the close of the Age of Pisces, and the Goddess as the primary personification of deity as we move into the Age of Aquarius, with Pisces rising as the Cardinal Ascendant. This is a good "bridge book" for anyone who is still experiencing some conflict between Neo-Pagan leanings in reconciliation with a strong Judeo-Christian background.

Slater, Herman, Ed. *A Book of Pagan Rituals.* York Beach, ME: Samuel Weiser, Inc., 1978.

A book of rituals for major seasonal holidays and a number of other purposes, with lists of symbols and correspondences, material on herbs and spells. Includes a Dedication ritual nearly identical to that in general use among a number of San Diego circles.

Starhawk. *The Spiral Dance*. San Francisco: Harper & Row, 1979.

This "classic" is frequently the first one a newcomer to Wicca reads, or is referred to by a Wiccan teacher. It's easy to read; contains a wealth of information on Wiccan philosophy and practice. Good source for ritual ideas.

Stein, Diane. *The Women's Spirituality Book*. St. Paul, MN: Llewellyn Publications, 1987.

The working in my Aquarius Full Moon ritual was derived from the Introduction to this book, and my Lughnasad ritual was adapted from Stein's Fall Equinox ritual. You should be able to get lots more ideas for ritual from the wealth of material throughout this work.

Walker, Barbara G. *The Woman's Encyclopedia of Myths and Secrets*. San Francisco: Harper & Row, 1983.

A big, thick book in which you can look up, in alphabetical order, about every topic you could possibly think of in regard to Goddess mythology and women's issues.

Waverly translation. *Ptolemy's Tetrabiblos*. North Hollywood, CA: Symbols & Signs, 1976.

Translation from the ancient Greek text.

Weinstein, Marion. *Positive Magic: Occult Self-Help*. Custer, WA: Phoenix Publishing, Inc., 1981.

Lady Beckett recommends this one to beginners at Circle Atheneum, because it is so strongly ethical in its approach. I repeat that recommendation. An excellent book.

Zain, C.C. *Ancient Masonry*. Brotherhood of Light.

I've looked high and low for this small soft-cover book—I know it is lost in my house somewhere. I don't remember the date of publication. It is very old and undoubtedly out of print.

Other Recommended Book Resources

There are so many good books out now on astrology, Wicca, Goddess, women's and men's myths and mysteries, the emerging feminine … it's difficult to know where to stop. What I am listing below are the ones, in addition to many of those cited above, that I'm most likely to grab off the shelf when I need to look something up in the course of my work with my circle—either planning rituals or classes, or trying to answer someone's questions.

Astrology

Burt, Kathleen. *Archetypes of the Zodiac.* St. Paul, MN: Llewellyn Publications, 1988.

> Here's a wealth of information on the mythology of the astrological sign archetypes, with questionnaires at the end of each chapter to help the reader understand when and how s/he may be experiencing the sign archetype within. (Remember, no matter what your personal chart, you have every sign somewhere in it!)

Forrest, Steven. *The Night Speaks, A Meditation on the Astrological Worldview.* San Diego: ACS Publications, 1993.

> This is an important book for articulating the significance of modern astrology's place in the emerging world view. The author masterfully blends a rational and intuitive approach to his topic. He deals with relevant scientific research in a manner that is easily readable, arguing for the intellectual plausibility of astrology. And yet throughout, he gives us his deeply personal insights of the Universe as Goddess—alive, awe-inspiring, calling us—now, as She has been throughout the ages.

Pottenger, Maritha. *Astro Essentials.* ACS Publications, 1991.

> I think this is the best "cookbook" on astrology currently available. "Cookbook" is the trade term for a book that gives you an easy look-up paragraph for every sign, house, and aspect in a chart. If you are experienced in astrology, this book will give you strong insight into the upside and downside of everything. (That's true, you know—nothing is all good or all bad!) If you are a complete novice, and you don't have an astrologer friend handy to calculate a chart for you, I recommend you get a color Student Chart from ACS, that has all the glyphs for signs, houses, and aspects in the chart listed below the chart wheel with identifying words, so you can easily look up the meanings in any "cookbook." This is a great way to get started in learning how to interpret your own chart or those of your friends and family. (The Student Chart is only $5. Call 800-888-9983. You need birth place, date, and time.)

River, Lindsay and Sally Gillespie. *The Knot of Time: Astrology and the Female Experience.* New York: Harper & Row, 1987.

> The subtitle says it all. This is a book that balances the predominant masculine archetypes in classical astrology with a feminine perspective. It correlates Goddess mythology with all the planets and signs—well worth reading.

Starck, Marcia. *Earth Mother Astrology.* St. Paul, MN: Llewellyn Publications, 1989.

> This is a good basic book on astrology for Craft-oriented readers. Good for herb/healing correspondences, ritual ideas.

Thorston, Geraldine. *God Herself.* New York: Avon Books, 1980.

Another very Goddess-oriented book on the mythology and the interpretation of the astrological signs.

Wicca

Buckland, Raymond. *Buckland's Complete Book of Witchcraft.* St. Paul, MN: Llewellyn Publications, 1987.

Fifteen detailed lessons on just about everything to do with the Craft. Interesting first-hand background on the introduction of the Craft (traditional Gardnerian) into the U.S. by the one who introduced it!

Campanelli, Pauline. *The Wheel of the Year.* St. Paul, MN: Llewellyn Publications, 1989.

Campanelli, Pauline. *Ancient Ways.* St. Paul, MN: Llewellyn Publications, 1991.

The only criticism I have of the two very helpful books by Campanelli, listed above, are that the titles should be reversed—but I realize this probably happened the way it did only because when the second title was written, the more appropriate first title had already been taken! *The Wheel of the Year* gives a wealth of lore and practice for each month of the year. *Ancient Ways* does the same, but is organized according to the eight Sabbats of the Wheel of the Year.

Cunningham, Scott. *Cunningham's Encyclopedia of Magical Herbs.* St. Paul, MN: Llewellyn Publications, 1985.

If you're getting one book on herbs, get this one. It has clear illustrations of each herb, so that you can learn to recognize them, and provides details about the correspondences and uses of each one.

Cunningham, Scott. *The Complete Book of Incense, Oils and Brews.* St. Paul, MN: Llewellyn Publications, 1985.

Cunningham, Scott. *The Magic of Incense, Oils and Brews.* St. Paul, MN: Llewellyn Publications, 1986.

The first of the two listed above is bigger. Both have lots of good recipes, with correspondences and helpful hints.

Cunningham, Scott. *Earth Power.* St. Paul, MN: Llewellyn Publications, 1983.

A small book, but with lots of good ideas, formulas, things to do.

Cunningham, Scott. *Encyclopedia of Crystal, Gem and Metal Magic.* St. Paul, MN: Llewellyn Publications, 1987.

Cunningham, Scott. *Wicca: A Guide for the Solitary Practitioner.* St. Paul, MN: Llewellyn Publications, 1988.

This clear guide to practically everything one might need to get started in Wiccan worship as a solitary (practicing alone); also has applications for group practice.

Cunningham, Scott. *The Truth about Witchcraft Today.* St. Paul, MN: Llewellyn Publications, 1988.

Inexpensive paperback that is packed with lots of information. Good introduction.

Farrar, Janet and Stewart. *A Witches Bible Compleat.* New York: Magickal Childe, 1984.

Very traditional Gardnerian/Alexandrian/British Wicca. Important both as a source of ritual ideas and for understanding the roots of many common Wiccan practices that have found their way into the various eclectic traditions.

Farrar, Janet and Stewart. *The Witches' God.* Custer, WA: Phoenix Publishing, Inc., 1989.

Farrar, Janet and Stewart. *The Witches' Goddess.* Custer, WA: Phoenix Publishing, Inc., 1987.

Mythology and rituals in both of the above, with extensive lists of God/dess names, origins, and meanings.

Fitch, Ed. *Magical Rites from the Crystal Well.* St. Paul, MN: Llewellyn Publications, 1984.

A beautifully illustrated sourcebook for ritual ideas, especially if you prefer a more archaic, poetic style of wording.

Hope, Murry. *The Psychology of Ritual.* Longmead, Shaftsbury, Dorset, UK: Element Books Limited, 1988.

This contains only a few actual rituals. It is mostly theory—good for understanding of what ritual is, why it has been important throughout history, and why it works.

Mariechild, Diane. *Mother Wit: A Feminist Guide to Psychic Development.* Trumansberg, NY: Crossing Press, 1981.

Excellent for meditation techniques, and ideas for guided meditation you can use in ritual.

Valiente, Doreen. *Witchcraft for Tomorrow.* Custer, WA: Phoenix Publishing, Inc., 1978.

Author calls it her "Book of Shadows," and several rituals are given, including a self-initiation—her famous Charge of the Goddess is not in this book. It's fascinating reading, for her first-hand information on the early years of the Gardnerian tradition, with extensive material about practice, tools, runes, sex magic, etc.—and there are a number of photographs of the author.

Walker, Barbara G. *Women's Rituals: A Sourcebook*. San Francisco: Harper & Row, 1990.

Although I can't specifically trace the origin of any of my ideas expressed in my book to this book, this is, as its subtitle indicates, a good sourcebook—one of those that I thumb through when I'm having mental block trying to think up what to do on the next ritual. It has lots of ideas for things to do, dances, chants, etc.

Weinstein, Marion. *Earth Magic: A Dianic Book of Shadows*. Custer, WA: Phoenix Publishing, Inc., 1980.

Another good source of ritual ideas; supplement to her *Positive Magic*, cited above.

Neither Astrology nor Wiccan, but Relevant

Hoffmann, David. *The New Holistic Herbal*. Rockport, MA: Element Books Limited, 1991.

If you are interested in learning how to understand and use herbs for health and home remedies, this is the best current reference I've found.

Periodicals

These are the ones that I read. There are others, here and there around the country. If you are looking for a circle, or like-minded people to help you start one, or looking for materials, reading periodicals such as these will help you find contacts.

Circle Network News. P.O. Box 219, Mt. Horeb, WI 53572.

Large international tabloid newspaper full of news, contacts, gatherings, etc. Published quarterly.

Green Egg. P.O. Box 1542, Ukiah, CA 95482.

Quarterly journal of the Church of All Worlds. Very professional quality, with many interesting articles, and an extensive reader write-in forum.

HAM, or How About Magic? P.O. Box 1542, Ukiah, CA 95482.

This is a quarterly magazine for Pagan youth, containing instructive and fun articles, pictures, stories and letters by and for Pagans aged 6 through 16. Has great line art.

New Moon Rising: A Journal of Magick and Wicca. 12345 SE Fuller Road #119, Milwaukie, OR 97222.

Another quality journal, not quite as thick as *Green Egg,* but containing lots of good articles, as well as rituals, songs, letters, etc. Published six times a year.

Llewellyn's New Worlds of Mind and Spirit. Llewellyn Publications, P.O. Box 64383, Dept. K657-2, St. Paul, MN 55164-0383.

Also available at many bookstores. This is not an all-Wiccan magazine, but it always includes several articles on Wicca, or of interest to Wiccans. Also has news and events around the country, as well as reader polls and letters from readers.

Astrological Services

Astro Communications Services, Inc. P.O. Box 34487, San Diego, CA 92163-4487, (619) 429-9919, order line 800-888-9983.

Offers fast service (orders in by 3 P.M. Monday through Friday are mailed the same day) on a huge range of services—everything for the interested layperson or the professional astrologer; from a wide variety of interpreted reports to the most complex calculations. You can call and request a free catalog.

Mail Order Sources for Wiccan Products

Abyss, RR1, Box 213, Chester Road, (413) 623-2155.

One of the most comprehensive mail order catalogs I've come across is this one cited in Chapter 10, in regard to the ordering of the crescent crowns for the spin-off gift. Their list of products is very extensive, and their prices are reasonable.

Mystic Moon, 8818 Troy Street, Spring Valley, CA 91977

A good mail order list of magickal supplies is available from the Mystic Moon bookshop in San Diego, which was mentioned at the beginning of Chapter 6.

Wren Faire Designs, 4290 Pepper Drive, San Diego, CA 92105, (619) 282-2889.

The maker of the custom silver crowns and rings described in the Chapter 10 handfasting. A small catalog of jewelry designs is available.

Music to Play During Ritual

New age music, I find, is generally best for ritual background. Some classical music works, if the tape stays in a similar mood, not suddenly jarring you with a fugue or drastic change of tempo. Because of those changes, however, it's probably best to make up your own tape of classical selections by copying bits and pieces of others. Much new age music is written for meditation, so it doesn't make those drastic changes as often. The problem with it, though, is sometimes it just isn't musical, or it gets stuck on one or two tones that are slightly dissonant for so long that it becomes distracting—"When is this going to get pretty again?" All too often I've purchased a new age tape because one little piece of it that could be played for me at the store sounded "right" for ritual, but then when I got it home and played the whole thing, I hated it. You may not agree with my taste, of course—but if, after reading this book, you think you might, I will give you my list of what works for ritual, to save you from wasting your money, too, in buying things that don't work.

My personal favorites in new age are the CDs or tapes by Gerald Jay Markoe:

> *Music from the Pleiades*
> *Pleiadian Danses*
> *Sacred Music from Seven Stars*
> *Melodies from the Pleiades*

Markoe is an accomplished classical musician, too, and it shows. His compositions combine the very best of new age synthesizer with a quality of musicianship that is all too often missing in the new age venue. This music is a beautiful background for ritual, healing, meditation, or just listening. Available at many local tape outlets, or through Astromusic, P.O. Box 118, New York, NY 10033.

Others that I especially like include (all should be available at local outlets):

Gibson, Dan. *Solitudes: The Classics: Exploring Nature with Music.*

A classical tape that *does* work all the way through.

Enya, or most anything by Enya—*Shepherd Moons, Watermark.*

Enya's music won't work for everything because it has vocals, but it is very good for some ritual moods or themes that can take a little stronger, more dynamic background.

Valentino, Chris. *The Musical Sea of Tranquility.*

> Harp over ocean waves.

Valentino, Chris. *The Romantic Sea of Tranquility.*

> Accoustic guitar over ocean waves. Both of these Valentino tapes use popular classics in an especially nice way that stays in the background and contributes to a romantic mood.

Roth, Gabrielle and the Mirrors. *Totem.* Raven Recording, P.O. Box 2034, Red Bank, NJ 07701.

> This is drumming. It's a great background for a theme in which you want to build a strong, sensual energy, or charge up a group—or yourself—when you're tired.

Terrell's Magic Flutes. *Kokopelli: The Indian Legend.* Diane and Terrell Jones, P.O. Box 184, Copper Hill, VA 24079, (703) 929-5239.

> We recently received this one, unsolicited, at ACS to review. We don't sell music, Terrell, but here's your review. Your tape of flutes, Pan pipes, guitars, drums, etc. is great for ritual—contributes to the building of group energy without distracting. Everyone in my circle liked it, so I imagine we'll use it often.

Additionally, I recommend any of the environmental tapes in which you hear natural sounds only—ocean waves, fire, rain, etc. These are easy to find—pick the environment that matches your theme.

Music Cited in the Text

Agápe. *The Genesis Songbook.* Main Place, Carol Stream, IL 60187.

> Contains a melody line for "Lord of the Dance."

Bethencourt, Joe. *Celtic Circle Dances.* P.O. Box 35190, Phoenix, AZ 85069.

> Contains the lyrics to "Lord of the Dance" given in Chapter 11, as well as several other lively, good-for-circle-dancing songs, and one lovely slow one called "The Dream Song."

DreaMaker. *Sing Along Tapes Hot 25: Phantom of the Opera.*

> The accompaniment for the theme song has a strong, steady rhythm that, similar to *Totem,* is a good energy-builder. We taped it over and over to play in the background for casting circle, right up to the Charge of the Goddess, then quick-switched to the original tape set to start playing at "Music of the Night," which provided the accompaniment for my "Magic of the Night" sung Charge for the Leo Full Moon. If

you'd like to use the song with a different kind of accompaniment, the sheet music for "Music of the Night" by Andrew Lloyd Webber is easily available through any music store.

First Chants. *Prana*. The Creative Source, P.O. Box 11024, Costa Mesa, CA 92627, (714) 722-7375.

Audio cassette tape that features many traditional chants. Much of it is quite nice to play as background during a ritual. You could sing along with it, too, but the pitch is set just a little high for the comfort of average voices.

James, Tamara and Jennifer Holding. *Libation*. 1988.

This is the tape from which we copied the "Handfasting Song" mentioned in Chapter 10. There's nothing on it to tell where to contact them to request permission to use the words to the song, which is why I haven't. Mark remembers buying the tape at Mystic Moon, so you could probably still get it through that source (listed above under Wiccan products). There are other great songs on the tape, too.

McBroom, Amanda. *The Rose*.

Sheet music for piano with guitar chords is easily available in the popular music section of any music store. This is the tune to use for "The Goddess and the Rose" in Chapter 11, which I wrote for my Pisces Full Moon ritual.

Schutte, S.J., Dan. "Here I Am, Lord," *Glory and Praise,* Vol. 3. Northern Liturgy Resources, Phoenix, AZ.

Melody and guitar chords for "Spirits of the Elements" (Chapter 11).

Glossary

In writing this book, I've tried to carefully explain terms as they were introduced, for the benefit of readers who are Wiccan but not astrologers, or who are astrologers but not Wiccan. In a final read-through of this book, before production began, I can see places where a reader who is skipping around might encounter jargon the meaning of which is not evident. In remembrance of the times that I have passed over jargon in reading or in listening to a conversation, in order to avoid interrupting the flow with a question just then, I decided that a easily accessible glossary of jargon might be useful. Here is, first of all, a list of commonly used Wiccan terms.

Glossary of Wiccan Jargon

athame—(a-THA-me, short "a" on the first two syllables, sometimes pronounced with the last syllable more like "may," also sometimes pronounced with the first syllable accented, rather than the second) The ritual dagger used in Wiccan ritual. It is the most personal tool of priestess or priest, usually used only by

439

the owner. Traditionally, it has a double-edged blade and a black handle. Symbolizes the masculine aspect.

banishing—To clear away, to dispel.

binding—To magickally hold, tie, restrict, or confine.

boline—(bow-leen, bow pronounced with long "o" as in bow and arrow) A white-handled, consecrated ritual knife that is kept sharp. Used for various tasks such as to harvest herbs, make magical tools, fix stubborn candle wicks or charcoal during ritual, cut fruit during ritual.

broom closet—Refers to the anonymity within which some Wiccans practice. One who does not let others know that s/he is a Witch is said to be "in the broom closet."

cast—A term used to refer to a ritual designed to "set" a particular intent, as in casting the circle (preparing sacred space) or casting a spell (directing focused mental energy).

cauldron—A term that refers to the Goddess' womb of rebirth, which has the capacity both to create and to destroy, as is needed for perpetuation of life. The physical symbol of the cauldron used in ritual is usually a black, cast-iron kettle, and it is used for many purposes, some of which are noted in the rituals.

chalice—A cup, usually a stemmed goblet, used on the ritual altar. Symbolizes the feminine aspect and the water element.

charge, charging—To infuse with energy, as in charging an altar tool; also to instruct, as in the Charge of the Goddess, as delivered by the High Priestess after the Goddess has been invoked into her.

circle/coven—A group of Wiccans who worship together regularly. An old tradition has it that the number of an official coven is 13, but this is not the case in most contemporary groups. The number of a group is usually a minimum of those who are interested—more than one—and a maximum of however many will fit into the High Priestess' ritual area. Another old tradition has it that if you have more than 13 in your group, you should call it a "grove." This tradition is only loosely followed, if at all. Circle also refers to the way a group stands together during ritual, and to the consecrated area in which they have "cast circle" to hold their ritual. The consecrated area in which ritual is held is also sometimes referred to as a temple, or as a sphere, indicating that the circle is not flat, but rather spherical.

cleansing—An act of purification, or of banishing impurities and unwanted energies.

cord—A long, flexible material like a string or rope. Used as a tool in magickal acts such as binding, or knotting to focus intent. Also used in specified colors to denote a particular degree or rank.

coven—See **circle**.

Craft—Short for Witchcraft. A term that summarizes the practice of Wicca.

Crone—The aspect of the Threefold Goddess that represents maturity of wisdom. Also used as a title of great respect for an elder woman.

Dedicate, Dedication—A Dedicate is one who makes a formal commitment to the path of the Goddess and the Horned God. The act of making that commitment is called Dedication. Dedication also refers to the opening statement at the beginning of a ritual that states the intent and purpose for the ritual.

degree—A rank denoting a level of training in a Wiccan tradition.

deocil—(JESS-ill) Clockwise motion, or "forward" motion, used to build energy. It is also described as sun-wise, in that it mirrors the daily apparent motion of the Sun.

directions—Refers to the four Watchtowers, or compass points.

elemental—Refers to the spirits of air, fire, water, and earth.

Esbat—The regular meeting of a circle/coven in which a ritual of worship is performed, including a magickal working or healing, and group business/announcements are taken care of. Full Moon Esbats are most common, although some groups also meet at New Moon.

evoke—To call forth, to summon, as to call an elemental to a Watchtower.

God—The masculine aspect of the Life Force, the Divine, the One, the Whole, the Order of the Universe, or whatever you want to call it. Known by thousands of proper names, and also defined by such terms as Bright Lord, Dark Lord, Horned One, Great Stag, Green Man, Oak King, Holly King, etc.

Goddess—The feminine aspect of the Life Force, the Divine, the One, the Whole, the Order of the Universe, or whatever you want to call it. Known by thousands of proper names, and also defined by such terms as The Lady and Maiden, Mother or Crone.

Great Rite—A ritual act of sexual intercourse. This may be actual or symbolic, the latter involving the thrusting of the athame into the chalice. The purpose is to merge or balance the masculine and feminine polarities.

handfasting—The ritual commitment of two people to live together as lovers and domestic partners. This may or may not be a legal marriage. Sometimes the commitment is made as a sort of trial marriage, for "a year and a day," after which the arrangement may be reevaluated.

High Priest, High Priestess—A priest or priestess who is a leader of a Wiccan circle. The High Priestess is usually the primary leader and the High Priest is her "working partner."

hive—See **spin-off**. Hiving is a term alternatively used for the same purpose.

initiation—A ritual that represents a final test of a person's intent to become a Wiccan priest or priestess, or to be elevated to a particular rank within a Wiccan circle, and that acknowledges such a passage by the initiators, and before the Goddess and the God.

intent—A clearly focused statement of will and purpose.

invoke—To petition for help or support, as to invoke Goddess or God.

Maiden—The aspect of the Threefold Goddess that represents such things as youth, freedom, independence, springtime. Also refers to a female member of a circle who is designated as the special assistant to the High Priestess.

magick—An act which draws upon the unseen source of energy for a focused intent. Spelled with a "k" to differentiate from the type of magic that suggests trickery or slight of hand, or just a "sparkly feeling" without focused intent.

Mother—The central aspect of the Threefold Goddess. Represents fulfillment—the full power of the feminine—creative, nurturing, sensual.

muse—A source of inspiration, derived from the nine Goddesses of Greek mythology who were said to be the inspiration for various specified fields. One of them, Urania, is the muse for astrology (or astronomy, if you prefer—but remember, until the eighteenth century the two terms were virtually synonymous).

pentacle/pentagram—A primary symbol of Wicca. Represents the four elements and the fifth element of Spirit, or Mind, through which humanity transcends the four elements. Usually depicted as a continuously drawn five-pointed star within a circle, although sometimes it is not enclosed within a circle, and indeed Wiccans are likely to favor any five-pointed star motif in jewelry, decor, etc., as representative of the pentacle. A Wiccan altar usually includes a pentagram as a central tool, and pentagrams are drawn in the air during acts of evocation, invocation, and banishing.

poppet—A small image of a person, perhaps made of cloth or plant life, which is used in a magickal act.

priest/priestess—Anyone who has been initiated into a Wiccan tradition.

quarters—Another term used to refer to the directions or Watchtowers.

raising energy—The act of building mental focus and emotion toward the directing of an intent.

Red Priest—A Wiccan priest who is designated to serve as special assistant to the High Priest.

rede—Creed. "The" Wiccan Rede is a statement of basic principles. The Wiccan Way, given in this book, is an adaptation of the rede.

robe—Loose-fitting garment especially made for ritual, and only worn for that purpose.

Sabbat—A holy day of the seasonal cycle of Sun and Earth. There are eight: the lesser Sabbats are the two equinoxes and the two solstices. The greater Sabbats are the holidays that fall half-way in between, or at the cross-quarters. See also **Wheel of the Year.**

scrying—To gaze into something in order to gain insight or psychic impressions. The obvious example of "something" is a crystal ball, but there are many other tools for scrying—black mirrors, pools of still water, water in a dark bowl, flames, cloud formations ...

shield—A thought form or psychic barrier of protection.

spell—A clearly focused intent that is directed through a ritual raising of energy.

spin-off—A ritual in which one leaves the circle with which one has trained in order to form a new circle. Also called **hiving.**

spiral dance—Refers to the "dance" of life, seen as a never-ending spiral. Also refers to an actual circle dance in which a group holds hands in a chain, spiraling inward to the center of the circle and out again, often snaking in and out in the process, but never dropping hands.

tradition—An established system of Wiccan practice that is handed down through circle spin-offs or through family generations.

wand—A magical tool used to invoke or conduct energy. This is generally a very personal tool of one priest or priestess, in the manner of the athame, and is often hand-crafted by its user.

ward—To shield an area, to perform a ritual to erect a psychic barrier around an area or person to be protected.

Watchtowers—The four directional points at the perimeter of a magick circle. The four elementals, air, fire, water, and earth, are called to be guardians of the directional points, to lend their energies to the magick, and to guard the circle.

Wheel of the Year—A term for the seasonal cycle of Sun and Earth. Also called the **Sabbats.**

wiccaning—A ritual for the naming and blessing of a new baby or a small child.

widdershins—(wid-der-shins, pronounced just like it's spelled, short vowels) Counterclockwise motion.

Witch—A term commonly used interchangeably with Wiccan. Denotes either a female or a male practitioner of Wicca. Witch is also used to refer to non-Wiccans, in other words: a Wiccan can also be called a Witch, but a witch is not necessarily a Wiccan.

working—an act of magick, e.g. "a working," or merely, the process of doing ritual.

working center—Performing the function of High Priestess or High Priest for a ritual.

working partner—The priest or priestess with whom one customarily works ritual. More often than not, the relationship also includes that of spouse, lover, and/or domestic partner, but this is not always the case. There are working partners who are married, those who are lovers, and there are also those who are each happily and faithfully married to others, yet have an effective working partnership as High Priestess and High Priest of their circle.

Glossary of Astrological Jargon

Following is a list of the astrological jargon used in this book, which is far from the only jargon for astrology, but enough for the present purpose. At my business we call it "Astrospeak." Astrospeak is a language unto itself, spoken freely by astrologers on elevators between conference room floors and eliciting dumbfounded expressions from non-astrologers sharing the same elevators. The overuse of this language tends to discourage further study in those who might otherwise be interested, which is exactly the opposite of that which I hope to accomplish! Much of what is given below has very little relevance to using astrology in ritual, but just in case a few readers really want more definition of the astrological terms than I gave in the text.

age—A controversial and much argued measurement of time of around 2000 years, give or take a few hundred, depending on the system you use (and in my opinion, how much you are vested in being in or getting to the Age of Aquarius within your lifetime). The ancients (according to scholarly sources— see *Hamlet's Mill* in the bibliography) defined the shift of the ages by observing, through generations, the actual constellations as they rise heliacally (before the Sun) at the equinoxes. When a constellation became totally "lost" in the rising Sun at vernal equinox, a new age was born, named for the constellation that now was the last to be fully visible just above the eastern horizon before sunrise. This implies an offset of equinoctial points (reference points for the zodiac of signs) against the unequal, actual, observable constellations. If this is so, we are still in the Age of Pisces for a long time yet. Most people seem to prefer to define ages by sign-based interpretations of the times in which they live, rather than by measurement. The flaw in this is the fact that sign symbolism can be universally applied, and life is not that simple—you can find plenty of things in our culture anytime, anywhere, to justify any sign, if that's what you are trying to do.

angle—The relationship of points on the horoscope circle. Most commonly refers to the start of the 1st, 4th, 7th, and 10th houses of an astrological chart, also called Ascendant, I.C., Descendant, and Midheaven, respectively. These points form a cross, and are considered to be especially important. A planet very near an angle is a good key to interpretation of the horoscope, because the characteristics symbolized by that planet will probably be much more dominant in the personality than those of other planets not so near angles. Such a planet will be referred to, by those speaking Astrospeak, as "angular," e.g.: "Well! What do you expect, with her angular Neptune?" To which one might respond, "Yeah, especially with that semi-square to her Mercury—hopelessly confused!" (That's me. I'm not—at least, I don't think so!)

Ascendant—Cusp of the 1st house of an astrological chart. The degree and sign of the Ascendant is determined by the degree of the ecliptic that rises in the east, according to the Sun's daily motion, at the time of a birth. Thus, the Ascendant is also called the Rising Sign. Significant information about a person's outward personality, one-to-one relationships, and environment are interpreted from the position of the Ascendant and its exact opposition degree, called the Descendant.

aspect—Refers to significant angular relationships between points on the horoscope circle. The aspects that are most universally considered to be significant are the conjunction 0°, sextile 60°, square 90°, trine 120° and opposition 180°. Opinions vary on others. For example, this author finds the semisquare 45° and the sesquisquare 135° to be more important than the sextile or trine. Others would not think to interpret a chart without the quincunx 150°. And there are more ...

asteroid—There are thousands of minor bodies orbiting between the orbits of Mars and Jupiter. They may be either a planet that disintegrated, or one that never quite formed. Hundreds of individual asteroids have been named and orbital data for many of them has been identified and published. Interpretive meanings for those used in astrology has generally been derived from the mythology associated with their names, and developed through observation of their themes within charts. Only the first four to be discovered are in common use by a great many astrologers. These are Ceres (discovered in 1801), Pallas (discovered in 1802), Juno (discovered in 1804), and Vesta (discovered in 1807).

astrologer—One who observes, studies, and interprets correspondences between celestial phenomena and life on Earth, particularly the behavior of humans and the events in their lives, individually or collectively.

astronomer—one who observes, studies, and measures celestial phenomena, but is usually not particularly interested in and/or denies, without attempting serious investigation, that such phenomena has any but the most remote correspondence with human behavior or human events. This is a "modern" definition. Until the last two or three centuries, astronomers were also astrologers. Johann Kepler (1571-1630), lauded in history books as the father of modern astronomy, was also a life-long practioner of astrology. Currently, there are a few notable exceptions to my definition of astronomer, who have, indeed, attempted serious investigation, e.g.: British astronomer Percy Seymour who wrote *The Scientific Basis of Astrology,* New York: St. Martin's Press, 1992.

cardinal—One of the four principal compass points, corresponding to sunrise at the equinoxes and solstices. The most commonly used form of measuring the signs of the zodiac in western civilization, called the tropical zodiac, uses the vernal equinox (east) as its starting point, which is designated 0° Aries. Aries, then, is the first cardinal sign and the first sign of the zodiac. The other cardinal signs are Cancer (north), which starts at summer solstice, Libra (west), which starts at the autumnal equinox, and Capricorn (south), which starts at winter solstice. All four of them form the Cardinal Cross. Interpretively, cardinal symbolizes action and initiative. The four cardinal signs are one of three families of four signs each, called (in Astrospeak) quadruplicities, and also called qualities or modes.

celestial longitude—A term of measurement for degrees on the ecliptic. This is the most common form of measurement used by astrologers, e.g. if I tell you I have the Sun in my chart at 26° Scorpio 06', that means that the position of the Sun at the moment of my birth, projected onto the ecliptic, was at 26°06' of celestial longitude within the 30° sign sector called Scorpio, or if measured from 0° Aries (the vernal equinox point), it would be at 236°06' celestial longitude.

complementary—Refers to the signs that are opposite each other in the zodiac: Aries-Libra, Taurus-Scorpio, Gemini-Sagittarius, Cancer-Capricorn, Leo-Aquarius, Virgo-Pisces.

Composite Chart—A chart of a relationship which is formed by the midpoint positions of the chart positions of the individuals who are part of the relationship, e.g.: the midpoint between two people's Sun positions becomes the Composite Sun, the midpoint between their Moons becomes the Composite Moon. A Composite Chart can be constructed for a group, as well as for a couple. The chart is interpreted for information about the dynamics of the relationship.

conjunction—Two or more planets in or very near the same degree of the zodiac. See aspect.

constellation—A group of stars that has been perceived to form a picture or image, is named, and then the image is conveyed to others, who also "see" it (or wonder, "How can anyone possibly see a bull [or whatever] in that?"). Thus the image is handed down through time, inspiring the imagination of stargazers and aiding them in identifying the changing positions of planets. The constellations that visually lie in the path of the ecliptic, seen in an arc across the southern sky, are called the constellations of the zodiac.

cross-quarters—The halfway points between the four quarters of the year—the equinoxes and solstices. There are four cross-quarter points in a year which come when the Sun is in 15° of a fixed sign (see **fixed**). These times correspond with the four Greater Sabbats.

declination—Refers to the number of degrees a planet (or other body) is north or south of the great circle known as the equator. The great circles of ecliptic (Sun's apparent path around Earth) and equator are tilted in relation to each other. They intersect at the equinoxes, and at the solstices they are 23°26' apart. At summer solstice the Sun is as far north of the equator as it gets, and that is why we have long days in the northern hemisphere. At winter solstice the Sun is as far south of the equator as it gets, so we have long nights. In magickal directions, this translates to: Sun at "home" in the fire-south-Summerland, at winter solstice is farthest away from Earth-north-winter. The Sun is reborn and travels steadily northward until summer solstice, warming the Earth as sunlight increases. After the fulfillment of light, Sun returns steadily south again. (So why do we say the Sun goes west into the Summerland? A question for another book ... maybe.)

degree—A unit of measurement in a circle, the glyph of which is a tiny superscript circle after a number. A full circle equals 360°.

eclipse—Either the Moon, in its orbit around Earth, gets so exactly between Earth and Sun that the sunlight is obscured (solar eclipse), or Earth is so exactly between Moon and Sun that Earth's shadow on the Moon obscures the normal fullness we would expect to see at that time (lunar eclipse). Solar eclipses happen at New Moon about twice a year. Lunar eclipses happen at Full Moon usually between two and four times a year. (From the vantage point of Earth, a New Moon is a conjunction of Sun and Moon, meaning the two are "seen" as together—if we could see the Moon, which at that time we can't, because the Sun is too bright when they're "up" together. A Full Moon is an opposition of Sun and Moon, meaning one of them is on this side of us and the other one on the opposite side.) In astrological interpretation, an eclipse denotes special focus on whatever part of one's chart the eclipse aspects. Also, mundane astrologers will cast a chart for the moment of an eclipse and use it for the interpretation of world events.

ecliptic—The celestial Great Circle that defines Earth's orbit around the Sun, or if you prefer, as seen from our earthly perspective, the apparent path of the Sun around the Earth.

element—The 12 signs of the zodiac are grouped into four families called triplicities. Each family of three signs each is assigned to one of the four elements of the ancients: fire, earth, air, and water. The elemental nature of each family defines many characteristics that the signs in that family have in common, although each of the three will express the element in a different way.

fixed—One of the three quadruplicity families of signs. The fixed signs (in this age, Taurus, Leo, Scorpio, and Aquarius) share common characteristics of persistence and stubbornness. Where cardinal signs initiate, fixed signs sustain. Fixed signs resist change—yes, even Aquarius, which may have a radical idea, but once fixed on it, will stubbornly resist change. Fixity, then, symbolizes stability and dependability.

house—There are enough ways of dividing the horoscope circle into twelve sections to practically insure that any group of astrologers will disagree on the "right" way to do it. (At least it is generally agreed that there should be 12 sections!) The methods are mathematically complicated, and the most popular house systems (Placidus and Koch, named after the mathematicians who figured them out) result in unequal house divisions. This greatly confuses most novices, who expect them to be equal in degrees, like the signs. They are not. Houses are designated by numbers and are interpreted according to departments of life that are fairly commonly agreed upon, even by those who do not agree on where the dividing degrees between houses are. For example, the 2nd house (for one thing) is the "department" for personal resources— money, possessions, values, etc. Information about that area of the individual's life is derived from the planets, aspects, and signs associated with the 2nd house.

ingress—Means a planet's entrance into a sign. "Ingress charts" (complete charts cast for the moment of a planet's ingress) are important for people studying mundane astrology (world events). The most notable of these are the seasonal ingresses, such as the Aries Ingress, which is a chart for the vernal equinox.

lunar phase—As Moon orbits Earth, the amount of sunlight we see reflected from her face changes regularly. Dane Rudhyar defined eight distinct phases, which in this book and in previous writings, I have corresponded to the eight seasonal Sabbats.

Midheaven—The cusp* of the 10th house of a horoscope. Mathematically, the degree of celestial longitude where ecliptic intersects the local meridian. Like the Ascendant, Midheaven is considered to be a very important sensitive point. Planets near Midheaven or Ascendant are very focal in a natal chart, and aspects to these points in birth chart or in movements in time are also very significant in astrological interpretation.

*Oops! A new Astrospeak word that I didn't use in the text has slipped in to explain another word that I did use. "Cusp" refers to the first degree of a house, which may or may not be the first degree of a sign. (See **house**.) "Cusp" may also be used in reference to a person being born "on the cusp," which means that their Sun (in their birth chart) comes at the very end of a sign, or at the very beginning of one.

mutable—The third quadruplicity family of signs (see also **cardinal** and **fixed**). The mutable signs in this age are Gemini, Virgo, Sagittarius, and Pisces. They symbolize change, adaptability, and dissemination of ideas.

natural zodiac—The zodiac of signs with its associated house numbers and planetary rulers. In the natural zodiac houses and signs are considered to be sort of a universal house system. A planet is assigned to each sign, and astrologers consider that Aries, the first sign of the zodiac (as designated by the classical Greeks and still in general use), is then always naturally associated with number 1 and with Mars; Taurus is naturally associated with number 2 and Venus, and so on around: Gemini-3-Mercury; Cancer-4-Moon; Leo-5-Sun; Virgo-6-Mercury; Libra-7-Venus; Scorpio-8-Pluto; Sagittarius-9-Jupiter; Capricorn-10-Saturn; Aquarius-11-Uranus; Pisces-12-Neptune. Most astrologers use the affinities derived from this system to some extent. Some, most notably Zipporah Dobyns, Ph.D., have developed effective systems of chart synthesis based on it.

planets—The term "planets," as generally used in astrology, means also the Sun and Moon, which are more properly termed "lights," but more often, for short, get lumped in with the planets. Including Sun and Moon, ten "planets" are considered "traditional" in horoscope interpretation: Mercury, Venus, Mars, Jupiter, Saturn, Uranus, Neptune and Pluto. Earth doesn't count because we are on it. (A horoscope is seen from our perspective—unless you are a heliocentric astrologer, in which case you leave out Sun and put in Earth.) Volumes of interpretive material has been written about all the planets. "Planets" can also refer to non-traditional bodies, including some that haven't been discovered yet and may not, in fact, exist as physical entities. (Did I ever say this made perfect sense? If I did, I lied.)

progressed—Refers to a system of symbolically moving a horoscope in time. The basic theory is one day equals one year. So if, for example, you want a progressed horoscope for the year you are 30, you calculate it for the 30th day after birth.

polarity—Used to refer to opposites. Complementary opposites are the polarity of signs that are opposite each other in the zodiac. They share the same mode or quality (cardinal, fixed, or mutable) and the same gender (masculine or feminine), but each is said to have characteristics that are opposite, although complementary, in that each provides what the other most lacks in a particular area—the "other side of the same coin," one could say. The other use of polarity refers to alternating signs of the zodiac. Six are said to be masculine, active (the author prefers kinetic), yang, and positive (as in a battery charge). The other six are said to be feminine, passive (the author prefers magnetic), yin, and negative (as in a battery charge).

ruler—A planet assigned to a sign according to an arbitrary system set up at the dawn of this age by Ptolemy, which is still in use today with some modifications. "Ruler" could be also taken as a reflection of the relative importance of planets to signs and houses. Planets and their relationships (aspects) are by far the most significant factors in "reading" a chart.

sign—An equal 30° segment of the ecliptic. In western civilization, when one refers to their "sign" they usually mean the sectors of the ecliptic that were named according to the constellations that lay approximately in their sectors during the time of the classical Greeks (about 2000 years ago), and are called the tropical zodiac. Due to the precession of the equinoxes, a slow backward movement of the vernal equinox (0° Aries) and the zodiac of signs against the backdrop of the constellations, the signs and the constellations no longer coincide. The vernal equinox Sun now rises in about the 4th degree of the constellation Pisces. Because these ancient Greeks (like most humans) were primarily conveniencing their own time, instead of thinking about what might happen far into the future, astrologers today are frequently challenged by scientific types who assume that we are not aware that the signs and constellations are out-of-sync. We are aware. A sign is not a constellation, nor is a constellation a sign—but our interpretive systems still "work." (See also **zodiac**.)

zenith—The point directly overhead of wherever you are, extended upward into infinity. The opposite point, directly and infinitely below wherever you are, is called the nadir.

zodiac—Refers to the 12 signs or constellations: Aries, Taurus, Gemini, Cancer, Leo, Virgo, Libra, Scorpio, Sagittarius, Capricorn, Aquarius, Pisces. "Zodiac" may refer to the tropical zodiac, with its reference points of the seasons—equinoxes and solstices, commonly referred to as "the signs." It may also refer to one of the various sidereal zodiacs, which have a moveable vernal point in reference to the fixed stars, in the attempt to keep the signs (which are still equal 30° sectors) more in alignment with the constellations. The constellational zodiac is made up of the group of star "pictures" that can be seen arcing across the southern sky (a visible ecliptic). These do not divide themselves neatly into equal sections at all. They range from very small (Libra, about 18°) to very large (Virgo, about 46°), with a few gaps in between and (for purists) a few embarrassing intrusions by pieces of other constellations. However, the symbolic system of 12 has held through time, in spite of a few very minor attempts to change it—a magickal number, perhaps?

Index

Passing references to words that are used a great many times in the text (e.g.: air, east, God, Goddess, etc.) are not individually page-indexed unless as part of a discussion of their meaning, and not indexed within the rituals. Numbers in bold type refer to major discussions of the topic.

455

STAY IN TOUCH

On the following pages you will find listed, with their current prices, some of the books now available on related subjects. Your book dealer stocks most of these and will stock new titles in the Llewellyn series as they become available. We urge your patronage.

TO GET A FREE CATALOG

You are invited to write for our catalog, *Llewellyn's New Worlds of Mind and Spirit*. A sample copy is free. Or you may subscribe for just $10 in the United States and Canada ($20 overseas, first class mail). Many bookstores also have *New Worlds* available to their customers. Ask for it.

In *New Worlds* you will find news and features about new books, tapes and services; announcements of meetings and seminars; helpful articles; author interviews and much more. Write to:

Llewellyn's New Worlds of Mind and Spirit
P.O. Box 64383, Dept. K657-2, St. Paul, MN 55164-0383, U.S.A.

TO ORDER BOOKS AND TAPES

If your book store does not carry the titles described on the following pages, you may order them directly from Llewellyn by sending the full price in U.S. funds, plus postage and handling (see below).

Credit Card Orders: VISA, Master Card, and American Express are accepted. Call toll-free in the USA and Canada at 1-800-THE-MOON.

Special Group Discount: Because there is a great deal of interest in group discussion and study of the subject matter of this book, we offer a 20% quantity discount to group leaders or agents. Our Special Quantity Price for a minimum order of five copies of *The Witch's Circle* is $79.80 cash-with-order. Include the postage and handling charges noted below.

Postage and Handling: Include $4 postage and handling for orders $15 and under; $5 for orders *over* $15. There are no postage and handling charges for orders over $100. Postage and handling rates are subject to change. We ship UPS whenever possible within the continental United States; delivery is guaranteed. Please provide your street address as UPS does not deliver to P.O. boxes. Orders shipped to Alaska, Hawaii, Canada, Mexico and Puerto Rico will be sent via first class mail. Allow 4-6 weeks for delivery. **International orders:** Airmail – add retail price of each book and $5 for each non-book item (audiotapes, etc.); Surface mail – add $1 per item. Minnesota residents please add 7% sales tax.

Mail orders to:
Llewellyn Worldwide,
P.O. Box 64383, Dept. K657-2,
St. Paul, MN 55164, USA

For customer service, call 1-800-THE-MOON
In Minnesota, call (612) 291-1970.

GREEN WITCHCRAFT
Folk Magic, Fairy Lore & Herb Craft

Aoumiel

Very little has been written about traditional family practices of the Old Religion simply because such information has not been offered for popular consumption. If you have no contacts with these traditions, Green Witchcraft will meet your need for a practice based in family and natural Witchcraft traditions. *Green Witchcraft* describes the worship of nature and the use of herbs that have been part of human culture from the earliest times. It relates to the Lord & Lady of Greenwood, the Primal Father and Mother, and to the Earth Spirits called Faeries.

Green Witchcraft traces the historic and folk background of this path and teaches its practical techniques. Learn the basics of Witchcraft from a third-generation, traditional family Green Witch who openly shares from her own experiences. Through a how-to format you'll learn rites of passage, activities for Sabbats and Esbats, Fairy lore, self-dedication, self-initiation, spellwork, herbcraft and divination. This practical handbook is an invitation to explore, identify and adapt the Green elements of Witchcraft that work for you, today.

1-56718-690-4, 6 x 9, 288 pp., illus. $14.95

To order, call 1-800-THE-MOON

Prices subject to change without notice

FAERY WICCA, BOOK ONE
Theory & Magick • A Book of Shadows & Lights

Kisma K. Stepanich

Many books have been written on Wicca, but never until now has there been a book on the tradition of Irish Faery Wicca. If you have been drawn to the kingdom of Faery and want to gain a comprehensive understanding of this old folk faith, *Faery Wicca* offers you a thorough apprenticeship in the beliefs, history and practice of this rich and fulfilling tradition.

First, you'll explore the Irish history of Faery Wicca, its esoteric beliefs and its survival and evolution into its modern form; the Celtic pantheon; the Celtic division of the year; and the fairies of the Tuatha De Danann and their descendants. The second part of *Faery Wicca* describes in detail magickal applications of the basic material presented in the first half: Faery Wicca ceremonies and rituals; utilizing magickal Faery tools, symbols and alphabets; creating sacred space; contacting and working with Faery allies; and guided visualizations and exercises suitable for beginners.

This fascinating guide will give you a firm foundation in the Faery Wicca tradition, which the upcoming *Faery Wicca, Book Two: The Shamanic Practices of Herbcraft, Spellcraft and Divination* will build upon.

1–56718–694–7, 320 pp., 7 x 10, illus., softcover $17.50

To order, call 1-800-THE-MOON

Prices subject to change without notice

FAERY WICCA, BOOK TWO
The Shamanic Practices of the Cunning Arts

Kisma Stepanich

Faery Wicca, Book Two continues the studies undertaken in *Faery Wicca, Book One*, with a deepening focus on the tradition's shamanic practices, including energy work, the Body Temple, healing techniques and developing Second-Sight; meditation techniques; journeys into the Otherworld; contacting Faery Guardians, Allies, Guides and Companions; herbcraft and spellcasting; different forms of Faery divination; rites of passages; the four minor holidays; and a closing statement on the shamanic technique known as "remembering."

The Oral Faery Tradition's teachings are not about little winged creatures. They are about the primal earth and the power therein, the circles of existence, Ancient Gods, the ancestors and the continuum. *Faery Wicca, Book Two* is not a how-to book but a study that provides extensive background information and mystery teachings for both novices and adepts alike.

1-56718-695-5, 320 pp., 7 x 10, illus., softcover $17.50

To order, call 1-800-THE-MOON

Prices subject to change without notice

BUCKLAND'S COMPLETE BOOK OF WITCHCRAFT

Raymond Buckland

Here is the most complete resource to the study and practice of modern, non-denominational Wicca. This is a lavishly illustrated, self-study course for the solitary or group. Included are rituals; exercises for developing psychic talents; information on all major "sects" of the Craft; sections on tools, beliefs, dreams, meditations, divination, herbal lore, healing, ritual clothing and much, much more. This book unites theory and practice into a comprehensive course designed to help you develop into a practicing Witch, one of the "Wise Ones." It is written by Ray Buckland, a very famous and respected authority on Witchcraft who first came public with the Old Religion in the United States. Large format with workbook-type exercises, profusely illustrated and full of music and chants. Takes you from A to Z in the study of Witchcraft.

Never before has so much information on the Craft of the Wise been collected in one place. Traditionally, there are three degrees of advancement in most Wiccan traditions. When you have completed studying this book, you will be the equivalent of a Third-Degree Witch. Even those who have practiced Wicca for years find useful information in this book, and many covens are using this for their textbook. If you want to become a Witch, or if you merely want to find out what Witchcraft is really about, you will find no better book than this.

0-87542-050-8, 272 pp., 8½ x 11, illus., softcover $14.95

To order, call 1-800-THE-MOON

Prices subject to change without notice

LIVING WICCA
A Further Guide for the Solitary Practitioner

Scott Cunningham

Living Wicca is the long-awaited sequel to Scott Cunningham's wildly successful *Wicca: a Guide for the Solitary Practitioner*. This new book is for those
who have made the conscious decision to bring their Wiccan spirituality into
their everyday lives. It provides solitary practitioners with the tools and added
insights that will enable them to blaze their own spiritual paths—to become
their own high priests and priestesses.

Living Wicca takes a philosophical look at the questions, practices, and differences within Witchcraft. It covers the various tools of learning available
to the practitioner, the importance of secrecy in one's practice, guidelines to
performing ritual when ill, magical names, initiation, and the Mysteries. It
discusses the benefits of daily prayer and meditation, making offerings to the
gods, how to develop a prayerful attitude, and how to perform Wiccan rites
when away from home or in emergency situations.

Unlike any other book on the subject, *Living Wicca* is a step-by-step guide
to creating your own Wiccan tradition and personal vision of the gods,
designing your personal ritual and symbols, developing your own book of
shadows, and truly living your Craft.

0-87542-184-9, 208 pp., 6 x 9, illus., softcover   **$12.95**

To order, call 1-800-THE-MOON

WHEEL OF THE YEAR
Living the Magical Life

Pauline Campanelli, illus. by Dan Campanelli

If you feel elated by the celebrations of the Sabbats and hunger for that feeling during the long weeks between Sabbats, *Wheel of the Year* can help you put the joy and fulfillment of magic into your everyday life. This book shows you how to celebrate the lesser changes in Nature. The wealth of seasonal rituals and charms are all easily performed with materials readily available and are simple as well as concise enough that the practitioner can easily adapt them to work within the framework of his or her own Pagan tradition.

Learn to perform fire magic in November, the secret Pagan symbolism of Christmas tree ornaments, the best time to visit a fairy forest or sacred spring and what to do when you get there. Learn the charms and rituals and the making of magical tools that coincide with the nesting season of migratory birds. Whether you are a newcomer to the Craft or have found your way back many years ago, *Wheel of the Year* will be an invaluable reference book in your practical magic library. It is filled with magic and ritual for everyday life and will enhance any system of Pagan Ritual.

0-87542-091-5, 176 pp., 7 x 10, illus., softcover $9.95

To order, call 1-800-THE-MOON

CAULDRON OF TRANSFORMATION
A New Vision of Wicca

Lady Sabrina

Thousands of people, tired of the politics and dogma of the Christian Church but longing for deity and spirituality, have found the answer in Co-Creation spirituality, a progressive formulation of doctrine and ritual that bridges the gap between Wiccan-Pagan ideology and the original intent of the Christian mysteries.

Cauldron of Transformation refreshingly approaches spirituality from an unbiased view and proclaims the truth and beauty of all positive religions. It explains the finer points of Paganism and teaches you how to blend and combine the wisdom of different traditions into a loving spiritual system of your own. You will be introduced to the origins, customs and beliefs of five religious traditions: Celtic Druidism, Buddism, Christianity, Santeria and Shamanism.

This book also provides both new and dynamic tools to help extend and expand personal spiritual awareness. One such tool, the Vessel of Creation, provides a method of actually talking to your deity as well as receiving an answer in return.

1-56718-600-9
320 pp., 6 x 9, illus., photos, softcover $16.95

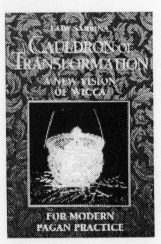

To order, call 1-800-THE-MOON